THE
BRONTË SISTERS

SELECTED SOURCE MATERIALS
FOR COLLEGE RESEARCH PAPERS

Edited by
RUTH H. BLACKBURN
STATE UNIVERSITY OF NEW YORK AT STONY BROOK

D. C. HEATH AND COMPANY *Boston*

For
G. Stuart Demarest
and
David Lilien
In gratitude and affection.

TABLE OF CONTENTS

The student using this book is in much the same position as many professional research scholars in that the texts available to him vary greatly in reliability. Some are good, notably in the case of the reviews, which in most cases have been photostatted straight from the periodicals. Other documents, for example the report on the Brontë children at Cowan Bridge, are reprinted from secondary sources. It has not usually been possible to check manuscript sources, and it is a matter for regret that printed texts of the Brontë letters are frequently unreliable. Mrs. Gaskell in particular is known to have hastily copied material lent to her, sometimes consciously or unconsciously editing as she copied. Understandably, she also left blanks for the names of persons still living when she wrote. Some of these have been filled in in the present edition. Later collections than hers are still imperfect, and a definitive edition is much needed. One is in preparation, but details about it are not available at present. All students of the Brontë family must await it with impatience.

The following abbreviations are used for the texts most commonly referred to in this collection:

G. for Mrs. Gaskell's book, *The Life of Charlotte Brontë,* Everyman Edition, New York: E. P. Dutton and Co., 1958. In this reprinting of the text, the following editorial apparatus has been adopted to show Mrs. Gaskell's deviations from the manuscript texts of letters she quotes: brackets around words indicate additions and emendations made by Mrs. Gaskell; brackets around ellipsis marks — [. . .] — indicate passages Mrs. Gaskell has omitted without acknowledgment; three asterisks — * * * — indicate omissions which Mrs. Gaskell has acknowledged; simple ellipses indicate passages omitted in this reprinting.

S. H. for *The Brontës: Their Lives, Friendships and Correspondence,* ed. Thomas James Wise and John Alexander Symington, 4 vols., Oxford: Basil Blackwell, 1932. These volumes are part of the Shakespeare Head Brontë.

B. S. T. *Brontë Society Transactions,* published by The Brontë Society, are cited. (Note: Membership in the Society includes the annual *Transactions* volume and costs ten shillings (about $1.50). Americans wishing to join should write to the Hon. Representative in the U. S. A., Mrs. H. Greene Arnold, 55 Emmonsdale Road, West Roxbury 32, Mass.)

Acknowledgments

My thanks are due to Messrs. E. P. Dutton of New York, Messrs. Basil Blackwell of Oxford, and Messrs. Lawson and Dunn of London for the use of their texts. Lawson and Dunn publish an inexpensive edition of Emily's poems which students might like to own. Called *Selected Poems* and edited by Philip Henderson, it may be obtained from Barmerlea Book Sales, Ltd., 10 Bayley St., Bedford Square, London, for about $1.50.

I should also like to express my gratitude to members of the Brontë Society who made me feel at home in Haworth and helped me in many ways. Finally, I should like to thank my friend, Lynn Montgomery, for her constant and stimulating interest in this project. Her enthusiasm helped to diminish the burden of the work and more than doubled its pleasures.

INTRODUCTION

The Gondals are discovering the interior of Gaaldene. Sally Mosely is washing in the back kitchen.

At sixteen Emily Brontë recorded this snapshot of the passing scene at Haworth Parsonage. Fancy and fact are casually set down side by side. Jottings made by Charlotte indicate that for her, too, the world of imagination sometimes seemed as actual as the real people and things around her. Once, lonely and homesick at boarding school, she wrote that she saw before her, vivid as flesh and blood, the Queen of Angria in her jewelled robes and a "swart and sinewy Moor . . . his broad chest heaving wildly" — when suddenly "the dining-room door opened and Miss Wooler [her teacher] came in with a plate of butter in her hand." This juxtaposition of the life of fantasy and the life of every day is part of the fascination of the Brontës and explains in part the charm they have exerted for more than a century over biographers and critics. The life lived in imagination and recorded in stories was always most important to them; their novels remain the most important evidence about them. Though their lives have seemed to generations of biographers as dramatic, as absorbing and intense, as their stories — and more tragic — both the novels and the records of their lives must be studied by anyone who wants to explore their peculiar geniuses, for their two worlds illuminate each other. Reread, then, *Jane Eyre* and *Wuthering Heights* as you study the records in this book, and consider not only "What do the records and letters say?" but also, always, "What do the novels mean? What do they tell us about the women who wrote them?"

Using this Book   With this proviso firmly in mind, you are ready to examine this book. In it you will find a variety of documents — school reports on Charlotte and Emily when they were very small, stories the Brontë children wrote to amuse each other, fragments of diaries, many personal letters, a sampling of Emily's poems, reviews of the novels, and letters and accounts people composed about the Brontës after they were dead. You probably know already that such documents are known as "primary sources," that is, firsthand statements and opinions, based usually on the writer's own observations, as opposed to "secondary sources" in which the original facts and opinions have been selected and arranged in a pattern which expresses the truth of the matter as the author sees it — or perhaps as he wishes his audience to see it. Primary sources such as you find here are the raw materials from which the historians and biographers usually work in preparing their books, which for us are secondary sources. You will not read any secondary sources on the Brontës at present except for the editor's headnotes. Rather, you will study the primary sources and try to reconstruct from them the truth as you see it. You will establish as accurately as you can what the facts were and then try to interpret them and show what they reveal about the personalities and convictions of the Brontë sisters. In short, you will become a "secondary source" yourself.

You will soon find that not all the documents are of equal accuracy and value. The two prospectuses of Cowan Bridge in Section I, for example, both date from the early days of the school and purport to recommend it, but why should they be so alike and yet so different? Why should there be two? Should we accept both? Select one to use? In the case of the quarrel between Charlotte and Harriet Martineau, how does Miss Martineau's account differ from Charlotte's, as far as it can be pieced together from her letters? Mrs. Gaskell's official life of Charlotte (Section V) is in many ways an admirable work, a classic in the history of biography, but since she only knew Charlotte for the last five years of her life, her account of earlier events are, strictly speaking, secondary; moreover, there are important matters which from motives of prudence she passes over in silence. The whole matter of evaluating the reliability of a source is a most delicate one, for which no exact rules can be given. The passage of time since the event, the experiences of the observer, his general reliability or lack of it, his relationship with the persons involved, his own preoccupations and prejudices — all these have to be taken into account.

Before you begin to read, study the table of contents to get a clear idea of what you may expect to find. Roughly speaking, the groups of documents are arranged in the order that they were written, so that you get, for example, the early records of Cowan Bridge School at the beginning of the book and the dispute about it, which took place after Charlotte was dead, at the end. However, the letters and papers of Charlotte (II), the papers and poems of Emily and Anne (III), and the letters and reminiscences (V) are all approximately contemporary with one another, and it may often be necessary for readers to cross-refer from one to another of these sections. Early and late book reviews have been grouped in a separate section (IV). Within the sections, the order is usually chronological; departures from this rule are indicated in the notes.

Mastering the Material   It is important before embarking on a research project to have a broad general grasp of the subject, so that particular problems can be seen in proper relationship to the whole. Your instructor may divide the reading matter up into sections, assigning short papers as you read, or he may leave you to work on the whole book yourself. In either case, go to work systematically. Read the headnotes to the first two sections and get a general idea of their contents. Section II, Charlotte's correspondence, is the backbone of the book, and the connecting headnote will give you a running narrative of events. If you were looking up this material in the library, as you will be for research papers later, it would be wise at this point to start making a chronology of the most important dates. Such a date-list saves much valuable time later and helps you to be accurate in matters of fact. In this book a short chronology has been provided, but you should add to it as your knowledge and needs suggest. As you read through the letters, if you are curious to know, for instance, what Emily and Anne were doing, or how Mary Taylor or Ellen Nussey remembered Charlotte in her school days, turn forward to the appropriate sections. Then go back to the letters again. You should be sure to read, as well as I through III, all the reminiscences (V), the excerpts from Mrs. Gaskell's *Life* (V), and Charlotte's memoir of her sisters in Section II. It is probably not absolutely necessary for every student to read Sections IV and VI, although some of you will want to and will find there challenging subjects for investigation. Students who do choose topics using these sections might report to the class on their findings and recommend sample readings.

Deciding on a Topic   As you read, jot down a list of possible topics for papers. Do not be hasty in deciding. Master the bulk of the material first. You will probably modify your ideas as your acquaintance with the family grows. Your instructor will perhaps devote some class or conference time to helping you make your final selection.

Remember that you are trying to be a historian, an interpreter as well as a recorder of facts, although as a matter of fact, the closer to a chronicle of events your first paper is, the easier it will be to do a competent job. Take, for example, the matter of the Bell pseudonym under which the Brontë girls wrote. Finding how they came to use a pseudonym, what confusion resulted, and how the truth finally came out, is not difficult, nor is the planning of the paper hard, as it falls naturally into a chronological pattern. A lively narrative, some enquiry into the girls' intense concern for secrecy, and you have a good paper. But even a short investigation where the facts are not so certain requires careful exercise of judgment.

Suppose, for instance, you embark on a short paper on "The Original of Helen Burns," whom you vaguely understand to be Charlotte's eldest sister Maria. You find out all you can about Maria, you locate Charlotte's allusions to her, you read what Ellen Nussey and Mary Taylor remember having heard and, of course, you read over the early chapters of *Jane Eyre*. You may find this account of Helen moving, irritating, convincing, unbelievable — you have to decide which and why (allowing for your own prejudices, if you are astute enough to recognize them) — and your decision becomes part of your evidence and affects your conclusion. If you later write a longer paper in which you try to decide whether Lowood School is a fair picture of Cowan Bridge as it was when the Brontë children were there, your problems of making correct judgments are multiplied: you not only have the fact-fiction problem, but must consider the characters involved — the parson, the cruel teacher, the good teacher — and of course Charlotte herself — as well as a sampling of the mass of contradictory letters which poured out from the clergyman's family and Charlotte's family after Mrs. Gaskell published *her* account in 1857.

Perhaps the most baffling and intriguing topics are those which have irritating gaps just where you most need facts. Take the question of Charlotte's relationship to M. Heger, her Belgian teacher, about which biographers have long argued with some violence. You want to know the heart of the matter — so you read carefully Charlotte's letters during and after the Brussels stay, you note that Mrs. Gaskell breathes not a word of romance (a little reflection will tell you why, and perhaps will whet your curiosity to read *her* letters as she was writing). You study *Villette* and perhaps *The Professor* for clues. There is a fair amount of evidence, but what does it tell? Charlotte got so worked up in Brussels that, though a rabid Protestant, she sought consolation in the confessional — but what did she confess? Why does *Villette* end so equivocally? How much is Charlotte saying when she writes, "May God bless you my dear Master, and crown you with peculiar blessings"? The professional biographer or historian knows no more than you do: like him, you are now driven to guess, to interpret, to make a series of interconnected decisions — against as broad a knowledge as possible of Charlotte's life and character. Finally, like the professional, you must tell your readers what the various possibilities are, but you may decide where you think the truth lies and marshall your facts accordingly.

Making the Outline   But this is to anticipate. Once you have chosen your topic, you should go back through the documents looking for data. Make some rough notes and put down a few page numbers if you wish, but do not do any formal note-taking yet. Soak yourself in your subject, reading everything you can find and thinking of ways it might be organized. Make two or three tentative outlines. Perhaps there will be class time in which you can describe what the purpose of your research is, how you plan to treat your topic, and what problems you see ahead. This experience will help you to clarify your ideas and may raise points you hadn't thought of. It will also make you more aware of the audience for which you are writing — the instructor and the other students in the class. Revise your tentative outline accordingly. Sometimes you will find that a paper "arranges itself" (in this case be sure you have not over-simplified), but more often you will have something of a struggle at this stage, a struggle which may not be over when you have rearranged your outline for the sixth time! — for you are continually adding to your knowledge and understanding. It is very important that you should not feel tied down by your early outline, no matter how neat it looked or how well your instructor thought of it. Be flexible and clear-headed, and make changes in accordance with your evidence and with clarity of presentation.

This is more difficult with a more abstract and complex subject. To take another example from the Brontës: let us suppose you have been struck by Charlotte's passionate declaration to Harriet Martineau, beginning "I know what love is, as I understand it," and have decided to explore and sort out Charlotte's attitudes to love and marriage. This is an "idea" topic more difficult to handle than a purely factual one. It will lead you back to Charlotte's early notions of romance, forward to her marriage, back again to *Jane Eyre* and *Villette,* to her statements to Miss Martineau and others. You will also have to take into consideration her apparent shifts of opinion, your own interpretation of the novels, and her life-long insistence in the primacy of love. A great many approaches are possible here. Obviously your paper will be hard to organize — and very rewarding. Obviously, too, you will have to be flexible in your thinking and planning.

A useful clarifying device at this point may be to make a thesis statement, a sentence which sets down the central point or issue, proved if possible. If carefully prepared, the thesis statement can contain the entire structure of the paper microcosmically. This statement should be continually referred to and the outline and organization of your paper revised accordingly.

Taking the Notes Flexibility and accuracy will be achieved if you learn from the start to make careful notes. Of course, with the material all in front of you as it is in this book, you could write short papers without bothering with note cards. But as you are training yourself for more advanced research, it is important to practice good habits from the start. Head your cards in accordance with your carefully planned outline. Limit each card to a single and specific part of your outline, e.g., not just "Newby" but "Newby's deceit re *Wildfell Hall.*" You may need several cards with the same heading. Duplicates can be discarded later. Resist the temptation to write on the backs of your note cards; this may save space, but usually wastes time, as topics or sub topics often need to be split at some later stage in the development of your paper. For example, having started a card on "Charlotte on nature and truth," you may find that you want cards on both "Nature" and "Truth." You can then cut your cards horizontally instead of writing them over. Also, when you spread out your cards to study them before you write, you need to be able to see all the information at once.

Summarize and paraphrase as you work, for you do not want to produce an essay which is merely a patchwork of quotations. Such papers are turgid and dry reading and, however exquisitely footnoted, are a dreadful bore. Remember, too, that too many quotations suggest to the reader that your grasp of the subject is inadequate. Quote only passages which are particularly striking or which are really needed to prove your point. Develop skill in using short, telling quotations instead of long ones. Avoid in particular long inset blocks which the reader will very likely skip. Whenever you do copy a quotation, re-read and re-check with the source before going on. You will probably be surprised to find how inexact you are.

Be accurate in noting (on *each* card) details, abbreviated where suitable, of your sources. The page numbers of the originals are provided in the margins of this book. Your instructor may wish to give you some practice in making correct footnotes and bibliography entries at this point. The form recommended by the Modern Language Association is set out in its Style Sheet, obtainable (with a deduction for quantity orders) from the Treasurer of the M. L. A., 100 Washington Square, New York 3, N. Y.

Writing the Paper When you have completed your note cards, spread them out on a flat surface, in the order suggested by your latest outline, and study them. You may find you have to make some changes in grouping and order. Set aside cards which are repetitive and irrelevant, being careful to preserve any which, though they do not fit your plan, are clearly relevant to it. You may need to modify your outline or even your thesis. Make a new outline, put your cards neatly together and, if possible, put the whole project away for a day or so, so that you can begin to write with some freshness of approach. After such an interval remarkable insights and inspirations sometimes occur — a clearer transition for that awkward link, a brighter guess about that point of difference. It might be well to look through the documents again. You sometimes find the evidence you were looking for staring you in the face.

Now you are ready to compose your first draft. Clear your desk and your mind of other subjects and plan on some hours of concentrated work. Write your first draft rather swiftly; you may refer to your notes and outline, but concentrate on making each point clear and making it "tell" toward your conclusion. Do not bother about complete footnotes at this stage, keep your style simple, straightforward and fresh, and remember that you are trying to interest as well as inform your audience. After your first draft is completed, again allow an interval before you continue: a "jelling" period is almost always beneficial. Then check the whole thing through for correctness of fact and quotation and for clarity of presentation. A useful device here is to make a new outline *directly from your paper,* without looking at your previous one. You will find this an excellent method of spotting fallacious reasoning, inadequate transitions, obscurely made points, and even awkwardness of style. Ask yourself insistently: Is it clear? Is it honest? Is it interesting? and rewrite accordingly. When you are satisfied that you have done your very best work, rewrite, completing your footnotes and checking for mechanical accuracy and consistency. In its final form, a research paper should include title page, table of contents, and a bibliography, annotated or not as your instructor recommends.

If you have worked thoroughly and carefully at every stage of this process, you will find that you have learned a tremendous amount from your first research project. You have dealt with a sizeable number of documents, decided on a problem, used your judgment in selecting facts and weighing evidence, and combined and marshalled your data so as to create your own pattern which will show the truth as you see it. You should follow up this experience with another and more complex research paper, in which you practice the facility you have acquired.

A final word of warning. "There has always been a tendency on the part of almost all those who have ever written about the Brontës to lose their heads," wrote E. M. Delafield some years ago.[1] Today her judgment would seem sweeping, for since she wrote we have had many sound, balanced studies; even so, students should be aware that wild and unfounded guesses still flourish, and pot-boiling journalists may present in popular magazines notions for which there is not a scrap of real evidence. So do not swallow indiscriminately any article or book on the Brontës which you may happen to run across. Some idealize Charlotte and in the process fail to show how complex, how faulty, yet how likeable and human she was. Branwell has always had his detractors and defenders. The very absence of evidence about Emily has encouraged a variety of portraits. Anne's reputation has only recently come in for some long-deserved rehabilitation. Be guided by the reading lists below and by your instructor, but, above all, study the evidence, keep your head, and make your own judgments with good sense and compassion.

As novices in the art of honest research, you may like to think about the invocation below, which M. Heger used to recite at the beginning of his classes.

> *Esprit de Sagesse, conduisez-nous;*
> *Esprit de Vérité, enseignez-nous;*
> *Esprit de Charité, vivifiez-nous;*
> *Esprit de Prudence, préservez-nous;*
> *Esprit de Force, défendez-nous;*
> *Esprit de Justice, éclairex-nous;*
> *Esprit de Consolateur, apaisez-nous.*

[1] *The Brontës: Their Lives Recorded by Their Contemporaries.* London: Hogarth Press, 1935, p. 4.

BIOGRAPHICAL SKETCHES AND PERSONAL ABBREVIATIONS

The following abbreviations are used for persons frequently referred to throughout this collection:

C. B. for Charlotte Brontë — A. B. for Anne Brontë — E. B. for Emily Jane Brontë — E. N. for Ellen Nussey — E. G. for Elizabeth Cleghorn Gaskell

The following are brief accounts of some of the less well-known persons in the Brontë circle:

Dobell, Sydney Thompson (1824–74) was a literary critic and a poet of the so-called spasmodic school, characterized by its extravagance in emotion, metaphor, and tone. He was also a Broad Churchman, an advocate of social reform, and a warm partisan of Italian and Hungarian liberty. His generosity of temper, evident in his article, is also reflected in his correspondence with Charlotte which followed its publication.

Heger, Romain Constantin Georges (1809–96), was a professor at the Athenée Royale in Brussels and teacher of literature at the Heger Pensionnat, whose head, Claire Zöe Parent (1804–90) was his second wife. Their relative ages are of some interest; he was only seven years older than Charlotte. He was evidently an exceptional teacher; the Abbé Richardson (whose sister's *Secret of Charlotte Brontë* is quoted below, V), left the following account of him: "The method M. Heger revealed to me . . . was no easy or royal road to teaching. His first requirement was perfect self-sacrifice of self: *un devou absolu* were his words. 'If, young man, you do not feel ready to give this *devou absolu* to your pupils, in heaven's name ask your superiors to give you other work, for you will never do any good as a professor.' For him the foundation, and the essential requirement for success were order and discipline, but order and discipline obtained not by fear, but by patience and unfailing watchfulness. For him the first point was to establish a perfect discipline in a class, even if for a time, say a month or more, little direct classical work was done. Once obtain order and an absolute command over a class, and progress was assured to a professor without brilliant talents, whereas the most brilliant master with an unruly or undisciplined class could obtain nothing except perhaps the success of one or two exceptional pupils. His next precept was to study the pupils, to know each one of them, to neglect none, and above all, never to allow an aversion towards any one even to enter into the heart of the teacher. . . . M. Heger was kind enough to come into my schoolroom and to give me a model lesson. Never shall I forget that lesson and the magic his genial presence and clever and almost dramatic manner had on my boys." (Mrs. Ellis H. Chadwick, *In the Footsteps of the Brontës*, London: Sir Isaac Pitman and Sons, 1914, p. 215.) The Hegers were people of note in educational circles and their obituaries (see Chadwick, Ch. XVII) show the respect they commanded in Brussels. See also Raymond, Ch. 15.

Lewes, George Henry (1817–78) was a literary critic with an exceptionally broad background. He had studied medicine, physiology, and biology, as well as dramatic literature and the novel, before he became editor of the *Fortnightly Review* in 1865. Many of his literary judgments, though hastily set down for magazines and other periodicals, have stood the test of time, thanks to the soundness of his taste. His enthusiasm for Jane Austen's novels, his admiration for *Jane Eyre*, and his disappointment in *Shirley* are all indicated in his letters to Charlotte from 1847 on. He was a man who was not easily swayed by argument and who did not fear to act unconventionally when he felt he was in the right. Although his legal wife was still living, Lewes' union with Mary Ann Evans (George Eliot) was regarded by both as a real marriage and was marked by loyalty and devotion.

Nussey, Ellen (1817–97) came from a large family with good connections. Several of her relatives were court physicians or filled other important public offices. She seems to have been a pretty, sensible, placid girl, loyal and affectionate, bright enough to know that her friendship with Charlotte was an important thing in her life, but otherwise undistinguished. She was devoted to her friend and faithful to her memory; but her attempts to capitalize on it by making money out of the letters would have shocked both Charlotte and Mary Taylor. Her childhood home, Rydings, Birstall, Yorkshire, was the original of Thornfield in *Jane Eyre,* and she is thought to have contributed some traits to Caroline Helstone in *Shirley.*

Smith, George Murray (1824–1901) went into his father's publishing company at fourteen and came into control of it in 1846, at his father's death. Its business multiplied thirteen times in twenty years. He was the friend of Thackeray, the Brownings, Arnold, and many other literary figures. His three most important publishing ventures were the *Cornhill Magazine,* the *Pall Mall Gazette,* and the *Dictionary of National Biography,* of which the first volume was issued in 1882.

Shaen, Winkworth. Charlotte met the Winkworth girls, Susanna, Catherine, and Emily, through Mrs. Gaskell, whose husband tutored them in Greek, literature, and science. (Harriet Martineau's brother James taught them logic and philosophy.) Emily Winkworth married William Shaen, the lawyer who later represented Mrs. Gaskell when she was threatened with libel suits. His sisters Ann and Emma were also friends of the Gaskells.

Taylor, Mary (1817–93), one of Charlotte's most refreshing friends, came from a large family where independent thinking and frank speech were encouraged. Her father, Joshua Taylor, was a banker and woolen manufacturer known for his radical opinions and his sympathy for the oppressed. Politics and religion were freely discussed at home and at school. Mary never was afraid to speak up for her own opinions. This sometimes got her into trouble. Ellen recalls that once when Miss Wooler set Charlotte and Mary a long piece to learn by heart, the docile Charlotte did it, but Mary refused and was deprived of supper for a month. However, she and her sister Martha were both popular and attractive. They visited the parsonage in 1838.

After Mr. Taylor's death in 1840, Mary and Martha were sent to school in Brussels and were thus the direct cause of Charlotte's interest in that city. Martha died there tragically in 1842 and Mary travelled and taught in Germany. Later, in 1845, she emigrated with her youngest brother to New Zealand, where they ran a food and clothing store. There Charlotte generously, on some pretext, sent her £10, probably, Mary told Mrs. Gaskell, a tenth of her income. She returned to England in 1859 and spent the rest of her life quietly in Yorkshire, refusing to the last to be lionized by Brontë enthusiasts.

Mary Taylor had strong and (for the time) unconventional views on the position of women. She believed they should work and make themselves independent, and she wrote a series of articles in which she enlarges on this principle, also touched on in her novel, *Miss Miles.*

It is certainly a misfortune that Mary did not keep most of Charlotte's letters. She was altogether more intellectual and broader in outlook than the conventional Ellen, and it seems likely that Charlotte would have discussed literature, politics, religion, and perhaps other matters more freely with her. Mary's own letters are vigorous and entertaining. Clement Shorter reprints some of them in *The Brontës and Their Circle,* Ch. IX. Incidentally, the Taylor family inspired the Yorkes in *Shirley.*

Williams, William Smith (1800–75), to whom Charlotte was to address so many of her letters, had as a youth known Keats, Leigh Hunt, and Hazlitt. G. M. Smith discovered him wasting his literary talents in accounting and brought him into the firm of Smith and Elder, which he served to the year of his death.

Winkworth, see Shaen.

CHRONOLOGY OF THE BRONTË FAMILY

1777	Patrick Brontë born
1783	Maria Branwell born
1812	Patrick Brontë and Maria Branwell married
1813	Maria Brontë born
1815	Elizabeth Brontë born
April 21, 1816	Charlotte Brontë born
June 26, 1817	Patrick Branwell Brontë born
July 30, 1818	Emily Jane Brontë born
Jan. 17, 1820	Anne Brontë born
1820	The Rev. Patrick Brontë becomes perpetual curate of Haworth
September 1821	Mrs. Brontë dies and Miss Branwell comes to The Parsonage
July 1, 1824	Maria and Elizabeth Brontë at Cowan Bridge
Aug. 10, 1824	Charlotte at Cowan Bridge
Nov. 25, 1824	Emily at Cowan Bridge
February 1825	Maria leaves Cowan Bridge
May 6, 1825	Maria dies
May 31, 1825	Elizabeth leaves Cowan Bridge
June 1, 1825	Charlotte and Emily leave Cowan Bridge
June 15, 1825	Elizabeth dies
1825	Tabitha Aykroyd comes as parsonage servant
1826	The plays of The Young Men, Our Fellows, and The Islanders established
January 1831	Charlotte goes to Roe Head School, stays until July 1832
July 1835	Charlotte returns to Roe Head as a teacher
July 1835	Emily enters Roe Head as a pupil, stays until October
1835	Branwell visits London, supposedly to enter the Royal Academy, but comes home without doing so
January 1836	Anne at Roe Head as a pupil
1837	The school removed to Dewsbury Moor
c. 1836–7	Emily teaches at Law Hill, Halifax (period of stay debated)
December 1837	Anne leaves Dewsbury Moor
May 1838	Charlotte leaves Dewsbury Moor
April 1839	Anne governess to the Ingrams at Mirfield, leaves in December
May 1839	Charlotte governess to the Sidgwicks at Stone Gappe Hall, Lothersdale
August 1839	The Reverend William Weightman becomes curate at Haworth
September 1839	Charlotte and Ellen at Bridlington
March 1841	Anne governess to the Robinsons at Thorpe Green Hall
March 1841	Charlotte governess to the Whites, Upperwood House, Rawdon, leaves December 1841
February 1842	Charlotte and Emily go to Brussels
Fall 1842	Weightman and Miss Branwell die
November 1842	Charlotte and Emily return to Haworth
December 1842	Branwell goes as tutor to the Robinson boy at Thorpe Green
January 1843	Charlotte goes back to teach at the Pensionnat Heger
January 3, 1844	Charlotte returns to Haworth
1844	The Rev. Arthur Bell Nicholls becomes curate at Haworth
June 1845	Anne leaves Thorpe Green, followed by Branwell in July
May 1846	Poems by Currer, Ellis, and Acton Bell published; the girls all working on their novels by this year
August 1846	Charlotte takes her father to Manchester for cataract operation and there begins Jane Eyre

October	1847	*Jane Eyre* published, second edition December 1847
December	1847	*Wuthering Heights* and *Agnes Grey* published
July	1848	Charlotte and Anne visit their publishers
July	1848	*The Tenant of Wildfell Hall* published
Sept. 24,	1848	Branwell dies
Dec. 19,	1848	Emily dies
May 28,	1849	Anne dies at Scarborough
Oct. 26,	1849	*Shirley* published
Nov.–Dec.	1849	Charlotte in London, meets Thackeray and Miss Martineau
March	1850	Charlotte visits Sir James Kay-Shuttleworth at Gawthorpe Hall, Lancashire
June	1850	Charlotte visits London, meets Lewes, sees Wellington, attends Thackeray's dinner party, has portrait painted by Richmond
July	1850	Charlotte visits Edinburgh with George Smith
August	1850	Charlotte visits the Kay-Shuttleworths at Briery Close, Windermere, and meets Mrs. Gaskell
Fall	1850	Charlotte edits her sisters' works
December	1850	Charlotte visits Miss Martineau at The Knoll, Ambleside, Windermere
May–June	1851	Charlotte visits London, hears Thackeray, visits the Crystal Palace
June	1851	Charlotte visits Mrs. Gaskell in Manchester
June	1852	Charlotte visits Filey and Scarborough
December	1852	Mr. Nicholls proposes
January	1853	Charlotte visits London: *Villette* published
April	1853	Charlotte visits Mrs. Gaskell
September	1853	Mrs. Gaskell visits Haworth
January	1854	Mr. Nicholls stays with a friend near Haworth
April	1854	Charlotte engaged to Mr. Nicholls
May	1854	Mr. Nicholls again curate at Haworth
May	1854	Charlotte visits Mrs. Gaskell
June 29,	1854	Charlotte and Mr. Nicholls are married, and visit Wales and Ireland
February	1855	Tabitha Aykroyd dies, aged 84
March 31,	1855	Charlotte dies
	1857	*The Professor* published
	1857	Mrs. Gaskell's *Life of Charlotte Brontë* published
June	1861	Mr. Brontë dies
	1906	Mr. Nicholls dies

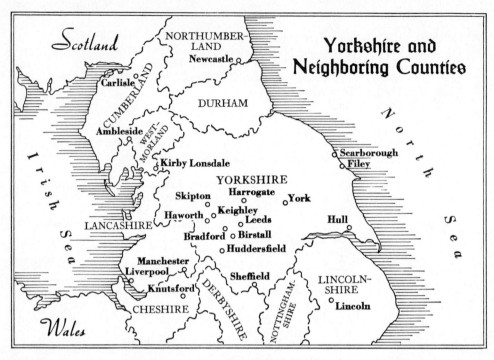

Yorkshire and Neighboring Counties

Scotland

NORTHUMBER-LAND
Newcastle

Carlisle

CUMBERLAND

DURHAM

North Sea

WEST-MORLAND

Ambleside

Irish Sea

Kirby Lonsdale

YORKSHIRE

Scarborough
Filey

Skipton

Harrogate

York

Keighley

Haworth

Leeds

LANCASHIRE

Bradford

Birstall

Hull

Huddersfield

Manchester
Liverpool

Sheffield

LINCOLN-SHIRE

Knutsford

DERBYSHIRE

NOTTINGHAM-SHIRE

Lincoln

CHESHIRE

Wales

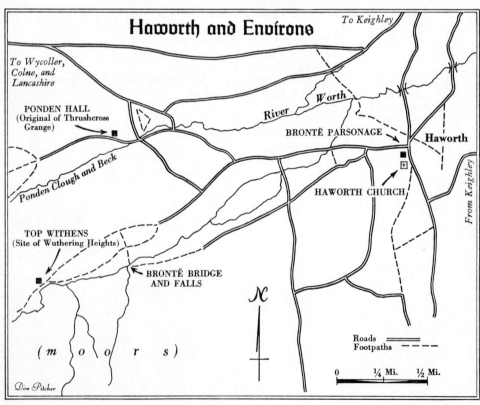

Haworth and Environs

To Keighley

To Wycoller,
Colne, and
Lancashire

River Worth

PONDEN HALL
(Original of Thrushcross
Grange)

BRONTË PARSONAGE

Haworth

Ponden Clough and Beck

HAWORTH CHURCH

From Keighley

TOP WITHENS
(Site of Wuthering Heights)

BRONTË BRIDGE
AND FALLS

(m o o r s)

N

Roads
Footpaths

0   ¼ Mi.   ½ Mi.

Don Pitcher

I. The Childhood of the Brontës

"Oh, God, my poor children — Oh, God, my poor children!" So Maria Branwell Brontë, dying of cancer at Haworth in 1821. She could not even bear to have the children in her sick room, for she dreaded to have them see her suffer, and their presence increased her own misery over their motherless future. She would have understood the recurrence of the orphan motif in their writings.

The Reverend and Mrs. Patrick Brontë had come to Haworth with their six children less than a year before. There were three girls, one little boy, then two baby girls. We can picture the young family, with their furniture and baggage loaded in seven carts, climbing for the first time the steep hill to the grey straggling village, the ancient church, and finally, highest of all, the parsonage, which looked out on the graveyard with the moors stretching beyond it.[1]

We may imagine that the little Brontës were left much to themselves during their mother's illness. Doubtless Maria and Elizabeth, seven and six respectively, often shepherded little Charlotte and Branwell, Emily and Anne when they were old enough, out on the moors to play.[2] After his wife's death and the failure of his attempts to remarry, Mr. Brontë became more aloof from his family, taking most of his meals alone and spending much time in his study. He did eat breakfast with the children, entertaining them with tales of the old days in Ireland, of heroic Methodism, and of the machine-smashing Luddite riots. But a woman was needed to supervise the children and keep the house, and eventually it was settled that Miss Elizabeth Branwell, Mrs. Brontë's sister, would stay permanently in the parsonage to look after the children.

About this time Mr. Brontë must have heard of the Clergy Daughters' School at Cowan Bridge, recently founded by the Reverend W. Carus Wilson, then Vicar of Tunstall, later (1825) Rector of Whittington. The governess or supervisor of the school was a Miss Evans. Maria and Elizabeth Brontë were sent here in July 1824 and Charlotte and Emily soon followed them. From here Maria (now twelve) and Elizabeth returned home to die early the next summer, leaving Charlotte, who had looked up to Maria as a mother, for the second time motherless. Now, at nine, she was the eldest child. From her misery and grief at Cowan Bridge sprang the early chapters of *Jane Eyre,* and Maria Brontë was the prototype of Helen Burns. The fact that Charlotte was so emotionally involved in the sufferings of Helen and Jane has given rise to some very interesting questions. Is Lowood, with its hardships and its loveless travesty of Christianity, a fair picture of Cowan Bridge? And what was the founder of the school, the Mr. Brocklehurst of *Jane Eyre,* really like? Was he the monster of hypocrisy Charlotte pictured? Or was he the admirable exemplar of Christian "good works" he thought himself? Fortunately for the curious, the essential facts about Mr. Carus Wilson and a large number of his works survive.

William Carus Wilson was an evangelical clergyman in the Church of England, known to his contemporaries for his piety and charitable works, particularly for the founding of this school, which in 1833 was moved to a better site at Casterton, where it still flourishes. He was a prolific writer and editor of juvenile literature of an evangelical cast, for example, *The Infant's Magazine, The Children's Friend,* and (for Sunday school teachers) *The Teachers' Visitor.* All three periodicals and another volume

---

[1] American students may need to be reminded that "the church" means the Church of England.
[2] Find, if you can, Joan Hassall's imaginative picture of this in Margaret Lane, *The Brontë Story,* London: William Heinemann, Ltd., 1953, p. 41.

1

entitled *Youthful Memoirs*, abound in anecdotes relating to the sayings, deeds, and deathbeds of extremely pious and articulate small children who prefer heaven to earth and the Bible to any other reading, perform acts of self-sacrifice and self-denial, learn psalms and hymns with alacrity, and die reciting verses of Scripture. Other stories recount hangings, massacres, and the sudden deaths of naughty children. A few of the anecdotes — out of hundreds which still exist — are printed below, together with some verses from Carus Wilson's hymns.

There seems no particular reason to question Mr. Carus Wilson's sincerity or good intentions. He probably lived and wrote according to his convictions, yet we are bound to ask "Was he wise?" and "Is Mr. Brocklehurst a fair picture of him?" When he died in 1859, the Bishop of Rochester wrote in his obituary, "He had the singular felicity of improving, if not anticipating, in his various plans for benevolence, the leading ideas of his age, and his name has long been a household word in every Christian family. In church building, in the diffusion of cheap Christian literature, and in education, his exertions for half a century have earned him the blessings of rich and poor." Ernest Raymond, who quotes this passage in his *In the Steps of the Brontës* (p. 56–7), comments, "A better man than many; but it was his misfortune that while he was lecturing to his girls at Cowan Bridge on the need for righteousness if they were not to perish everlastingly, there was among them a child of eight, but so small as to look no more than five, who was listening. Why did not the Spirit of the Future touch him on the arm and whisper:

> A chiel's among you takin' notes,
> And, faith, he'll prent it!

For the Bishop might write what he liked, but he had no power against the child. His words perished the day after they were published, but the black marble clergyman which the child created endures like a monument."

The student who wishes to decide between Charlotte and the bishop should read, in addition to this section, Charlotte's relevant letters (especially that to Miss Wooler of August 28, 1848, and those to W. S. Williams of Oct. 28, 1847, Jan. 4, 1848, Nov. 5, 1849); *Jane Eyre*, Chapters I–X; Mrs. Gaskell's observations on Cowan Bridge (V); and the letters of controversy between Charlotte's husband and the defenders of the school (VI). Mrs. Gaskell's account, which gave rise to this controversy, was somewhat colored by Charlotte's recollections and by her own indignation on behalf of the Brontës. Some of her inaccuracies can be corrected by a careful reading of the school documents below.

For five and a half years after the Cowan Bridge catastrophe, Mr. Brontë made no attempt to send any of his children away to school. Under Miss Branwell's direction, the household ran like clockwork and the girls were educated in the household arts. Aunt also impressed on the children some of the teachings of the emotional, evangelical Methodism she had brought from Penzance. Under her direction they learned by heart Wesleyan hymns and prayers and read pious stories reeking of hellfire and brimstone and of the glories of triumphant living in Christ. None escaped some effect of this teaching.

Otherwise, however, the children were left much to their own devices by both father and aunt. They did not play with other children but, happily free from grown-up interference, entertained each other with their "plays" which were at first acted out and later written down, blossoming into a corporate day-dream shared and lived intensely by all of them. The games absorbed all they read and heard — *Arabian Nights*,

Aesop's Fables, Pilgrim's Progress, the Methodist magazines, Homer, Scott, Shakespeare, the Bible, even the *Imitation of Christ* — and, primary influences, the poetry of Byron and the political talk for which Mr. Brontë had such a passion. The Duke of Wellington (strangely metamorphosed) and his two sons, the Marquis of Douro and Lord Charles Wellesley, played gaudy roles in the adventures, while the children themselves were genii, presiding spirits who could come in a flash of lightning to raise the dead, rescue a favorite from savages, or (like Homer's gods) direct the course of a battle.

"I am the Chief Genius Brannii," wrote Branwell. "With me are three others. She Wellesley, who protects you, is named Tallii; she who protects Parry is named Emmii; she who protects Ross is called Annii. Those lesser ones whom ye saw are Genii and Fairies, our slaves and minions. . . . We are the guardians of you all."[3] So the children held the destinies of men and nations in their small hands and could at will bring their entire world to life. An ancient geography book provided some place-names and perhaps, along with the current Ashanti Wars on the Gold Coast, suggested the move to an Africa no explorer had ever seen. There, Branwell tells us, the "Twelves" invaded the land and made their capital at Glass Town which the Genii obligingly raised up for them, and eventually founded and settled in a cluster of townships known as the Glass Town Confederacy; later an Eastern province, Angria, gave its name to the whole saga. War, politics, intrigues were the stuff of these blood-and-thunder dramas. Branwell handled the battles and the Parliamentary debates, while Charlotte planned the romances, developed the characters, and described the scenery.

The various events were chronicled in histories, tales, and novelettes, and in periodicals such as the *Young Men's Magazine.* These periodicals, in imitation of the ones the children saw at home, contained poems, plays, book reviews, speeches, pen-portraits, and advertisements. They were written in different styles and under different pen names; for example, Branwell wrote as Captain Bud, Captain Flower, and the poet Young Soult; while Charlotte wrote in the persons of Captain Tree, Lord Charles Wellesley, and the Marquis of Douro. Over a hundred of these tiny booklets still survive, some only an inch and a half long, printed (for economy and secrecy) in microscopic script and often neatly stitched into covers of blue or brown wrapping paper. Some of the tiny pages contain as many as 1500 words.

Twice the series of adventures was interrupted. Charlotte's departure for the Roe Head School was evidently regarded as the end of an era, for the four genii in conclave decided to destroy Great Glass Town. Charlotte celebrated the city's destruction in a poem "The Trumpet Hath Sounded." But the game was too delightful to be given up. Presently Branwell was sending Charlotte "Letters from an Englishman," in which he reported the latest military and political events from the Angria Confederacy. The plays were resumed on Charlotte's return and when at nineteen she went back to Roe Head to teach, the Angria dreams accompanied her. (See her diary fragments of August and October, 1836.) She continued the saga whenever she could until she resolved, with obvious pain, to cut herself off from the fantasy when she was twenty-three. Even so, as late as 1843, alone and homesick in Brussels, she wrote Branwell that her thoughts in her desolation returned nostalgically to "the world below." Meanwhile, probably after Charlotte left for Roe Head, Emily and Anne started a rival saga dealing with the islands of Gondal and Gaaldine. The tales of civil war, heroic deeds and loves, imprisonments, escapes by land and sea are as melodramatic as the Angrian stories, but are more

[3] See Branwell's "History of the Young Men," *Miscellaneous and Unpublished Writings of Charlotte and Patrick Branwell Brontë,* ed. Thomas James Wise and John Alexander Symington, 2 vols., Oxford: Basil Blackwell, 1936, 1938, I, 78–9; cited below as S. H. *Misc.* Parry and Ross were two of the heroes.

austere and less amoral. See comments by Phylis Bentley (*The Brontës*, pp. 23–4) and the Hansons (*The Four Brontës*, p. 22).

Anonymous

Cowen [sic] Bridge College advertisement, reprinted in *B.S.T.*, XI (Pt. 56).

This advertisement, copied from an unknown newspaper, was found among some old papers in an office in Kirkby Lonsdale, Yorkshire. With it were the next two items, the Prospectus, which we shall call Prospectus A, and the "New Song," written to the tune of "St. Patrick's Day." Both the Prospectus and the verses are handwritten in the copybook style of the period. Compare it with Item 2 and decide if either or both should be accepted or rejected. If you reject any part of these documents as not bona fide, how do you account for their existence? Can you date Prospectus A on internal evidence?

1

20 CLERGYMEN's daughters are liberally Boarded and clothed, supplied with Books, and carefully instructed by The Rev. W. Wilson and skillful assistants in every department of Classical and Polite Literature, English, French and Italian Languages, Geography (with the use of the Globe), Arithmetic, Music, Fine Needle Work for £14.0.0. per Annum each. N.B. Utmost attention is paid in rendering the students accomplished. The only extras are for instructions in Dancing and Riding — half a guinea per quarter each.

A doctor visits the College regularly once a week. No doctor's Bills. No vacations allowed.

The utmost attention is paid to their Moral and Religious instruction, and due care is taken to inculcate Religious principles, and Habits, as the surest Basis of sound Learning and pious conduct.

Further particulars may be had by applying to The Rev. W. Wilson, Whittington Rectory, or to W. W. Wilson, M.P., Casterton Hall, who will give references to clergymen of the greatest respectability who have placed their daughters under their care at this College. . . .

Anonymous

[Prospectus A] Cowan Bridge College, printed in *B.S.T.*, XI (Pt. 56).

2

20 Patron —— W. W. C. Wilson, M.P.
Rector and Theological Lecturer ——
    Rev. W. Wilson, M.A.
Assistant Lecturers
    In Housekeeping, Domestic Economy ——
    Rev. R. Wilson, M.A.
Elocution, Ventriloquy ——
    Rev. Edward Wilson

Latin, Greek, and Philosophy ——
    Rev. Ian Blythe
Female managing Assistants, Teachers, Head Manager and teacher in Arithmetic and Dress-making ——
    Mrs. W. Wilson
Foreign Language, Dancing, Riding ——
    Mrs. Ann Wilson

English, Reading, and Poetry ——
   Miss Jane Thompson
Singing and Scourgemistress ——
   Miss Finch
Physician ——
   W. Batty, M.D., M.L.H.L.
Chemist, Dentist —— Mrs. Batty
Solicitor, Law Agent ——
   John Hartley, Esq. . . .

21 The object of this Institution may simply be said to afford a comfortable home and all the Blessings of a Pious Liberal and Refined Education to the daughters of necessitous Clergy.

To provide the future success of this Scheme, pecuniary assistance from the pious and Charitable is absolutely necessary.

It is truly painful to reflect how many Poor Clergymen are utterly unable to bestow that on their female offspring to which their rank in Society entitles them.

This civilized Island is blessed with various laudable institutions for the promotion of Classical and Scientific Learning and clergymen can send their sons to the University where ample scope is afforded for those Bright talents which are so frequently found in an humble sphere of life. But hitherto, no colleges, no liberal institutions of learning for their daughters where they can reap those blessings their Brethren enjoy, and it by no means unfrequently happens that we see these pious girls busy — perhaps in a Dairy or employed in some menial occupation in a kitchen, and at the very same time their brothers are enjoying Fellowship or Scholarship in a University or some other valuable employment, the reward of their Assiduity and Literary Attainments.

Such circumstances, together with repeated Solicitations of my father, family and friends, have at length induced me to open a Clerical School, approaching as nigh as possible in resemblance (as to mode of Instruction, Rules, Dress, etc.) to a College. For this purpose I have already engaged professional teachers of more than ordinary talent to assist me in superintending the Education of the Students. Their abilities need no comment from me; they have already distinguished themselves by their accomplishments. I could afford instances of such, but seeing they are members for the most part of my own family, I refrain from motives of delicacy.

These gentlemen I have engaged in the various classes of Lecturers, Etc. (vide Prospectus) at a Salary of £100 each. Attendance required — three days per week, 8 hours per day.

The Female Teachers I have engaged to be constantly resident at College (excepting my sister whom domestic afflictions must necessarily detain at her father's house during the winter session), at a salary of 50 guineas per an. each.

All the teachers named in the prospectus receive the above mentioned sum as being teachers, etc., excepting Miss Finch (a lady well known for the pious fortitude and resignation with which she has borne various trying afflictions) who has engaged for a very trifling annual remuneration to assist me in regulating the *Discipline* of the College.

Doctor Batty has engaged for the sum of £120 per annum to supply the students with all needful Medicines and to visit professionally every Friday in the week. His wife has also volunteered for a trifling gratuity to impart those portions of Chemical and Dental knowledge. . . .

Anonymous

Cowen [*sic*] Bridge College: A New Song, printed in *B.S.T.*, XI (Pt. 56).[1]

3

23   The following was written on sight of an Advertisement (to which was attached a prospectus of what is termed a collegiate Academy) (vide contra) in a Country Newspaper of the date of August, 1824.

All the various particulars "set forth" in the above advertisement are related in the following verses, with the utmost veracity, and in as concise and correct a manner as possible.

F. Neydhame.

1.

Come hither good neighbours, and cease from
your Labours,
And ye Reverend Clergy attend,
Whilst I tell of a College, replenished with
Knowledge,
To which ye your daughters may send.

2.

We've had many troubles, and various
Bubbles,[2]
Of Schemes both on Land and On Water,
And a pious good man, has commenced a
Cheap Plan,
Of Rearing each clergyman's Daughter. . . .

24   #### 5.

The Students are clothed, and liberally
Boarded,
For Fourteen pounds sterling per Annum;
And well-vers'd in Knowledge, returning
from College,
Each Lass will amaze her old Gran'num. . . .

8.

Both French and Italian each Student shall
speak;
Shall warble in Hymns and quote Scripture;

[1] As the "song" is very long, only some of the verses are printed.
[2] Inflated speculation in stocks followed by a crash.

And the Rector, in person, shall thrice in the
Week,
On various Sciences lecture.

9.

He will Modesty preach, by example he'll
teach,
'Em Gratitude, Meekness and Tact,
Meantime his Young Wife, the Sole prop of
his Life,
Instructs them to add and Subtract.

10.

Next Roger, his Brother, by all ranks esteem'd,
Shall lecture on Breeding and Marriage,
For to steal a Rich heiress he's cleverly schem'd
And his plans cannot fail from Miscarriage.
. . .

14.   25

Now to keep all in order, and punish disorder,
And all kinds of Rows which may rise,
They'll a Mistress require, full of spirit and
fire,
Who can flog with false tears in her eyes.

15.

Miss Finch famed for Strength, and in pun-
gency skill'd,
The Flogg-mistress' office shall fill,
With Rods steep'd in pickle, she'll charmingly
tickle,
The Nun who conducts herself ill. . . .

26.

The Reverend Rector has tried every plan   26
Of procuring the Students choice food.
And buys Butchers meat (wholesale) as cheap
as he can,
Providing 'tis wholesome — and good. . . .

27   32.

The House Mistress enacts a most rigorous
    Law;
    That at College no flipp'ry be seen;
That instead of Caps, students wear Bonnets
    of Straw,
And instead of Gowns — robes of Nankeen.
    . . .

    37.

28 Then haste, Oh, ye parsons — no longer delay

In sending your daughters to college,
Fair Science stands ready to light up their way
    On the true Path of Virtue and
    Knowledge. . . .

    40.

This Scheme to its Rector will lucre unfold,
    Before 'tis reduced to a level,
And his pockets well-cramm'd with Simonical
    Gold,
    He'll a school keep at last with the Devil.

Anonymous

[Prospectus B] School for Clergymen's Daughters, reprinted in *B.S.T.*, XII (Pt. 63).

4

190   It has long been a subject of regret among the friends of the established Church, that the provision for a considerable portion of the Clergy is inadequate to their support; and whether we consider the happiness of individuals, or the welfare of parishes and congregations, few projects can more strongly recommend themselves to our benevolence, than those which aim at the alleviation of this evil. Efforts of this nature have long been made with considerable success. The salutary effects of Queen Anne's Bounty[1] are felt throughout the kingdom. The Corporation of the Sons of the Clergy, and the Clergy Orphan Society, are the means of relieving much misery; while in most of our dioceses, Clerical Charities have been established, and are in successful operation.

In addition to the means already adopted, of administering to the wants of the poorer Clergy, a School is now opened for the education of their Daughters, at Cowen Bridge in the parish of Tunstall; and on the turnpike road from Leeds to Kendall; between which towns a Coach runs daily. The property is transferred to Trustees;

[1] Queen Anne's Bounty (1703), grant of the first fruits and tithes which Henry VIII had confiscated for the crown; used to increase the incomes of clergy whose benefices were small.

thereby to guard against the uncertainties of the life of the projector; and to perpetuate the establishment for the benefit of those for whom it is designed.

The house is enlarged and altered for the accommodation of sixty or seventy pupils; each pupil pays £14 a year (half in advance) for clothing, lodging, boarding, and educating; and £1 entrance towards the expense / of books &c. The education is 191 directed according to the capacities of the pupils, and the wishes of their friends. In all cases, the great object in view is their intellectual and religious improvement; and to give that plain and useful education, which may best fit them to return with respectability and advantage to their own homes, or to maintain themselves in the different stations of life to which Providence may call them.

In cases where the parents are unable to pay the whole of the annual sum of £14, (which unhappily must frequently occur) it is hoped that more affluent parishioners, and other friends, who are locally interested in a Clergyman, will gladly avail themselves of this method of administering to his wants.

It is calculated, that the sum of £14 will so far defray the whole annual expenditure, as not to require more than £200, or

£250 a year, to be raised by subscription.

The school is open to the whole kingdom. Donors and Subscribers will gain the first attention in the recommendation of pupils; and every effort will be made to confine the benefits of the school to the *really* necessitous clergy.

Several additions have been made to the original plan; but it is expected that about £500 more will cover the first expenditure.

The undertaking is an arduous and responsible one; but it has been ventured upon in a confident expectation, that the plan will recommend itself to the benevolent members of our Church, and ensure their liberal assistance. It were indeed to be wished, that the Clergy could be relieved from the necessity of accepting such aid as is now proposed to them; but until that object is effected, it is clearly incumbent on the friends of religion, to do what they can on behalf of a class of persons, on whose welfare so much depends that of the community at large.

Donations and subscriptions are received by the Rev. Wm. Carus Wilson, M.A., Vicar of Tunstall, near Kirkby Lonsdale, who will be happy to give further particulars; and to receive recommendations of proper pupils. He may be addressed under cover to W. W. Carus Wilson, Esq., M.P., Casterton Hall, Kirkby Lonsdale. Contributions will also be received by Messrs. Hatchard, 187 Piccadilly, London; George Thorne, Esq., Bristol; the Rev. J. Scholefield, Fellow of Trinity College, Cambridge; John Ingleby, Esq., Walthamstow; and Messrs. Heywood and Co. Bankers, Manchester.

Tunstall Vicarage, August 1824

ENTRANCE RULES, &C.

I   The terms for clothing, lodging, boarding, and educating are £14 a year; half to be paid in advance when the pupils are sent: and also £1 entrance money for the use of books &c. The system of education comprehends History, Geography, the Use of the Globes, Grammar, Writing and Arithmetic; all kinds of Needlework, and the nicer kinds of household-work, such as getting up fine linen, &c. If Accomplishments are required, an additional charge is made, for French, Music, or Drawing, of £3 a year each.

II   It is particularly requested that the wishes of the friends may be stated regarding the line of education for each pupil; as it will be desirable to give it that direction, which will best suit their future prospects, as well as their respective dispositions and abilities.

III   Each pupil must bring with her, a Bible and Prayer Book, a Workbag, with necessary Sewing Implements, &c., Combs, Brushes, Pair of Pattens, Gloves, and the following Articles of clothing, &c.

 4 Day Shifts
 3 Night do.
 3 Night Caps
 2 Pair of Stays
 2 Flannel Petticoats
 3 White Upper Petticoats
 1 Grey Stuff do.
 2 Pair of Pockets
 4 Pair of White Cotton Stockings
 3 Pair of Black worsted do.
 1 Nankeen Spencer
 4 Brown Holland Pinafores
 2 White do.
 1 Short coloured Dressing Gown.
 2 Pair of Shoes

The pupils all appear in the same dress. They wear plain straw cottage bonnets; in summer, white frocks on Sundays, and nankeen on other days. In winter, purple stuff frocks and purple cloth pelisses. For the sake of uniformity, therefore, it is requested that each pupil may bring £3 in lieu of frocks, pelisse, bonnet, tippet, and frills. They may however bring with them such bonnet, spencer or pelisse, as they may happen to be wearing at the time of their coming: as they will answer for walking out and playing.

IV   There are five weeks holiday at Midsummer; but any of the pupils may remain at the school during the holidays, for which £1 1s. is to be paid.

V The parents are requested to state what diseases incidental to children each girl has had.

VI A quarter's notice is requested previous to the removal of a pupil.

VII All letters and parcels will be inspected by the Governess.

Cowan Bridge School Records

[Entries on the Brontë children] printed in Ernest Raymond, *In the Steps of the Brontës*. London: Rich and Cowan, 1948. Reprinted by permission.

5

54 Maria Brontë, aged 10½ (daughter of Patrick Brontë, Haworth, near Keighley, Yorks), July 21st, 1824: Reads tolerably. Writes pretty well. Ciphers a little. Works [i.e. sews] very badly. Knows a little grammar, geography and history. Has made some progress in reading French, but knows nothing of the language grammatically. Left February 14th, 1825, in ill-health, and died May 6, 1825.

55 Elizabeth Brontë, aged 9. (Vaccinated. Scarlet fever. Whooping cough.) Reads little. Writes pretty well. Works very badly. Knows nothing else. Left in ill-health, May 31st, 1825. Died June 15, 1825, in decline.

Charlotte Brontë. Entered school August 10, 1824. Writes indifferently. Ciphers a little and works neatly. Knows nothing of grammar, geography, history, or accomplishments. Altogether clever for her age, but knows nothing systematically. Left school June 1, 1825. Governess.

Emily Brontë. Entered Nov. 25, 1824, aged 5¾. Reads very prettily and works a little. Left June 1, 1825. Subsequent career, governess.

William Carus Wilson

From W. Carus Wilson [ed.] *The Children's Friend*. Published in Kirkby Lonsdale, Westmoreland.

6

(V, No. li, March, 1828)

71 'Tis he that keeps me strong and well
  While many others die;
And if they're naughty, go to hell,
  Who are as young as I.

(V, No. liii, May, 1828)[1]

[An editorial called "The Last Day" reflects on this inscription seen on a child's tomb.]

[1] Each volume of *The Children's Friend* has a biblical text on its title page. The text for this volume is "Suffer the little children to come unto me."

When the archangel's trump shall sound, 97
And souls to bodies join;
Thousands will wish their stay on earth
Had been as short as mine.

. . . You have passed the age of infancy. 99
. . . [continues the editor] You have now entered the season of either childhood or youth; and have become responsible. . . .

'Tis dang'rous to provoke a God
  Whose power and vengeance none can
  tell.
One stroke of his almighty rod
  Can send young sinners quick to hell.

From *Youthful Memoirs*. Philadelphia: American Sunday School Union, 1829.[2]

7

JANE BROWN

41   New bonnets had been given at school to the children. A person, who doubtless wished to show a mark of her approval of Jane, trimmed her bonnet, and made it appear more showy than the rest. She took it home, and said to her mother, [sic] "mother, I can't wear this bonnet; I can't /
42 for shame put it on . . . and bursting into tears, she said, "What am I, a poor vile sinner, that I should be better dressed than the rest!" [Soon after she was taken ill, but professed to have no fears of death]. . . . "I was talking before my sickness about having a new frock this summer, if spared, but I shall have a better robe to wear, than the one I thought of having — I shall have a robe, washed, and made white in the blood of the Lamb." [She died in great pain, quoting Scripture to the last.]

LITTLE GEORGE

59   The Rev. Mr. —— was preaching at the town of C—— on behalf of the Church Missionary Society. . . . Little George was at Church that day, and after the clergyman had ended his sermon, George felt his heart open to give all he had . . . and run-
60 ning breathless / into the house, said, "mother will you let me have my guinea to give to the Missionary Society?" George's mother said "my dear, your feelings are warm now, but perhaps by and by you will be sorry you have given so much . . . "no," said George "I would like to give it all, mother, there are so many ignorant little children. . . . If I had a guinea I could put it between two half-pence and nobody

2 The Memoirs include many accounts of pious deaths, even of children so holy that they prefer death to life, usually expiring while reciting the Lord's Prayer or a pious hymn from *The Children's Friend* (a periodical by W. C. W.). One story tells of a girl who dies urging her Jewish father to follow Christ, of whom she had never been taught, but who appeared to her in her sickness (pp. 37–40).

would know a thing about it." [Later George died.]

DAUGHTER OF THE REV. T. SCOTT

[This account was supplied by the father of the child.] / At the age of three years 27 and a half, she had a very painful and uncommon illness. For many weeks she could take neither medicine nor food, but what was poured down her throat. . . . I often and most earnestly besought the Lord, that He would not take her from me without some token of her repentance, and faith in his mercy through the Lord Jesus Christ. To the surprize of all she came round; and lived just another year . . . . on my return home one evening, my wife told me that the child had been very naughty. . . . I took her between my knees and . . . . told her, she had often heard / that she was a sin- 28 ner before God . . . . that she had disobeyed her mother and thus sinned against God, and made him angry at her — far more angry than her mother had been: that she had often heard that she must have a new heart . . . without which she could not be happy after death. I went on to talk with her, in language suited to her age, about the love and mercy of Christ . . . . I ended by pressing upon her to pray to Jesus Christ to forgive her sins, to give her a new heart, and not to let her die until he had done so. [From then on the child prayed every day for a new heart / and learned 29 many of the Olney (Cowper's) hymns by heart, and rebuked other sinners.] Our servant sometimes used the name of God in an improper manner; and the child would kindly talk to her and say "do not use such words, Kitty; you will indeed go to hell if you say such naughty words." [She died very suddenly, aged 4½, praying 30–3 for patience and reciting the Lord's Prayer.]

A—— G——

At the end of each Sunday's teaching I 100

used to read a certain text of Scripture.... / Scripture which she statedly repeated to
101 The children were requested in addition to her teacher always far more than her
their catechisms and hymns, to commit to allotted task.
memory this text; and on the next Sunday [She became a teacher and taught with
to bring me an explanation of it, and as pleasure and delight for some time until
many parallel passages as they could find she went into consumption.] / Though her 102
in their Bible. The explanation given by sufferings were great, she always showed a
little Ann was generally so good, the texts sweet spirit of resignation to the will of
which she had noted down so many and so her heavenly Father.... / "Speak not of 103
properly chosen, that I was fully convinced my goodness (she said) for what I have
she was truly in earnest. She also far ex- been, it was grace that made me; and in-
ceeded the greater part of her schoolfellows stead of weeping, you ought rather to re-
in the number of hymns and verses of joice, that I am going to glory."

From W. Carus Wilson [ed.], *Original Hymns for Maternal Meetings.* London: Piper
and Co., 1844.

8

21 Lord! give us grace, that we may train   But if correction's rod they need
    Our children up for Thee!   The stubborn will to bow,
    From every evil way restrain,   Let not mistaken fondness plead,
    And evil company. . . .   But wisdom them bestow.

Extracts from *Thoughts Suggested to the Superintendent and Ladies of the 'Clergy
Daughters' School' at Casterton, on their Re-Assembling* by The Rev. W. Carus-Wilson,
M.A. 1858: T. Butler, Printer.

9

39 The pupils are necessarily put into a very   that trivial and useless work is discounte-
simple and a uniform attire. Many of them   nanced amongst the pupils the better. My
no doubt feel it. They have been unfortu-   earnest desire is, that they should be brought
nately accustomed perhaps even to excess   up usefully, not tawdrily. The tinsel and
in this very prevailing and increasing love   varnish are of little moment compared with
of dress; for, alas! clergymen's families are excellence in plain useful work. It will be
not exempt from the mania, — not even the   a sorry look-out for a clergyman's daughter,
poorest. With me it was always an object   if she is sent out from the school, for into nip in the bud any growing symptoms   stance, a first-rate performer in crotchet and
of vanity. . . .   worsted work, and that sort of thing — how-
                                               ever useful this may be — but unable to cut
                                               out, and make, and mend her own garments.
40 And let me add, that I am sure the more

Charlotte Brontë

"History of the Year 1829" [G.][1]

10

[March 12, 1829]
55 Once Papa lent my sister Maria a book. It was an old geography book; she wrote on its blank leaf, "Papa lent me this book." This book is a hundred and twenty years old; it is at this moment lying before me. While I write this I am in the kitchen of the Parsonage, Haworth; Tabby, the servant, is washing up the breakfast-things, and Anne, my youngest sister (Maria was my eldest), is kneeling on a chair, looking at some cakes which Tabby had been baking for us. Emily is in the parlour, brushing the carpet. Papa and Branwell are gone to Keighley. Aunt is up-stairs in her room, and I am sitting by the table writing this in the kitchen. Keighley is a small town four miles from here. Papa and Branwell are gone for the newspaper, the *Leeds Intelligencer,* a most excellent Tory newspaper, edited by Mr. Wood, and the proprietor, Mr. Henneman.[2] We take two and see three newspapers a week. We take the *Leeds Intelligencer,* Tory, and the *Leeds Mercury,* Whig, edited by Mr. Baines, and his brother, son-in-law, and his two sons, Edward and Talbot. We see the *John Bull;* it is a high Tory, very violent. Mr. Driver lends us it, as likewise *Blackwood's Magazine,* the most able periodical there is. The Editor is Mr. Christopher North, an old man seventy-four years of age; the 1st of April is his birth-day; his company are Timothy Tickler, Morgan O'Doherty, Macrabin Mordecai, Mullion, Warnell, and James

Hogg, a man of most extraordinary genius, a Scottish shepherd. Our plays were established; *Young Men,* June, 1826; *Our Fellows,* July 1827; *Islanders,* December, 1827. These are our three great plays, that are not kept secret. Emily's and my best plays[3] were established the 1st of December, 1827; the others March, 1828. Best plays mean secret plays; they are very nice ones. All our plays are very strange ones. Their nature I need not write on paper, for I think I shall always remember them. The *Young Men's* play took its rise from some wooden soldiers Branwell had; *Our Fellows* from *Æsop's Fables;* and the *Islanders* from several events which happened. I will sketch out the origin of our plays more explicitly if I can. First, *Young Men.* Papa bought Branwell some wooden soldiers at Leeds; when Papa came home it was night, and we were in bed, so next morning Branwell came to our door with a box of soldiers. Emily and I jumped out of bed, and I snatched up one and exclaimed, "This is the Duke of Wellington! This shall be the / Duke!" When I had said this Emily 56 likewise took one up and said it should be hers; when Anne came down, she said one should be hers. Mine was the prettiest of the whole, and the tallest, and the most perfect in every part. Emily's was a grave-looking fellow, and we called him "Gravey." Anne's was a queer little thing, much like herself, and we called him "Waiting-boy." Branwell chose his, and called him "Buonaparte."

---

[1] The "History" mentions all the "plays," but is placed first because it describes the origin of the first game, "the Young Men."

[2] Edward Wood and John *Hernaman.*

[3] The word "best" is Mrs. Gaskell's emendation. The manuscript clearly reads "bed plays."

"The Play of the Islanders" [G.]4

11

53   June the 31st, 1829.
The play of the *Islanders* was formed in December, 1827, in the following manner. One night, about the time when the cold sleet and stormy fogs of November are succeeded by the snow-storms, and high piercing night-winds of confirmed winter, we were all sitting round the warm blazing kitchen fire, having just concluded a quarrel with Tabby concerning the propriety of lighting a candle, from which she came off victorious, no candle having been produced. A long pause succeeded, which was at last broken by Branwell saying, in a lazy manner, "I don't know what to do." This was echoed by Emily and Anne.

Tabby. "Wha ya may go t' bed."

54 *Branwell.* "I'd rather do anything than that."

Charlotte. "Why are you so glum tonight, Tabby? Oh! suppose we had each an island of our own."

Branwell. "If we had I would choose the Island of Man."

Charlotte. "And I would choose the Isle of Wight."

Emily. "The Isle of Arran for me."

Anne. "And mine should be Guernsey."

We then chose who should be chief men in our islands. Branwell chose John Bull, Astley Cooper, and Leigh Hunt; Emily, Walter Scott, Mr. Lockhart, Johnny Lockhart; Anne, Michael Sadler, Lord Bentinck, Sir Henry Halford. I chose the Duke of Wellington and two sons, Christopher North and Co., and Mr. Abernethy.5 Here our conversation was interrupted by the, to us, dismal sound of the clock striking seven, and we were summoned off to bed. The next day we added many others to our list of men, till we got almost all the chief men of the kingdom. After this, for a long time, nothing worth noticing occurred. In June, 1828, we erected a school on a fictitious island, which was to contain 1,000 children. The manner of the building was as follows. The Island was fifty miles in circumference, and certainly appeared more like the work of enchantment than anything real, * * * [Here the MS. unfortunately breaks off.]

Fragment from "Tales of the Islanders," written 1829 [G.]6

12

56 Parliament was opened, and the great Catholic question was brought forward, and the Duke's measures were disclosed, and all was, slander, violence, party-spirit, and confusion. Oh, those six months, from

4 The second game, *The Islanders,* was also popular and perhaps provided the germ of the island saga of Gondal later invented by Emily and Anne. Notice here that Charlotte had already developed an ear for dialogue and a feeling for atmosphere.

5 John Bull, generic name for "typical" honest, plain-dealing Englishman; Astley Cooper, noted surgeon, experimentalist, surgeon to George IV; Leigh Hunt, liberal poet, essayist; Walter Scott, novelist and poet; John Gibson Lockhart, biographer, Scott's son-in-law; Johnny Lockhart was *his* son; Michael Sadler, social reformer, opponent of child labor; Lord Bentinck, either William Cavendish the Governor General of India or Lord George Bentinck, a supporter of Catholic Emancipation and the Reform Bill; Sir Henry Halford, a noted physician (note that seven-year-old Anne's choices were all benefactors of mankind); Arthur Wellesley, Duke of Wellington, the victor of Waterloo; Christopher North (pseud.), publisher of *Blackwood's;* Mr. Abernethy, surgeon at St. Bartholomew's. The physicians and surgeons were needed to take care of the wounded in Branwell's battles.

6 Charlotte inserted this note into Volume II of the "Tales" to explain why she had neglected them. It illustrates further the children's interest in politics.

the time of the King's speech to the end! Nobody could write, think, or speak on any subject but the Catholic question, and the Duke of Wellington, and Mr. Peel. I remember the day when the *Intelligence Extraordinary* came with Mr. Peel's speech in it, containing the terms on which the / 57 Catholics were to be let in! With what eagerness papa tore off the cover, and how we all gathered round him, and with what breathless anxiety we listened, as one by one they were disclosed, and explained, and argued upon so ably, and so well; and then when it was all out, how aunt said that she thought it was excellent, and that the Cath-olics could do no harm with such good security. I remember also the doubts as to whether it would pass the House of Lords, and the prophecies that it would not; and when the paper came which was to decide the question, the anxiety was almost dreadful with which we listened to the whole affair: the opening of the doors; the hush; the royal dukes in their robes, and the great duke in green sash and waistcoat; the rising of all the peeresses when he rose; the reading of his speech — papa saying that his words were like precious gold; and lastly, the majority of one to four (sic) in favour of the Bill. But this is a digression. . . .

"Characters of Celebrated Men of the Present Time" [S. H. *Misc.*]

13

I,37
CHAPTER THE FIRST.
CHARACTER AND DESCRIPTION OF THE
DUKE OF WELLINGTON.

The first time I saw his Grace was about twenty or 21 years ago. He was then in the 19th year of his age and very much like what the Marquis of Duro[7] is now, except that his countenance was more manly and there was a certain expression of sarcasm about his mouth which showed that he considered many of those with whom he associated much beneath him. The next time is only 3 or 4 years since. He was attired in his Field-Marshal's uniform and was standing in Cloud Square surrounded by his staff. His appearance came up to my highest notions of what a great General ought to be — the high stern forehead, noble Roman nose, compressed disdainful lip, and in short, the whole contour of his features were exactly what I should have wished for in the hero of Waterloo, conqueror of Buonaparte. And now for his Grace's character. He is without dispute one of the greatest men that ever lived.

In his disposition he is decisive, calm, courageous and noble-minded. His genius is not confined merely to military affairs. He is equally irresistible in the Cabinet as in the field. The campaigns in the Peninsula prove that the resources of his great mind are inexhaustible. On his bravery and prudence the fortune of all Europe hung for 6 years, and how nobly he returned the trust that was reposed in him is known to every man.

There was no neglect in him, no wavering in his determination. When once a thing was decided it was decided and acted upon. All his conduct was calculated to inspire confidence into the minds of his soldiers and to make them more resolute in the defence of their King and Country. And now some dare to say that this man, this great, this mighty man, knows not how to defend England to save her in her present terrible situation — that he who saved her when the star of destruction cast its livid wasting beams over all her rolling fields and stately cities cannot now save her when no foreign foe threatens her desolation.[8] Let those who say so remember the time when the haughty Napoleon went on conquering and to conquer — when every

---

[7] Usually spelled Douro.

[8] The Duke of Wellington's Tory ministry was voted out of office in 1830.

general that was sent against him withered and died at the blast of his trumpet and fled in terror and dismay at every victory, leaving the victor haughtier than before.

38   When at length the glorious Wellington arose, and the joyous heart-gladdening news rang on the ears of a fainting dying nation that Buonaparte was beaten and vanquished, who was the terrible vanquisher? It was the Immortal Wellington. If he saved England in that hour of tremendous perils, shall he not save her again? . . . I leave the question to be answered by those of my readers who have the mind to comprehend it.

C.B. Captain T [Tree]
December 12, 1829.

CHAPTER THE 2.

CHARACTER OF THE MARQUIS OF DURO

The eldest of these young noblemen, the Marquis of Duro is now in the 22 year of his age. In appearance he strongly resembles his noble mother. He has the same tall slender shape, the same fine and slightly Roman nose. His eyes, however, are large and brown like his father's, and his hair is dark auburn, curly and glossy much like what his father's was when he was young. His character also resembles the Duchess's, mild and humane but very courageous, grateful for any favour that is done, and ready to forgive injuries, kind to others and disinterested in himself.

His mind is of the highest order, elegant and cultivated. His genius is lofty and soaring, but he delights to dwell among pensive thoughts and ideas rather than to roam in the bright regions of fancy. The Meditations of a lonely traveller in the wilderness or the mournful song of a solitary exile are the themes in which he most delights and which he chiefly indulges in, though often his songs consist of grand and vivid descriptions of storms and tempests — of the wild roaring of the ocean mingling with the tremendous voice of thunder when the flashing lightning gleams in unison with the bright lamp of some wicked spirit striding over the face of the troubled waters, or sending forth his cry from the bosom of a black and terrible cloud. Such is the Marquis of Duro. . . .

C.B. Captain Tree Dec 16 1829

"Retrospection," (Written Dec. 19, 1835), from *The Complete Poems of Charlotte Brontë*, ed. Clement Shorter, rev. with Bibliography and Notes, by C. W. Hatfield. London: Hodder and Stoughton, 1923. Reprinted by permission of the publisher.

14

193   We wove a web in childhood,
    A web of sunny air;
We dug a spring in infancy
    Of water pure and fair;

We sowed in youth a mustard seed,
    We cut an almond rod;

We are now grown up to riper age:
    Are they withered in the sod?

Are they blighted, failed and faded   194
    Are they mouldered back to clay?
For life is darkly shaded,
    And its joys fleet fast away!

The Last of Angria, written at Roe Head, 1839 [S.H. *Misc.*]

15

II,403   I have now written a great many books and for a long time have dwelt on the same characters and scenes and subjects. I have shown my landscapes in every variety of shade and light which morning, noon, and evening — the rising, the meridian and the setting sun can bestow upon them. Sometimes I have filled the air with the whitened tempest of winter: snow has embossed the dark arms of the beech and oak and filled with drifts the parks of the lowlands or the mountain-pass of wilder districts. Again, the same mansion with its woods, the same moor with its glens, has been softly coloured with the tints of moonlight in summer, and in the warmest June night the trees have clustered their full-plumed heads over glades flushed with flowers. So it is with persons. My readers have been habituated to one set of features, which they have seen now in profile, now in full face, now in outline, and again in finished painting — varied but by the change of feeling or 404 temper or age; lit with / love, flushed with passion, shaded with grief, kindled with ecstasy; in meditation and mirth, in sorrow and scorn and rapture; with the round outline of childhood, the beauty and fulness of youth, the strength of manhood, and the furrows of thoughtful decline; but we must change, for the eye is tired of the picture so oft recurring and now so familiar.

Yet do not urge me too fast, reader: it is no easy theme to dismiss from my imagination the images which have filled it so long; they were my friends and my intimate acquaintances, and I could with little labour describe to you the faces, the voices, the actions, of those who peopled my thoughts by day, and not seldom stole strangely even into my dreams by night. When I depart from these I feel almost as if I stood on the threshold of a home and were bidding farewell to its inmates. When I strive to conjure up new inmates I feel as if I had got into a distant country where every face was unknown and the character of all the population an enigma which it would take much study to comprehend and much talent to expound. Still, I long to quit for awhile that burning clime where we have sojourned too long — its skies flame — the glow of sunset is always upon it — the mind would cease from excitement and turn now to a cooler region where the dawn breaks grey and sober, and the coming day for a time at least is subdued by clouds.

II. Letters and Papers of Charlotte Brontë

Like many shy people, Charlotte found letter writing a great outlet and to many people probably wrote more easily than she talked. Modern readers will be amused at the formality, stately phraseology, and sometimes heavy-handed humor of her early letters to friends and family — a reflection, no doubt, of the models set in school. Some of this stiffness disappeared later, though only when most moved did she write with ringing simplicity. Her style and subject matter varied according to her correspondent. As Mrs. Sparks remarks in her edition of the letters:

> Her letters to Ellen Nussey, her friend from school days to the end of her life, show Charlotte's inner being only so far as she wished to reveal it, except for some early letters belonging to a particular phase in the relationship. To Ellen she gave few confidences, and much gossip; to her father she was respectful, conventional and patient; to Emily, gay and confiding; and to Branwell, she appears frank, sisterly, sometimes slangy. In her letters to eminent writers and literary friends, Charlotte made an effort to give the best of her intelligence while preserving a subtle appearance of modesty; to her discarded suitor, Henry Nussey, her tone was polite and patronizing; and to M. Hegér, impetuous, passionate and distracted. But this polygonal shape of Charlotte's personality has led to much immoderate interpretation of it, and only by observing each facet of her personality as a part of a whole and in due proportion can we form an integrated idea of this complex woman (pp. 18–19).

Roe Head and Haworth, 1831 to 1835

In January, 1831, Charlotte was sent away to Miss Margaret Wooler's School at Roe Head, near Huddersfield, and remained there until the following spring. Mingling for the first time with girls from comfortable homes, she realized acutely that the future of her sisters depended on her and that any security she could attain must be her own work, as all would have to support themselves if Mr. Brontë died and the parsonage was no longer their home. Branwell was expected to make his way in the world easily, talented as he was in both music and art. He was already taking lessons from a portrait painter in Leeds and planning to go to the Royal Academy. In fact, however, he already had an unwholesome amount of free time, much of which he spent wandering around the village and cracking jokes at the local pub, the Black Bull. The girls also had drawing lessons in this period and all but Charlotte had piano lessons. In their spare time, naturally, they continued to play at Angria and Gondal.

Academic knowledge was not all that Charlotte had brought back from Roe Head. Her imagination was fired by Miss Wooler's account of the Luddite Riots, which had taken place in that very district between the textile workers and the mill owners. Recollections of these tales (and her father's) resulted in an Angrian story about industrial riots in Glass Town and, much later, in *Shirley*. Charlotte also made two life-long friends at Roe Head, Mary Taylor and Ellen Nussey.

Charlotte and Ellen, who exchanged visits in 1832 and '33 (see Ellen's reminiscences), kept up a steady correspondence for the rest of their lives, valuable for details of everyday life at the parsonage. Their friendship in these years was the emotional and sentimental kind sometimes experienced by girls of their age. It was heightened on Charlotte's side by her isolation and by morbid religious doubts and fears, the result, no doubt, of Aunt Branwell's religious teaching, reinforced by much reading of Cowper, whom all the Brontës admired (see his "Castaway" and "I Was a Stricken Deer That Left the Herd").

Footnote numbers in this section run from one to nine or ten and repeat.

1. TO BRANWELL BRONTË [S. H.][1]

Roe Head, May 17th, 1831

I,87 DEAR BRANWELL, — As usual I address my weekly letter to you, because to you I find the most to say. I feel exceedingly anxious to know how and in what state you arrived at home 88 after / your long and (I should think) very fatiguing journey. I could perceive when you arrived at Roe Head that you were very much tired, though you refused to acknowledge it. After you were gone, many questions and subjects of conversation recurred to me which I had intended to mention to you, but quite forgot them in the agitation which I felt at the totally unexpected pleasure of seeing you. Lately I had begun to think that I had lost all the interest which I used formerly to take in politics, but the extreme pleasure I felt at the news of the Reform Bill's being thrown out by the House of Lords, and of the expulsion or resignation of Earl Grey, etc., etc., convinced me that I have not as yet lost *all* my penchant for politics. I am extremely glad that aunt has consented to take in "Fraser's Magazine," for though I know from your description of its general contents it will be rather uninteresting when compared with "Blackwood," still it will be better than remaining the whole year without being able to obtain a sight of any periodical publication whatever; and such would assuredly be our case, as in the little wild, moorland village where we reside, there would be no possibility of borrowing or obtaining a work of that description from a circulating library. I hope with you that the present delightful weather may con-

tribute to the perfect restoration of our dear papa's health, and that it may give aunt pleasant reminiscences of the salubrious climate of her native place.

With love to all, — Believe me, dear Branwell, to remain your affectionate sister,
Charlotte.

2. TO E. N. [G.]

[Haworth, July 21st, 1832]

[My dearest Ellen, —] [. . .] An account of 78 one day is an account of all. In the morning, from nine o'clock till half-past twelve, I instruct my sisters, and draw; then we walk till dinner-time. After dinner I sew till tea-time, and after tea I either write, read, or do a little fancy work, or draw, as I please. Thus, in one delightful, though somewhat monotonous course, my life is passed.[2] I have been only out twice to tea since I came home. We are expecting company this afternoon, and on Tuesday next we shall have all the female teachers of the Sunday-school to tea. [. . .]

[. . . from Your real friend
Charlotte Brontë . . .]

3. TO E. N. [G.]

Haworth, February 20th, 1834

[Dearest Ellen, —] . . . I was greatly amused 82 at the tone of nonchalance which you assumed, while treating of London and its wonders. Did you not feel awed while gazing at St. Paul's and Westminster Abbey? Had you no feeling of intence and ardent interest, when in St. James's you saw the palace where so many of England's kings have held their courts, and beheld the representations of their persons on the walls? / You should not be too much afraid of appearing *country-bred*; the magnificence of 83 London has drawn exclamations of aston-

---

[1] Toward the end of Charlotte's eighteen months at Roe Head, her loyal co-author walked the twenty miles over the high moors to see her. Her next letter to him gives an idea of her taste in magazines at fifteen, her notion of stylistic elegance, and her affection for her brother.

[2] Charlotte does not mention that the monotony is varied by the effortless shift to the Angrian fantasy.

ishment from travelled men, experienced in the world, its wonders and beauties. Have you yet seen anything of the great personages whom the sitting of Parliament now detains in London — the Duke of Wellington, Sir Robert Peel, Earl Grey, Mr. Stanley, Mr. O'Connell? If I were you, I would not be too anxious to spend my time in reading whilst in town. Make use of your own eyes for the purposes of observation now, and, for a time at least, lay aside the spectacles with which authors would furnish us.   [. . . Your affectionate friend
C. Brontë . . .]

4. TO E. N. [G.]

Haworth, July 4th, 1834
84 [Dear Ellen, —] . . . I am not grown a bit, but as short and dumpy as ever. You ask
85 me to / recommend you some books for your perusal. I will do so in as few words as I can. If you like poetry, let it be first-rate; Milton, Shakspeare, Thomson, Goldsmith, Pope (if you will, though I don't admire him), Scott, Byron, Campbell, Wordsworth, and Southey. Now don't be startled at the names of Shakspeare and Byron. Both these were great men, and their works are like themselves. You will know how to choose the good, and to avoid

the evil; the finest passages are always the purest, the bad are invariably revolting; you will never wish to read them over twice. Omit the comedies of Shakspeare and the "Don Juan," perhaps the "Cain," of Byron, though the latter is a magnificent poem, and read the rest fearlessly; that must indeed be a depraved mind which can gather evil from *Henry VIII.,* from *Richard III.,* from *Macbeth,* and *Hamlet,* and *Julius Cæsar.* Scott's sweet, wild, romantic poetry can do you no harm. Nor can Wordsworth's, nor Campbell's, nor Southey's — the greatest part at least of his; some is certainly objectionable. For history, read Hume, Rollin, and the *Universal History,* if you *can;* I never did. For fiction, read Scott alone; all novels after his are worthless. For biography, read Johnson's *Lives of the Poets,* Boswell's *Life of Johnson,* Southey's *Life of Nelson,* Lockhart's *Life of Burns,* Moore's *Life of Sheridan,* Moore's *Life of Byron, Wolfe's Remains.* For natural history, read Bewick and Audubon, and Goldsmith, and White's *History of Selborne.* For divinity, your brother will advise you there. I can only say, adhere to standard authors, and avoid novelty. [. . .]
[. . . for ever yours,
Charlotte Brontë]

ROE HEAD, DEWSBURY MOOR, AND LAW HILL, 1835 TO 1838

In 1835 Miss Wooler invited Charlotte to teach at Roe Head. Part of the agreement was that another sister would be educated at the school. First Emily attended; when she became ill and homesick, Anne took her place. In 1837, the school was moved to a less wholesome site, Dewsbury Moor. Anne left in ill health late that year.

Emily soon left home again to teach at Law Hill School, a fashionable establishment near Halifax. Very little is known about her stay there, even the length of time she served, six or eighteen months, being disputed. However, biographers have pointed out that the quantity of writing done by Emily there, including fourteen poems in the first three months, argues some surplus energy and leisure. According to a tradition from this period, Emily once told her class of little girls that she liked the dog better than any of them.

Meantime, Branwell's plans to attend the Royal Academy came to nothing, and he remained at home, finding some social life in the (Freemason) Lodge of the Three Graces, writing Angrian prose and verse, penning tactless and emotional appeals to *Blackwood's Magazine* and to Wordsworth, and paying occasional visits to his artist friends in Bradford. His failure to fulfill the family's hopes for him depressed Charlotte, already disappointed in Emily, worried over Anne, and frustrated by work which she did not like and which did not pay. She missed the Angrian world intensely and continued to suffer from morbid religious doubts and fears. She left Dewsbury Moor in poor health and spirits in May, 1838.

5. TO E. N. [G.]

Haworth, July 6th [2], 1835

89 [Dear Ellen, —] I had hoped to have had the extreme pleasure of seeing you at Haworth this summer, but human affairs are mutable, and human resolutions must bend to the course of events. We are all about to divide, break up, separate. Emily is going to school, Branwell is going to London, and I am going to be a governess. This last determination I formed myself, knowing that I should have to take the step some time, "and better sune as syne," to use the Scotch proverb; and knowing well that papa would have enough to do with his limited income, should Branwell be placed at the Royal Academy, and Emily at Roe Head. Where am I going to reside? you will ask. Within four miles of you, at a place neither of us are unacquainted with, being no other than the identical Roe Head mentioned above. Yes! I am going to teach in the very school where I was myself taught. Miss Wooler made me the offer, and I preferred it to one or two proposals of private governess-ship, which I had before received. I am sad — very sad — at the thoughts of leaving home; but duty — necessity — these are stern mistresses, who will not be disobeyed. Did I not once say you ought to be thankful for your independence? I felt what I said at the time, and I repeat it now with double earnestness; if anything would cheer me, it is the idea of being so near you. Surely, you and Polly [Mary Taylor] will come and see me; it would be wrong in me to doubt it; you were never unkind yet. Emily and I leave home on the 27th of this month; the idea of being together consoles us both somewhat, and, truth, since I must enter a situation, "My lines have fallen in pleasant places." I both love and respect Miss Wooler. [. . .]

[Affectionately, warmly Yours
C. Brontë]

6. TO E. N. [G.]

[Roe Head, prob. 1836]

My dear dear E., — . . . I will no longer 94 shrink from answering your questions. I *do* wish to be better than I am. I pray fervently sometimes to be made so. I have stings of conscience, visitings of remorse, glimpses of holy, of inexpressible things, which formerly I used to be a stranger to; it may all die away, and I may be in utter midnight, but I implore a merciful Redeemer, that, if this be the dawn of the gospel, it may still brighten to perfect day. Do not mistake me — do not think I am good; I only wish to be so. I only hate my former flippancy and forwardness. Oh! I am no better than ever I was. I am in that state of horrid, gloomy uncertainty that, at this moment, I would submit to be old, grey-haired, to have passed all my youthful days of enjoyment, and to be settling on the verge of the grave, if I could only thereby ensure the prospect of reconciliation to God, and redemption through His Son's merit. I never was exactly careless of these matters, but I have always taken a clouded and repulsive view of them; and now, if possible, the clouds are gathering darker, and a more oppressive despondency weighs on my spirits. You have cheered me, my darling; for one moment, for an atom of time, I thought I might call you my own sister in the spirit; but the excitement is past, and I am now as wretched and hopeless as ever. This very night I will pray as you wish me. May the Almighty hear me compassionately! and I humbly hope he will, for you will strengthen my polluted petitions with your own pure requests. All is bustle and confusion round me, the ladies pressing with their sums and their lessons. * * * If you love me, *do, do, do* come on Friday . . .

— farewell, my blessed Ellen,
Charlotte

7. DIARY[3]

255   All this day I have been in a dream, half miserable, half-ecstatic, — miserable because I could not follow it out uninterruptedly, ecstatic because it showed almost in the vivid light of reality the ongoings of the infernal world. I had been toiling for nearly an hour with Miss Lister, Miss Marriott, and Ellen Cook, striving to teach them the distinction between an article and a substantive. The parsing lesson was completed; a dead silence had succeeded it in the schoolroom, and I sat sinking from irritation and weariness into a kind of lethargy. The thought came over me: Am I to spend all the best part of my life in this wretched bondage, forcibly suppressing my rage at the idleness, the apathy, and the hyperbolical and most asinine stupidity of these fat-headed oafs, and of compulsion assuming an air of kindness, patience and assiduity? Must I from day to day sit chained to this chair, prisoned within these four bare walls, while these glorious summer suns are burning in heaven and the year is revolving in its richest glow, and declaring, at the close of every summer day, the time I am losing will never come again? Stung to the heart with this reflection, I started up and mechanically walked to the window. A sweet August morning was smiling without. The dew was not yet dried off the field, the early shadows were stretching cool and dim from the hay-stacks and the roots of the /

256 grand old oaks and thorns scattered along the sunk fence. All was still except the murmur of the scribes about me over their tasks. I flung up the sash. An uncertain sound of inexpressible sweetness came on a dying gale from the south. I looked in that direction. Huddersfield and the hills beyond it were all veiled in blue mist, the woods of Hopton and Heaton Lodge were clouding the water's edge, the Calder, silent but bright, was shooting among them like a silver arrow. I listened — the sound sailed full and liquid down the descent: it was

[3] These extracts from Charlotte's fragmentary diary were written between August and October, 1836. They are printed in S. H. *Misc.*

the bells of Huddersfield Parish Church. I shut the window and went back to my seat. Then came on me, rushing impetuously, all the mighty phantasm that this had conjured from nothing, — from nothing to a system strange as some religious creed. I felt as if I could have written gloriously. The spirit of all Verdopolis — of all the mountainous North — of all the woodland West — of all the river-watered East, came crowding into my mind. If I had had time to indulge it I felt that the vague suggestions of that moment would have settled down into some narrative better at least than anything I ever produced before. But just then a dolt came up with a lesson . . .

About a week since I got a letter from Branwell containing a most exquisitely characteristic epistle from Northangerland to his daughter. It is astonishing what a soothing and delightful tone that letter seemed to speak. I lived on its contents for days; in every pause of employment it came chiming in like some sweet bar of music — bringing with it agreeable thoughts such as I had for many weeks been a stranger to. . . . A curtain seemed to rise and discover to me the Duchess as she might appear when newly risen and lightly dressed for the morning — discovering her father's letter in the contents of the mail which lies on her breakfast-table. . . . / The localities of the 257 picture were so graphic, the room so distinct, the clear fire of morning, the window looking upon no object but a cold October sky, except when you draw very near and look down on a terrace far beneath, and, at a still dizzier distance, on a green court with a fountain and rows of stately limes — beyond, a wide road and wider river, and a vast metropolis. You feel it to be the Zamorna Palace, for buildings on buildings piled round embosom this little verdant circle with its marble basin to receive the jet, and its grove of mellowing foliage. Above fifty windows look upon the court admitting light into you know what splendid and spacious chambers. The Duchess. . . . looks from the window, and there is the high, vast and lordly front of Northangerland

House, towering like some great theatre above the streets of Adrianopolis. . . .

8. TO E. N. [S. H.]

Roe Head [Dec. 6, 1836]

I,147   . . . If I could always live with you and daily read the bible with you, if your lips and mine could at the same time drink the same draught from the same pure fountain of mercy, I hope, I trust, I might one day become better, far better, than my evil wandering thoughts, my corrupt heart, cold to the spirit, and warm to the flesh will now permit me to be. I often plan the pleasant life which we might lead together, strengthening each other in that power of self-denial, that hallowed and glowing devotion which the past saints of God often attained to. My eyes fill with tears when I contrast the bliss of such a state brightened by hopes of the future with the melancholy state I now live in, uncertain that I have ever felt true contrition, wandering in thought and deed, longing for holiness which I shall *never, never* attain — smitten at times to the heart with the conviction that ——'s ghastly Calvinistic doctrines are true — darkened in short by the very shadows of Spiritual Death! . . .

148   Good-bye, Ellen, C. Brontë. . . .

9. TO ROBERT SOUTHEY [G.][4]

[Roe Head] March 16th [1837]

103   Sir, — I cannot rest till I have answered your letter, even though by addressing you a second time I should appear a little intrusive; but I must thank you for the kind and wise advice you have condescended to

[4] In the Christmas holidays of 1836, Charlotte wrote a letter, now lost, to Robert Southey, then Poet Laureate. His reply, to which he referred elsewhere as a "cooling admonition," brought about a short correspondence between them. (See V.)

give me. I had not ventured to hope for such a reply; so considerate in its tone, so noble in its spirit. I must suppress what I feel, or you will think me foolishly enthusiastic.

At the first perusal of your letter, I felt 104 only shame and regret that I had ever ventured to trouble you with my crude rhapsody; I felt a painful heat rise to my face when I thought of the quires of paper I had covered with what once gave me so much delight, but which now was only a source of confusion; but, after I had thought a little and read it again and again, the prospect seemed to clear. You do not forbid me to write; you do not say that what I write is utterly destitute of merit. You only warn me against the folly of neglecting real duties, for the sake of imaginative pleasures; of writing for the love of fame; for the selfish excitement of emulation. You kindly allow me to write poetry for its own sake, provided I leave undone nothing which I ought to do, in order to pursue that single, absorbing, exquisite gratification. I am afraid, sir, you think me very foolish. . . . Following my father's advice — who from my childhood has counselled me just in the wise and friendly tone of your letter — I have endeavoured not only attentively to observe all the duties a woman ought to fulfil, but to feel deeply interested in them. I don't always succeed, for sometimes when I'm teaching or sewing I would rather be reading or writing; but I try to deny myself; and my father's approbation amply rewarded me for the privation. Once more allow me to thank you with sincere gratitude. I trust I shall never more feel ambitious to see my name in print; if the wish should rise I'll look at Southey's letter, and suppress it. It is honour enough for me that I have written to him, and received an answer. . . .   C. Brontë

NEW VENTURES, 1838 TO 1841

Mary Taylor and her sister Martha visited the parsonage in the summer of 1838 and in 1839 Charlotte for the first time saw the sea. But during these years, while Emily took over much of the house-keeping at the parsonage, Charlotte, Anne, and Branwell all worked for varying periods (for details see chronology). From May to July, 1839, Charlotte was governess to the Sidgwick family, and says E. F. Benson in his life of her, "appears to have fallen among fiends." He did not comment further, but the sly irony of his remark is apparent when one realizes that Mr. Sidgwick was his own cousin. Another cousin to both was the Archbishop of Canterbury, whose son, A. C. Benson, wrote of this episode,

> Charlotte Brontë acted as governess to my cousin at Stonegappe for a few months in 1839. Few traditions of her connection with the Sidgwicks survive. She was, according to her own account, very unkindly treated, but it is clear that she had no gifts for the management of children, and was also in a very morbid condition the whole time. My cousin Benson Sidgwick, now vicar of Ashby Parva, certainly on one occasion threw a Bible at Miss Brontë! and all that another cousin can recollect of her is that if she was invited to walk to church with them, she thought she was being ordered about like a slave; if she was not invited, she imagined she was excluded from the family circle. Both Mr. and Mrs. John Sidgwick were extraordinarily benevolent people, much beloved, and would not wittingly have given pain to any one connected with them.[5]

Her second situation, with the Whites at Rawdon, seems to have been slightly more bearable.

Branwell still had literary ambitions, wrote verse and many letters, but was drinking and probably taking laudanum, then a dangerously inexpensive and common remedy for coughs, nerves, diarrhoea, and other ills, which dulled pain and misery and released the power of fantasy.

10. TO E. N. [S. H.]

I,162

Dewsbury Moor,
October 2nd, 1837 [1836]

Dear, dear Ellen, — . . . My sister Emily is gone into a situation as teacher in a large school of near forty pupils, near Halifax. I have had one letter from her since her departure; it gives an appalling account of her duties — hard labour from six in the morning until eleven at night, with only one-half hour of exercise between. This is slavery. I fear she will never stand it. . . .
. . . Your friend, C. Brontë

11. TO E. N. [G.][6]

112

[Haworth] March 12, 1839
[My dearest Ellen, —] * * * I had a kindly

leaning towards him, because he is an amiable and well-disposed man. Yet I had not, and could not have, that intense attachment which would make me willing to die for him; and if ever I marry, it must be in that light of adoration that I will regard my husband. Ten to one I shall never have the chance again; but *n'importe*. Moreover, I was aware that he knew so little of me he could hardly be conscious to whom he was writing. Why! it would startle him to see me in my natural home character; he would think I was a wild, romantic enthusiast indeed. I could not sit all day long making a grave face before my husband. I would laugh, and satirise, and say whatever came into my head first. And if he were a clever

---

[5] *The Life of Edward White Benson*, 2 vols., London: Macmillan and Co., 1900, I, 12.

[6] In this letter Charlotte tells Ellen why she refused the proposal of her brother, Henry Nussey, who apparently was in need of a housekeeper for his pupils. The incident may have suggested to Charlotte the St. John episode in *Jane Eyre*. Charlotte refused another clerical suitor later in the year.

man, and loved me, the whole world, weighed in the balance against his smallest wish, should be light as air. [. . .]

[. . . Good-bye, my dear Ellen. C. Brontë]

12. TO E. B. [G.]

[Stonegappe] June 8th, 1839

115 [Dearest Lavinia, —] [. . .] I have striven hard to be pleased with my new situation. The country, the house and the grounds are, as I have said, divine; but, alack-a-day, there is such a thing as seeing all beautiful around you — pleasant woods, white paths, green lawns, and blue sunshiny sky — and not having a free moment or a free thought left to enjoy them. The children are constantly with me. As for correcting them, I quickly found that was out of the question; they are to do as they like. A complaint to the mother only brings black looks on myself, and unjust, partial excuses to screen the children. I have tried that plan once, and succeeded so notably, I shall try no more. I said in my last letter that Mrs. [Sidgwick] did not know me. I now begin to find she does not intend to know me; that she cares nothing about me, except to contrive how the greatest possible quantity of labour may be got out of me; and to that end she overwhelms me with oceans of needlework; yards of cambric to hem, muslin nightcaps to make, and, above all things, dolls to dress. I do not think she likes me at all, because I can't help being shy in such an entirely novel scene, surrounded as I have hitherto been by strange and constantly changing faces. * * * I used to think I should like to be in the stir of grand folks' society; but I have had enough of it — it is dreary work to look on and listen. I see more clearly than I have ever done before, that a private governess has no existence, is not considered as a living rational being, except as connected with the wearisome duties she has to fulfil. * * * One of the pleasantest afternoons I have spent here — indeed, the only one at all pleasant — was when Mr. [Sidgwick] walked out with his children, and I had orders to follow a little behind. As he strolled on through his fields,

with his magnificent Newfoundland dog at his side, he looked very like what a frank, wealthy, Conservative gentleman ought to be. He spoke freely / and unaffectedly to 116 the people he met, and, though he indulged his children and allowed them to tease himself far too much, he would not suffer them grossly to insult others. * * *   [C. Brontë]

13. TO E. B. [G.]

[July, 1839]

Mine bonnie love, I was as glad of your 117 letter as tongue can express: it is a real, genuine pleasure to hear from home; a thing to be saved till bed-time, when one has a moment's quiet and rest to enjoy it thoroughly. Write whenever you can. I could like to be at home. I could like to work in a mill. I could like to feel some mental liberty. I could like this weight of restraint to be taken off. But the holidays will come. Coraggio.

14. TO E. N. [G.]

[Haworth] Oct. 24th [1839]

[My dear Ellen, —] [. . .] Have you forgot- 121 ten the sea by this time, E.? Is it grown dim in your mind? Or you can still see it, dark, blue, and green, and foam-white, and hear it roaring roughly when the wind is high, or rushing softly when it is calm. * * * I am as well as need be, and very fat. I think of Easton very often, and of worthy Mr. H[udson] and his kind-hearted helpmate, and of our pleasant walks to H[arlequin] Wood, and to Boynton, our merry evenings, our romps with little Hancheon, etc., etc. If we both live, this period of our lives will long be a theme for pleasant recollection. . . .   [Your old friend C. Brontë]

15. TO E. N. [G.]

May 15th, 1840

[My dear Ellen, —] [. . .] Do not be over- 129 persuaded to marry a man you can never respect — I do not say *love*; because, I think, if you can respect a person before marriage, moderate love at least will come after; and as to intense *passion*, I am convinced that that is no desirable feeling. In the first

place, it seldom or never meets with a re-
quital; and, in the second place, if it did,
the feeling would be only temporary: it
would last the honeymoon, and then, perhaps, give place to disgust, or indifference
worse, perhaps, than disgust. Certainly this
would be the case on the man's part; and on
the woman's — God help her, if she is left
to love passionately and alone.

I am tolerably well convinced that I shall
never marry at all. Reason tells me so, and
I am not so utterly the slave of feeling but
that I can *occasionally hear* her voice.

[C. Brontë]

16. TO E. N. [S. H.]

March 3rd, 1841

1,227 My dear Ellen, — . . . I dare say you have
received a valentine this year from our
bonny-faced friend the curate of Haworth.[7]
I got a precious specimen a few days before
I left home, but I knew better how to treat
it than I did those we received a year ago.
I am up to the dodges and artifices of his
lordship's character. He knows I know him,
and you cannot conceive how quiet and
respectful he has long been. Mind I am
not writing against him — I never *will* do
that. I like him very much. I honour and
admire his generous, open disposition, and
sweet temper — but for all the tricks, wiles,
and insincerities of love, the gentleman has
not his match for twenty miles round. He
would fain persuade every woman under
thirty whom he sees that he is desperately
in love with her. I have a great deal more
to say, but I have not a moment's time to
write it in. My dear Ellen, *do* write to me
soon, don't forget. — Good-bye.

17. TO E. N. [G.]

[Rawdon] March 21 [1841]

[My dearest Ellen, —] You must excuse a 136
very short answer to your most welcome
letter; for my time is entirely occupied.
Mrs. [White] expected a good deal of sewing from me. 1 cannot sew much during
the day, on account of the children, who
require the utmost attention. I am obliged,
therefore, to devote the evenings to this
business. Write to me often; very long letters. It will do both of us good. This place
is far better than [Swarcliffe], but, God
knows, I have enough to do to keep a good
heart in the matter. What you said has
cheered me a little. I wish I could always
act according to your advice. Home-sickness affects me sorely. I like Mr. [White]
extremely. [. . .] The children [. . .] are
over-indulged, and consequently hard at
times to manage. *Do, do,* do come and see
me; if it be a breach of etiquette, never
mind. If you can only stop an hour, come.
Talk no more about my forsaking you; my
darling, I could not afford to do it. I find
it is not in my nature to get on in this weary
world without sympathy and attachment in
some quarter; and seldom indeed do we
find it. It is too great a treasure to be ever
wantonly thrown away when once secured.
[. . .]   [Fare-thee-well, Nell. C. B.]

The School Project and Brussels, 1841 to 1843

All the girls disliked being governesses. How could they achieve a degree of independence and security and be together? The only solution that seemed feasible was to
start their own school, and for this only Charlottee was in some degree prepared. The
steps they took toward a more thorough grounding can be traced in the letters below.

The school finally chosen for their training was the Pensionnat Heger, Rue
d'Isabelle, Brussels. Mme. Heger[8] (aged thirty-six) ran the school, while her husband,
Constantin Heger (thirty-one) taught at the nearby Athenée Royale, but held French
classes at his wife's establishment. Charlotte and Emily worked hard and did well. By

---

[7] William Weightman, the gayest and most attractive of a long line of Mr. Brontë's curates.

[8] Contrary to the practice of many Brontë biographers, the Heger family did *not* use an accent.

fall Charlotte was entrusted with English classes. Then followed a series of disasters: early in September William Weightman, the curate at Haworth, died of cholera; in October Martha Taylor died and was buried in the Protestant cemetery (see *The Professor*, Ch. XIX). A few days later news reached the girls that Aunt Branwell was seriously ill. She was dead and the funeral was over before they arrived home where Emily remained, Charlotte returning to Brussels for another year. The Brussels years were central in Charlotte's emotional experience and provided the basis for *The Professor* and *Villette*. Many characters and events in both novels are founded on her experiences in Belgium, notably the portraits of the Hegers — how far colored by her own emotions the reader may decide — as Mme. Beck and M. Paul Emanuel in *Villette*.

18. TO E. N. [S. H.]

July 19th, '41

1,236 My dear Ellen, — . . . To come to the point, papa and aunt talk, by fits and starts of our — *id est*, Emily, Anne, and myself — commencing a school. I have often, you know, said how much I wished such a thing; but I never could conceive where the capital was to come from for making such a speculation. I was well aware, indeed, that aunt had money, but I always considered that she was the last person who would offer a loan for the purpose in question. A loan, however, she *has* offered, or rather intimates that she perhaps *will* offer, in case pupils can be secured, an eligible situation obtained, etc. This sounds very fair, but still there are matters to be considered which throw something of a damp upon the scheme. I do not expect that aunt will risk more than £150 on such a venture; and would it be possible to establish a respectable (not by any means a *showy*) school and to commence housekeeping with a capital of only that amount? . . . As to getting into debt, that is a thing we could none of us reconcile our minds to for a moment. We do not care how modest, how humble a commencement be, so it be made on sure ground, and have a safe foundation. . . . Much inquiry and consideration will be necessary, of course, before any place is decided on; and I fear much time will elapse before any plan is executed.

Our reverend friend, William Weightman, is quite as bonny, pleasant, lighthearted, good-tempered, generous, careless, fickle, and unclerical as ever.

. . . Good-bye, dear Ellen. C. B.

19. TO E. N. [G.]

[Upperwood House] August 7th, 1841 138 [My dear Ellen, —] This is Saturday evening; I have put the children to bed; now I am going to sit down and answer your letters. I am / again by myself — [H]ouse- 139 keeper and [G]overness — for Mr. and Mrs. [White] are staying [near Tadcaster]. To speak truth, though I am solitary while they are away, it is still by far the happiest part of my time. The children are under decent control, the servants are very observant and attentive to me, and the occasional absence of the master and mistress relieves me from the duty of always endeavouring to seem cheerful and conversable. [. . .]

Martha [Taylor], it appears, is in the way of enjoying great advantages; so is Mary, for you will be surprised to hear that she is returning immediately to the Continent with her brother; not, however, to stay there, but to take a month's tour and recreation. I have had a long letter from Mary, and a packet containing a present of a very handsome black silk scarf, and a pair of beautiful kid gloves, bought at Brussels. . . .

Mary's letters spoke of some of the pictures and cathedrals she had seen — pictures the most exquisite, cathedrals the most venerable. I hardly know what swelled to my throat as I read her letter: such a vehement impatience of restraint and steady work; such a strong wish for wings — wings such as wealth can furnish; such an urgent thirst to see, to know, to learn; something internal seemed to expand bodily for a minute. I was tantalised by the consciousness of faculties unexercised, — then all collapsed, and I despaired. My dear, I would hardly make that confession to any one but yourself; and to you, rather in a letter than *vivâ voce*. These rebellious and absurd emotions were only momentary; I quelled them in five minutes. I hope they will not revive, for they were acutely painful. No further steps have been taken about the project I mentioned to you, nor probably will be for the present; but Emily, and Anne, and I, keep it in view. It is our polar star, and we look to it in all circumstances of despondency. I begin to suspect I am writing in a strain which will make you think I am unhappy. This is far from being the case; on the contrary, I know my place is a favourable one, for a governess. What dismays and haunts me sometimes, is a conviction that I have no natural knack for my vocation. If teaching only were requisite, it would be smooth and easy; but it is the living in other people's houses — the estrangement from one's 140 real character — / the adoption of a cold, rigid, apathetic exterior, that is painful. * * * You will not mention our school project at present. A project not actually commenced is always uncertain. Write to me often, my dear Nell; you *know* your letters are valued. Your "loving child" (as you choose to call me so),

C. B.

P.S. I am well in health; don't fancy I am not; but I have one aching feeling at my heart (I must allude to it, though I had resolved not to). It is about Anne; she has so much to endure: far, far more than I ever had. When my thoughts turn to her, they always see her as a patient, persecuted stranger. I know what concealed susceptibility is in her nature, when her feelings are wounded. I wish I could be with her, to administer a little balm. She is more lonely — less gifted with the power of making friends, even than I am: Drop the subject.

20. TO AUNT BRANWELL [G.]

[Upperwood House, Rawdon]
[Sept. 29th, 1841]

141 Dear Aunt, — I have heard nothing of Miss Wooler yet since I wrote to her, inti-mating that I would accept her offer. I cannot conjecture the reason of this long silence, unless some unforeseen impediment has occurred in concluding the bargain. Meantime, a plan has been suggested and approved by Mr. and Mrs. [White] and others, which I wish now to impart to you. My friends recommend me, if I desire to secure permanent success, to delay commencing the school for six months longer, and by all means to contrive, by hoo[k] or by crook, to spend the intervening time in some school on the continent. They say schools in England are so numerous, competition so great, that without some such step towards attaining superiority, we shall probably have a very hard struggle, and may fail in the end. They say, moreover, that the loan of £100, which you have been so kind as to offer us, will, perhaps, not be all required now, as Miss Wooler will lend us the furniture; and that, if the speculation is intended to be a good and successful one, half the sum, at least, ought to be laid out in the manner I have mentioned, thereby insuring a more speedy repayment both of interest and principal.

I would not go to France or to Paris. I would go to Brussels, in Belgium. The cost of the journey there, at the dearest rate of travelling, would be £5; living is there little more than half as dear as it is in England, and the facilities for education are equal or superior to any other place in Europe. In half a year, I could acquire a thorough familiarity with French. I could improve greatly in Italian, and even get a dash of German; *i.e.*, providing my health continued as good as it is now. Mary is now staying at Brussels, at a first-rate establishment there. I / should not think of going 142 to the Château de Kokleberg, where she is resident, as the terms are much too high; but if I wrote to her, she, with the assistance of Mrs. Jenkins, the wife of the British Chaplain, would be able to secure me a cheap decent residence and respectable protection. I should have the opportunity of seeing her frequently; she would make me acquainted with the city; and, with the assistance of her cousins, I should probably be introduced to connections far more improving, polished, and cultivated, than any I have yet known.

These are advantages which would turn to real account, when we actually commenced a school; and, if Emily could share them with me, we could take a footing in the world afterwards which we can never do now. I say Emily instead of Anne; for Anne might take her turn at some future period, if our school answered. I feel certain, while I am writing, that you will see the propriety of what I say. You always like to use your money to the best advantage. You are not fond of making shabby purchases; when you do confer a favour, it is often done in style; and, depend upon it, £50 or £100 thus laid out, would be well employed. Of course, I know no other friend in the world to whom I could apply, on this subject, except yourself. I feel an absolute conviction that, if this advantage were allowed us, it would be the making of us for life. Papa will, perhaps, think it a wild and ambitious scheme; but who ever rose in the world without ambition? When he left Ireland to go to Cambridge University, he was as ambitious as I am now. I want us *all* to get on. I know we have talents and I want them to be turned to account. I look to you, aunt, to help us. I think you will not refuse. I know, if you consent, it shall not be my fault if you ever repent your kindness. [. . .]

[Believe me, dear aunt, your affectionate niece, C. Brontë]

21. TO E. N. [G.]

[Rawdon] Nov. 2, 1841

143 [Dear E. N., —] . . . The plain fact is, I *was* not, I am not now, certain of my destiny. On the contrary, I have been most uncertain, perplexed with contradictory schemes and proposals. . . . Miss W. did most kindly propose that I should come to Dewsbury Moor, and attempt to revive the school her sister had relinquished. She offered me the use of her furniture, for the consideration of her board. At first, I re-

ceived the proposal cordially, and prepared to do my utmost to bring about success; but a fire was kindled in my very heart, which I could not quench. I so longed to increase my attainments — to become something better than I am; a glimpse of what I felt, I showed to you in one of my former letters — only a glimpse; Mary cast oil upon the flames — encouraged me, and in her own strong, energetic language, heartened me on. I longed to go to Brussels; but how could I get? I wished for one, at least, of my sisters to share the advantage with me. I fixed on Emily. She deserved the reward, I knew. How could the point be managed? In extreme excitement, I wrote a letter home, which carried the day. I made an appeal to aunt for assistance, which was answered by consent. Things are not settled; yet it is sufficient to say we have a *chance* of going for half a year. Dewsbury Moor is relinquished. Perhaps, fortunately so, for it is an obscure, dreary place, not adapted for a school. In my secret soul, I believe there is no cause to regret it. My plans for the future are bounded to this intention: if I once get to Brussels, and if / my health is spared, I will do my best to 144 make the utmost of every advantage that shall come within my reach. When the half-year is expired, I will do what I can. * * *

Believe me, though I was born in April, the month of cloud and sunshine, I am not changeful. My spirits are unequal, and sometimes I speak vehemently, and sometimes I say nothing at all; but I have a steady regard for you, and if you will let the cloud and shower pass by, be sure the sun is always behind, obscured, but still existing. [. . .]   [C. B.]

22. TO E. N. [S. H.]

Brussels, May 1842. I,259

Dear Ellen, — / . . . I was twenty-six years 260 old a week or two since, and at this ripe time of life I am a schoolgirl, a complete schoolgirl, and, on the whole, very happy in that capacity. It felt very strange at first to submit to authority instead of exercising it — to obey orders instead of giving them; but I like that state of things. I returned to it with the same avidity that a cow, that has long been kept on dry hay, returns to fresh grass. Don't laugh at my simile. It is natural to me to submit, and very unnatural to command.

This is a large school, in which there are about forty *externes* or day-pupils, and twelve *pensionnaires* or boarders. Madame Heger, the head, is a lady of precisely the same cast of mind, degree of cultivation, and quality of intellect as Miss Catherine Wooler. I think the severe points are a little softened, because she has not been disappointed, and consequently soured. In a word, she is a married instead of a maiden lady. There are three teachers in the school — Mademoiselle Blanche, Mademoiselle Sophie, and Mademoiselle Marie. The two first have no particular character. One is an old maid, and the other will be one. Mademoiselle Marie is talented and original, but of repulsive and arbitrary manners, which have made the whole school, except myself and Emily, her bitter enemies. No less than seven masters attend to teach the different branches of education — French, Drawing, Music, Singing, Writing, Arithmetic, and German. All in the house are Catholics except ourselves, one other girl, and the *gouvernante* of Madame's children, an Englishwoman, in rank something between a lady's-maid and nursery governess. The difference in country and religion makes a broad line of demarcation between us and all the rest. We are completely isolated in the midst of numbers. Yet I think I am never unhappy; my present life is so delightful, so congenial to my own nature, compared with that of a governess. My time, constantly occupied, passes too rapidly. Hitherto both Emily and I have had good health, and therefore we have been able to work well. There is one individual of whom I have not yet spoken — M. Heger, the husband of Madame. He is professor of rhetoric, a man of power as to mind, but very choleric and irritable as to temperament; a little black ugly being, with a face that varies in expression. Some-

times he borrows the lineaments of an insane tom-cat, sometimes those of a delirious hyena; occasionally, but very seldom, he discards these perilous attractions and assumes an air not above 100 degrees removed from mild and gentleman-/like. He is very 261 angry with me just at present, because I have written a translation which he chose to stigmatise as *peu correcte*. He did not tell me so, but wrote the accusation on the margin of my book, and asked in brief, stern phrase, how it happened that my compositions were always better than my translations? adding that the thing seemed to him inexplicable. The fact is, some weeks ago, in a high-flown humour, he forbade me to use either dictionary or grammar in translating the most difficult English compositions into French. This makes the task rather arduous, and compels me now and then to introduce an English word, which nearly plucks the eyes out of his head when he sees it. Emily and he don't draw well together at all. When he is very ferocious with me I cry; that sets all things straight. Emily works like a horse, and she has had great difficulties to contend with, far greater than I have had. Indeed, those who come to a French school for instruction ought previously to have acquired a considerable knowledge of the French language, otherwise they will lose a great deal of time, for the course of instruction is adapted to natives and not to foreigners; and in these large establishments they will not change their ordinary course for one or two strangers. The few private lessons M. Heger has vouchsafed to give us are, I suppose, to be considered a great favour, and I can perceive they have already excited much spite and jealousy in the school. . . .

— Yours, sundered by the sea, C. Brontë.

23. TO E. N. [G.]

Brussels, 1842 [July] 159

[Dear Ellen, —] [. . .] I consider it doubtful whether I shall come home in September or not. Madame Heger has made a proposal for both me and Emily to stay another half year, offering to dismiss her English master, and take me as English teacher; also to employ Emily some part of each day in teaching music to a certain number of the pupils. For these services we are to be allowed to continue our studies in French and German, and to have board, etc., without paying for it; no salaries, however, are offered. The proposal is kind, and in a great selfish city like Brussels, and a great selfish school, containing nearly ninety pupils (boarders and day-pupils included), implies a degree of interest which demands gratitude in return. I am inclined to accept it. What think you? I don't deny I sometimes wish to be in England, or that I have brief attacks of home-sickness; but, on the whole, I have borne a very valiant heart so far; and I have been happy in Brussels, because I have always been fully occupied with the employments that I like. Emily is making rapid progress in French, German, music, and drawing. Monsieur and Madame Heger begin to recognise the valuable parts of her character, under her singularities. If the national character of the Belgians is to be measured by the character of most of the girls in this school, it is a character singularly cold, selfish, animal, and inferior. They are very mutinous and difficult for the teachers to manage; and their principles are rotten to the core. We avoid them, which it is not difficult to do, as we have the brand of Protestantism and Anglicism upon us. . . .   [– believe me present occasionally in spirit when absent in flesh   C. B.]

24. TO BRANWELL BRONTË [S. H.]

I,296   Brussels, May 1st, 1843.
Dear Branwell, – I hear you have written a letter to me. This letter, however, as usual, I have never received, which I am exceedingly sorry for, as I have wished very much to hear from you. Are you sure that you put the right address and that you paid the English postage, 1s. 6d.? Without that, letters are never forwarded. I heard from papa a day or two since. All appears to be going on reasonably well at home. I grieve only that Emily is so solitary; but, however, you and Anne will soon be returning for

the holidays, which will cheer the house for a time. Are you in better health and spirits, and does Anne continue to be pretty well? I understand papa has been to see you. Did he seem cheerful and well? Mind when you write to me you answer these questions, as I wish to know. Also give me a detailed account as to how you get on with your pupil and the rest of the family. I have received a general assurance that you do well and are in good odour, but I want to know particulars.

As for me, I am very well and wag on as usual. I perceive, however, that I grow exceedingly misanthropic and sour. You / will say that this is no news, and that you 297 never knew me possessed of the contrary qualities — philanthropy and sugariness. *Das ist wahr* (which being translated means, that is true); but the fact is, the people here are no go whatsoever. Amongst 120 persons which compose the daily population of this house, I can discern only one or two who deserve anything like regard. This is not owing to foolish fastidiousness on my part, but to the absence of decent qualities on theirs. They have not intellect or politeness or good-nature or good-feeling. They are nothing. I don't hate them — hatred would be too warm a feeling. They have no sensations themselves and they excite none. But one wearies from day to day of caring nothing, fearing nothing, liking nothing, hating nothing, being nothing, doing nothing — yes, I teach and sometimes get red in the face with impatience at their stupidity. But don't think I ever scold or fly into a passion. If I spoke warmly, as warmly as I sometimes used to do at Roe Head, they would think me mad. Nobody ever gets into a passion here. Such a thing is not known. The phlegm that thickens their blood is too gluey to boil. They are very false in their relations with each other, but they rarely quarrel, and friendship is a folly they are unacquainted with. The black Swan, M. Heger, is the only sole veritable exception to this rule (for Madame, always cool and always reasoning, is not quite an exception). But I rarely speak to Monsieur now, for not being a pupil I have little or nothing to do with him. From time to time he shows his kind-heartedness by loading me with books, so that I am still indebted to him for all the pleasure or amusement I have. Except for the total want of companionship I have nothing to complain of. I have not too much to do, sufficient liberty, and I am rarely interfered with. I lead an easeful, stagnant, silent life, for which, when I think of Mrs. Sidgwick, I ought to be very thankful. Be sure you write to me soon, and beg of Anne to inclose a small billet in the same letter; it will be a real charity to do me this kindness. Tell me everything you can think of.

It is a curious metaphysical fact that always in the evening when I am in the great dormitory alone, having no other company than a number of beds with white curtains, I always recur as fanatically as ever to the old ideas, the old faces, and the old scenes in the world below. Give my love to Anne, and believe me   Yourn! Dear Anne, — Write to me, — Your affectionate Schwester,   C. B.

Mr. Heger has just been in and given me a little German Testament as a present. I was surprised, for since a good many days he has hardly spoken to me.

25. TO E. B. [S. H.]

I,299   Brussels, May 29th, 1843 Dear E. J., — . . . Of late days, M. and Mde. Heger rarely speak to me, and I really don't pretend to care a fig for any body else in the establishment. You are not to suppose by that expression that I am under the influence of *warm* affection for Mde. Heger. I am convinced that she does not like me — why, I can't tell, nor do I think she herself has any definite reason for the aversion; but for one thing, she cannot comprehend why I do not make intimate friends of Mesdames Blanche, Sophie, and Haussé. M. Heger is wondrously influenced by Madame, and I should not wonder if he disapproves very much of my unamiable want of sociability. He has already given me a brief lecture on universal *bienveillance,* and, perceiving that

I don't improve in consequence, I fancy he has taken to considering me as a person to be let alone — left to the error of her ways; and consequently he has in a great measure withdrawn the light of his countenance, and I get on from day to day in a Robinson-Crusoe-like condition — very lonely. That does not signify. In other respects I have nothing substantial to complain of, nor is even this a cause for complaint. Except the loss of M. Heger's good will (if I have lost it) I care for none of 'em. I hope you are well and hearty. Walk out often on the moors. . . .   — Your C. B.

26. TO E. N. [S. H.]

Brussels, August 6th, 1843 I,301 Dear Ellen, — / . . . Alas! I can hardly write, 302 I have such a dreary weight at my heart; and I do so wish to go home. Is not this childish? Pardon me, for I cannot help it. However, though I am not strong enough to bear up cheerfully, I can still bear up; and I will continue to stay (D. V.) some months longer, till I have acquired German; and then I hope to see all your faces again. Would that the vacation were well over! it will pass so slowly. Do have the Christian charity to write me a long, long letter; fill it with the minutest details; nothing will be uninteresting. Do not think it is because people are unkind to me that I wish to leave Belgium; nothing of the sort. Everybody is abundantly civil, but homesickness keeps creeping over me. I cannot shake it off. . . . Remember me to your mother and Mercy, and believe me, very merrily, vivaciously, gaily yours,   C. B.

27. TO E. B. [S. H.]

Bruxelles, September 2nd, 1843 I,303 Dear E. J., —

. . . I should inevitably fall into the gulf of low spirits if I stayed always by myself here without a human being to speak to, so I go out and traverse the Boulevards and streets of Bruxelles sometimes for hours together. Yesterday I went on a pilgrimage to the cemetery, and far beyond it on to a hill where there was nothing but fields as far as the horizon. When I came back it was evening; but I had such a repugnance to return to the house, which contained nothing that I cared for, I still kept threading the streets in the neighbourhood of the Rue d'Isabelle and avoiding it. I found myself opposite to Ste Gudule, and the bell, whose voice you know, began to toll for evening *salut*. I went in, quite alone (which procedure you will say is not much like me), wandered about the aisles where a few old women were saying their prayers, till vespers begun. I stayed till they were over. Still I could not leave the church or force myself to go home — to school I mean. An odd whim came into my head. In a solitary part of the Cathedral six or seven people still remained kneeling by the confessionals. In two confessionals I saw a priest. I felt as if I did not care what I did, provided it was not absolutely wrong, and that it served to vary my life and yield a moment's interest. I took a fancy to change myself into a Catholic and go and make a real confession to see what it was like. Knowing me as you do, you will think this odd, but when people are by themselves they have singular fancies. A penitent was occupied in confessing. They do not go

304 into the sort of pew or / cloister which the priest occupies, but kneel down on the steps and confess through a grating. Both the confessor and the penitent whisper very low, you can hardly hear their voices. After I had watched two or three penitents go and return, I approached at last and knelt down in a niche which was just vacated. I had to kneel there ten minutes waiting, for on the other side was another penitent invisible to me. At last that went away and a little wooden door inside the grating opened, and I saw the priest leaning his ear towards me. I was obliged to begin, and yet I did not know a word of the formula with which they always commence their confessions. It was a funny position. I felt precisely as I did when alone on the Thames at midnight. I commenced with saying I was a foreigner and had been brought up a Protestant. The priest asked

if I was a Protestant then. I somehow could not tell a lie, and said 'yes.' He replied that in that case I could not '*jouir du bonheur de la confesse*'; but I was determined to confess, and at last he said he would allow me because it might be the first step towards returning to the true church. I actually did confess — a real confession. When I had done he told me his address, and said that every morning I was to go to the rue du Parc — to his house — and he would reason with me and try to convince me of the error and enormity of being a Protestant!!! I promised faithfully to go. Of course, however, the adventure stops there, and I hope I shall never see the priest again. I think you had better not tell papa of this. He will not understand that it was only a freak, and will perhaps think I am going to turn Catholic. Trusting that you and papa are well, and also Tabby and the Hoyles, and hoping you will write to me immediately, — I am, yours,   C. B.[9]

28.   TO E. B. [S. H.]

Oct. 1, 1843. I,304

Dear E. J., — This is Sunday morning. They are at their idolatrous "messe," and I am here — that is, in the *réfectoire*. I should like uncommonly to be in the dining-room at home, or in the kitchen, or in the back kitchen. I should like even to be cutting up the hash, with the clerk and some register people at the other / table, and you 305 standing by, watching that I put enough flour, and not too much pepper, and, above all, that I save the best pieces of the leg of mutton for Tiger and Keeper, the first of which personages would be jumping about the dish and carving-knife, and the latter standing like a devouring flame on the kitchen floor. To complete the picture, Tabby blowing the fire, in order to boil the potatoes to a sort of vegetable glue! How divine are these recollections to me at this moment! Yet I have no thought of coming home just now. I lack a real pretext for doing so; it is true this place is dismal to

9 For Charlotte's use of this incident in fiction, see *Villette*, Ch. XV.

me, but I cannot go home without a fixed prospect when I get there; and this prospect must not be a situation; that would be jumping out of the frying-pan into the fire. *You* call yourself idle! absurd, absurd! . . . Is papa well? Are you well? and Tabby? You ask about Queen Victoria's visit to Brussels. I saw her for an instant flashing through the Rue Royale in a carriage and six, surrounded by soldiers. She was laughing and talking very gaily. She looked a little stout, vivacious lady, very plainly dressed, not much dignity or pretension about her. . . . Tell me whether papa really wants me very much to come home, and whether you do likewise. I have an idea that I should be of no use there — a sort of aged person upon the parish. I pray, with heart and soul, that all may continue well at Haworth; above all in our grey, half-inhabited house. God bless the walls thereof! Safety, health, happiness, and prosperity to you, papa, and Tabby. Amen.   C. B.

29. TO E. B. [S. H.]

Brussels, December 19th, 1843 I,309
Dear E. J., — I have taken my determination. I hope to be at home the day after New Year's Day. I have told Mme. Heger. But in order to come home I shall be obliged to draw on my cash for another £5. . . . / Low spirits have afflicted me much lately, I,310 but I hope all will be well when I get home — above all, if I find papa and you and B. and A. well. I am not ill in body. It is only the mind which is a trifle shaken — for want of comfort.

I shall try to cheer up now. — Good-bye.
C. B.

THE FAILURE OF THE SCHOOL PLAN, 1843 TO 1845

The girls now possessed the training needed to start their school. Anne, though still not happy at Thorpe Green, had been brushing up her music and (more important, as she was probably the only one of the girls who knew it) her Latin. Thanks to Aunt Branwell's legacy, there was some capital to enlarge the parsonage to house their pupils. But though they assiduously circulated prospectuses and wrote to their friends, no pupils were forthcoming. It is probable that Charlotte and Anne felt the disappointment more keenly than Emily, whose birthday letter of 1845 (III) is buoyant and whose poetry of this period suggests an increasing absorption in her deepening inner life.

Charlotte's private preoccupation and suffering are apparent in her letters to M. Heger. Since Mrs. Gaskell's time, biographers have taken sides about the exact nature of her feelings for him. To take some diverse samples, May Sinclair (*The Three Brontës,* London: Hutchinson, 1912) thought Charlotte so pure as to be without sentiment, incapable of passion. Frederika Macdonald (*The Secret of Charlotte Brontë*) was sure Charlotte was really in love; Phyllis Bentley (*The Brontës*) thinks the letters to Heger are real love letters, but that Charlotte was not conscious of this until later. Laura Hinkley (*The Brontës*) thinks Charlotte sought "companionship, counsel, compassion" (p. 75), not love. The letters are here; the reader may try to decide for himself.

This seems to be a good place to give a short account of Branwell's vicissitudes, since his condition by the summer of 1845 put an absolute and final end to the possibility of holding school in the parsonage, not to mention the shame and distress it caused his family. For a while he had stuck to his railway job and even been promoted, but the uneventful life drove him to his usual forms of escape and in March, 1842, he was dismissed for negligence and haphazard bookkeeping. He was at home and deeply upset when his aunt and Weightman died. Thanks to Anne, he got one more chance to support himself: this time as tutor to the Robinson boy at Thorpe

Green. Charlotte who wrote Ellen from Brussels (January, 1844) that her brother and sister were "wondrously valued" by the Robinsons, was certainly not prepared for the explosion that took place in the summer of 1845.

The exact truth about what happened will probably never be known. We are not even sure why Anne left before Branwell did. It is usually thought that his attachment for Mrs. Robinson became known to the Reverend Robinson, but direct evidence is lacking. A habitual romancer, Branwell himself gave different accounts of the affair to different people, all probably at variance with the facts. In early days, Branwell's references to the estate which would one day come to Mrs. Robinson suggest that the prospect of a competency and leisure to write may have attracted him. Later he certainly believed that she loved him in return. Whether he imagined this, whether she innocently or intentionally encouraged him is uncertain. It seems highly unlikely that she ever (as he insisted) intended to marry him. When Mr. Robinson did die, in May 1846, Branwell put about a story that the terms of her husband's will prevented Mrs. Robinson from marrying him. This was a fabrication, as an examination of the will makes clear; but by this time poor Branwell probably believed the extravagant romance he recounted to anyone he could get to listen to him. Probably his *grande passion,* so much like those he had often described in his stories, was his last remaining reason for living, a last effort to bolster his self-esteem. His suffering was certainly real to him. He continued to write poetry and letters, and boasted of a three-volume novel, but his creative power was spent.

Branwell's degradation was a tragedy to his family, but he himself merits our pity and compassion. Too much had been expected of him and his failure to achieve even a modicum of success made his destruction sure. Only day-dreams, self-pity, opium, and drink were left.

Readers fascinated by the puzzle of talent that mysteriously fails should look at the books on Branwell by du Maurier or Gérin and at the discussion of the problem in *B.S.T.* XIV, Pt. 72, by Dame Myra Curtis *et al.*

30. TO E. N. [G.]

[Haworth, January 23rd, 1844]

182 [My dear Ellen, —] [. . .] Every one asks me what I am going to do, now that I am returned home; and every one seems to expect that I should immediately commence a school. In truth it is what I should wish to do. I desire it above all things. I have sufficient money for the undertaking, and I hope now sufficient qualifications to give me a fair chance of success; yet I cannot yet permit myself to enter upon life — to touch the object which seems now within my reach, and which I have been so long straining to attain. You will ask me why? It is on papa's account; he is now, as you know, getting old, and it grieves me to tell you that he is losing his sight. I have felt for some months that I ought not to be away from him; and I feel now that it would be too selfish to leave him (at least, as long as Branwell and Anne are absent), in order to pursue selfish interests of my own. With the help of God, I will try to deny myself in this matter, and to wait.

I suffered much before I left Brussels. I think, however long I live, I shall not forget what the parting with M. Héger cost me. It grieved me so much to grieve him who has been so true, kind, and disinterested a friend. At parting he gave me a kind of diploma certifying my abilities as a teacher, sealed with the seal of the Athénée Royal, of which he is professor. I was surprised also at the degree of regret expressed by my Belgian pupils, when they knew I was going to leave. I did not think it had been in their phlegmatic nature. * * * I do not know whether you feel as I do, but there are times now when it appears to me

as if all my ideas and feelings, except a few friendships and affections, are changed from what they used to be; something in me, which used to be enthusiasm, is tamed down and broken. I have fewer illusions; what I wish for now is active exertion — a stake in life. Haworth seems such a lonely, quiet spot, buried away from the world. I no longer regard myself as young — indeed, I shall soon be twenty-eight; and it seems as if I ought to be working and braving the rough realities of the world, as other people do. It is, however, my duty to restrain this feeling at present, and I will endeavour to do so. [. . .]   [your *unchanged* friend,
C. Brontë]

31. TO M. HEGER[10]

July 24th, [1844]

10 Monsieur, — I am well aware that it is not my turn to write to you, but as Mrs. Wheelwright is going to Brussels and is kind enough to take charge of a letter — it seems to me that I ought not to neglect so favourable an opportunity of writing to you.

I am very pleased that the school-year is nearly over and that the holidays are approaching. — I am pleased on your account, Monsieur — for I am told that you are working too hard and that your health has suffered somewhat in consequence. For that reason I refrain from uttering a single complaint for your long silence — I would rather remain six months without receiving news from you than add one grain to the weight, already too heavy, which overwhelms you. I know well that it is now the period of compositions, that it will soon be that of examinations, and later on of prizes — and during all that time you are condemned to breathe the stifling atmosphere of the class-rooms — to spend yourself — to explain, to question, to talk all day, and then in the evening you have all those wretched compositions to read, to correct, almost to re-write — Ah, Monsieur! I once wrote you a

10 This and the following letters to M. Heger are reprinted from *The* [London] *Times*, July 29, 1913. [Translated from the original French by Marion H. Spielmann. Reprinted by permission of the *Times*.]

letter that was less than reasonable, because sorrow was at my heart; but I shall do so no more. — I shall try to be selfish no longer; and even while I look upon your letters as one of the greatest felicities known to me, I shall await the receipt of them in patience until it pleases you and suits you to send me any. Meanwhile, I may well send you a little letter from time to time: — you have authorised me to do so.

I greatly fear that I shall forget French, for I am firmly convinced that I shall see you again some day — I know not how or when — but it must be, for I wish it so much, and then I should not wish to remain dumb before you — it would be too sad to see you and not be able to speak to you. To avoid such a misfortune I learn every day by heart half a page of French from a book written in familiar style; and I take pleasure in learning this lesson, Monsieur; as I pronounce the French words it seems to me as if I were chatting with you.

I have just been offered a situation as first governess in a large school in Manchester, with a salary of £100 (*i.e.* 2,500 francs) per annum. I cannot accept it, for in accepting it I should have to leave my father, and that I cannot do. Nevertheless I have a plan — (when one lives retired the brain goes on working; there is the desire of occupation, the wish to embark on an active career). Our parsonage is rather a large house — with a few alterations there will be room for five or six boarders. If I could find this number of children of good family I should devote myself to their education. Emily does not care much for teaching, but she would look after the housekeeping, and, although something of a recluse, she is too good-hearted not to do all she could for the well-being of the children. Moreover she is very generous, and as for order, economy, strictness — and diligent work — all of them things very essential in a school — I willingly take that upon myself.

That, Monsieur, is my plan, which I have already explained to my father and which he approves. It only remains to find the pupils — rather a difficult thing — for we live rather far from towns and people do not greatly care about crossing the hills which form as it were a barrier around us. But the task that is without difficulty is almost without merit; there is great interest in triumphing over obstacles. I do not say I shall succeed but I shall *try* to succeed — the effort alone will do me good. There is nothing I fear so much as idleness, the want of occupation, inactivity, the lethargy of the faculties: when the body is idle, the spirit suffers painfully.

I should not know this lethargy if I could write. Formerly I passed whole days and weeks and months in writing, not wholly without result, for [Southey] and Coleridge — two of our best authors, to whom I sent certain manuscripts — were good enough to express their approval; but now my sight is too weak to write. — Were I to write much I should become blind. This weakness of sight is a terrible hindrance to me. Otherwise do you know what I should do, Monsieur? — I should write a book, and I should dedicate it to my literature-master — to the only master I ever had — to you, Monsieur. I have often told you in French how much I respect you — how much I am indebted to your goodness, to your advice; I should like to say it once in English. But that cannot be — it is not to be thought of. The career of letters is closed to me — only that of teaching is open. It does not offer the same attractions; never mind, I shall enter it, and if I do not go far it will not be from want of industry. You too, Monsieur — you wished to be a barrister — destiny or Providence made you a professor; you are happy in spite of it.

Please convey to Madame the assurance of my esteem. I fear that Maria, Louise, Claire have already forgotten me. Prospère and Victorine never knew me well; I remember well all five of them, especially Louise. She had so much character — so much naïveté in her little face. — Good-bye, Monsieur, — Your grateful pupil C. Brontë.

I have not begged you to write to me soon as I fear to importune you — but you are too kind to forget that I wish it all the same — yes, I wish it greatly. Enough; after all, do as you wish, Monsieur. If, then, I received a letter, and if I thought that you had written it *out of pity* — I should feel deeply wounded.

It seems that Mrs Wheelwright is going to Paris before going to Brussels — but she will post my letter at Boulogne. Once more good-bye, Monsieur; it hurts to say good-bye even in a letter. Oh, it is certain that I shall see you again one day — it must be so — for as soon as I shall have earned enough money to go to Brussels I shall go there — and I shall see you again if only for a moment.

32. TO E. N. [S. H.]

[Oct. 2nd, 1844]

Dear Ellen, — I, Emily, and Anne are truly 17 obliged to you for the efforts you have made on our behalf, and if you have not been successful you are only like ourselves. Every one wishes us well, but there are no pupils to be had. We have no present intention, however, of breaking our hearts on the subject, still less of feeling mortified at defeat. The effort must be beneficial whatever the result may be, because it teaches us experience and an additional knowledge of the world. — Yours faithfully,   C. Brontë.

33. TO M. HEGER

October 24th, 1844. 10

Monsieur, I am in high glee this morning — and that has rarely happened to me these last two years. It is because a gentleman of my acquaintance is going to Brussels, and has offered to take charge of a letter for you — which letter he will deliver to you himself, or else his sister, so that I shall be certain that you have received it.

I am not going to write a long letter; in the first place, I have not the time — it must leave at once; and then, I am afraid of worrying you. I would only ask of you if you heard from me at the beginning of May and again in the month of August? For six months I have been awaiting a letter from Monsieur — six months' waiting is very long, you know! However, I do not complain, and I shall be richly rewarded for a little sorrow if you will now write a letter and give it to this gentleman — or to his sister — who will hand it to me without fail.

I shall be satisfied with the letter however brief it be — only do not forget to tell me of your health, Monsieur, and how Madame and the children are, and the governesses and pupils.

My father and my sister send you their respects. My father's infirmity increases little by little. Nevertheless he is not yet entirely blind. My sisters are well, but my poor brother is still ill.

Farewell, Monsieur; I am depending on soon having your news. The idea delights me for the remembrance of your kindness will never fade from my memory, and as long as that remembrance endures the respect with which it has inspired me will endure likewise. Your very devoted pupil,
C. Brontë

34. TO M. HEGER

10   January 8th, [1845.]

Mr. Taylor has returned. I asked him if he had a letter for me. "No; nothing." "Patience," said I — "his sister will be here soon." Miss Taylor has returned. "I have nothing for you from Monsieur Heger," says she; "neither letter nor message."

Having realized the meaning of these words, I said to myself what I should say to another similarly placed: "You must be resigned, and above all do not grieve at a misfortune which you have not deserved." I strove to restrain my tears, to utter no complaint.

But when one does not complain, when one seeks to dominate oneself with a tyrant's grip, the faculties start into rebellion, and one pays for external calm with an internal struggle that is almost unbearable.

Day and night I find neither rest nor peace. If I sleep I am disturbed by tormenting dreams in which I see you, always severe, always grave, always incensed against me.

Forgive me then, Monsieur, if I adopt the course of writing to you again. How can I endure life if I make no effort to ease its sufferings?

I know that you will be irritated when you read this letter. You will say once more that I am hysterical [or neurotic] — that I have black thoughts, &c. So be it, Monsieur; I do not seek to justify myself; I submit to every sort of reproach. All I know is that I cannot, that I will not, resign myself to lose wholly the friendship of my master. I would rather suffer the greatest physical pain than always have my heart lacerated by smarting regrets.

If my master withdraws his friendship from me entirely I shall be altogether without hope; if he gives me a little — just a little — I shall be satisfied — happy; I shall have reason for living on, for working.

Monsieur, the poor have not need of much to sustain them — they ask only for the crumbs that fall from the rich men's table. But if they are refused the crumbs they die of hunger. Nor do I, either, need much affection from those I love. I should not know what to do with a friendship entire and complete — I am not used to it. But you showed me of yore a *little* interest, when I was your pupil in Brussels, and I hold on to the maintenance of that *little* interest — I hold on to it as I would hold on to life.

You will tell me perhaps — "I take not the slightest interest in you, Mademoiselle Charlotte. You are no longer an inmate of my House; I have forgotten you."

Well, Monsieur, tell me so frankly. It will be a shock to me. It matters not. It would be less dreadful than uncertainty.

I shall not re-read this letter. I send it as I have written it. Nevertheless, I have a hidden consciousness that some people, cold and common-sense, in reading it would say — "She is talking nonsense." I would avenge myself on such persons in no other way than by wishing them one single day of the torments which I have suffered for eight months. We should then see if they would not talk nonsense too.

One suffers in silence so long as one has

the strength so to do, and when that strength gives out one speaks without too carefully measuring one's words.

I wish Monsieur happiness and prosperity.   C. B.

35. TO E. N. [G.]

March 24, 1845.

190 [Dear Ellen, —] [. . .] I can hardly tell you how time gets on at Haworth. There is no event whatever to mark its progress. One day resembles another; and all have heavy, lifeless physiognomies. Sunday, baking-day, and Saturday, are the only ones that have any distinctive mark. Meantime, life wears away. I shall soon be thirty; and I have done nothing yet. Sometimes I get melancholy at the prospect before and behind me. Yet it is wrong and foolish to repine. Undoubtedly, my duty directs me to stay at home for the present.[1] There was a time when Haworth was a very pleasant place to me; it is not so now. I feel as if we were all buried here. I long to travel; to work; to live a life of action. Excuse me, dear [Ellen], for troubling you with my fruitless wishes. I will put by the rest, and not trouble you with them.

You *must* write to me. If you knew how welcome your letters are, you would write very often. Your letters, and the French newspapers, are the only messengers that come to me from the outer world beyond our moors; and very welcome messengers they are. [. . .]   [Write very soon — Goodbye dear Ellen. C. Brontë]

36. TO E. N. [S. H.]

II,43   July 31st, '45

Dear Ellen, —. . . It was ten o'clock at night when I got home. I found Branwell ill; he is so very often owing to his own fault. I was not therefore shocked at first, but when Anne informed me of the immediate cause of his present illness, I was very greatly shocked. He had last Thursday re-ceived a note from Mr Robinson sternly dismissing him, intimating that he had discovered his proceedings, which he characterised as bad beyond expression, and charging him on pain of exposure to break off instantly and for ever all communication with every member of his family. We have had sad work with Branwell since. He thought of nothing but stunning or drowning his distress of mind. No one in the house could have rest. At last we have been obliged to send him from home for a week, with some one to look after him;[2] he has written to me this morning, and expresses some sense of contrition for his frantic folly; he promises amendment on his return, but so long as he remains at home I scarce dare hope for peace in the house. We must all, I fear, prepare for a season of distress and disquietude. When I left you I was strongly impressed with the feeling that I was going back to sorrow. I cannot now ask Miss Wooler or any one else. . . . Good-bye, dear Nell,   C. Brontë.

37. TO M. HEGER

November 18th[, 1845.]

Monsieur, — The six months of silence have 10 run their course. It is now the 18th of Novr.; my last letter was dated (I think) the 18th of May. I may therefore write to you without failing in my promise.

The summer and autumn seemed very long to me; truth to tell, it has needed painful efforts on my part to bear hitherto the self-denial which I have imposed on myself. You, Monsieur, you cannot conceive what it means; but suppose for a moment that one of your children was separated from you, 160 leagues away, and that you had to remain six months without writing to him, without receiving news of him, without hearing him spoken of, without knowing aught of his health, then you would understand easily all the harshness of such an obligation. I tell you frankly that I have tried mean-/while to forget you, for the remembrance of a person whom one thinks

---

[1] Mary Taylor, who emigrated to New Zealand in the spring of this year, had strongly advised Charlotte to get away from home. She was never reconciled to Charlotte's sacrifice of her own wishes to her father's comfort. See Section V.

[2] He was sent to Liverpool with John Brown, the sexton.

never to see again, and whom, nevertheless, one greatly esteems, frets too much the mind; and when one has suffered that kind of anxiety for a year or two, one is ready to do anything to find peace once more. I have done everything; I have sought occupations; I have denied myself absolutely the pleasure of speaking about you — even to Emily; but I have been able to conquer neither my regrets nor my impatience. That, indeed, is humiliating — to be unable to control one's own thoughts, to be the slave of a regret, of a memory, the slave of a fixed and dominant idea which lords it over the mind. Why cannot I have just as much friendship for you, as you for me — neither more nor less? Then should I be so tranquil, so free — I could keep silence then for ten years without an effort.

My father is well but his sight is almost gone. He can neither read nor write. Yet the doctors advise waiting a few months more before attempting an operation. The winter will be a long night for him. He rarely complains; I admire his patience. If Providence wills the same calamity for me, may He at least vouchsafe me as much patience with which to bear it! It seems to me, Monsieur, that there is nothing more galling in great physical misfortunes than to be compelled to make all those about us share in our sufferings. The ills of the soul one can hide, but those which attack the body and destroy the faculties cannot be concealed. My father allows me now to read to him and write for him; he shows me, too, more confidence than he has ever shown before, and that is a great consolation.

Monsieur, I have a favour to ask of you: when you reply to this letter, speak to me a little of yourself, not of me; for I know that if you speak of me it will be to scold me, and this time I would see your kindly side. Speak to me therefore of your children. Never was your brow severe when Louise and Claire and Prosper were by your side. Tell me also something of the School, of the pupils, of the Governesses. Are Mesdemoiselles Blanche, Sophie, and Justine still at Brussels? Tell me where you travelled during the holidays — did you go to the Rhine? Did you not visit Cologne or Coblentz? Tell me; in short, *mon maître,* what you will, but tell me something. To write to an ex-assistant-governess (No! I refuse to remember my employment as assistant-governess — I repudiate it) — anyhow, to write to an old pupil cannot be a very interesting occupation for you, I know; but for me it is life. Your last letter was stay and prop to me — nourishment to me for half a year. Now I need another and you will give it me; not because you bear me friendship — you cannot have much — but because you are compassionate of soul and you would condemn no one to prolonged suffering to save yourself a few moments' trouble. To forbid me to write to you, to refuse to answer me, would be to tear from me my only joy on earth, to deprive me of my last privilege — a privilege I never shall consent willingly to surrender. Believe me, *mon maître,* in writing to me it is a good deed that you will do. So long as I believe you are pleased with me, so long as I have hope of receiving news from you, I can be at rest and not too sad. But when a prolonged and gloomy silence seems to threaten me with the estrangement of my master — when day by day I await a letter, and when day by day disappointment comes to fling me back into overwhelming sorrow, and the sweet delight of seeing your handwriting and reading your counsel escapes me as a vision that is vain, then fever claims me — I lose appetite and sleep — I pine away.

May I write to you again next May? I would rather wait a year, but it is impossible — it is too long. C. Brontë.

I must say one word to you in English — I wish I could write to you more cheerful letters, for when I read this over, I find it to be somewhat gloomy — but forgive me my dear master — do not be irritated at my sadness — according to the words of the Bible: "Out of the fulness of the heart, the mouth speaketh" and truly I find it difficult to be cheerful so long as I think I shall never see you more. You will perceive by the defects in this letter that I am forgetting the French language — yet I read all the French books I can get, and learn daily a portion by heart — but I have never heard French spoken but once since I left Brussels — and then it sounded like music in my ears — every word was most precious to me because it reminded me of you — I love French for your sake with all my heart and soul.

Farewell my dear Master — may God protect you with special care and crown you with peculiar blessings.   C. B.[3]

The *Poems* and the First Novels, 1845 to 1847

The future must have looked bleak in the summer of 1845. In addition to their private miseries — and Anne's poems and diary[4] of the period show that she as well as Charlotte experienced frustration and unhappiness — and the anxiety over Branwell,[5] Mr. Brontë's eyesight was getting steadily worse. But Charlotte's discovery of Emily's poems and the acceptance of *Poems by Currer, Ellis, and Acton Bell* (at the cost of £31:10 of Aunt's legacy) plunged them into work, choosing and revising their poems, settling on pseudonyms, studying various qualities of paper, writing inquiries and directions to the publishers.[6] The volume came out in May, 1846, was reviewed by only three critics,[7] and did not sell. This failure did not deter the sisters, who were already hard at work on the novels.[8] No one wanted *The Professor,* but eventually *Wuthering Heights* and *Agnes Grey* were accepted by T. C. Newby. No one, not even Ellen, was told about these ventures.

Meanwhile Mr. Brontë had become nearly blind and Charlotte and Emily, overriding his objections, went to Manchester to arrange for a cataract operation. Charlotte stayed with her father throughout this ordeal and under these unpropitious circumstances began the writing of *Jane Eyre.* For its reception by its publishers, by the critics, and finally by her father, see the reviews and the accounts by George Smith and Mrs. Gaskell (IV, V).

[3] These verses may throw some light on Charlotte's state of mind in these months.

He saw my heart's woe, discovered my soul's anguish,
   How in fever, in thirst, in atrophy it pined;
Knew he could heal, yet looked and let it languish, —
   To its moans spirit-deaf, to its pangs spirit-blind.

But once a year he heard a whisper low and dreary
   Appealing for aid, entreating some reply;
Only when sick, soul-worn, and torture-weary,
   Breathed I that prayer, heaved I that sigh.

He was mute as is the grave, he stood stirless as a tower;
   At last I looked up and saw I prayed to stone:
I asked help of that which to help had no power,
I sought love where love was utterly unknown.
   . . .
    (C. B., *Poems,* ed. Shorter, rev. Hatfield, pp. 220–221)

[4] See Section III and contrast her mood with Emily's.

[5] Yet Branwell, like his sisters, was still planning to write. In a letter to his friend Joseph Leyland, the sculptor, he wrote on September 10, 1845 (S. H. II, 60–61), "In the present state of the publishing world, a Novel is the most saleable article"; his projected book, "the result of years of thought," would give a vivid picture of good and evil and could, he said, be compared to *Hamlet* and *Lear.*

[6] See the Biographical Notice.

[7] Charlotte had listed ten periodicals to which she wished review copies sent. She should have been pleased with the *Athenaeum* critic who detected some "inspiration" in the work of Ellis Bell. "A Fine, quaint spirit has the latter," he wrote, ". . . and an evident power of wing that may reach heights here not attempted . . . How musical he can be, and how lightly and eagerly the music falls from his heart and pen. . . . He is no copyist. There is not enough in this volume to judge him by, but, to our mind, an impression of originality is conveyed beyond what his contributions to these pages embody." — *Athenaeum,* July 1846, p. 46.

[8] Laura Hinkley (*The Brontës: Charlotte and Emily,* p. 146–9) argues cogently that Emily may have begun her book much earlier, perhaps as early as 1840.

38. TO E. N. [S. H.]

II,83 March 3rd [1846]

Dear Ellen — I reached home a little after 2 o'clock all safe and right — yesterday — I found papa very well — his sight much the same — Emily and Anne were gone to Keighley to meet me — unfortunately I had returned by the old road while they were /

84 gone by the new — and we missed each other — they did not get home till ½ past 4 — and were caught in the heavy shower of rain which fell in the afternoon — I am sorry to say Anne has taken a little cold in consequence — but I hope she will soon be well. . . .

I went into the room where Branwell was to speak to him about an hour after I got home — it was very forced work to ad-dess him — I might have spared myself the trouble as he took no notice and made no reply — he was stupefied — My fears were not vain. Emily tells me that he got a sov-ereign from Papa while I have been away under the pretence of paying a pressing debt — he went immediately and changed it at a public-house — and has employed it as was to be expected — she concluded her account with saying he was a hopeless being — it is too true — In his present state it is scarcely possible to stay in the room where he is — what the future has in store I do not know. . . .

Believe me dear Nell, — Yours faithfully,
C. B.

39. TO E. N. [G.]

[Manchester, August 21, '46]

210 [Dear Ellen, —] I just scribble a line to you to let you know where I am, in order that you may write to me here, for it seems to me that a letter from you would relieve me from the feeling of strangeness I have in this big town. Papa and I came here on Wednesday; we saw Mr. Wilson, the ocu-list, the same day; he pronounced papa's eyes quite ready for an operation, and has fixed next Monday for the performance of it. Think of us on that day [. . . .] Mr. Wilson says we shall have to stay here for a month at least. [. . .] I wonder how Emily and Anne will get on at home with Bran-

well. They, too, will have their troubles. What would I not give to have you here! One is forced, step by step, to get experience in the world; but the learning is so disagree-able. One cheerful feature in the business is, that Mr. Wilson thinks most favourably of the case. [Yours, C. Brontë.]

40. TO E. N. [G.][9]

August 26th, 1846.

[Dear Ellen, —] The operation is over; it 211 took place yesterday. Mr. Wilson per-formed it; two other surgeons assisted. Mr. Wilson says, he considers it quite succes-ful; but papa cannot yet see anything. The affair lasted precisely a quarter of an hour . . . Papa displayed extraordinary patience and firmness; the surgeons seemed surprised. I was in the room all the time, as it was his wish that I should be there; of course, I neither spoke nor moved till the thing was done, and then I felt that the less I said, either to papa or the surgeons, the better. Papa is now confined to his bed in a dark room, and is not to be stirred for four days; he is to speak and be spoken to as little as possible. . . . [C. Brontë]

41. TO E. N. [S. H.][10]

[September 22nd, '46]

Dear Ellen, — I have nothing new to tell II,110 you except that papa continues to do well though the process of recovery appears to me very tedious — I dare-say it will yet be many weeks before his sight is completely restored — yet every time Mr. Wilson comes he expresses his satisfaction at the perfect success of the operation — and assures me Papa will ere long be able both to read and write — he is still a prisoner in his darkened room — into which however a little more light is admitted than formerly. The nurse goes to day — her departure will certainly

9 "Charlotte Brontë told me that her tale [*The Professor*] came back upon her hands, curtly re-jected by some publisher, on the very day when her father was to submit to his operation." — Mrs. Gaskell, *Life*, p. 213.

10 Notice that Charlotte does not breathe a word about *Jane Eyre*, at which she was working at a furious pace.

be a relief though she is I daresay not the worst of her class. . . .

Yours faithfully   C. Brontë

42. TO E. N. [S. H.]

II,114   Octr. 14th, '46

Dear Ellen, — [In the first part of this letter, Charlotte refuses to leave home to join Ellen in setting up a school.] . . . / But if I *could* leave home Ellen — I should not be at Haworth now — I know life is passing away and I am doing nothing — earning nothing a very bitter knowledge it is at moments — but I see no way out of the mist — More than one very favorable opportunity has now offered which I have been obliged to put aside — probably when I am free to leave home I shall neither be able to find place nor employment — perhaps too I shall be quite past the prime of life — my faculties will be rusted — and my few acquirements in a great measure forgotten — These ideas sting me keenly sometimes — but whenever I consult my Conscience it affirms that I am doing right in staying at home — and bitter are its upbraidings when I yield to an eager desire for release — I returned to Brussels after Aunt's death against my conscience — prompted by what then seemed an irresistible impulse — I was punished for my selfish folly by a total withdrawal for more than two years of happiness and peace of mind — I could hardly expect success if I were to err again in the same way — . . . .
C. Brontë

43. TO THOMAS DE QUINCEY [S. H.]

II,136   June 16th, 1847.

Sir, — My relatives, Ellis and Acton Bell,[1] and myself, heedless of the repeated warnings of various respectable publishers, have committed the rash act of printing a volume of poems.

The consequences predicted have, of course, overtaken us: our book is found to be a drug; no man needs it or heeds it. In the space of a year our publisher has disposed but of two copies, and by what painful efforts he succeeded in getting rid of these two, himself only knows.

Before transferring the edition to the trunkmakers, we have decided on distributing as presents a few copies of what we cannot sell — we beg to offer you one in acknowledgement of the pleasure and profit we have often and long derived from your works. — I am, sir, yours very respectfully,
Currer Bell

44. TO E. N. [S. H.]

June 29th, '47 II,136

Dear Ellen, — . . . I was amused by what she [Miss Ringrose] says respecting her wish that when she marries, her husband will at least have a will of his own, even should he be a tyrant — Tell her when she forms that aspiration again she must make it conditional — if her husband has a strong will, he must also have a strong sense — a kind heart — a thoroughly correct notion of justice — because a man with a *weak brain, chill affections* and *strong will* — is merely an intractable fiend — you can have no hold of him — you can never lead him right. A Tyrant under any circumstances is a curse. When can you come to Haworth? . . .
Yours faithfully, C. Brontë

45. TO SMITH, ELDER & CO. [G.]

August 24th [1847] 224

[Gentlemen, —] I now send you per rail a MS. entitled *Jane Eyre,* a novel in three volumes, by Currer Bell. I find I cannot prepay the / carriage of the parcel, as money 225 for that purpose is not received at the small station-house where it is left. If, when you acknowledge the receipt of the MS., you would have the goodness to mention the amount charged on delivery, I will immediately transmit it in postage stamps. It is better in future to address Mr. Currer Bell, under cover to Miss Brontë, Haworth, Bradford, Yorkshire, as there is a risk of letters otherwise directed not reaching me at pres-

---

[1] Biographers have speculated about the origin of the pseudonyms. Was "Bell" for the Bell Chapel at Thornton, where they were baptised? There is a Currer in an early story by Branwell and an "Elles" in an Angrian tale. Incidentally, Charlotte also sent copies of the *Poems* to Lockhart and other writers.

ent. To save trouble, I enclose an envelope.

[Currer Bell]

46. TO SMITH, ELDER & CO. [S. H.]

II,142   September 24th, 1847

Gentlemen, — I have to thank you for punctuating the sheets before sending them to me, as I found the task very puzzling, and, besides, I consider your mode of punctuation a great deal more correct and rational than my own. I am glad you think pretty well of the first part of "Jane Eyre," and I trust, both for your sakes and my own, the public may think pretty well of it too.

Henceforth I hope I shall be able to return the sheets promptly and regularly. — I am, Gentlemen, Yours respectfully,

C. Bell.

47. TO E. N. [S. H.]

II,148   Oct. 15th, 1847

Dear Ellen, — . . . We are getting on here the same as usual[2] only that Branwell has been more than ordinarily troublesome and annoying of late; he leads Papa a wretched life. Mr. Nicholls is returned just the same; I cannot for my life see those interesting germs of goodness in him you discovered; his narrowness of mind always strikes me chiefly. I fear he is indebted to your imagination for his hidden treasure. . . .

Yours faithfully, C. Brontë.

48. TO SMITH, ELDER & CO. [S. H.]

October 19th, 1847. II,149

Gentlemen, — The six copies of "Jane Eyre" reached me this morning. You have given the work every advantage which good paper, clear type, and a seemly outside can supply; if it fails the fault will lie with the author; you are exempt.

I now await the judgment of the press and the public. — I am gentlemen, yours respectfully,   C. Bell.

49. TO SMITH, ELDER & CO. [G.]

Oct. 26th, 1847. 227

Gentlemen, — I have received the newspapers. They speak quite as favourably of *Jane Eyre* as I expected them to do. The notice in the *Literary Gazette* seems certainly to have been indited in rather a flat mood, and the *Athenæum* has a style of its own, which I respect, but cannot exactly relish; still when one considers that journals of that standing have a dignity to maintain which would be deranged by a too cordial recognition of the claims of an obscure author, I suppose there is every reason to be satisfied.

Meantime a brisk sale would be effectual support under the hauteur of lofty critics. — I am, Gentlemen, yours respectfully,   C. Bell.

THE THREE BELLS, 1847 TO 1848

In December, 1847, T. C. Newby,[3] prompted no doubt by the success of *Jane Eyre,* finally brought out *Wuthering Heights* and *Agnes Grey,* by Ellis and Acton Bell respectively. This precipitated the confusion about the Bells which so mystified and delighted the public. The Brontës were, of course, eager to remain anonymous. Privacy was precious and publicity foreign to their retired way of life. Charlotte in particular, because she had used so many recognizable models, needed her invisibility.

Yet it is remarkable that they thought the secret could be kept, for Currer Bell was now an important figure in the literary world. Now the fame she had dreamed of when she was a little girl writing the tales of the Young Men was hers. Now she was a part of the great world of art and culture which she had so deeply longed for. Now she could — and did — write freely and frankly to other members of that world, such as Lewes and Dobell and Thackeray. It was Thackeray, long one of her heroes,

---

[2] This sentence was penned the day before the publication of *Jane Eyre!*

[3] The first of his misdeeds was his failure to incorporate into the text the careful corrections the authors had made on the proofs.

to whom she dedicated the second edition of *Jane Eyre,* eliciting the comment "I am quite vexed that by some blundering of mine I should have delayed answering Currer Bell's enormous compliment so long. I didn't know what to say in reply; it quite flustered and upset me. Is it true, I wonder? I'm — But a truce to egotism.

"Thank you for your kindness in sending me the volumes, and (indirectly) for the greatest compliment I ever received in my life" (Thackeray to W. S. Williams, S. H. II, 182–3). She was not aware that his life paralleled Rochester's in one spectacularly unfortunate respect; his wife had become mentally incapable in 1840. The dedication only whetted the public curiosity about the Bells, and probably hastened the breakdown of the precious incognito.

If Charlotte needed anonymity for practical reasons, Emily valued its shelter most highly because of her shyness and reserve. And, stoical as she was, she cannot have found the reviews of her novel easy to take. Charlotte said later that much of her pleasure in her own success was spoilt by the spectacle of Emily's silent suffering.

Agnes Grey was only mildly praised or written off as not important. *Douglas Jerrold's Weekly* pronounced it "a tale worth telling" and the *Atlas* critic found it "sunny and level." Anne was not disheartened. She was well along with her second novel, *The Tenant of Wildfell Hall,* in which she tried to depict with complete honesty the effects on a weak young man of vice and depravity. The novel was ahead of its time in being relentlessly naturalistic and gave almost as much offence as *Wuthering Heights.* Anne was probably as baffled as Emily.

It was *Wildfell Hall,* too, which brought the Bell incognito further into jeopardy. Charlotte's publishers would have taken another Bell novel, but Anne felt committed to Newby, who repaid her loyalty by deceit (see Charlotte's letter of September 4, 1848). It is typical of the Brontë integrity that when, thanks to Newby's machinations, the honesty of the Bells was questioned, Charlotte and Anne did not hesitate to reveal the secret of the pseudonym to Smith and Elder (V). Publicly the incognito was maintained. Anne's Preface to the new edition of *Wildfell Hall* (London, 1848) contained the sentence "Respecting the author's identity, I would have it be distinctly understood that Acton Bell is neither Currer nor Ellis Bell and therefore let not his faults be attributed to them." A pleasant byproduct of this visit was that Smith and Elder took over the sheets of the neglected *Poems.* The girls evidently had it out with Newby, but of this there are no details.

50. TO W. S. WILLIAMS [S. H.]
II,150   Haworth, October 28th, 1847.

Dear Sir, — Your last letter was very pleasant to me to read, and is very cheering to reflect on. I feel honoured in being approved by Mr Thackeray, because I approve Mr Thackeray. This may sound presumptuous perhaps, but I mean that I have long recognised in his writings genuine talent, such as I admired, such as I wondered at and delighted in. No author seems to distinguish so exquisitely as he does dross from ore, the real from the counterfeit. I believed too he had deep and true feelings under his seeming sternness. Now I am sure he has. One good word from such a man is worth pages of praise from ordinary judges.

You are right in having faith in the reality of Helen Burns's character; she was real enough. I have exaggerated nothing there. I abstained from recording much that I remember respecting her, lest the narrative should sound incredible. Knowing this, I could not but smile at the quiet self-complacent dogmatism with which one of the journals lays it down that "such creations as Helen Burns are very beautiful but very untrue."

The plot of "Jane Eyre" may be a hackneyed one. Mr Thackeray remarks that it is familiar to him. But having read comparatively few novels I never chanced to meet with it, and I thought it original. The work referred to by the critic of the "Athenæum" I had not the good fortune to hear of. . . .

I would still endeavour to keep my expectations low respecting the ultimate success of "Jane Eyre." But my desire that it / should succeed augments, for you have taken much trouble about the work, and it would grieve me seriously if your active efforts should be baffled and your sanguine hopes disappointed. Excuse me if I again remark that I fear they are rather *too* sanguine: it would be better to moderate them. What will the critics of the monthly reviews and magazines be likely to see in "Jane Eyre" (if indeed they deign to read it), which will win from them even a stinted modicum of approbation? It has no learning, no research, it discusses no subject of public interest. A mere domestic novel will, I fear, seem trivial to men of large views, and solid attainments.

Still, efforts so energetic and indefatigable as yours ought to realise a result in some degree favourable, and I trust they will. — I remain, dear sir, yours respectfully,
C. Bell.

51. TO G. H. LEWES [G.]

233   Nov. 6th, 1847.
Dear Sir, — Your letter reached me yesterday[.] I beg to assure you, that I appreciate fully the intention with which it was written, and I thank you sincerely both for its cheering commendation and valuable advice.

You warn me to beware of melodrama, and you exhort me to adhere to the real. When I first began to write, so impressed was I with the truth of the principles you advocate, that I determined to take Nature and Truth as my sole guides, and to follow in their very footprints; I restrained imagination, eschewed romance, repressed excitement; over-bright colouring, too, I avoided, and sought to produce something which should be soft, grave, and true.

My work (a tale in one volume) being completed, I offered it to a publisher. He said it was original, faithful to nature, but he did not feel warranted in accepting it; such a work / would not sell. I tried six 234 publishers in succession; they all told me it was deficient in "startling incident" and "thrilling excitement," that it would never suit the circulating libraries, and, as it was on those libraries the success of works of fiction mainly depended, they could not undertake to publish what would be overlooked there.

Jane Eyre was rather objected to at first, on the same grounds, but finally found acceptance.

I mention this to you, not with a view of pleading exemption from censure, but in order to direct your attention to the root of certain literary evils. If, in your forthcoming article in *Frazer,* you would bestow a few words of enlightenment on the public who support the circulating libraries, you might, with your powers, do some good.

You advise me, too, not to stray far from the ground of experience, as I become weak when I enter the region of fiction; and you say, "real experience is perennially interesting, and to all men."

I feel that this also is true; but, dear Sir, is not the real experience of each individual very limited? And, if a writer dwells upon that solely or principally, is he not in danger of repeating himself, and also of becoming an egotist? Then, too, imagination is a strong, restless faculty, which claims to be heard and exercised: are we to be quite deaf to her cry, and insensate to her struggles?

When she shows us bright pictures, are we never to look at them, and try to reproduce them? And when she is eloquent, and speaks rapidly and urgently in our ear, are we not to write to her dictation?

I shall anxiously search the next number of *Frazer* for your opinions on these points. — Believe me, dear Sir, yours gratefully,
C. Bell.[4]

---

[4] See Section IV, for a note on Lewes and his review of *Jane Eyre.*

52. TO W. S. WILLIAMS [S. H.]

II,153

Novbr. 10th, 1847

Dear Sir, — I have received the "Britannia" and the "Sun," but not the "Spectator," which I rather regret, as censure, though not pleasant, is often wholesome.

Thank you for your information regarding Mr. Lewes. I am glad to hear that he is a clever and sincere man: . . . even if it /
154 goes against me I shall not murmur; ability and honesty have a right to condemn, where they think condemnation is deserved. From what you say, however, I trust rather to obtain at least a modified approval.

Your account of the various surmises respecting the identity of the brothers Bell amused me much: were the enigma solved it would probably be found not worth the trouble of solution; but I will let it alone; it suits ourselves to remain quiet and certainly injures no one else.

The Reviewer who noticed the little book of poems, in the "Dublin Magazine," conjectured that the *soi-disant* three personages were in reality but one who, endowed with an unduly prominent organ of self-esteem, and consequently impressed with a somewhat weighty notion of his own merits, thought them too vast to be concentrated in a single individual and accordingly divided himself into three, out of consideration, I suppose, for the nerves of the much-to-be-astounded public! This was an ingenious thought in the Reviewer — very original and striking, but not accurate. We are three.

A prose work by Ellis and Acton, will soon appear: it should have been out, indeed, long since; for the first proof-sheets were already in the press at the commencement of last August, before Currer Bell had placed the MS. of "Jane Eyre" in your hands. Mr. Newby however does not do business like Messrs Smith & Elder; a different spirit seems to preside at 172 Mortimer Street to that which guides the helm at 65 Cornhill. Mr. Newby shuffles, gives his word and breaks it; Messrs Smith & Elders performance is always better than their promise. My relatives have suffered from exhausting delay and procrastination, while I have to acknowledge the benefits of a management at once businesslike and gentlemanlike, energetic and considerate.

I should like to know if Mr Newby often acts as he has done to my relatives, or whether this is an exceptional instance of his method. Do you know, and can you tell me anything about him? You must excuse me for going to the point at once, when I want to learn anything — if my questions are impertinent you are, of course, at liberty to decline answering them. — I am yours respectfully, C. Bell.

53. TO SMITH, ELDER & CO. [G.]

Dec. 10th, 1847

Gentlemen, — I beg to acknowledge the re- 228 ceipt of your letter inclosing a bank post bill, for which I thank you.[5] Having already expressed my sense of your kind and upright conduct, I can now only say that I trust you will always have reason to / be 229 as well content with me as I am with you. If the result of any future exertions I may be able to make should prove agreeable and advantageous to you, I shall be well satisfied; and it would be a serious source of regret to me if I thought you ever had reason to repent being my publishers.

You need not apologise, Gentlemen, for having written to me so seldom; of course I am always glad to hear from you, but I am truly glad to hear from Mr. Williams likewise; he was my first favourable critic; he first gave me encouragement to persevere as an author, consequently I naturally respect him and feel grateful to him.

Excuse the informality of my letter, and believe me, Gentlemen, yours respectfully,

Currer Bell.

54. TO W. S. WILLIAMS [S. H.]

Jany 4th, 1848 II,173

Dear Sir, —/. . . "Jane Eyre" has got down 174 into Yorkshire; a copy has even penetrated into this neighbourhood: I saw an elderly clergyman reading it the other day, and

[5] Charlotte received £500 for *Jane Eyre* at this point, £100 on February 17, 1848.

had the satisfaction of hearing him exclaim "Why — they have got —— school, and Mr. —— here, I declare! and Miss ——" (naming the original of Lowood, Mr. Brocklehurst and Miss Temple) He had known them all: I wondered whether he would recognize the portrait, and was gratified to find that he did and that moreover he pronounced them faithful and just — he said too that Mr —— (Brocklehurst) "deserved the chastisement he had got."

He did not recognize "Currer Bell" — What author would be without the advantage of being able to walk invisible? One is thereby enabled to keep such a quiet mind. I make this small observation in confidence. . . . Believe me &c. Currer Bell

55. TO G. H. LEWES [G.]

239   [Haworth, January 12th, 1848]
Dear Sir, — I thank you then sincerely for your generous review; and it is with the sense of double content I express my gratitude, because I am now sure the tribute is not superfluous or obtrusive. You were not severe on *Jane Eyre*; you were very lenient. I am glad you told me my faults plainly in private, for in your public notice you touch on them so lightly, I should perhaps have passed them over, thus indicated, with too little reflection.

I mean to observe your warning about being careful how I undertake new works; my stock of materials is not abundant, but very slender; and, besides, neither my experience, my acquirements, nor my powers, are sufficiently varied to justify my ever becoming a frequent writer. I tell you this, because your article in *Frazer* left in me an uneasy impression that you were disposed to think better of the author of *Jane Eyre* than that individual deserved; and I would rather you had a correct than a flattering opinion of me, even though I should never see you.

If I ever *do* write another book, I think I will have nothing of what you call "melodrama;" I think so, but I am not sure. I *think*, too, I will endeavour to follow the counsel which shines out of Miss Austen's

"mild eyes," "to finish more and be more subdued;" but neither am I sure of that. When authors write / best, or, at least, 240 when they write most fluently, an influence seems to waken in them, which becomes their master — which will have its own way — putting out of view all behests but its own, dictating certain words, and insisting on their being used, whether vehement or measured in their nature; new-moulding characters, giving unthought of turns to incidents, rejecting carefully-elaborated old ideas, and suddenly creating and adopting new ones.

Is it not so? And should we try to counteract this influence? Can we indeed counteract it? . . .

Why do you like Miss Austen so very much? I am puzzled on that point. What induced you to say that you would have rather written *Pride and Prejudice,* or *Tom Jones,* than any of the Waverley Novels?

I had not seen *Pride and Prejudice* till I read that sentence of yours, and then I got the book. And what did I find? An accurate, daguerreotyped portrait of a commonplace face! a carefully-fenced, highly-cultivated garden, with neat borders and delicate flowers; but no glance of a bright, vivid physiognomy, no open country, no fresh air, no blue hill, no bonny beck. I should hardly like to live with her ladies and gentlemen, in their elegant but confined houses. These observations will probably irritate you, but I shall run the risk. . . .

Am I wrong — or, were you hasty in what you said? If you have time, I should be glad to hear further on this subject; if not, or if you think the questions frivolous, do not trouble yourself to reply. — I am, yours respectfully,   C. Bell.

56. TO G. H. LEWES [G.]

Jan. 18th, 1848. 241
Dear Sir, — I must write one more note, though I had not intended to trouble you again so soon. I have to agree with you, and to differ from you.

You correct my crude remarks on the subject of the "influence"; well, I accept your definition of what the effects of that influence should be; I recognize the wisdom of your rules for its regulation. * * *

What a strange lecture comes next in your letter! You say I must familiarise my mind with the fact, that "Miss Austen is not a poetess, has no 'sentiment' (you scornfully enclose the word in inverted commas), no eloquence, none of the ravishing enthusiasm of poetry," — and then you add, I *must* "learn to acknowledge her as *one of the greatest artists, of the greatest painters of human character*, and one of the writers with the nicest sense of means to an end that ever lived."

The last point only will I ever acknowledge.

Can there be a great artist without poetry?

What I call — what I will bend to, as a great artist then — cannot be destitute of the divine gift. But by *poetry*, I am sure, you understand something different to what I do, as you do by "sentiment." It is *poetry*, as I comprehend the word, which elevates that masculine George Sand, and makes out of something coarse, something Godlike. It is "sentiment," in my sense of the term — sentiment jealously hidden, but genuine, which extracts the venom from that formidable Thackeray, and converts what might be corrosive poison into purifying elixir.

If Thackeray did not cherish in his large heart deep feeling for his kind, he would delight to exterminate; as it is, I believe, he wishes only to reform. Miss Austen being, as you say, without "sentiment," without *poetry*, maybe *is* sensible, real (more *real* than *true*), but she cannot be great.

I submit to your anger, which I have now excited (for have I not questioned the perfection of your darling?); the storm may pass over me. Nevertheless, I will, when I can (I do not know when that will be, as I have no access to a circulating library), diligently peruse all Miss Austen's works, as you recommend. * * * You must forgive me for not always being able to think as you do, and still believe me, yours gratefully,   C. Bell.

57. TO W. S. WILLIAMS [S. H.]
Jany. 22nd, 1848. II,181
Dear Sir, — I have received the Morning Herald, and was much pleased with the notice, chiefly on account of the reference made to that portion of the preface which concerns Messrs Smith & Elder: if my tribute of thanks can benefit my publishers, it is desirable that it should have as much publicity as possible.

I do not know if the part which relates to Mr Thackeray is likely to be as well received; but whether generally approved and understood or not, I shall not regret having written it, for I am convinced of its truth.

I see I was mistaken in my idea that the "Athenæum" and others wished to ascribe the authorship of "Wuthering Heights" to Currer Bell; the contrary is the case; "Jane Eyre" is given to Ellis Bell, and Mr Newby, it appears, thinks it expedient so to frame his advertisements as to favour the misapprehension — if Mr Newby had much sagacity he would see that Ellis Bell is strong enough to stand without being propped by Currer Bell — and would have disdained what Ellis himself of all things disdains — recourse to trickery. However, Ellis, Acton and Currer care / nothing for the matter II,182 personally — . . .   Yours faithfully, C. Bell

58. TO W. S. WILLIAMS [S. H.]
Haworth, January 28th, 1848. II,183
Dear Sir, — I need not tell you that when I saw Mr Thackeray's letter enclosed under your cover, the sight made me very happy. It was some time before I dared to open it, lest my pleasure in receiving it should be mixed with pain on learning its contents — lest, in short, the dedication should have been, in some way, unacceptable to him.

And, to tell you the truth, I fear this must have been the case; he does not say so, his letter is most friendly in its noble simplicity, but he apprises me, at the commencement, of a circumstance which both surprised and dismayed me.

I suppose it is no indiscretion to tell you this circumstance, for you doubtless know it already. It appears that his private position is in some points similar to that I have ascribed to Mr Rochester, that thence arose a report that "Jane Eyre" had been written by a governess in his family, and that the dedication coming now has confirmed everybody in the surmise.

Well may it be said that fact is often stranger than fiction! The coincidence struck me as equally unfortunate and extraordinary. Of course I knew nothing whatever of Mr Thackeray's domestic concerns, he existed for me only as an author. Of all regarding his personality, station, connections, private history, I was, and am still in a great measure, totally in the dark; but I am *very very* sorry that my inadvertent blunder should have made his name and affairs a subject for common gossip.

The very fact of his not complaining at all and addressing me with such kindness, notwithstanding the pain and annoyance I must have caused him, increases my chagrin. I could not half express my regret to him in my answer, for I was restrained by the consciousness that that regret was just worth nothing at all — quite valueless for healing the mischief I had done.

Can you tell me anything more on this subject? or can you guess in what degree the unlucky coincidence would affect him — whether it would pain him much and 184 deeply: for he says so / little himself on the topic, I am at a loss to divine the exact truth — but I fear. . . . yours with regard and respect, Currer Bell.

59. TO W. S. WILLIAMS [S. H.]

,203   April 20th, 1848
My dear Sir, — . . . I trust your firm will not lose by the third edition of "Jane / 204 Eyre" what has been made by the first, but I must say I think you enterprising to run the risk; however you have all along been the reverse of timid in the business. Success to the fearless!

It is very kind and right in you to answer "Currer Bell" to all queries respecting the authorship of "Jane Eyre." That is the only name I wish to have mentioned in connection with my writings. "Currer Bell" only I am and will be to the Public, if acci-

dent or design should deprive me of that name, I should deem it a misfortune — a very great one. Mental tranquility would then be gone; it would be a task to write, a task which I doubt whether I should continue. If I were known, I should ever be conscious in writing that my book must be read by ordinary acquaintances, and that idea would fetter me intolerably. . . .

          Yours sincerely, Currer Bell

60. TO E. N. [G.]

            April 28th, '48 245
[Dear Ellen, —] Write another letter, and explain that last note of yours distinctly. If your allusions are to myself, which I suppose they are, understand this, I have given no one a right to gossip about me, and am not to be judged by frivolous conjectures, emanating from any quarter whatever. Let me know what you heard, and from whom you heard it. [. . .] [C. Brontë]

61. TO E. N. [G.]

            May 3rd, 1848. 245
[Dear Ellen, —] All I can say to you about a certain matter is this: the report — if report there be — and if the lady, who seems to have been rather mystified, had not dreamt what she fancied had been told to her — must have had its origin in some absurd misunderstanding. I have given *no one* a right either to affirm, or to hint, in the most distant manner, that I was "publishing" — (humbug!) Whoever has said it — if any one has, which I doubt — is no friend of mine. Though twenty books were ascribed to me, I should own none. I scout the idea utterly. Whoever, after I have distinctly rejected the charge, urges it upon me, will do an unkind and an ill-bred thing. The most profound obscurity is infinitely preferable to vulgar notoriety; and that notoriety I neither seek nor will have. If then any B——an, or G——an,[6] should presume to bore you on the subject, — to ask you what "novel" Miss Brontë has been "publishing," you can just say, with the

[6] Inhabitants of Birstall and Gomersal, villages near Ellen's home.

distinct firmness of which you are perfect
246 mistress / when you choose, that you are
authorised by Miss Brontë to say, that she
repels and disowns every accusation of the
kind. . . . Laugh or scold A—— out of the
publishing notion; and believe me, through
all chances and changes, whether calumni-
ated, or let alone, — Yours faithfully,
C. Brontë.

62. TO E. N. [S. H.]

II,226   Haworth, June 26th, '48
227 Dear Ellen, —/. . . I was glad to hear that
you were well received at London and that
you got safe to the end of your journey —
Your naïveté in gravely inquiring my opinion of the "last new novel" amuses me: we
do not subscribe to a circulating library at
Haworth and consequently "new novels"
rarely indeed come in our way, and consequently again we are not qualified to give
opinions thereon. . . .
Yours faithfully, C. Brontë[7]

63. TO W. S. WILLIAMS [S. H.]

II,241   Haworth, July 31st, 1848
My dear Sir, — . . . Permit me to caution
you not to speak of my sisters when you
write to me. I mean, do not use the word
in the plural. Ellis Bell will not endure to
be alluded to under any other appellation

[7] Among Ellen's papers was a note which ran:
The naïveté respecting the last new novel was
on Charlotte's side in supposing that I, though
silent, was uninformed. *Specially* informed I was
not; but I had seen proof-sheets corrected (at
Brookroyd) and passed them to the house letter-
bag without glancing at the address. Perceiving
that confidence was not volunteered, it was not
sought. Charlotte confessed afterwards what a
struggle it cost her to retain silence; but the sisters
had pledged themselves to keep their attempts at
Authorship unknown to any but themselves.
When I reached London I found there was
quite a fureur about the authorship of the new
novel. The work was quickly obtained, and as
soon as it arrived it was seized upon and the first
half page read aloud. It was as though Charlotte
Brontë herself was present in every word, her
voice and spirit thrilling through and through,
till a rapid escape was imperative for the outlet of
feeling; hence the enquiry on the last new novel,
which Charlotte Brontë in vain tries to suppress
knowledge of. She succeeded for a time — till
"Martin Yorke" [in *Shirley*; the youngest Taylor
boy.] found out the secret and soon made it an
open one. (S. H. II, 228)

than the *nom de plume*. I committed a
grand error in betraying his identity to you
and Mr Smith. It was inadvertent — the
words "we are three sisters" escaped me
before I was aware. I regretted the avowal
the moment I had made it; I regret it bitterly now, for I find it is against every feeling and intention of Ellis Bell.
I was greatly amused to see in the "Examiner" of this week one of Newby's little
cobwebs neatly swept away by some dex-
terous brush. If Newby is not too old to
profit by experience, such an exposure
ought to teach him that "Honesty is indeed
the best policy."
Your letter has just been brought to me.
I must not pause to thank you, I should
say too much. Our life is, and always has
been, one of few pleasures, as you seem in
part to guess, and for that reason we feel
what passages of enjoyment come in our
way very keenly; and I think if you knew
how pleased I am to get a long letter from
you, you would laugh at me.
In return, however, I smile at you for
the earnestness with which you urge on us
the propriety of seeing something of London society. There would be an advantage
in it — a great advan-/tage; yet it is one that 242
no power on earth could induce Ellis Bell,
for instance, to avail himself of. And even
for Acton and Currer, the experiment of an
introduction to society would be more formidable than you, probably, can well imagine. An existence of absolute seclusion and
unvarying monotony, such as we have long
— I may say, indeed, ever — been habituated to, tends, I fear, to unfit the mind for
lively and exciting scenes, to destroy the
capacity for social enjoyment. . . .
I thank both you and your family for 243
keeping our secret. It will indeed be a kindness to us to persevere in doing so; and I
own I have a certain confidence in the
honourable discretion of a household of
which you are the head. — Believe me,
yours very sincerely,   C. Brontë.

64. TO W. S. WILLIAMS [S. H.]

August 14th, 1848 II,24
My dear Sir, — . . . The first duty of an

author is, I conceive, a faithful allegiance to Truth and Nature; his second, such a conscientious study of Art as shall enable him to interpret eloquently and effectively the oracles delivered by those two great deities. The Bells are very sincere in their worship of Truth, and they hope to apply themselves to the consideration of Art, so as to attain one day the power of speaking the language of conviction in the accents of persuasion; though they rather apprehend that whatever pains they take to modify and soften, an abrupt word or vehement tone will now and then occur to startle ears 244 polite, whenever the / subject shall chance to be such as moves their spirits within them.

I have already told you, I believe, that I regard Mr Thackeray as the first of modern masters, and as the legitimate high priest of Truth; I study him accordingly with reverence. He, I see, keeps the mermaid's tail below water, and only hints at the dead men's bones and noxious slime amidst which it wriggles; *but,* his hint is more vivid than other men's elaborate explanations, and never is his satire whetted to so keen an edge as when with quiet mocking irony he modestly recommends to the approbation of the public his own exemplary discretion and forbearance. The world begins to know Thackeray rather better than it did two years or even a year ago, but as yet it only half knows him. His mind seems to me a fabric as simple and unpretending as it is deep-founded and enduring — there is no meretricious ornament to attract or fix a superficial glance; his great distinction of the genuine is one that can only be fully appreciated with time. There is something, a sort of "still profound," revealed in the concluding part of *Vanity Fair* which the discernment of one generation will not suffice to fathom. . . .

You say Mr Huntingdon[8] reminds you of Mr Rochester. Does he? Yet there is no likeness between the two; the foundation of each character is entirely different.

Huntingdon is a specimen of the naturally selfish, sensual, superficial man, whose one merit of a joyous temperament only avails him while he is young and healthy, whose best days are his earliest, who never profits by experience, who is sure to grow worse the older he grows. Mr Rochester has a thoughtful nature and a very feeling heart; he is neither selfish nor self-indulgent; he is ill-educated, misguided; errs, when he does err, through rashness and inexperience: he / lives for a time as too many 245 other men live, but being radically better than most men, he does not like that degraded life, and is never happy in it. He is taught the severe lessons of experience and has sense to learn wisdom from them. Years improve him; the effervescence of youth foamed away, what is really good in him still remains. His nature is like wine of a good vintage, time cannot sour, but only mellows him. Such at least was the character I meant to portray.

Heathcliff, again, of "Wuthering Heights" is quite another creation. He exemplifies the effects which a life of continued injustice and hard usage may produce on a naturally perverse, vindictive, and inexorable disposition. Carefully trained and kindly treated, the black gipsy-cub might possibly have been reared into a human being, but tyranny and ignorance made of him a mere demon. The worst of it is, some of his spirit seems breathed through the whole narrative in which he figures: it haunts every moor and glen, and beckons in every fir-tree of the Heights. . . .

I hope Mrs Williams's health is more satisfactory than when you last wrote. With every good wish to yourself and your family, — Believe me, my dear sir, yours sincerely,

C. Brontë.

65. TO MARGARET WOOLER [S. H.]

Haworth, August 28th, 1848 II,247
My dear Miss Wooler, —/ . . . You said Mrs 248 Carter had some thoughts of sending Ellen to school, and wished to know whether the Clergy Daughters' School at Casterton was an eligible place.

---

[8] The hero of *Wildfell Hall.*

My personal knowledge of that institution is very much out of date, being derived from the experience of twenty years ago; the establishment was at that time in its infancy, and a sad, ricketty infancy it was. Typhus fever decimated the school periodically, and consumption and scrofula in every variety of form, [which] bad air and water, and bad, insufficient diet can generate, preyed on the ill-fated pupils. It would not *then* have been a fit place for any of Mrs Carter's children. But, I understand, it is very much altered for the better since those days. The school is removed from Cowan Bridge (a situation as unhealthy as it was picturesque — low, damp, beautiful with wood and water) to Casterton; the accommodation, the diet, the discipline, the system of tuition, all are, I believe, entirely altered and greatly improved. I was told that such pupils as behaved well and remained at the School till their educations were finished, were provided with situations as governesses, if they wished to adopt that vocation, and that much care was exercised in the selection; it was added they were also furnished with an excellent wardrobe on quitting Casterton. . . .

I heard from Mary Taylor in June; she wrote in excellent spirits: her proceedings seem prosperous, and she says she is leading an active, happy and joyous life. She had lately bought a cow, and had some thoughts of purchasing a section of land. She expressed pity for my comparatively dull, uneventful, and unoccupied existence. . . .

yours affectionately and respectfully,
C. Brontë

66. TO MARY TAYLOR [S. H.]

II,250   Haworth, September 4th, 1848.
Dear Polly, — I write you a great many more letters than you write me, though whether they all reach you, or not, Heaven knows! I dare say you will not be without a certain desire to know how our affairs get on; I will give you therefore a notion as briefly as may be. Acton Bell has published another book; it is in three volumes, but I do not like it quite so well as "Agnes Grey"

— the subject not being such as the author had pleasure in handling; it has been praised by some reviews and blamed by others. As yet, only £25 have been realised for the copyright, / and as Acton Bell's 251 publisher is a shuffling scamp, I expect no more.

About two months since I had a letter from my publishers — Smith and Elder — saying that "Jane Eyre" had had a great run in America, and that a publisher there had consequently bid high for the first sheets of a new work by Currer Bell, which they had promised to let him have.

Presently after came another missive from Smith and Elder; their American correspondent had written to them complaining that the first sheets of a new work by Currer Bell had been already received, and not by their house, but by a rival publisher, and asking the meaning of such false play; it enclosed an extract from a letter from Mr Newby (A. and E. Bell's publisher) affirming that to the best of his belief "Jane Eyre," "Wuthering Heights," and "Agnes Grey," and "The Tenant of Wildfell Hall" (the new work) were all the production of one author.

This was a *lie,* as Newby had been told repeatedly that they were the production of three different authors, but the fact was he wanted to make a dishonest move in the game to make the public and the trade believe that he had got hold of Currer Bell, and thus cheat Smith and Elder by securing the American publisher's bid.

The upshot of it was that on the very day I received Smith and Elder's letter, Anne and I packed up a small box, sent it down to Keighley, set out ourselves after tea, walked through a snowstorm to the station, got to Leeds, and whirled up by the night train to London with the view of proving our separate identity to Smith and Elder, and confronting Newby with his *lie.*[9]

We arrived at the Chapter Coffee-House (our old place, Polly, we did not well know

[9] This account should be compared with George Smith's, Section V.

where else to go) about eight o'clock in the morning. We washed ourselves, had some breakfast, sat a few minutes, and then set off in queer inward excitement to 65 Cornhill. Neither Mr Smith nor Mr Williams knew we were coming — they had never seen us — they did not know whether we were men or women, but had always written to us as men.

We found 65 to be a large bookseller's shop, in a street almost as bustling as the Strand. We went in, walked up to the counter. There were a great many young men and lads here and there; I said to the first I could accost: "May I see Mr Smith?" He hesitated, looked a little surprised. We sat down and waited a while, looking at some books on the counter, publications of theirs well known to us, of many of which they had sent us copies as presents. At last we were shown up to Mr Smith. "Is it Mr Smith?" I said, looking up through my spectacles at a tall young man. "It is." I then put his own letter into his hand directed to Currer Bell. He looked at it and then at me again. "Where did you get this?" he said. I laughed at his perplexity — a recognition took place. I gave my real name: Miss Brontë. We were in a small room — ceiled with a great skylight — and there explanations were rapidly gone into; Mr Newby being anathematised, I fear, with undue vehemence. Mr Smith hurried out and returned quickly with one whom he introduced as Mr Williams, a pale, mild, stooping man of fifty, very much like a faded Tom Dixon. Another recognition and a long, nervous shaking of hands. Then followed talk — talk — talk; Mr Williams being silent, Mr Smith loquacious.

Mr Smith said we must come and stay at his house, but we were not prepared for a long stay and declined this also; as we took our leave he told us he should bring his sisters to call on us that evening. We returned to our inn, and I paid for the excitement of the interview by a thundering headache and harassing sickness. Towards evening, as I got no better and expected the Smiths to call, I took a strong dose of sal-volatile. It roused me a little; still, I was in grievous bodily case when they were announced. They came in, two elegant young ladies, in full dress, prepared for the Opera — Mr Smith himself in evening costume, white gloves, etc. We had by no means understood that it was settled we were to go to the Opera, and were not ready. Moreover, we had no fine, elegant dresses with us, or in the world. However, on brief rumination I thought it would be wise to make no objections — I put my headache in my pocket, we attired ourselves in the plain, high-made country garments we possessed, and went with them to their carriage, where we found Mr Williams. They must have thought us queer, quizzical-looking beings, especially me with my spectacles. I smiled inwardly at the contrast, which must have been apparent, between me and Mr Smith as I walked with him up the crimson-carpeted staircase of the Opera House and stood amongst a brilliant throng at the box door, which was not yet open. Fine ladies and gentlemen / glanced at us 253 with a slight, graceful superciliousness quite warranted by the circumstances. Still, I felt pleasantly excited in spite of headache and sickness and conscious clownishness, and I saw Anne was calm and gentle, which she always is.

The performance was Rossini's opera of the "Barber of Seville," very brilliant, though I fancy there are things I should like better. We got home after one o'clock; we had never been in bed the night before, and had been in constant excitement for twenty-four hours. You may imagine we were tired.

The next day, Sunday, Mr Williams came early and took us to church. He was so quiet, but so sincere in his attentions, one could not but have a most friendly leaning towards him. He has a nervous hesitation in speech, and a difficulty in finding appropriate language in which to express himself, which throws him into the background in conversation; but I had been his correspondent and therefore knew with what intelligence he could write, so that I was not in danger of undervaluing him. In the afternoon Mr Smith came in his carriage with his mother, to take us to his house to dine. Mr Smith's residence is at Bayswater, six miles from Cornhill; the rooms, the drawing-room especially, looked splendid to us. There was no company — only his mother, his two grown-up sisters, and his brother, a lad of twelve or thirteen, and a little sister, the youngest of the family, very like himself. They are all dark-eyed, dark-haired, and have clear, pale faces. The mother is a portly, handsome woman of her age, and all the children more or less well-looking — one of the daughters decidedly pretty. We had a fine dinner, which neither Anne nor I had appetite to eat, and were glad when it was over. I always feel under an awkward constraint at table. Dining out would be hideous to me. . . .

II,254   On Monday we went to the Exhibition of the Royal Academy and the National Gallery, dined again at Mr Smith's, then went home with Mr Williams to tea and saw his comparatively humble but neat residence and his fine family of eight children. A daughter of Leigh Hunt's was there. She sang some little Italian airs which she had picked up among the peasantry in Tuscany, in a manner that charmed me.

On Tuesday morning we left London laden with books which Mr Smith had given us, and got safely home. A more jaded wretch than I looked when I returned it would be difficult to conceive. I was thin when I went, but was meagre indeed when I returned; my face looked grey and very old, with strange, deep lines ploughed in it; my eyes stared unnaturally. I was weak and yet restless. In a while, however, the bad effects of excitement went off and I regained my normal condition. We saw Mr Newby, but of him more another time. Good-bye. God bless you. Write.   C. B.

67. TO W. S. WILLIAMS [S. H.]

[September, 1848]

My dear Sir, — . . . Defects there are both II,255 in "Jane Eyre" and "Wildfell Hall" which it will be the authors' wisdom and duty to endeavour to avoid in future. Other points there are to which they deem it incumbent on them firmly to adhere, whether such adherence bring popularity or unpopularity, praise or blame. The standard heroes and heroines of novels are personages in whom I could never from childhood upwards take an interest, believe to be natural, or wish to imitate. Were I obliged to copy these characters I would simply not write at all. Were I obliged to copy any former novelist, even the greatest, even Scott, in anything, I would not write. Unless I have something of my own to say, and a way of my own to say it in, I have no business to publish. Unless I can look beyond the greatest Masters, and study Nature herself, I have no right to paint. Unless I can have the courage to use the language of Truth in preference to the jargon of Conventionality, I ought to be silent. . . .

Believe me, Yours sincerely, C. Bell

The Deaths of Branwell, Emily, and Anne, 1848 to 1849

"A year ago — had a prophet warned me how I should stand in June 1849 — how stripped and bereaved . . . I should have thought — this never can be endured. It is over — Branwell — Emily — Anne are gone like dreams — gone as Maria and Elizabeth went twenty years ago" (Charlotte to W. S. Williams, June 13, 1849, S. H. II, 340).

The summer of 1848 was the height of the Brontë fortunes. Charlotte could look with pride on her achievement — for it was hers — poverty, isolation, and suffering surmounted, a place in the sun for herself and her sisters. The girls could look forward to some financial security, the writing they loved, and at least a modest fame. They could feel that their lives and talents had not been thrown away. All were planning new books; Charlotte had started *Shirley.* Was it absorption in their plans or familiarity with his sufferings that inured them to Branwell's condition? Though he continued to write self-pitying letters, though he went to the village and even to Halifax to drink and meet friends, their brother was dying. His faithful friend Grundy gives[10] a fearful description of Branwell when he last visited him in 1846: "Presently the door opened cautiously, and a head appeared. It was a mass of red, unkempt, uncut hair, wildly floating round a great, gaunt forehead; the cheeks yellow and hollow, the mouth fallen, the thin white lips not trembling but shaking, the sunken eyes, once small, now glaring with the light of madness, — all told the sad tale but too surely. I hastened to my friend, greeted him in my gayest manner, as I knew he best liked, drew him quickly into the room, and forced upon him a stiff glass of hot brandy. Under its influence, and that of the bright, cheerful surroundings, he looked frightened — frightened of himself. He glanced at me a moment, and muttered something of leaving a warm bed to come out into the cold night. Another glass of brandy, and returning warmth gradually brought him back to something like the Brontë of old. He even ate some dinner, a thing which he said he had not done for long; so our last interview was pleasant, though grave. I never knew his intellect clearer. He described himself as waiting anxiously for death — indeed, longing for it, and happy, in these his sane moments, to think that it was so near. He once again declared that that death would be due to the story I knew, and to nothing else."

Branwell died in September.

Emily caught cold at the funeral service and never left the house again. Her insistence on carrying out all her household tasks and her absolute refusal to go to bed or to accept any medical care greatly increased the suffering of her family. Her motives remain a mystery. She died on the horsehair sofa in the dining room just before Christmas. Anne fell ill within three weeks and a doctor from Leeds pronounced her already far gone in consumption. She willingly tried various remedies and for her the course of the disease was less rapid and painful. She was hopeful of recovery if she could revisit her beloved Scarborough, the seaside resort where she had worked as a governess, but died there and was buried there, the only member of the family not buried at Haworth.

68. TO W. S. WILLIAMS [S. H.]

October 2nd, 1848.

II,261

My Dear Sir, — "We have buried our dead out of our sight." A lull begins to succeed the gloomy tumult of last week. It is not permitted us to grieve for him who is gone as others grieve for those they lose. The removal of our only brother must necessarily be regarded by us rather in the light of a mercy than a chastisement. Branwell was his father's and his sisters' pride and hope in boyhood, but since manhood the case has been otherwise. It has been our lot to see him take a wrong bent; to hope, expect, wait his return to the right path; to know

10 Francis H. Grundy, *Pictures of the Past,* London: Griffith and Farrar, 1879, pp. 41–2; Grundy incorrectly dates the incident 1848.

the sickness of hope deferred, the dismay of prayer baffled; to experience despair at last — and now to behold the sudden early obscure close of what might have been a noble career.

I do not weep from a sense of bereavement — there is no prop withdrawn, no consolation torn away, no dear companion lost — but for the wreck of talent, the ruin of promise, the untimely dreary extinction of what might have been a burning and a shining light. My brother was a year my junior. I had aspirations and ambitions for him once, long ago — they have perished mournfully. Nothing remains of him but a memory of errors and sufferings. There is such a bitterness of pity for his life and death, such a yearning for the emptiness of his whole existence as I cannot describe. I trust time will allay these feelings.

My poor father naturally thought more of his *only* son than of his daughters, and, much and long as he had suffered on his account, he cried out for his loss like David for that of Absalom — my son! my son! — and refused at first to be comforted. And then when I ought to have been able to collect my strength and be at hand to support him, I fell ill with an illness whose approaches I had felt for some time previ-
262 ously, and of which the crisis was / hastened by the awe and trouble of the death-scene — the first I had ever witnessed. The past has seemed to me a strange week. Thank God, for my father's sake, I am better now, though still feeble. I wish indeed I had more general physical strength — the want of it is sadly in my way. I cannot do what I would do for want of sustained animal spirits and efficient bodily vigour.

My unhappy brother never knew what his sisters had done in literature — he was not aware that they had ever published a line.[1] We could not tell him of our efforts for fear of causing him too deep a pang of remorse for his own time misspent, and talents misapplied. Now he will *never* know. I cannot dwell longer on the subject at present — it is too painful.

I thank you for your kind sympathy, and pray earnestly that your sons may all do well, and that you may be spared the sufferings my father has gone through. — Yours sincerely,   C. Brontë.

69. TO E. N. [G.]

[October 9th, '48]
253 [My dear Ellen, —] [. . .] The past three weeks have been a dark interval in our /
254 humble home. Branwell's constitution had been failing fast all the summer; but still,

neither the doctors nor himself thought him so near his end as he was. He was entirely confined to his bed but for one single day, and was in the village two days before his death. He died, after twenty minutes' struggle, on Sunday morning, September 24th. He was perfectly conscious till the last agony came on. His mind had undergone the peculiar change which frequently precedes death, two days previously; the calm of better feelings filled it; a return of natural affection marked his last moments. He is in God's hands now; and the All-Powerful is likewise the All-Merciful. A deep conviction that he rests at last — rests well, after his brief, erring, suffering, feverish life — fills and quiets my mind now.

The final separation, the spectacle of his pale corpse, gave me more acute bitter pain than I could have imagined. Till the last hour comes, we never know how much we can forgive, pity, regret a near relative. All his vices were and are nothing now. We remember only his woes. Papa was acutely distressed at first, but, on the whole, has borne the event well. Emily and Anne are pretty well, though Anne is always delicate, and Emily has a cold and cough at present. It was my fate to sink at the crisis, when I should have collected my strength. Headache and sickness came on first on the Sunday; I could not regain my appetite. Then internal pain attacked me. I became at once much reduced. It was impossible to touch a morsel. At last, bilious fever declared itself. I was confined to bed a week, — a dreary week. But, thank God! health seems now returning. I can sit up all day, and take moderate nourishment. The doctor said at first, I should be very slow in recovering, but I seem to get on faster than he anticipated. I am truly *much better*. [. . .]
[Yours faithfully, C. Brontë]

[1] This seems extremely unlikely, with all the girls writing steadily, with Branwell's knowledge of their writing habits, with packages of manuscripts and author's copies coming and going. Perhaps Charlotte meant that she hoped (for his sake) that he did not know of her success, or that she and her sisters no longer discussed their work with him. George Searle Philips, who reviewed *Jane Eyre* unfavorably in the *Mirror*, claimed later that Branwell discussed the novel with him in Haworth. If this story is true, Philips must have exerted great self-control in not revealing such a scoop.

70. TO W. S. WILLIAMS [S. H.]

II,286   November 22nd, 1848.

My dear Sir, — I put your most friendly letter into Emily's hands as soon as I had myself perused it, taking care, however, not to say a word in favour of homœopathy — that would not have answered. It is best usually to leave her to form her own judgment, and *especially* not to advocate the side you wish her to favour; if you do, she is sure to lean in the opposite direction, and ten to one will argue herself into non-compliance. Hitherto she has refused medicine, rejected medical advice; no reason-287 ing, / no entreaty, has availed to induce her to see a physician. After reading your letter she said, "Mr Williams's intention was kind and good, but he was under a delusion: Homœopathy was only another form of quackery." Yet she may reconsider this opinion and come to a different conclusion; her second thoughts are often the best.

The "North American Review" [see Section IV] is worth reading; there is no mincing the matter there. What a bad set the Bells must be! What appalling books they write! To-day, as Emily appeared a little easier, I thought the "Review" would amuse her, so I read it aloud to her and Anne. As I sat between them at our quiet but now somewhat melancholy fireside, I studied the two ferocious authors. Ellis, the "man of uncommon talents, but dogged, brutal, and morose," sat leaning back in his easy-chair drawing his impeded breath as he best could, and looking, alas! piteously pale and wasted; it is not his wont to laugh, but he smiled half-amused and half in scorn as he listened. Acton was sewing, no emotion ever stirs him to loquacity, so he only smiled too, dropping at the same time a single word of calm amazement to hear his character so darkly portrayed. I wonder what the reviewer would have thought of his own sagacity could he have beheld the pair as I did. Vainly, too, might he have looked round for the masculine partner in the firm of "Bell & Co." How I laugh in my sleeve when I read the solemn assertions that "Jane Eyre" was written in part-nership, and that it "bears the marks of more than one mind and one sex."

. . . However, the view they take of the matter rather pleases me than otherwise. If they like, I am not unwilling they should think a dozen ladies and gentlemen aided at the compilation of the book. Strange patchwork it must seem to them — this chapter being penned by Mr, and that by Miss or Mrs Bell; that character or scene being delineated by the husband, that other by the wife! The gentleman, of course, doing the rough work, the lady getting up the finer parts. I admire the idea vastly. . . .

Yours sincerely, Currer Bell

71. TO E. N. [S. H.]

November 23rd, '48. II,288

Dear Ellen, — Whatever my inclination may be to let all correspondence alone for the present, I feel that to *you* at least I ought to write a line. I told you Emily was ill, in my last letter. She has not rallied yet. She is *very* ill. I believe, if you were to see her, your impression would be that there is no hope. A more hollow, wasted, pallid aspect I have not beheld. The deep, tight cough continues; the breathing after the least exertion is a rapid pant; and these symptoms are accompanied by pains in the chest and side. Her pulse, the only time she allowed it to be felt, was found to beat 115 per minute. In this state she resolutely refuses to see a doctor; she will not give an explanation of her feelings, she will scarcely allow her illness to be alluded to. Our position is, and has been for some weeks, exquisitely painful. God only knows how all this is to terminate. More than once, I have been forced boldly to regard the terrible event of her loss as possible and even probable. But nature shrinks from such thoughts, I think Emily seems the nearest thing to my heart in this world. . . . Mrs Robinson is now Lady Scott.[2] Her daughters say she is in the highest spirits. Write to me soon, dear Ellen, and believe me, yours faithfully,   C. Brontë.

[2] The lady whom Branwell had been in love with.

72. TO W. S. WILLIAMS [S. H.]

II,289   December 7th, 1848
290 My Dear Sir, — / . . . I am indeed surprised
that Mr Newby should say that he is to
publish another work by Ellis and Acton
Bell. Acton has had quite enough of him.
I think I *have* before intimated that that
author never more intends to have Mr
Newby for a publisher. Not only does he
seem to forget that engagements made
should be fulfilled, but by a system of petty
and contemptible manoeuvring he throws
an air of charlatanry over the works of
which he has the management. This does
not suit the "Bells"; they have their own
rude north-country ideas of what is delicate, honourable, and gentlemanlike. . . .
291   / yours sincerely, C. Brontë

73. TO E. N. [S. H.]

II,293   Tuesday, [December 19th, 1848]
Dear Ellen, — I should have written to you
before, if I had had one word of hope to
say; but I had not. She grows daily weaker.
The physician's opinion was expressed too
obscurely to be of use. He sent some medicine which she would not take. Moments
so dark as these I have never known. I pray
for God's support to us all. Hitherto He has
granted it,   Yours faithfully, C. Brontë.

74. TO E. N. [G.]

258   Dec. 21st [poss. 23rd], 1848.
[My dear Ellen, —] Emily suffers no more
from pain or weakness now. She never will
suffer more in this world. She is gone, after
a hard, short conflict. She died on *Tuesday,*
the very day I wrote to you. I thought it
very possible she might be with us still for
weeks; and a few hours afterwards, she
was in eternity. Yes; there is no Emily in
time or on earth now. Yesterday we put
her poor, wasted, mortal frame quietly under the church pavement. We are very
calm at present. Why should we be otherwise? The anguish of seeing her suffer is
over; the spectacle of the pains of death is
gone by; the funeral day is past. We feel

she is at peace. No need now to tremble
for the hard frost and the keen wind. Emily
does not feel them. She died in a time of
promise. We saw her taken from life in its
prime. But it is God's will, and the place
where she is gone is better than that she
has left.

God has sustained me, in a way that I
marvel at, through such agony as I had not
conceived. I now look at Anne, and / wish 259
she were well and strong; but she is neither;
nor is papa. Could you now come to us for
a few days? I would not ask you to stay
long. . . . You will, I trust, find us tranquil.
Try to come. I never so much needed the
consolation of a friend's presence. . . .

[No signature.]

75. TO E. N. [G.][3]

Jany. 10th, '49 261
[Dear Ellen, —] [. . .] Anne had a very tolerable day yesterday, and a pretty quiet night
last night, though she did not sleep much.
Mr. Wheelhouse ordered the blister to be
put on again. She bore it without sickness.
I have just dressed it, and she is risen and
come down-stairs. She looks somewhat pale
and sickly. She has had one dose of the
cod-liver oil; it smells and tastes like train
oil. I am trying to hope, but the day is
windy, cloudy, and stormy. My spirits fall
at intervals very low; then I look where
you counsel me to look, beyond earthly
tempests and sorrows. I seem to get strength,
if not consolation. It will not do to anticipate. I feel that hourly. In the night, I
awake and long for morning; then my heart
is wrung. Papa continues much the same;
he was very faint when he came down to
breakfast. * * * Dear [Ellen], your friendship is some comfort to me. I am thankful
for it. I see few lights through the darkness
of the present time; but amongst them the
constancy of a kind heart attached to me
is one of the most cheering and serene. [. . .]
Yours faithfully, C. Brontë.

[3] Readers of Section IV will notice that Elizabeth
Rigby's unkind review came out in this month.
See letters of Feb. 4 and March 2, 1849.

76. TO W. S. WILLIAMS [S. H.]

II,306   Feby 4th, '49.

My Dear Sir, — I send the parcel up without delay according to your request. The manuscript has all its errors upon it, not having been read through since copying. I have kept "Madeleine" along with the two other books I mentioned; I shall consider it the gift of Miss Kavanagh[4] and shall value it both for its literary excellence and for the modest merit of the giver. We already possess Tennyson's Poems and "Our Street", Emerson's essays I read with much interest and often with admiration, but they are of mixed gold and clay — deep and invigorat-
307 ing truth — dreary / and depressing fallacy seem to me combined therein. In George Borrow's works I found a wild fascination, a vivid graphic power of description, a fresh originality, an athletic simplicity (so to speak) which give them a stamp of their own. After reading his "Bible in Spain" I felt as if I had actually travelled at his side, had seen the "wild sil" rush from its mountain cradle, wandered in the hilly wilderness of the Sierras — encountered and conversed with Manchegan, Castillian, Andalusian, Arragonese, and above all with the savage gitanos.[5]

Your mention of Mr Taylor[6] suggests to me that possibly you and Mr Smith might wish him to share the little secret of the MS. — that exclusion might seem invidious — that it might make your mutual evening chat less pleasant. If so — admit him to the confidence by all means — he is attached to the firm and will no doubt keep its secrets. I shall be glad of another censor — and if a severe one, so much the better, provided he is also just. I court the keenest criticism: far rather would I never publish more than publish anything inferior to my first effort. Be honest therefore all three of you — If you think this book promises less favour-

ably than "Jane Eyre" say so: it is but trying again — i.e. if life and health be spared.

Anne continues a little better: the mild weather suits her. At times — I hear the renewal of Hope's whisper — but I dare not listen too fondly — she deceived me cruelly before. A sudden change to cold would be the test — I dread such change but must not anticipate. Spring lies before us — and then summer — surely we may hope a little.

Anne expresses a wish to see the notices of the poems — you had better therefore send them. We shall expect to find painful allusions to one now above blame and beyond praise — but these must be borne. For ourselves — we are almost indifferent to censure. I read the "Quarterly" without a pang — except that I thought there were some sentences disgraceful to the critic. He seems anxious to let it be understood that he is a person well acquainted with the habits of the upper classes — be this as it may — I am afraid he[7] is no gentleman — and moreover that no training could make him such. Many a poor man — born and bred to labour — would disdain that reviewer's cast of feeling. — Yours sincerely,

C. Brontë.

77. TO W. S. WILLIAMS [S. H.]

March 2nd, 1849. II,313

My dear Sir, — My sister still continues better: she has less languor and weakness; her spirits are improved. This change gives cause, I think, both for gratitude and hope.

I am glad that you and Mr Smith like the commencement of my present work. I wish it were *more than a commencement*; for how it will be reunited after the long break, or how it can gather force of flow when the current has been checked or rather drawn off so long, I know not.

I sincerely thank you both for the candid expression of your objections. What you say with reference to the first chapter shall be duly weighed. At present I feel reluctant to withdraw it, because, as I formerly said of the Lowood part of "Jane Eyre," *it is*

---

4 Julia Kavanagh (1824–1877), novelist and biographer, author of *Women in France during the Eighteenth Century, Women of Christianity, Daisy Burns,* etc.

5 Gypsies.

6 James Taylor, another reader of the firm.

7 See IV; Charlotte soon found out that "he" was a Miss Rigby, later Lady Eastlake.

true. The curates and their ongoings are merely photographed from the life. I should like you to explain to me more fully the ground of your objections. Is it because you think this chapter will render the work liable to severe handling by the press? Is it because knowing as you now do the identity of "Currer Bell," this scene strikes you as unfeminine? It is because it is intrinsically defective and inferior? I am afraid the two first reasons would not weigh with me — the last would. . . .

314   Your generous indignation against the "Quarterly" touched me. But do not trouble yourself to be angry on Currer Bell's account; except where the May-Fair gossip and Mr Thackeray's name were brought in he was never stung at all, but he certainly thought that passage and one or two others quite unwarrantable. However, slander without a germ of truth is seldom injurious: it resembles a rootless plant and must soon wither away.

The critic would certainly be a little ashamed of herself if she knew what foolish blunders she had committed, if she were aware how completely Mr Thackeray and Currer Bell are strangers to each other, that "Jane Eyre" was written before the author had seen one line of "Vanity Fair." . . . — Believe me, my dear sir, yours sincerely,   C. Brontë.

78. TO E. N. [S. H.]

II,314   March 8th, 1849.
Dear Ellen, — Anne's state has apparently varied very little during the last fortnight or three weeks. I wish I could say she gains either flesh, strength, or appetite, but there is no progress on these points, nor I hope, as far as regards the two last at least, any falling off; she is piteously thin. Her cough, and the pain in her side continue the same.

I write these few lines that you may not think my continued silence strange; anything like frequent correspondence I cannot keep up and you must excuse me. I trust you and Miss Ringrose and all at Brookroyd are happy and well. Give my love to your mother and all the rest, and believe me, yours sincerely,   C. Brontë.

79. TO MARGARET WOOLER [G.]

[Haworth, March 24th, '49]
[My dear Miss Wooler, —] [. . .] Anne's 263 decline is gradual and fluctuating; but its nature is not doubtful. * * * In spirit she is resigned: at heart she is, I believe, a true Christian. * * * May God support her and all of us through the trial of lingering sickness, and aid her in the last hour, when the struggle which separates soul from body / must be gone through! We saw Emily torn 264 from the midst of us when our hearts clung to her with intense attachment. * * * She was scarce buried when Anne's health failed. * * * These things would be too much, if reason, unsupported by religion, were condemned to bear them alone. I have cause to be most thankful for the strength that has hitherto been vouchsafed both to my father and to myself. . . . Yet I must confess that, in the time which has elapsed since Emily's death, there have been moments of solitary, deep, inert affliction, far harder to bear than those which immediately followed our loss. The crisis of bereavement has an acute pang which goads to exertion; the desolate after-feeling sometimes paralyses. I have learnt that we are not to find solace in our own strength; we must seek it in God's omnipotence. Fortitude is good; but fortitude itself must be shaken under us to teach us how weak we are! [. . .]   [yours faithfully, C. Brontë.]

80. TO W. S. WILLIAMS [S. H.]

April 16, 1849 II,325
My dear Sir, — / . . . Do not ask me to men- 326 tion what books I should like to read. Half the pleasure of receiving a parcel from Cornhill consists in having its contents chosen for us. We like to discover, too, by the leaves cut here and there, that the ground has been travelled before us. I may however say, with reference to works of fiction, / that I should much like to see 327 one of Godwin's works, never having hitherto had that pleasure — "Caleb Wil-

liams" or "Fleetwood," or which you thought best worth reading.

. . . I try to write now and then. The effort was a hard one at first. It renewed the terrible loss of last December strangely. Worse than useless did it seem to attempt to write what there no longer lived an "Ellis Bell" to read; the whole book, with every hope founded on it, faded to vanity and vexation of spirit. . . .

Yours sincerely, C. Brontë

81. TO W. S. WILLIAMS [S. H.][8]

II,337   2, Cliff, Scarbro,' June 4th, 1849

My dear Sir, — . . . You have been informed of my dear sister Anne's death. Let me now add that she died without severe struggle, resigned, trusting in God — thankful for release from a suffering life — deeply

[8] For Anne's last letter and verses, see Section III; for Ellen Nussey's account of her death, see Section V.

assured that a better existence lay before her. She believed, she hoped — and declared her belief and hope with her last breath. Her quiet, Christian death did not rend my heart as Emily's stern, simple, undemonstrative end did. I let Anne go to God, / and felt He had a right to her. I 338 could hardly let Emily go. I wanted to hold her back then, and I want her back now. Anne, from her childhood, seemed preparing for an early death. Emily's spirit seemed strong enough to bear her to fulness of years. They are both gone, and so is poor Branwell, and Papa has now me only — the weakest, puniest, least promising of his six children. Consumption has taken the whole five.

For the present Anne's ashes rest apart from the others. I have buried her here at Scarbro', to save Papa the anguish of the return and a third funeral. . . .

Yours sincerely, C. Brontë

CHARLOTTE ALONE: SOCIETY AND SOLITUDE, 1849 TO 1851

For the next few years, Charlotte's life was one of incongruous and often painful contrasts. In Raymond's phrase (p. 246), she was "world-famous and alone." The loneliness must have filled her mind at first. In nine months she had lost all the contemporaries in her family and was left to care for her father and old Tabby, both elderly and ailing. She suffered much from insomnia and depression and admitted to becoming dependent on the letters and book packages from Cornhill. She tried to write, but it was an imperfect escape. After Anne died she took up *Shirley,* begun before Branwell's death and headed the next chapter "The Valley of the Shadow of Death." The revision of her sisters' works in the fall of 1850 brought back painful memories.

Yet Charlotte was now a popular and successful novelist, with the money, the leisure, and the literary contacts to enter, if she wished, the cosmopolitan world whose imaginary counterpart she and Branwell had created so long ago. She did indeed make some attempts to enjoy her inheritance, visiting London several times, staying with the hospitable Smiths, and, though hampered by her shyness, meeting some of the notable people of the day. A trip to Edinburgh with the Smiths and a visit to Mrs. Gaskell were enjoyable. Sir John Kay-Shuttleworth, a wealthy physician who was ambitious to be known as a patron of literature, invited her to his home and to the Lakes and was eager to take her to London for the season. Charlotte would have steeled herself to go for the sake of her father, whose pride in her success was enormous, but luckily Mr. Brontë's illness gave her an excuse to stay at home.

In many ways the fame and the wider world she had longed for came to her too late. She was too tired, too sad, perhaps too little flexible to enjoy it fully. After every excursion the return to Haworth was painful; the exhaustion, the silence of the parsonage where she was conscious of the ticking of the clock, the desolating loneliness which once more pressed in upon her. Even the power to write sometimes deserted her: the fact that two years passed between the publication of *Shirley* and the commencement of *Villette* is some indication of her state of mind.

82. TO E. N. [S. H.]

[June 23rd, 1849].

II,347 Dear Ellen, — I intended to have written a line to you to-day if I had not received yours.

We did indeed part suddenly — it made my heart ache that we were severed without the time to exchange a word — and yet perhaps it was better.

I got home a little before eight o'clock. All was clean and bright waiting for me — Papa and the servants were well — and all received me with an affection which should have consoled. The dogs seemed in strange ecstasy. I am certain they regarded me as the harbinger of others — the dumb creatures thought that as I was returned — those who had been so long absent were not far behind.

I left Papa soon and went into the dining-room — I shut the door — I tried to be glad that I was come home — I have always been glad before — except once — even then I was cheered, but this time joy was not to be the sensation. I felt that the house was all silent — the rooms were all empty — I remembered where the three were laid — in what narrow dark dwellings — never were they to reappear on earth. So the sense of desolation and bitterness took possession of me — the agony that *was to be undergone* — and *was not* to be avoided came on — I underwent it and passed a dreary evening and night and a mournful morrow — to-day I am better.

I do not know how life will pass — but I certainly do feel confidence in Him who has upheld me hitherto. Solitude may be cheered and made endurable beyond what I can believe. The great trial is when evening closes and night approaches — At that hour we used to assemble in the dining-room — we used to talk — Now I sit by myself — necessarily I am silent — I cannot help thinking of their last days — remembering their sufferings and what they said

and did and how they looked in mortal affliction — perhaps all this will become less poignant in time.

Let me thank you once more, dear Ellen, for your kindness to / me which I do not 348 mean to forget. . . . I am glad to hear a good account of your Mother and a tolerable one of Mercy — I hope she will soon recover her health — Give my love to her and to all. . . .

— Yours sincerely, C. Brontë.

83. TO W. S. WILLIAMS [S. H.]

June 25th, '49. II,348

My dear Sir, — I am now again at home where I returned last Thursday. I call it *home* still — much as London would be called London if an earthquake should shake its streets to ruins. But let me not be ungrateful: Haworth parsonage is still a home for me, and not quite a ruined or desolate home either. Papa is there — and two most affectionate and faithful servants — and two old dogs, in their way as faithful and affectionate — Emily's large house-dog which lay at the side of her dying-bed, and followed her funeral to the vault, lying in the pew couched at our feet while the burial service was being read — and Anne's little spaniel. The ecstasy of these poor animals when I came in was something singular — at former returns from brief absence they always welcomed me, warmly — but not in that strange, heart-touching way — I am certain they thought that, as I was returned, my sisters were not far behind, — but here my sisters will come no more, Keeper may visit Emily's little bed-room as he still does day by day — and Flossy may look wistfully round for Anne — they will never see them again — nor shall I — at least the human part of me.

I must not write so sadly — but how can I help thinking and feeling sadly? In the daytime effort and occupation aid me — but when evening darkens something within my heart revolts against the burden of solitude — the sense of loss and want grows almost too much for me. I am not good or amiable in such moments — I am rebellious — and it is only the thought of my dear Father in the next room, or of the kind servants in the kitchen — or some caress of the poor dogs which restores me to softer sentiments and more rational views. As to the night — could I do without bed — I would never seek it — waking I think — 349 sleeping / I dream of them — and I cannot recall them as they were in health — still they appear to me in sickness and suffering — Still my nights were worse after the first shock of Branwell's death — They were terrible then — and the impressions experienced on waking were at that time such as we do not put into language. Worse seemed at hand than was yet endured — in truth worse awaited us. . . .

Believe me, Yours sincerely, C. Brontë

84. TO E. N. [G.]

275   [Haworth,] July 14th, '49

[Dear Ellen, —] [. . .] My life is what I expected it to be. Sometimes when I wake in the morning, and know that Solitude, Remembrance, and Longing are to be almost my sole companions all day through — that at night I shall go to bed with them, that they will long keep me sleepless — that next morning I shall wake to them again, — sometimes, Nell, I have a heavy heart of it. But crushed I am not, yet; nor robbed of elasticity, nor of hope, nor quite of endeavour. I have some strength to fight the battle of life. I am aware, and can acknowledge, I have many comforts, many mercies. Still I can *get on*. But I do hope and pray, that never may you, or any one I love, be placed as I am. . . .

I write to you freely, because I believe you will hear me with moderation — that you will not take alarm or think me in any way worse off than I am. [. . .]

[Yours sincerely, C. B.]

85. TO W. S. WILLIAMS [G.]

279   Sept. 21st, 1849.

My dear Sir, — I am obliged to you for pre-serving my secret, being at least as anxious as ever (*more* anxious I cannot well be) / to keep quiet. You asked me in one of your 280 letters lately, whether I thought I should escape identification in Yorkshire. I am so little known, that I think I shall. Besides, the book is far less founded on the Real, than perhaps appears. It would be difficult to explain to you how little actual experience I have had of life, how few persons I have known, and how very few have known me.

As an instance how the characters have been managed, take that of Mr. Helstone. If this character had an original, it was in the person of a clergyman who died some years since at the advanced age of eighty. I never saw him except once — at the consecration of a church — when I was a child of ten years old. I was then struck with his appearance, and stern, martial air. At a subsequent period, I heard him talked about in the neighbourhood where he had resided: some mention him with enthusiasm — others with detestation. I listened to various anecdotes, balanced evidence against evidence, and drew an inference. The original of Mr. Hall I have seen; he knows me slightly; but he would as soon think I had closely observed him or taken him for a character — he would as soon, indeed, suspect me of writing a book — a novel — as he would his dog, Prince. . . .

No matter, — whether known or unknown — misjudged, or the contrary, — I am resolved not to write otherwise. I shall bend as my powers tend. . . . I must have my own way in the matter of writing. The loss of what we possess nearest and dearest to us in this world, produces an effect upon the character: we search out what we have yet left that can support, and, when found, we cling to it with a hold of new-strung tenacity. The faculty of imagination lifted me when I was sinking, three months ago; its active exercise has kept my head above water since; its results cheer me now, for I feel they have enabled me to give pleasure to others. I am thankful to God, who gave me the faculty; and it is for me a part of my religion to defend this gift, and to profit by its possession. — Yours sincerely,

Charlotte Brontë.

86. TO W. S. WILLIAMS [S. H.]

III,29   November 1st, 1849

My dear Sir, — . . . During my late visit [to Ellen] I have too often had reason, sometimes in a pleasant, sometimes in a painful form, to fear that I no longer walk invisible. "Jane Eyre," it appears, has been read all over the district — a fact of which I never dreamt — a circumstance of which the possibility never occurred to me. I met sometimes with new deference, with augmented kindness: old schoolfellows and old teachers, too, greeted me with generous warmth. And again, ecclesiastical brows lowered thunder on me. When I confronted one or two large-made priests, I longed for the battle to come on. I wish they would speak out plainly. You must not understand that my school-fellows and teachers were of the Clergy Daughters' School — in fact, I was never there but for one little year as a very little girl. I am certain I have long been forgotten; though for myself, I remember all and everything clearly: early impressions are ineffaceable. . . .   yours sincerely, C. B.

87. TO W. S. WILLIAMS [S. H.]

III,33   November 5th, 1849

My dear Sir, — . . . You ask me if I am related to Nelson. No, I never heard that I was. The rumour must have originated in our name resembling his title. I wonder who that former school-fellow of mine was that told Mr Lewes, or how she had been enabled to identify Currer Bell with C. Brontë. She could not have been a Cowan Bridge girl, none of them can possibly re-
34 member me. They / might remember my eldest sister, Maria; her prematurely-developed and remarkable intellect, as well as the mildness, wisdom, and fortitude of her character, *might* have left an indelible impression on some observant mind amongst her companions. My second sister, Elizabeth, too, may perhaps be remembered, but

I cannot conceive that I left a trace behind me. My career was a very quiet one. I was plodding and industrious, perhaps I was very grave, for I suffered to see my sisters perishing, but I think I was remarkable for nothing. — Believe, my dear sir, yours sincerely,   C. Brontë.

88. TO W. S. WILLIAMS [S. H.]

[November 20th, 1849] III,40

My dear Sir, — You said that if I wished for any copies of "Shirley" to be sent to individuals I was to name the parties. I have thought of one person to whom I should much like a copy to be offered — Harriet Martineau. For her character — as revealed in her works — I have a lively admiration — a deep esteem. Will you enclose with the volumes the accompanying note.

The letter you forwarded this morning was from Mrs Gaskell — authoress of "Mary Barton." She said I was not to answer it, but I cannot help doing so. Her note brought the tears to my eyes: she is a good — she is a great woman — proud am I that I can touch a chord of sympathy in souls so noble. . . . Both these ladies are above me — certainly far my superiors in attainment and experience — I think I could look up to them if I knew them. . . .

Yours sincerely, C. Brontë.

89. TO PATRICK BRONTË[9] [S. H.]

Dec. 4th, 1849 III,54

Dear Papa, — I must write another line to you to tell you how I am getting on. I have seen a great many things since I left home about which I hope to talk to you at future tea-times at home. I have been to the theatre and seen Macready in "Macbeth," I have seen the pictures in the National Gallery. I have seen a beautiful exhibition of Turner's paintings, and yesterday I saw Mr Thackeray. He dined here with some other gentlemen. He is a very tall man — above six feet high, with a peculiar face — not handsome, very ugly indeed, generally

[9] For Charlotte's meeting with Miss Martineau at this time, see V, Mrs. Gaskell to Ann Shaen, and Miss Martineau's autobiography.

somewhat stern and satirical in expression, but capable also of a kind look. He was not told who I was, he was not introduced to me, but I soon saw him looking at me through his spectacles; and when we all rose to go down to dinner he just stepped quietly up and said, "Shake hands"; so I shook hands. He spoke very few words to me, but when he went away he shook hands again in a very kind way. It is better, I should think, to have him for a friend than an enemy, for he is a most formidable-looking personage . . . — I remain, dear papa, your affectionate daughter,   C. Brontë

90. TO W. S. WILLIAMS [S. H.]

III,63   Jany 3rd, 1850.
My dear Sir, — I have to acknowledge the receipt of the "Morning Chronicle" with a good review — and of the "Church of England Quarterly" and the "Westminster" with bad ones: I have also to thank you for your letter which would have been answered sooner had I been alone, but just now I am enjoying the treat of my friend Ellen's society and she makes me indolent and negligent — I am too busy talking to her all day to do anything else. You allude to the subject of female friendship and express wonder at the infrequency of sincere attachments amongst women — As to married women, I can well understand that they should be absorbed in their husbands and children — but single women often like each other much and derive great solace from their mutual regard. Friendship however is a plant which cannot be forced — true friendship is no gourd springing in a night and withering in a day. When I first saw Ellen I did not care for her — we were schoolfellows — in the course of time we learnt each others faults and good points — we were contrasts — still we suited — affection was first a germ, then a sapling — then a strong tree: now — no new friend, however lofty or profound in intellect — not even Miss Martineau herself could be to me what Ellen is, yet she is no more than a conscientious, observant, calm, well-bred Yorkshire girl. She is without romance —

if she attempts to read poetry — or poetic prose aloud — I am irritated and deprive her of her book — if she talks of it I stop my ears — but she is good — she is true — she is faithful and I love her.

Since I came home Miss Martineau has written me a long and truly kind letter — she invites me to visit her at Ambleside — I like the idea, whether I can realize it or not — it is pleasant to have in prospect. . . .

Yours sincerely, C. Brontë 64

91. TO W. S. WILLIAMS [S. H.]

January 10th, 1850. III,66
My dear Sir, — . . . I have received and perused the "Edinburgh Review" — it is very brutal and savage. I am not angry with Lewes, but I wish in future he would let me alone, and not write again what makes me feel so cold and sick as I am feeling just now.

Thackeray's Christmas Book at once grieved and pleased me, as most of his writings do. I have come to the conclusion that / whenever he writes, Mephistopheles 67 stands on his right hand and Raphael on his left; the great doubter and sneerer usually guides the pen, the Angel, noble and gentle, interlines letters of light here and there. Alas! Thackeray, I wish your strong wings would lift you oftener above the smoke of cities into the pure region nearer heaven!

Good-bye for the present. — Yours sincerely,   C. Brontë

92. TO G. H. LEWES [S. H.]

[January, 1850].
I can be on my guard against my ene- III,67 mies, but God deliver me from my friends!
Currer Bell.

93. TO G. H. LEWES [G.]

Jan. 19th, 1850.
My dear Sir, — I will tell you why I was so 293 hurt by that review in the *Edinburgh*; not because its criticism was keen or its blame sometimes severe; not because its praise was stinted (for, indeed, I think you give me quite as much praise as I deserve), but be-

cause after I had said earnestly that I wished critics would judge me as an *author,* not as a woman, you so roughly—I even thought so cruelly—handled the question of sex. I dare say you meant no harm, and perhaps you will not now be able to understand why I was so grieved at what you will probably deem such a trifle; but grieved I was, and indignant too.

There was a passage or two which you did quite wrong to write.

However, I will not bear malice against you for it; I know what your nature is: it is not a bad or unkind one, though you would often jar terribly on some feelings with whose recoil and quiver you could not possibly sympathise. I imagine you are both enthusiastic and implacable, as you are at once sagacious and careless; you know much and discover much, but you are in such a hurry to tell it all you never give yourself time to think how your reckless eloquence 294 may affect others; and, what / is more, if you knew how it did affect them, you would not much care.

However, I shake hands with you: you have excellent points; you can be generous. I still feel angry, and think I do well to be angry; but it is the anger one experiences for rough play rather than for foul play.— I am yours, with a certain respect, and more chagrin,   Currer Bell.

94. TO E. N. [S. H.]

III,71   January 28, 1850
Dear Ellen,—I cannot but be concerned to hear of your mother's illness; write again soon, if it be but a line, to tell me how she gets on. This shadow will, I trust and believe, be but a passing one, but it is a foretaste and warning of what *must come* one day. Let it prepare your mind, dear Ellen, for that great trial which, if you live, it *must* in the course of a few years be your lot to undergo. . . .   C. B.

P. S.—Mr Nicholls has finished reading "Shirley," he is delighted with it. John Brown's wife seriously thought he had gone wrong in the head as she heard him giving

vent to roars of laughter as he sat alone, clapping his hands and stamping on the floor. He would read all the scenes about the curates aloud to papa, he triumphed in his own character. What Mr Grant will say is another thing. No matter.[1]

95. TO E. N. [S. H.]

February 4th, 1850. III,73
Dear Ellen,—I am truly glad to hear of the happy change in your mother's state, I hope nothing will occur to give it a check. . . .

Martha came in yesterday, puffing and blowing, and much excited. "I've heard sich news," she began. "What about?" "Please ma'am, you've been and written two books, the grandest books that ever was seen. My father has heard it at Halifax, and Mr George Taylor and Mr Greenwood, and Mr Merrall at Bradford; and they are going to have a meeting at the Mechanics' Institute, and to settle about ordering them." "Hold your tongue Martha, and be off." I fell into a cold sweat. "Jane Eyre" will be read by John Brown, by Mrs Taylor, and Betty. God help, keep, and deliver me! Good-bye.   C. B.

96. TO E. N. [S. H.]

February 16th, 1850 III,77
Dear Nell,— . . . The Haworth people have been making great fools of themselves about "Shirley." They take it in an enthusiastic light. When they got the volumes at the Mechanics' Institute, all the members wanted them. They cast lots for the whole three, and whoever got a volume was only allowed to keep it two days, and was to be fined a shilling per diem for longer detention. It would be mere nonsense and vanity to tell you what they say. . . .   C. B.

97. TO W. S. WILLIAMS [S. H.]

Feby 22nd, 1850 III,79
My dear Sir,—/ . . . I believe both "Shirley" 80 and "Jane Eyre" are being a good deal read in the North just now—but I only hear

---

[1] Mr. Nicholls was the original of the curate Malone.

fitful rumours from time to time — I ask nothing — and my life of anchorite seclusion shuts out all bearers of tidings. One or two curiosity-hunters have made their way to Haworth Parsonage — but our rude hills and rugged neighbourhood will I doubt not form a sufficient barrier to the frequent repetition of such visits. — believe me,   Yours sincerely, C. Brontë.

98. TO GEORGE SMITH [G.]

297   March 16th, 1850
[My dear Sir, —] . . . One thing . . . I see plainly enough, and that is, Mr. Currer Bell needs improvement, and ought to strive after it; and this (D. V.) he honestly intends to do

298 — taking his / time, however, and following as his guides Nature and Truth. If these lead to what the critics call art, it is all very well; but if not, that grand desideratum has no chance of being run after or caught. The puzzle is, that while the people of the South object to my delineation of Northern life and manners, the people of Yorkshire and Lancashire approve. They say it is precisely the contrast of rough nature with highly artificial cultivation which forms one of their main characteristics. Such, or something very similar, has been the observation made to me lately, whilst I have been from home, by members of some of the ancient East Lancashire families, whose mansions lie on the hilly border-land between the two counties. The question arises, whether do the London critics, or the old Northern squires, understand the matter best? . . .
                                      [C. Brontë.]

99. TO W. S. WILLIAMS [S. H.]

III,88   March 19th, 1850.
My dear Sir, — The books came yesterday evening just as I was wishing for them very much. There is much interest for me in opening the Cornhill parcel. I wish there was not pain too — but so it is. As I untie the cords and take out the volumes, I am reminded of those who once on similar occasions looked on eagerly. . . .

89,90   . . . I / deem it unwise to dwell much on these matters, but for once I must permit myself to remark, that the generous pride many of the Yorkshire people have taken in the matter has been such as to awake and claim my gratitude, especially since it has afforded a source of reviving pleasure to my father in his old age. The very curates, poor fellows! show no resentment: each characteristically finds solace for his own wounds in crowing over his brethren. Mr Donne was, at first, a little disturbed; for a week or two he was in disquietude, but he is now soothed down; only yesterday I had the pleasure of making him a comfortable cup of tea, and seeing him sip it with revived complacency. It is a curious fact that, since he read "Shirley," he has come to the house oftener than ever, and been remarkably meek, and assiduous to please. Some people's natures are veritable enigmas: I quite expected to have had one good scene at least with him, but as yet nothing of the sort has occurred.

I hope Mrs Williams continues well, and that she is beginning to regain composure after the shock of her recent bereavement. . . . — Believe me, dear sir, yours sincerely,
                                      C. Brontë.

100. TO W. S. WILLIAMS [S. H.]

                              April 12th, 1850 III,98
My dear Sir, — . . . The perusal of Southey's Life has lately afforded me much pleasure; the autobiography with which it commences is deeply interesting and the letters which follow are scarcely less so, disclosing as they do a character most estimable in its integrity and a nature most amiable in its benevolence, as well as a mind admirable in its talent. Some people assert that Genius is inconsistent with domestic happiness, and yet Southey was happy at home and made his home happy; he not only loved his wife and children *though* he was a poet, but he loved them the better *because* he was a poet. He seems to have been without taint of / worldliness; Lon- 99 don, with its pomp and vanities, learned coteries with their dry pedantry rather scared than attracted him; he found his prime glory in his genius, and his chief

felicity in home-affections. I like Southey.[2]

I have likewise read one of Miss Austen's works "Emma" — read it with interest and with just the degree of admiration which Miss Austen herself would have thought sensible and suitable — anything like warmth or enthusiasm; anything energetic, poignant, heartfelt, is utterly out of place in commending these works: all such demonstration the authoress would have met with a well-bred sneer, would have calmly scorned as outré and extravagant. She does her business of delineating the surface of the lives of genteel English people curiously well; there is a Chinese fidelity, a miniature delicacy in the painting: she ruffles her reader by nothing vehement, disturbs him by nothing profound: the Passions are perfectly unknown to her; she rejects even a speaking acquaintance with that stormy Sisterhood; even to the Feelings she vouchsafes no more than an occasional graceful but distant recognition; too frequent converse with them would ruffle the smooth elegance of her progress. Her business is not half so much with the human heart as with the human eyes, mouths, hands and feet; what sees keenly, speaks aptly, moves flexibly, it suits her to study, but what throbs fast and full, though hidden, what the blood rushes through, what is the unseen seat of Life and the sentient target of death — *this* Miss Austen ignores; she no more, with her mind's eye, beholds the heart of her race than each man, with bodily vision sees the heart in his heaving breast. Jane Austen was a complete and most sensible lady, but a very incomplete, and rather insensible (*not senseless*) woman, if this is heresy — I cannot help it. If I said it to some people (Lewes for instance) they would directly accuse me of advocating exaggerated heroics, but I am not afraid of your falling into any such vulgar error. — Believe me, Yours sincerely.

C. Brontë.

2 See Charlotte's letters to Southey in 1837. He had died in 1843.

101. TO JAMES TAYLOR [G.]

May 22nd, [1850] 302

[My dear Sir, —] . . . I have just received 303 yours of this morning; thank you for the enclosed note. The longings for liberty and leisure which May sunshine wakens in you, stir my sympathy. I am afraid Cornhill is little better than a prison for its inmates on warm spring or summer days. It is a pity to think of you all toiling at your desks in such genial weather as this. For my part, I am free to walk on the moors; but when I go out there alone, everything reminds me of the times when others were with me, and then the moors seem a wilderness, featureless, solitary, saddening. My sister Emily had a particular love for them, and there is not a knoll of heather, not a branch of fern, not a young bilberry leaf, not a fluttering lark or linnet, but reminds me of her. The distant prospects were Anne's delight, and when I look round, she is in the blue tints, the pale mists, the waves and shadows of the horizon. In the hill-country silence, their poetry comes by lines and stanzas into my mind: once I loved it; now I dare not read it, and am driven often to wish I could taste one draught of oblivion, and forget much that, while mind remains, I never shall forget. [C. Brontë.]

102. TO E. N. [G.]

June 12th, ['50] 304

[Dear Ellen, —] . . . Of course I cannot give you in a letter a regular chronicle of how my time has been spent. I can only just notify what I deem three of its chief incidents: — a sight of the Duke of Wellington at the Chapel Royal (he is a real grand old man), a visit to the House of Commons (which I hope to describe to you some day when I see you), and last, not least, an interview with Mr. Thackeray. He made a morning call, and sat above two hours. Mr. Smith only was in the room the whole time. He described it afterwards as a "queer scene," and I suppose it was. The giant sate before me; I was moved to speak to him of some of his short-comings (literary of course); one by one the faults came /

305 into my head, and one by one I brought them out, and sought some explanation or defence. He did defend himself, like a great Turk and heathen; that is to say, the excuses were often worse than the crime itself. The matter ended in decent amity; if all be well, I am to dine at his house this evening. . . . [Yours faithfully, C. B.]

III, 149   103. TO MRS. GASKELL [S. H.]
        August 27, 1850
150 . . . I have read Tennyson's "In Memoriam," or rather part of it; I closed the book when I had got about half-way. It is beautiful; it is mournful; it is monotonous. Many of the feelings expressed bear, in their utterance, the stamp of truth; yet, if Arthur Hallam had been somewhat nearer Alfred Tennyson — his brother instead of his friend — I should have distrusted this rhymed, and measured, and printed monument of grief. . . .   C. Brontë.

104. TO JAMES TAYLOR [G.]
[September 5th, 1850]
314 [My dear Sir, —] . . . I did indeed enjoy my trip to Scotland, and yet I saw little of the face of the country; nothing of its grandeur or finer scenic features; but Edinburgh, Melrose, Abbotsford — these three in themselves sufficed to stir feelings of such deep interest and admiration, that neither at the time did I regret, nor have I since regretted, the want of wider space over which to diffuse the sense of enjoyment. There was room and variety enough to be very happy, and "enough," the proverb 315 says, "is as good as / a feast." The queen, indeed, was right to climb Arthur's Seat with her husband and children. I shall not soon forget how I felt when, having reached its summit, we all sat down and looked over the city — towards the sea and Leith, and the Pentland Hills. No doubt you are proud of being a native of Scotland, — proud of your country, her capital, her children, and her literature. You cannot be blamed.

The article in the *Palladium*[3] is one of those notices over which an author rejoices

[3] By Sydney Dobell; see IV.

trembling. He rejoices to find his work finely, fully, fervently appreciated, and trembles under the responsibility such appreciation seems to devolve upon him. I am counselled to wait and watch — D. V. I will do so; yet it is harder to wait with the hands bound, and the observant and reflective faculties at their silent and unseen work, than to labour mechanically.

I need not say how I felt the remarks on *Wuthering Heights;* they woke the saddest yet most grateful feelings; they are true, they are discriminating, they are full of late justice, but it is very late — alas! in one sense, *too* late. Of this, however, and of the pang of regret for a light prematurely extinguished, it is not wise to speak much. Whoever the author of this article may be, I remain his debtor.

Yet, you see, even here, *Shirley* is disparaged in comparison with *Jane Eyre;* and yet I took great pains with *Shirley.* I did not hurry; I tried to do my best, and my own impression was that it was not inferior to the former work; indeed, I had bestowed on it more time, thought, and anxiety: but great part of it was written under the shadow of impending calamity; and the last volume, I cannot deny, was composed in the eager, restless endeavour to combat mental sufferings that were scarcely tolerable. . . . [Yours very sincerely, C. Brontë.]

105. TO W. S. WILLIAMS [S. H.]
September 13th, 1850 III, 156
My dear Sir, — Mr Newby undertook first to print 350 copies of "Wuthering Heights," but he afterwards declared he had only printed 250. I doubt whether he could be induced to return the £50 without a good deal of trouble — much more than I should / feel justified in delegating to Mr Smith. 157 For my part, the conclusion I drew from the whole of Mr Newby's conduct to my sisters was that he is a man with whom it is desirable to have little to do. I think he must be needy as well as tricky — and if he is, one would not distress him, even for one's rights.

If Mr Smith thinks proper to reprint

"Wuthering Heights" and "Agnes Grey," I would prepare a preface comprising a brief and simple notice of the authors, such as might set at rest all erroneous conjectures respecting their identity — and adding a few poetical remains of each.

In case this arrangement is approved, you will kindly let me know, and I will commence the task (a sad, but, I believe, a necessary one), and send it when finished.

I am, my dear sir, yours sincerely,

C. Brontë.

106. TO GEORGE SMITH [S. H.]
[September, 18th, 1850]

III, My Dear Sir, — "Wuthering Heights" and
160 "Agnes Grey" were published by Mr Newby on the condition that my sisters should share the risk. Accordingly they advanced £50. Mr Newby engaging to repay it as soon as the work should have sold a sufficient number of copies to defray expenses; and Mr Newby mentions in his letter to my sister on the subject that "the sale of 250 copies would leave a *surplus* of £100. to be divided." No portion of the sum advanced has yet been returned, and, as it appears that the work is now entirely out of print, I should feel greatly obliged if you would call upon Mr Newby and enquire whether it be convenient to him to refund the amount received.

For "The Tenant of Wildfell Hall" my sister Anne was to receive £25. on the day of publication, a second £25. on the sale reaching 250 copies, £50 more on its extending to 400 copies, and another £50. on 500 being sold.

Two instalments of £25. each were paid to my sister. I should be glad if you could learn how many copies of the work have been sold on the whole, and whether any further sum is now due. —

Yours sincerely,   C. Brontë.

107. TO MARGARET WOOLER [G.]
[Haworth, Sept. 27th, 1850]

311 [My dear Miss Wooler, —]. . . .
312 Sir James Kay Shuttleworth is residing near Windermere, at a house called the "Briery,"

and it was there I was staying for a little time this August. He very kindly showed me the neighbourhood, *as it can be seen from a carriage,* and I discerned that the Lake country is a glorious region, of which I had only seen the similitude in dreams, waking or sleeping. Decidedly I find it does not agree with me to prosecute the search of the picturesque in a carriage. A waggon, a spring-cart, even a post-chaise might do; but the carriage upsets everything. I longed to slip out unseen, and to run away by myself in amongst the hills and dales. . . .

During the month I spent in London in the spring, I kept very quiet, having the fear of lionising before my eyes. I only went out once to dinner; and once was present at an evening party; and the only visits I have paid have been to Sir James Kay Shuttleworth's and my publisher's. From this system I should not like to depart; as far as I can see, indiscriminate visiting tends only to a waste of time and a vulgarising of character. Besides, it would be wrong to leave Papa often; he is now in his seventy-fifth year, the infirmities of age begin to creep upon him; during the summer he has been much harassed by chronic bronchitis, but I am thankful to say that he is now somewhat better. I think my own health has derived benefit from change and exercise. . . .

[affectionately and respectfully, C. Brontë]

108. TO W. S. WILLIAMS [S. H.]
Octr 25th, 1850. III,

My dear Sir, — The box of books came last 174
night and — as usual — I have only gratefully to admire the selection made: Jeffrey's Essays, Dr Arnold's Life, the Roman, Alton Locke — these were all wished-for and welcome. . . .

I have already had Macaulay's Essays — Sydney Smith's lectures on Moral Philosophy, and Knox on Race. Pickering's work on the same subject I have not seen — nor all the vols of Leigh Hunt's Autobiography. However — I am now abundantly supplied for a long time to come. I liked Hazlitt's essays much.

175   The Autumn — as you say — has been very fine — I and Solitude and Memory have often profited by its sunshine on the Moors.

I had felt some disappointment at the non-arrival of the proofsheets of "Wuthering Heights" — a feverish impatience to complete the revision is apt to beset me — the work of looking over papers &c. could not be gone through with impunity or with unaltered spirits — associations too tender — regrets too bitter sprang out of it —

Meantime — the Cornhill books now as heretofore, are my best medicine — affording a solace which could not be yielded by the very same books procured from a common library. . . .   Yours sincerely, C. Brontë

109. TO GEORGE SMITH [S. H.]

III,   December 3rd, 1850
185 My dear Sir, — . . . As to Mr Newby, he charms me. First there is the fascinating coyness with which he shuns your pursuit. For a month, or nearly two months, have you been fondly hoping to win from him an interview, while he has been making himself as scarce as violets at Christmas, aristocratically absenting himself from town, evading your grasp like a publisher metamorphosed into a rainbow. Then when you come upon him in that fatal way in Regent Street, pin him down, and hunt him home with more promptitude than politeness, and with a want of delicate consideration for your victim's fine feelings calculated to awaken emotions of regret, that victim is still ready for the emergency. Scorning to stand on the defensive, he at once assumes the offensive. Not only has he realised no profit, he has sustained actual loss; and, to account for this, adds, with a sublime boldness of invention, that the author "wished him to spend all possible profits in advertisements."

Equally well acted too is the artless simplicity of his surprise at the news you communicate; and his pretty little menace of a "Chancery injunction" consummates the picture and makes it perfect.

Any statement of accounts he may send I shall at once transmit to you. In your hands I leave him; deal with him as you list, but I heartily wish you well rid of the business.

On referring to Mr Newby's letters I find in one of them a / boast that he is 186 "advertising vigorously." I remember that this flourish caused us to look out carefully for the results of his vast exertions; but though we everywhere encountered "Jane Eyre" it was as rare a thing to find an advertisement of "Wuthering Heights" as it appears to be to meet with Mr Newby in town. . . .   yours sincerely, C. Brontë

110. TO SYDNEY DOBELL [G.]

Haworth, near Keighley, Yorkshire 325
Dec. 8th, 1850

I offer this little book to my critic in the *Palladium*, and he must believe it accompanied by a tribute of the sincerest gratitude; not so much for anything he has said of myself, as for the noble justice he has rendered to one dear to me as myself — perhaps dearer; and perhaps one kind word spoken for her awakens a deeper, tenderer, sentiment of thankfulness than eulogies heaped on my own head. As you will see when you have read the biographical notice, my sister cannot thank you herself; she is gone out of your sphere and mine, and human blame and praise are nothing to her now. But to me, for her sake, they are something still; it revived me for many a day to find that, dead as she was, the work of her genius had at last met with worthy appreciation.

Tell me, when you have read the introduction, whether any doubts still linger in your mind respecting the authorship of *Wuthering Heights, Wildfell Hall*, etc. Your mistrust did me some injustice; it proved a general conception of character such as I should be sorry to call mine; but these false ideas will naturally arise when we only judge an author from his works. In fairness, I must also disclaim the flattering side of the portrait. I am no "young Penthesilea *mediis in millibus*," but a plain country parson's daughter.

Once more I thank you, and that with a full heart.   C. Brontë.

111. TO E. N. [G.]

[The Knoll, Ambleside,
Decbr 18th, 1850]

326 [Dear Ellen, —] I can write to you now, dear [Ellen], for I am away from home, and relieved, temporarily, at least, by change of air and scene, from the heavy burden of depression which, I confess, has for nearly three months been sinking me to the earth. I never shall forget last autumn! Some days and nights have been cruel; but now, having once told you this, I need say no more on the subject. My loathing of solitude grew extreme; my recollection of my sisters intolerably poignant. I am better now. I am at Miss Martineau's for a week. Her house is very pleasant, both within and without; arranged at all points with admirable neatness and comfort. Her visitors enjoy the most perfect liberty; what she claims for herself she allows them. I rise at my own hour, breakfast alone (she is up at five, takes a cold bath, and a walk by starlight, and has finished breakfast and got to her work by seven o'clock). I pass the morning in the drawing-room — she, in her study. At two o'clock we meet — work, talk, and walk together till five, her dinner-hour, spend the evening together, when she converses fluently and abundantly, and with the most complete frankness. I go to my own room soon after ten, — she sits up writing letters till twelve. She appears exhaustless in strength and spirits, and indefatigable in the faculty of labour. She is a great and a good woman; of course not without peculiarities, but I have seen none as yet that annoy me. She is both hard and warm-hearted, abrupt and affectionate, liberal and despotic. I believe she is not at all conscious of her own absolutism. When I tell her of it, she denies the charge warmly; then I laugh at her. I believe she almost rules Ambleside. Some of the gentry dislike her, but the lower orders have a great regard for her. * * *

[Yours faithfully, C. Brontë]

112. TO PATRICK BRONTË [S. H.]

Ambleside, December 21st, 1850 III, 190

Dear Papa, — I think I shall not come home till Thursday. If all be well I shall leave here on Monday and spend a day or two with Ellen Nussey. I have enjoyed my visit exceedingly. Sir. J. K. Shuttleworth has called several times and taken me out in his carriage. He seems very truly friendly; but, I am sorry to say, he looks pale and very much wasted. I greatly fear he will not live very long unless some change for the better soon takes place. Lady Shuttleworth is ill too, and cannot go out. I have seen a good deal of Dr. Arnold's family and like them much.[4] As to Miss Martineau, I admire her and wonder at her more than I can say. Her powers of labour, of exercise, and social cheerfulness are beyond my comprehension. In spite of the unceasing activity of her colossal intellect she enjoys robust health. She is a taller, larger, and more strongly made woman than I had imagined from that first interview with her. She is very kind to me, though she must think I am a very insignificant person compared to herself. She has just been into the room to show me a chapter of her / history which 191 she is now writing, relating to the Duke of Wellington's character and his proceedings in the Peninsula.[5] She wanted an opinion on it, and I was happy to be able to give a very approving one. She seems to understand and do him justice.

You must not direct any more letters here as they will not reach me after to-day. Hoping, dear papa, that you are well, and with

[4] See Arnold's note of this date (V).
[5] Miss Martineau gave Mrs. Gaskell her account of the incident mentioned in Charlotte's letter to her father:

One morning I brought her the first page of the chapter on the Peninsular War in my Introductory History, and said, "Tell me if this will do for a beginning," &c. I read the page or two to her, as we stood before the fire, and she looked up at me and stole her hand into mine, and to my amazement the tears were running down her cheeks. She said, "Oh, I do thank you! Oh, we are of one mind! Oh! I thank you for this justice to the man." I saw at once there was a touch of idolatry in the case, but it was a charming enthusiasm.

kind regards to Tabby and Martha, — I am, your affectionate daughter,   C. Brontë

113. TO W. S. WILLIAMS [S. H.]

January 3rd, 1851

III, 193 My dear Sir, — . . . I trust to have derived benefit from my visit to Miss Martineau. A visit more interesting I certainly never paid. If self-sustaining strength can be acquired from example, I ought to have got good. But my nature is not hers; I could not make it so though I were to submit it seventy times seven to the furnace of affliction and discipline it for an age under the hammer and anvil of toil and self-sacrifice. Perhaps if I was like her I should not admire her so much as I do. She is somewhat absolute, though quite unconsciously so; but she is likewise kind, with an affection at once abrupt and constant, whose sincer-

194 ity you cannot doubt. It was / delightful to sit near her in the evenings and hear her converse, myself mute. She speaks with what seems to me a wonderful fluency and eloquence. Her animal spirits are as unflagging as her intellectual powers. I was glad to find her health excellent. I believe neither solitude nor loss of friends would break her down. I saw some faults in her, but somehow I liked them for the sake of her good points. It gave me no pain to feel insignificant, mentally and corporeally, in comparison with her. . . .

yours sincerely, C. Brontë

114. TO E. N. [S. H.]

[Jan. 20th, 1851]

III, 201– 202 Dear Ellen, — / . . . Dear Nell — your last letter but one made me smile. I think you draw great conclusions from small inferences. I think those "fixed intentions" you fancy — are imaginary — I think the "undercurrent" amounts simply to this — a kind of natural liking and sense of something congenial. Were there no vast barrier of age, fortune &c. there is perhaps enough personal regard to make things possible which now are impossible. If men and women married because they like each others' temper, look, conversation, nature

and so on — and if besides, years were more nearly equal — the chance you allude to might be admitted as a chance — but other reasons regulate matrimony — reasons of convenience, of connection, of money. Meantime I am content to have him as a friend — and pray God to continue to me the commonsense to look on one so young, so rising and so hopeful in no other light.[6]

That hint about the Rhine disturbs me; I am not made of stone — and what is mere excitement to him — is fever to me. However it is a matter for the Future and long to look forward to — As I see it now, the journey is out of the question — for many reasons — I rather wonder he should think of it — I cannot conceive either his mother or his sisters relishing it, and all London would gabble like a countless host of geese —

Good-bye, dear Nell, Heaven grant us both some quiet wisdom — and strength not merely to bear the trial of pain — but to resist the lure of pleasure when it comes in such a shape as our better judgment disapproves.   C. Brontë

115. TO JAMES TAYLOR [G.]

Feb. 11th, 1851 329

My dear Sir, — Have you yet read Miss Martineau's and Mr. Atkinson's new work, *Letters on the Nature and Development of Man?*[7] If you have not, it would be worth your while to do so.

Of the impression this book has made on me, I will not now say much. It is the first exposition of avowed atheism and materialism I have ever read; the first unequivocal declaration of disbelief in the existence of a God or a future life I have ever seen. In judging of such exposition and declaration,

[6] Ellen was not the only person to wonder if Charlotte and her attractive young publisher were interested in each other. Years later George Smith admitted to Mrs. Humphrey Ward that there had been enough mutual interest to worry his mother, but that he had never actually proposed to Charlotte.

[7] The published correspondence between Henry Atkinson and Miss Martineau in which the miracle stories of the New Testament were described as legends and God was reduced to a first cause.

one would wish entirely to put aside the sort of instinctive horror they awaken, and to consider them in an impartial spirit and collected mood. This I find it difficult to do. The strangest thing is, that we are called on to rejoice over this hopeless blank — to receive this bitter bereavement as great gain — to welcome this unutterable desolation as a state of pleasant freedom. Who *could* do this if he would? Who *would* do it if he could?

Sincerely, for my own part, do I wish to find and know the Truth; but if this be Truth, well may she guard herself with mysteries, and cover herself with a veil. If this be Truth, man or woman who beholds her can but curse the day he or she was born. . . .   [yours sincerely, C. Brontë]

116. TO E. N. [s. h.]

III,
228
229

April 23rd, 1851

My dear Ellen, — / . . . My conscience, I can truly say, does not *now* accuse me of having treated Mr Taylor with injustice or unkindness. What I once did wrong in this way, I have endeavoured to remedy both to himself and in speaking of him to others, Mr Smith to wit. . . . It would sound harsh were I to tell even *you* of the estimate I felt compelled to form respecting him; dear Nell, I looked for something of the gentleman — something I mean of the *natural* gentleman; you know I can dispense with acquired polish, and for looks, I know myself too well to think that I have any right to be exacting on that point. I could not find one gleam, I could not see one passing glimpse, of true good-breeding; it is hard to say, but it is true. In mind too; though clever, he is second-rate; thoroughly second-rate. . . .

I am, dear Nell, your middle-aged friend.[8]
C. Brontë

---

[8] Taylor seems to have made a proposal to Charlotte — her third. She records elsewhere that her "veins ran ice" when he was near her.

[9] George Smith's sister, who accompanied Charlotte to the lecture, described the episode to Mrs. Gaskell, who wrote:

When the lecture was ended, Mr. Thackeray came down from the platform, and making his

117. TO E. N. [G.][9]

[Gloucester Terrace, Hyde Park,]
June 2nd [1851]

[Dear Nell, —] I came here on Wednesday, 334 being summoned a day sooner than I expected, in order to be in time for Thackeray's second lecture, which was delivered on Thursday afternoon. This, as you may suppose, was a genuine treat to me, and I was glad not to miss it. It was given in Willis' Rooms, where the Almacks balls are held — a great painted and gilded saloon with long sofas for benches. The audience was said to be the cream of London society, and it looked so. I did not at all expect the great lecturer would know me or notice me under these circumstances, with admiring duchesses and countesses seated in rows before him; but he met me as I entered — shook hands — took me to his mother, whom I had not before seen, and introduced me. She is a fine, handsome, young-looking old lady; was very gracious, and called with one of her grand-daughters next day.

Thackeray called too, separately. I had a long talk with him, and I think he knows me now a little better than he did: but of this I cannot yet be sure; he is a great and strange man. There is quite a furor for his lectures. They are a sort of essays, characterised by his own peculiar originality and power, and delivered with a finished taste and ease, which is felt, but cannot be described. . . .

way towards her, asked her for her opinion. This she mentioned to me not many days afterwards, adding remarks almost identical with those which I subsequently read in *Villette*, where a similar action on the part of M. Paul Emanuel is related.

As they were preparing to leave the room, her companion saw with dismay that many of the audience were forming themselves into two lines, on each side of the aisle down which they had to pass before reaching the door. Aware that any delay would only make the ordeal more trying, her friend took Miss Brontë's arm in hers, and they went along the avenue of eager and admiring faces. During this passage through the "cream of society," Miss Brontë's hand trembled to such a degree, that her companion feared lest she should turn faint and be unable to proceed; and she dared not express her sympathy or try to give her strength by any touch or word, lest it might bring on the crisis she dreaded.

335   On Friday, I went to the Crystal Palace; it is a marvellous, stirring, bewildering sight — a mixture of a genii palace, and a mighty bazaar, but it is not much in my way; I liked the lecture better. On Saturday I saw the Exhibition at Somerset House; about half a dozen of the pictures are good and interesting, the rest of little worth. Sunday — yesterday — was a day to be marked with a white stone; through most of the day I was very happy, without being tired or over-excited. In the afternoon, I went to hear D'Aubigné, the great Protestant French preacher; it was pleasant, half sweet, half sad — and strangely suggestive to hear the French language once more. For health, I have so far got on very fairly, considering that I came here far from well. [...]   [faithfully yours, C. Brontë]

118. TO MRS. SMITH [S. H.]

III,   Haworth, July 1st, 1851
254 My dear Mrs. Smith, — . . . The visit to Mrs Gaskell formed a cheering break in the journey. She is a woman of many fine qualities and deserves the epithet which I find is generally applied to her — charming. Her family consists of four little girls[10] — all more or less pretty and intelligent — these scattered through the rooms of a somewhat spacious house — seem to fill it with liveliness and gaiety. . . .
Believe me very sincerely yours, C. Brontë

119. TO W. S. WILLIAMS [S. H.]

III,   [July 21st, 1851].
262 My dear Sir, . . .
263 . . . In the matter of friendship — I have observed — that disappointment here arises chiefly — *not* from liking our friends too well — or thinking of them too highly — but rather from an over-estimate of *their* liking for and opinion of *us;* and that if we guard ourselves with sufficient scrupulousness of care from error in this direction — and can be content, and even happy to give more

affection than we receive — can make just comparison of circumstances and be severely accurate in drawing inferences thence, and never let self-love blind our eyes — I *think* we may manage to get through life with consistency and constancy — unembittered by that misanthropy which springs from revulsions of feeling. All this sounds a little metaphysical — but it is good sense if you consider it. The Moral of it is that if we would build on a sure foundation in friendship — we must love our friends for *their* sakes rather than for *our own,* we must look at their truth to *themselves,* full as much as their truth to *us.* In the latter case — every wound to self-love would be a cause of coldness; in the former — only some painful change in the friend's character and disposition — some fearful breach in his allegiance to his better self — could alienate the heart. . . .   yours sincerely, C. Brontë

120. TO E. G. [G.]

[September 20th, 1851]
* * * Beautiful are those sentences out 344 of James Martineau's sermons; some of them gems most pure and genuine; ideas deeply conceived, finely expressed. I should like much to see his review of his sister's book. Of all the articles respecting which you question me, I have seen none, except that notable one in the *Westminster* on the Emancipation of Women.[1] But why are you and I to think (perhaps I should rather say to *feel*) so exactly alike on some points that there can be no discussion between us? Your words on this paper express my thoughts. Well-argued it is, — clear, logical, — but vast is the hiatus of omission; harsh the consequent jar on every finer chord of the soul. What is this hiatus? I think I know; and knowing, I will venture to say. I think the writer forgets there is such a thing as self-sacrificing love and disinterested devotion. When I first read the paper, I thought it was the work of a powerful-minded, clear-headed woman, who had a hard, jealous heart, muscles of iron, and

---

10 Her baby boy had died of scarlet fever in 1845. It was then that her husband, alarmed at her despair, urged her to try to write as an antidote to grief.

1 By Mrs. John Taylor, later wife of John Stuart Mill.

nerves of bend leather; of a woman who longed for power, and had never felt affection. To many women affection is sweet, and power conquered indifferent — though we all like influence won. I believe J. S. Mill would make a hard, dry, dismal world of it; and yet he speaks admirable sense through a great portion of his article — especially when he says, that if there be a natural unfitness in women for men's employment, there is no need to make laws on the subject; leave all careers open; let them try; those who ought to succeed will succeed, or, at least, will have a fair chance — the incapable will fall back into their right place. He likewise disposes of the "maternity" question very neatly. In short, J. S. Mill's head is, I dare say, very good, but I feel disposed to scorn his heart. You are right when you say that there is a large margin in human nature over which the logicians have no dominion; glad am I that it is so.

I send by this post Ruskin's *Stones of Venice,* and I hope you and Meta will find passages in it that will please you. Some parts would be dry and technical were it not for the character, the marked individuality which pervades every page. I wish Marianne had come to speak to me at the lecture; it would have given me such pleasure. What you say of that small sprite Julia, amuses me much. I believe you don't know that she has a great deal of her mama's nature (modified) in her; yet I think you will find she has as she grows up. . . .

345 You charge me to write about myself. What can I say on that precious topic? My health is pretty good. My spirits are not always alike. Nothing happens to me. I hope and expect little in this world, and am thankful that I do not despond and suffer more. Thank you for inquiring after our old servant; she is pretty well; the little shawl, etc., pleased her much. Papa likewise, I am glad to say, is pretty well; with his and my kindest regards to you and Mr. Gaskell — Believe me, sincerely and affectionately yours,   C. Brontë

121. TO GEORGE SMITH [S. H.]

[Undated, probably November 1851]

My dear Sir, — . . . I will tell you a thing III, to be noted, often in your letters and almost 292 always in your conversation, a psychological thing, and not a matter pertaining to style or intellect: I mean an undercurrent of quiet raillery, an inaudible laugh to yourself, a not unkindly but somewhat subtle playing on your correspondent or companion for the time being — in short, a sly touch of a Mephistopheles with the fiend extracted. In the present instance this speciality is perceptible only in the slightest degree — quite imperceptible for the world — but it *is* there, and more or less you have it always. I by no means mention this as a *fault,* I merely tell you you have it. And I can make the accusation with comfortable impunity, guessing pretty surely that you are too busy just now to deny this or any other charge. . . .

Sincerely yours, C. Brontë.

122. TO E. G. [S. H.]

November 6th, 1851 III,

If anybody would tempt me from home 286 you would; but just now, from home I must not, will not go. I feel greatly better at present than I did three weeks ago. For a month or six weeks about the equinox (autumnal or vernal) is a period of the year which, I have noticed, strangely tries me. Sometimes the strain falls on the mental, sometimes on the physical part of me; I am ill with neuralgic headache, or I am ground to the dust with deep dejection of spirits (not, however, such dejection but I can keep to myself). That weary time has, I think and trust, got over for this year. It was the anniversary of my poor brother's death, and of my sister's failing health: I need say no more.

As to running away from home every time I have a battle of this sort to fight, it would not do: besides the "weird" would follow. As to shaking it off, that cannot be. I have declined to go / to Mrs Forster, to 287 Miss Martineau, and now I decline to go to you. But listen! do not think that I throw your kindness away, or that it fails of doing the good you desire. On the contrary, the feeling expressed in your letter — proved by your invitation — goes *right home* where you would have it to go, and heals as you would have it to heal. . . .   C. Brontë

123. TO JAMES TAYLOR [G.]

[Haworth, November 15th, 1851]

348 [My dear Sir,] [. . .] I spent a few weeks in town last summer, as you have heard; and was much interested by many things I heard and saw there. What now chiefly dwells in my memory are Mr. Thackeray's lectures, Mademoiselle Rachel's[2] acting, D'Aubigné's, Melville's, and Maurice's preaching, and the Crystal Palace.[3]

Mr. Thackeray's lectures you will have seen mentioned and commented on in the papers; they were very interesting. I could not always coincide with the sentiments ex-

[2] The famous French tragédienne.
[3] Sir David Brewster (1781–1868), a famous scientist of the day, took Charlotte around and explained the exhibits to her.

pressed, or the opinions broached; but I admired the gentlemanlike ease, the quiet humour, the taste, the talent, the simplicity, and the originality of the lecturer.

Rachel's acting transfixed me with wonder, enchained me with interest, and thrilled me with horror. The tremendous force with which she expresses the very worst passions in their strongest essence forms an exhibition as exciting as the bull fights of Spain, and the gladiatorial combats of old Rome, and (it seemed to me) not one whit more moral than these poisoned stimulants to popular ferocity. It is scarcely human nature that she shows you; it is something wilder and worse; the feelings and fury of a fiend. The great gift of genius she undoubtedly has; but, I fear, she rather abuses it than turns it to good account.

With all the three preachers I was greatly pleased. Melville seemed to me the most eloquent, Maurice the most in earnest; had I the choice, it is Maurice whose ministry I should frequent. . . .

[I am, yours sincerely, C. Brontë]

THE WRITING OF *Villette*, 1851 TO 1852

Finally, in the fall of 1851, Charlotte began work on her fourth novel. Rejecting with horror George Smith's suggestion that she publish in installments like Dickens and Thackeray, she insisted on working at her own pace. Even so she progressed slowly and with difficulty. Charlotte's vitality was low. The deaths of her sisters and brother were still fresh in her memory and in *Villette* she was reliving the painful Brussels experience. Although she longed for companionship, she deprived herself of it because she feared she was not getting on fast enough with her book and would disappoint or displease her Cornhill friends. Moreover, she was trying to prepare her mind for the loneliness which seemed to be her portion. "I must absolutely get accustomed to a life of solitude," she wrote George Smith, "there is no other plan."

Her writing had many interruptions. Her father was ill, Tabby was ill, eventually Charlotte herself became ill. Bending over to write gave her pains in the chest, her liver was disordered, and she suffered from headaches and nausea. Finally, as she was completing the third volume, Mr. Brontë embarrassed her by insisting that she provide a happy ending to the romance. This Charlotte could not bring herself to do. A certain ambiguity was the most she would consent to. *Villette* was mailed to Smith and Elder late in November, 1852.

124. TO GEORGE SMITH [G.]

[Haworth, November 28th, 1851]

349 [My dear Sir, —] [. . .] It is not at all likely

that my book[4] will be ready at the time you mention. If my health is spared, I shall get

[4] *Villette*

on with it as fast as is consistent with its being done, if not *well*, yet as well as I can do it. *Not one whit faster*. When the mood leaves me (it has left me now, without vouchsafing so much as a word or a message when it will return) I put by the MS. and wait till it comes back again. God knows, I sometimes have to wait long — very long it seems to me. Meantime, if I might make a request to you, it would be this. Please to say nothing about my book till it is written, and in your hands. You may not like it. I am not myself elated with it as far as it is gone, and authors, you need not be told, are always tenderly indulgent, even blindly partial to their own. Even if it should turn out reasonably well, still I regard it as ruin to the prosperity of an ephemeral book like a novel, to be much talked of before-hand, as if it were something great. People are apt to conceive, or at least to profess, exaggerated expectation, such as no performance can realise; then ensue disappointment and the due revenge, detraction, and failure. If when I write, I were to think of the critics who, I know, are waiting for Currer Bell, ready "to break all his bones or ever he comes to the bottom of the den," my hand would fall paralyzed on my desk. However, I can but do my best, and then muffle my head in the mantle of Patience, and sit down at her feet and wait. [. . .]   [Sincerely yours, C. Brontë]

125. TO E. N. [S. H.]

III,
298

December, 1851

Dear Ellen, — I hope you have got on this last week well. It has been very trying here. Papa so far has borne it unhurt, but these winds and changes have given me a bad cold of influenza character. However, I am better now than I was. Poor old Keeper died last Monday morning; after being ill all night, he went gently to sleep. We laid his old faithful head in the garden. Flossy is dull and misses him. . . .

I am, yours faithfully, C. Brontë

126. TO E. G. [G.]

351

Feb. 6th, 1852.

Certainly, the past winter has been to me

a strange time, had I the prospect before me of living it over again, my prayer must necessarily be, "Let this cup pass from me." That depression of spirits, which I thought was gone by when I wrote last, came back again with a heavy recoil; internal congestion ensued, and then inflammation. I had severe pain in my right side, frequent burning and aching in my chest; sleep almost forsook me, or would never come, except accompanied by ghastly dreams; appetite vanished, and slow fever was my continual companion. It was some time before I could bring myself to have recourse to medical advice. I thought my lungs were affected, and could feel no confidence in the power of medicine. When, at last, however, a doctor was consulted, he declared my lungs and chest sound, and ascribed all my sufferings to derangement of the liver, on which organ it seems the inflammation had fallen. This information was a great relief to my dear father, as well as / to myself; but I 352 had subsequently rather sharp medical discipline to undergo, and was much reduced. Though not yet well, it is with deep thankfulness that I can say, I am *greatly better*. My sleep, appetite, and strength seem all returning.   [C. Brontë]

127. TO GEORGE SMITH [G.]

Feb. 14th, 1852. 352

My dear Sir, — It has been a great delight to me to read Mr. Thackeray's work;[5] and I so seldom now express my sense of kindness that, for once, you must permit me, without rebuke, to thank you for a pleasure so rare and special. Yet I am not going to praise either Mr. Thackeray or his book. I have read, enjoyed, been interested, and, after all, feel full as much ire and sorrow as gratitude and admiration. And still one can never lay down a book of his without the last two feelings having their part, be the subject or treatment what it may. In the first half of the book, what chiefly struck me was the wonderful manner in which the writer throws himself into the spirit and

5 *Henry Esmond*, Vol. I.

letters of the times whereof he treats; the allusions, the illustrations, the style, all seem to me so masterly in their exact keeping, their harmonious consistency, their nice, natural truth, their pure exemption from exaggeration. No second-rate imitator can write in that way; no coarse scene-painter can charm us with an allusion so delicate and perfect. But what bitter satire, what relentless dissection of diseased subjects! Well, and this, too, is right, or would be right, if the savage surgeon did not seem so fiercely pleased with his work. Thackeray likes to dissect an ulcer or an aneurism; he has pleasure in putting his cruel knife or probe into quivering, living flesh. Thackeray would not like all the world to be good; no great satirist would like society to be perfect.

As usual, he is unjust to women; quite unjust. There is hardly any punishment he does not deserve for making Lady Castlewood peep through a keyhole, listen at a door, and be jealous of a boy and a milkmaid. Many other things I noticed that, for my part, grieved and exasperated me as I read; but then, again, came passages so true, so deeply thought, so tenderly felt, one could not help forgiving and admiring. / * * *
353 But I wish he could be told not to care much for dwelling on the political or religious intrigues of the times. Thackeray, in his heart, does not value political or religious intrigues of any age or date. He likes to show us human nature at home, as he himself daily sees it; his wonderful observant faculty likes to be in action. In him this faculty is a sort of captain and leader; and if ever any passage in his writings lacks interest, it is when this master-faculty is for a time thrust into a subordinate position. I think such is the case in the former half of the present volume. Towards the middle, he throws off restraint, becomes himself, and is strong to the close. Everything now depends on the second and third volumes. If, in pith and interest, they fall short of the first, a true success cannot ensue. If the continuation be an improvement upon the commencement, if the stream

gather force as it rolls, Thackeray will triumph. Some people have been in the habit of terming him the second writer of the day; it just depends on himself whether or not these critics shall be justified in their award. He need not be the second. God made him second to no man. If I were he, I would show myself as I am, not as critics report me; at any rate, I would do my best. Mr. Thackeray is easy and indolent, and seldom cares to do his best. Thank you once more; and believe me yours sincerely,

C. Brontë.

128. TO E. N. [S. H.]
Haworth, March 4th, '52 III, 319
Dear Ellen, — The news of E. Taylor's death came to me last week in a letter from Mary — a long letter — which wrung my heart so — in its simple strong, truthful emotion — I have only ventured to read it once. It ripped up half-scarred wounds with terrible force — the death-bed was just the same — breath failing &c. . . .
Yours faithfully, C. Brontë. 320

129. TO MARGARET WOOLER [S. H.]
Haworth, March 12th, 1852 III, 323
My dear Miss Wooler, — Your kind note holds out a strong temptation, but one that *must be resisted.* From home I must not go unless health or some cause equally imperative render a change necessary. For nearly four months now (*i.e.* since I first became ill) I have not put pen to paper — my work has been lying untouched and my faculties have been rusting for want of exercise; further relaxation is out of the question, and I *will not permit myself to think of it.* My publisher groans over my long delays; I am sometimes provoked to check the expression of his impatience with short and crusty answers.

Yet the pleasure I now deny myself I would fain regard as only deferred. I heard something about your purposing to visit Scarbro' in the course of the summer, and could I — by the close of July or August bring my task to a certain point — how glad should I be to join you there for a while! . . .

yours always affectionately and respectfully,

C. Brontë.

130. TO GEORGE SMITH [S. H.]

III,   March 21st, 1852
324 My dear Sir, — I have read and now return
Mr Thackeray's second volume. The complaint, I suppose, will be that there is too
little story. I thought so myself in reading
the first part of this packet of MS. I felt
tedium in the first campaign of Harry
Esmond; the second and third seemed to
me to kindle the spirit. The character of
Marlborough I thought a masterly piece of
writing. But where is the use of giving
one's broken impressions of such a book? It
ought not to be judged piecemeal. . . .

Yours sincerely, C. Brontë.

131. TO E. G. [G.]

[April 26th, 1852]

358   [. . .] The sketch you give of your work
(respecting which I am, of course, dumb)
seems to me very noble; and its purpose
may be as useful in practical result as it is
high and just in theoretical tendency. Such
a book may restore hope and energy to
many who thought they had forfeited their
right to both; and open a clear course for
honourable effort to some who deemed that
they and all honour had parted company in
this world.

Yet — hear my protest!

Why should she die? Why are we to
shut up the book weeping?

My heart fails me already at the thought
of the pang it will have to undergo. And
yet you must follow the impulse of your
own inspiration. If *that* commands the slay-
ing of the victim, no bystander has a right
to put out his hand to stay the sacrificial
knife: but I hold you a stern priestess in
these matters.[6]   [C. Brontë]

132. TO PATRICK BRONTË [S. H.]

III,   Cliff House, Filey, June 2nd, 1852.
335 Dear Papa, — Thank you for your letter,
which I was so glad to get that I think I
must answer it by return of post. I had ex-

[6] The reference is to Mrs. Gaskell's *Ruth,* published in 1853.

pected one yesterday, and was perhaps a
little unreasonably anxious when disappointed, but the weather has been so *very*
cold that I feared either you were ill or
Martha worse. I hope Martha will take
care of herself. I cannot help feeling a little
uneasy about her.

On the whole, I get on very well here,
but I have not bathed yet, as I am told it is
much too cold and too early in the season.
The sea is very grand. Yesterday it was a
somewhat unusually high tide, and I stood
about an hour on the cliffs yesterday afternoon watching the tumbling in of great
tawny, turbid waves, that made the whole
shore white with foam and filled the air
with a sound hollower and deeper than
thunder. There are so very few visitors at
Filey yet that I and a few sea-birds and
fishing-boats have often the whole expanse
of sea, shore, and cliff to ourselves. When
the tide is out the sands are wide, long, and
smooth, and very pleasant to walk on. When
the high tides are in, not a vestige
of sand remains. I saw a great dog rush
into the sea yesterday, and swim and bear
up against the waves like a seal. I wonder
what Flossy would say to that.

On Sunday afternoon I went to a church
which I should like Mr Nicholls to see. It
was certainly not more than thrice the
length and breadth of our passage, floored
with brick, the walls green with mould, the
pews painted white, but the paint almost /
all worn off with time and decay. At one 336
end there is a little gallery for the singers,
and when these personages stood up to perform, they all turned their backs upon the
congregation, and the congregation turned
their backs on the pulpit and parson. The
effect of this manœuvre was so ludicrous,
I could hardly help laughing; had Mr
Nicholls been there he certainly would
have laughed out. Looking up at the gallery and seeing only the broad backs of the
singers presented to their audience was ex-
cessively grotesque. There is a well-mean-
ing but utterly inactive clergyman at Filey,
and Methodists flourish. . . .

your affectionate daughter, C. Brontë

133. TO E. N. [S. H.]

III,
336
Cliff House, Filey, June 6th, 1852.
Dear Ellen, — I am at Filey utterly alone.
Do not be angry. The step is right. I considered it and resolved on it with due de-
liberation. Change of air was necessary;
there were reasons why I should *not* go to
the South and why I should come here.
On Friday I went to Scarbro', visited the
church-yard and stone — it must be refaced
and re-lettered — there are 5 errors. I gave
the necessary directions — *that* duty then is
done — long has it lain heavy on my mind
— and that was a pilgrimage I felt I could
only make alone.

    . . . Filey seems to me much altered —
more lodging-houses — some of them very
handsome — have been built — the sea has
all its old grandeur — I walk on the sands a
good deal and try *not* to feel desolate and
337 melancholy/ . . . . Believe me — dearest Nell,
Yours faithfully, C. Brontë

134. TO W. S. WILLIAMS [S. H.]

IV,2
July 28th, 1852
3 My dear Sir, — / . . . Last autumn I got on
for a time quickly. I ventured to look forward to spring as the period of publication:
my health gave way; I passed such a winter
as, having been once experienced, will
never be forgotten. The spring proved little
better than a protraction of trial. The warm
weather and a visit to the sea have done
me much good physically; but as yet I have
recovered neither elasticity of animal spirits nor flow of the power of composition.
    . . . I am, yours sincerely, C. Brontë.

135. TO GEORGE SMITH [G.]

363
Oct. 30th, 1852.
My dear Sir, — You must notify honestly
what you think of *Villette* when you have
read it. I can hardly tell you how I hunger
to hear some opinion besides my own, and
how I have sometimes desponded, and almost despaired, because there was no one
to whom to read a line, or of whom to ask
a counsel. *Jane Eyre* was not written under
such circumstances, nor were two-thirds of

Shirley. I got so miserable about it, I could
bear no allusion to the book. It is not finished yet; but now I hope. / As to the 364
anonymous publication, I have this to say:
If the withholding of the author's name
should tend materially to injure the publisher's interest, to interfere with booksell-
ers' orders, etc., I would not press the point;
but if no such detriment is contingent, I
should be most thankful for the sheltering
shadow of an incognito. I seem to dread the
advertisements — the large-lettered "Currer
Bell's New Novel," or "New Work, by the
Author of Jane Eyre." These, however, I
feel well enough, are the transcendental-
isms of a retired wretch; so you must speak
frankly. * * * I shall be glad to see "Colonel
Esmond." My objection to the second volume lay here: I thought it contained decidedly too much history — too little story.

    You will see that *Villette* touches on no
matter of public interest. I cannot write
books handling the topics of the day; it is
of no use trying. Nor can I write a book
for its moral. Nor can I take up a philan-
thropic scheme, though I honour philanthropy; and voluntarily and sincerely veil
my face before such a mighty subject as
that handled in Mrs Beecher Stowe's work,
Uncle Tom's Cabin. To manage these great
matters rightly they must be long and
practically studied — their bearings known
intimately, and their evils felt genuinely;
they must not be taken up as a business
matter and a trading speculation. I doubt
not, Mrs Stowe had felt the iron of slavery /
enter into her heart, from childhood up-365
wards, long before she ever thought of writing books. The feeling throughout her work
is sincere, and not got up. Remember to
be an honest critic of *Villette*, and tell
Mr Williams to be unsparing: not that I
am likely to alter anything, but I want to
know his impressions and yours.

136. TO GEORGE SMITH [G.]

[Haworth, probably Nov., 1852]
    The third volume [of *Esmond*] seemed 364
to me to possess the most sparkle, impetus,
and interest. Of the first and second my

judgment was, that parts of them were admirable; but there was the fault of containing too much History — too little Story. I hold that a work of fiction ought to be a work of creation: that the *real* should be sparingly introduced in pages dedicated to the *ideal*. Plain household bread is a far more wholesome and necessary thing than cake; yet who would like to see the brown loaf placed on the table for dessert? In the second volume, the author gives us an ample supply of excellent brown bread; in his third, only such a portion as gives substance, like the crumbs of bread in a well-made, not too rich, plum-pudding.

[C. Brontë]

The Courtship of Arthur Bell Nicholls, 1852 to 1854

Charlotte's last novel, *Villette*, was received, as Mrs. Gaskell says, "with one burst of acclamation." Yet once again much of Charlotte's pleasure in her triumph was spoiled. After *Jane Eyre*, the harsh reviews of *Wuthering Heights*; after *Villette*, Harriet Martineau's criticisms. Charlotte could forgive a denial of Christian orthodoxy, but not a denial of the primacy of love. Otherwise Charlotte's last visit to London (January, 1853) was not eventful. George Smith was overworked and much taken up with his fiancée. Left on her own, Charlotte's sight-seeing was of a more serious kind — the prisons, the Foundling Hospital, Bethlehem Hospital for the mentally ill, the Bank of England, the Royal Exchange. Once more she must have looked with dread to the future. Smith was to be married, Taylor in India had long since stopped writing. Papa was old and ailing. She probably had not the energy to start another book. She must have still longed, without hope, for a satisfying marriage. Yet the situation with her father's curate was more of an embarrassment than a comfort.

Arthur Bell Nicholls, born of Scottish parents in County Antrim, Ireland (1818) was a graduate of Trinity College, Dublin (1844) and had been curate at Haworth since 1845. In spite of her scorn for curates, Charlotte's first impressions were good: he was respectable and read the service well. Otherwise the serious, rather narrow, puritanical clergyman did not appeal to her, though judging by gossip which reached Ellen, he was attracted to Charlotte from the early stages of their acquaintance.

He was interested in her primarily as a woman, and her fame as a writer probably inhibited his ambitions rather than otherwise, since his stipend was only £100 a year. The sequence of events — his declaration of love, Mr. Brontë's indignation, and Charlotte's and her father's change of heart — is clear enough in the letters which follow. Mr. Nicholls was so discouraged at one point that he offered his services as a missionary to the Society for the Propagation of the Gospel.

137. TO E. N. [S. H.]

December 15th, 1852

IV,28
29 Dear Nell, — ... / I know not whether you have ever observed him [Mr. Nicholls] specially when staying here, your perception is generally quick enough, *too* quick I have sometimes thought, yet as you never said anything, I restrained my own dim misgivings, which could not claim the sure guide of vision. What papa has seen or guessed I will not inquire though I may conjecture. He has minutely noticed all Mr Nicholls's low spirits, all his threats of expatriation, all his symptoms of impaired health, noticed them with little sympathy and much indirect sarcasm. On Monday evening Mr Nicholls was here to tea. I vaguely felt without clearly seeing, as without seeing, I have felt for some time, the meaning of his constant looks, and strange, feverish restraint. After tea I withdrew to the dining-room as usual. As usual, Mr

Nicholls sat with papa till between eight and nine o'clock, I then heard him open the the parlour door as if going. I expected the clash of the front-door. He stopped in the passage: he tapped: like lightning it flashed on me what was coming. He entered – he stood before me. What his words were you can guess; his manner – you can hardly realise – never can I forget it. Shaking from head to foot, looking deadly pale, speaking low, vehemently yet with difficulty – he made me for the first time feel what it costs a man to declare affection where he doubts response.

The spectacle of one ordinarily so statue-like, thus trembling, stirred, and overcome, gave me a kind of strange shock. He spoke of sufferings he had borne for months, of sufferings he could endure no longer, and craved leave for some hope. I could only entreat him to leave me then and promise a reply on the morrow. I asked him if he had spoken to papa. He said, he dared not. I think I half led, half put him out of the room. When he was gone I immediately went to papa, and told him what had taken place. Agitation and anger disproportionate to the occasion ensued; if I had *loved* Mr Nicholls and had heard such epithets applied to him as were used, it would have transported me past my patience; as it was, my blood boiled with a sense of injustice, but papa worked himself into a state not to be trifled with, the veins on his temples started up like whipcord, and his eyes became suddenly bloodshot. I made haste to promise that Mr Nicholls should on the morrow have a distinct refusal.

30 I wrote yesterday and got his note. There is no need to add to this statement any comment. Papa's vehement antipathy to the bare thought of any one thinking of me as a wife, and Mr Nicholls's distress, both give me pain. Attachment to Mr Nicholls you are aware I never entertained, but the poignant pity inspired by his state on Monday evening, by the hurried revelation of his sufferings for many months, is something galling and irksome. That he cared something for me, and wanted me to care for him, I have long suspected, but I did not know the degree or strength of his feelings. Dear Nell, good-bye. – Yours faithfully,   C. Brontë

138. TO E. N. [S. H.]
Haworth, December 18th, '52. IV,30
Dear Nell, – You may well ask, How is it? for I am sure I don't know. This business would seem to me like a dream, did not my reason tell me it has long been brewing. It puzzles me to comprehend how and whence comes this turbulence of feeling.

You ask how papa demeans himself to Mr Nicholls. I only wish you were here to see papa in his present mood: you would know something of him. He just treats him with a hardness not to be bent, and a contempt not to be propitiated. The two have had no interview as yet: all has been done by letter. Papa wrote, I must say, a most cruel note to Mr Nicholls on Wednesday. In his state of mind and health (for the poor man is horrifying his landlady, Martha's mother, by entirely rejecting his meals) I felt that the blow must be parried, and I thought it right to accompany the pitiless despatch by a line to the effect that, while Mr Nicholls must never expect me to reciprocate the feeling he had expressed, yet at the same time I wished to disclaim participation in sentiments calculated to give him pain; and I exhorted him to maintain his courage and spirits. On receiving the two letters, he set off from home. Yesterday came the enclosed brief epistle.

You must understand that a good share of papa's anger arises from the idea, not altogether groundless, that Mr Nicholls has behaved with disingenuousness in so long concealing his aim. . . . I am afraid also that papa thinks a / little too much about 31 his want of money; he says that the match would be a degradation, that I should be throwing myself away, that he expects me, if I marry at all, to do very differently; in short, his manner of viewing the subject is, on the whole, far from being one in which I can sympathise. My own objections arise from a sense of incongruity and uncongeniality in feelings, tastes, principles.

How are you getting on, dear Nell, and how are all at Brookroyd? Remember me kindly to everybody. Yours, wishing devoutly that papa would resume his tranquillity, and Mr N. his beef and pudding,

C. Brontë.

139. TO E. N. [S. H.]

IV,32　　　　　　　　　　　　Jany 2nd, 1853

Dear Nell, — . . . Mr N[icholls] is one of those who attach themselves to very few, whose sensations are close and deep — like an underground stream, running strong but in a narrow channel. He continues restless and ill — he carefully performs the occasional duty — but does not come near the church, procuring a substitute every Sunday.

A few days since he wrote to Papa requesting permission to withdraw his resignation. Papa answered that he should only do so on condition of giving his written promise never again to broach the obnoxious subject either to him or to me. This he has evaded doing, so the matter remains 33 unsettled./. . . Yours faithfully, C. Brontë

140. TO HARRIET MARTINEAU [S. H.]

IV,38　　　　　　　　　　　January 21st, 1853.

I know that you will give me your thoughts upon my book, as frankly as if you spoke to some near relative whose good you preferred to her gratification. I wince under the pain of condemnation, like any other weak structure of flesh and blood; but I love, I honor, I kneel to truth. Let her smite me on the one cheek — good! the tears may spring to the eyes; but courage! there is the other side; hit again, right sharply.

C. Brontë.[7]

---

[7] Miss Martineau's reply to this read in part:

As for the other side of the question, which you so desire to know, I have but one thing to say; but it is not a small one. I do not like the love, either the kind or the degree of it; and its prevalence in the book, and effect on the action of it, help to explain the passages in the reviews which you consulted me about, and seem to afford *some* foundation for the criticisms they offered. H. Martineau. (S. H. IV, 41.)

141. TO MARGARET WOOLER. [G.]

[112, Gloucester Terrace, Jany 27th, 1853]

[My dear Miss Wooler, —] [. . .] I read 375 attentively all you say about Miss Martineau; the sincerity and constancy of your solicitude touch me very much; I should grieve to neglect or oppose your advice, and yet I do not feel it would be right to give Miss Martineau up entirely. There is in her nature much that is very noble; hundreds have forsaken her, more, I fear, in the apprehension that their fair names may suffer, if seen in connection with hers, than from any pure convictions, such as you suggest, of harm consequent on her fatal tenets. With these fair-weather friends I cannot bear to rank; and for her sin, is it not one of those of which God and not man must judge?

To speak the truth, my dear Miss 376 [Wooler], I believe, if you were in my place, and knew Miss Martineau as I do, — if you had shared with me the proofs of her genuine kindliness, and had seen how she secretly suffers from abandonment, — you would be the last to give her up; you would separate the sinner from the sin, and feel as if the right lay rather in quietly adhering to her in her strait, while that adherence is unfashionable and unpopular, than in turning on her your back when the world sets the example. I believe she is one of those whom opposition and desertion make obstinate in error; while patience and tolerance touch her deeply and keenly, and incline her to ask of her own heart whether the course she has been pursuing may not possibly be a faulty course. [. . .]

[I am always, affectionately and respectfully yours, C. Brontë]

142. TO HARRIET MARTINEAU [S. H.]

[Early 1853]

My dear Miss Martineau, — I think I best IV,42 show my sense of the tone and feeling of your last, by immediate compliance with the wish you express that I should send your letter. I enclose it, and have marked with red ink the passage which struck me dumb. All the rest is fair, right, worthy of you, but I protest against this passage; and were I brought up before the bar of all the critics in England to such a charge I should respond, "Not guilty."

I know what *love* is as I understand it; and if man or woman should be ashamed of feeling such love, then is there nothing right, noble, faithful, truthful, unselfish in this earth, as I comprehend rectitude, nobleness, fidelity, truth, and disinterestedness. — Yours sincerely,   C. B.

To differ from you gives me keen pain.[8]

143. TO E. N. [G.]

[Haworth] Feb. 15th, 1853

373 [Dear Ellen, —] [. . .] I got a budget of no less than seven papers yesterday and to-day. The import of all the notices is such as to make my heart swell with thankfulness to Him, who takes note both of suffering, and work, and motives. Papa is pleased too. As to friends in general, I believe I can love them still, without expecting them to take any large share in this sort of gratification. The longer I live, the more plainly I see that gentle must be the strain on fragile human nature; it will not bear much. [. . .][9]

[Yours faithfully, C. Brontë]

144. TO E. N. [S. H.]

IV,49   March 4th, 1853

Dear Ellen, — . . . The Bishop has been, and is gone. . . . My penalty came on in a strong headache and bilious attack as soon as the Bishop was fairly gone: how thankful I was that it had politely waited his departure! I continue mighty stupid to-day: of course, it is the reaction consequent on several days of extra exertion and excitement. It is all very well to talk of receiving a Bishop without trouble, but you *must* prepare for him. We had the parsons to supper as well as to tea. Mr. Nicholls demeaned himself

not quite so pleasantly. I thought he made no effort to / struggle with his dejection; 50 but gave way to it in a manner to draw notice; the Bishop was obviously puzzled by it.[1] Mr Nicholls also showed temper once or twice in speaking to papa. Martha was beginning to tell me of certain "flaysome" looks also, but I desired not to hear of them. The fact is, I shall be most thankful when he is well away; I pity him, but I don't like that dark gloom of his. He dogged me up the lane after the evening service in no pleasant manner, he stopped also in the passage after the Bishop and the other clergy were gone into the room, and it was because I drew away and went upstairs that he gave that look which filled Martha's soul with horror. She, it seems, meantime, was making it her business to watch him from the kitchen door. If Mr Nicholls be a good man at bottom, it is a sad thing that nature has not given him the faculty to put goodness into a more attractive form. . . . Yours faithfully, C. Brontë

145. TO W. S. WILLIAMS [G.]

[Haworth, March 9th, '53]

My dear Sir, — Were a review to appear, 378 inspired with treble their animus, *pray* do not withhold it from me. I like to see the satisfactory notices, — especially I like to carry them to my father; but I *must* see such as are *unsatisfactory* and hostile; these are for my own especial edification; — it is in these I best read public feeling and opinion. To shun examination into the dangerous and disagreeable seems to me cowardly. I long always to know what really *is*, and am only unnerved when kept in the dark. * * *

[Yours sincerely, C. Brontë.]

146. TO GEORGE SMITH [S. H.]

March 26th, 1853 IV,55

My dear Sir, — . . . You express surprise

---

[8] For Miss Martineau's account, see V.

[9] Mrs. Gaskell (p. 373) thought the wistful note of the last sentence was a further reference to Miss Martineau's lack of understanding. Contrast with the favorable reviews is provided in a remark of Matthew Arnold (Letter to Mrs. Forster, April 14, 1853, *Letters of Matthew Arnold*, London: Macmillan, 1895, Vol. I, 34): . . . Why is *Villette*

disagreeable? Because the writer's mind contains nothing but hunger, rebellion, and rage, and therefore that is all she can, in fact, put into her book. No fine writing can hide this thoroughly, and it will be fatal to her in the long run. . . .

[1] Charlotte later discovered that in actual fact the Bishop had surmised what the trouble was and had spoken kindly to the sufferer.

that Miss Martineau should apply to *you* for news of *me*. The fact is, I have never written to her since a letter I received from her about eight weeks ago, just after she had read "Villette." What is more, I do not know when I can bring myself to write again. The differences of feeling between Miss M. and myself are very strong and marked; very wide and irreconcilable. Besides, I fear language does not convey to her apprehension the same meaning as to mine. In short, she has hurt me a good deal, and at present it appears very plain to me that she and I had better not try to be close friends; my wish, indeed, is that she should quietly forget me. . . .

56   Yours sincerely, C. Brontë.

147. TO E. N. [S. H.]

IV,56   Haworth, April 6th, 1853
Dear Ellen, — . . . You ask about Mr Nicholls. I hear he has got a curacy, but do not yet know where. I trust the news is true. He and papa never speak. He seems to pass a desolate life. He has allowed late circumstances so to act on him as to freeze up his manner and overcast his countenance not only to those immediately concerned but to every one. He sits drearily in his rooms. If Mr Croxton or Mr Grant, or any other clergyman calls to see, and as they think, to cheer him, he scarcely speaks. I find he tells them nothing, seeks no confidant, rebuffs all attempts to penetrate his
57 mind. I / own I respect him for this. He still lets Flossy go to his rooms and takes him to walk. He still goes over to see Mr Sowden sometimes, and, poor fellow, that is all. He looks ill and miserable. I think and trust in Heaven that he will be better as soon as he gets away from Haworth. I pity him inexpressibly. We never meet nor speak, nor dare I look at him, silent pity is just all I can give him, and as he knows nothing about that, it does not comfort. He is now grown so gloomy and reserved, that nobody seems to like him, his fellow-curates shun trouble in that shape, the lower orders dislike it. Papa has a perfect antipathy to him, and he, I fear, to papa.

Martha hates him. I think he might almost be *dying* and they would not speak a friendly word to or of him. How much of all this he deserves I can't tell, certainly he never was agreeable or amiable, and is less so now than ever, and alas! I do not know him well enough to be sure there is truth and true affection, or only rancour and corroding disappointment at the bottom of his chagrin. In this state of things I must be, and I am, *entirely passive*. I may be losing the purest gem, and to me far the most precious life can give — a genuine attachment — or I may be escaping the yoke of a morose temper. . . .

        Yours faithfully, C. Brontë.

148. TO MARGARET WOOLER [S. H.]

        Haworth, April 13th, '53 IV,57
My dear Miss Wooler, — . . . / "Extremes 58 meet," says the proverb; in proof whereof I would mention that Miss Martineau finds with "Villette" nearly the same fault as the Puseyites — She accuses me with attacking Popery "with virulence" — of going out of my way to assault it "passionately." In other respects she has shown with reference to the work a spirit so strangely and unexpectedly acrimonious — that I have gathered courage to tell her that the gulf of mutual difference between her and me is so wide and deep — the bridge of union so slight and uncertain — I have come to the conclusion that frequent intercourse would be most perilous and unadvisable — and have begged to adjourn *sine die* my long projected visit to her — Of course she is now very angry — and I know her bitterness will not be short-lived, but it cannot be helped.[2]
yours affectionately and sincerely, C. Brontë 59

149. TO E. N. [S. H.]

        May 16th, 1853 IV,64
Dear Ellen, — . . . / Yesterday was a strange 65 sort of a day at church. It seems as if I were to be punished for my doubts about the nature and truth of poor Mr. Nicholls's regard. Having ventured on Whit-Sunday

2 Compare Miss Martineau's account, Section V.

to stop to the sacrament,[3] I got a lesson not to be repeated. He struggled, faltered, then lost command over himself, stood before my eyes and in the sight of all the communicants, white, shaking, voiceless. Papa was not there, thank God! Joseph Redman spoke some words to him. He made a great effort, but could only with difficulty whisper and falter through the service. I suppose he thought this would be the last time; he goes either this week or the next. I heard the women sobbing round, and I could not quite check my own tears. What had happened was reported to papa either by Joseph Redman or John Brown; it excited only anger, and such expressions as "unmanly driveller." Compassion or relenting is no more to be looked for from Papa than sap from firewood.

. . . Yours faithfully, C. Brontë

150. TO E. N. [S. H.]

IV,68 Haworth, May 27th, 1853
Dear Ellen, — . . . The biscuits came all right, but I believe you have sent about twice the quantity I ordered. You *must* tell me how much they cost, dear Nell, or I shall never be able to ask you to render me a similar service again. . . .

You will want to know about the leave-taking; the whole matter is but a painful subject, but I must treat it briefly. The testimonial was presented in a public meeting. Mr T. and Mr Grant were there. Papa was not very well and I advised him to stay away, which he did. As to the last Sunday, it was a cruel struggle. Mr Nicholls ought not to have had to take any duty.

He left Haworth this morning at 6 o'clock. Yesterday evening he called to render into Papa's hands the deeds of the National School, and to say good-bye. They were busy cleaning, washing the paint, etc., in the dining-room, so he did not find me there. I would not go into the parlour to speak to him in Papa's presence. He went out thinking he was not to see me, and indeed, till the very last moment, I thought it best not. But perceiving that he stayed long before going out at the gate, and remembering his long grief, I took courage and went out trembling and miserable. I found him leaning against the garden door in a paroxysm of anguish, sobbing as women never sob. Of course I went straight / to him. 69 Very few words were interchanged, those few barely articulate. Several things I should have liked to ask him were swept entirely from my memory. Poor fellow! But he wanted such hope and such encouragement as I *could* not give him. Still I trust he must know now that I am not cruelly blind and indifferent to his constancy and grief. For a few weeks he goes to the South of England — afterwards he takes a curacy somewhere in Yorkshire, but I don't know where.

Papa has been far from strong lately. I dare not mention Mr Nicholls's name to him. He speaks of him quietly and without opprobrium to others, but to me he is implacable on the matter. However, he is gone — gone — and there's an end of it. I see no chance of hearing a word about him in future, unless some stray shred of intelligence comes through Mr Sowden or some other second-hand source. In all this it is not I who am to be pitied at all, and of course nobody pities me. They all think, in Haworth, that I have disdainfully refused him, etc. If pity would do Mr Nicholls any good, he ought to have and I believe has it. They may abuse me if they will; whether they do or not I can't tell.

Write soon and say how your prospects proceed. I trust they will daily brighten. — Yours faithfully, C. Brontë.

151. TO E. G. [G.]

[Haworth] July 9th, 1853 382
[My dear Mrs. Gaskell, —] Thank you for your letter; it was as pleasant as a quiet chat, as welcome as spring showers, as reviving as a friend's visit; in short, it was very like a page of *Cranford*. * * *

A thought strikes me. Do you, who have 383 so many friends, — so large a circle of acquaintance, — find it easy, when you sit

[3] Remain in church to receive communion.

down to write, to isolate yourself from all those ties, and their sweet associations, so as to be your *own woman,* uninfluenced or swayed by the consciousness of how your work may affect other minds; what blame or what sympathy it may call forth? Does no luminous cloud ever come between you and the severe Truth, as you know it in your own secret and clear-seeing soul? In a word, are you never tempted to make your characters more amiable than the Life, by the inclination to assimilate your thoughts to the thoughts of those who always *feel* kindly, but sometimes fail to *see* justly? Don't answer the question; it is not intended to be answered. * * *

[Yours with true attachment, C. Brontë]

152. TO E. N. [S. H.]

IV,
112
Haworth, April 11th, 1854

Dear Ellen, — . . . Mr Nicholls came on Monday, and was here all last week. Matters have progressed thus since July. He renewed his visit in September, but then matters so fell out that I saw little of him. He continued to write. The correspondence pressed on my mind. I grew very miserable in keeping it from Papa. At last sheer pain made me gather courage to break it — I told all. It was very hard and rough work at the time — but the issue after a few days was that I obtained leave to continue the communication. Mr N[icholls] came in Jan [uary]; he was ten days in the neighbourhood. I saw much of him; I had stipulated with Papa for opportunity to become better acquainted — I had it, and all I learnt inclined me to esteem and if not love — at least affection. Still papa was very, very hostile — bitterly unjust.

I told Mr. Nicholls the great obstacles that lay in his way. He has persevered. The result of this, his last visit, is that Papa's consent is gained — that his respect, I believe, is won, for Mr. Nicholls has in all things proved himself disinterested and forbearing. He has shown, too, that while his feelings are exquisitely keen — he can freely forgive. Certainly I must respect him, nor can I withhold from him more than mere cool respect. In fact, dear Ellen, I am engaged. . . .

For myself, dear Ellen, while thankful to One who seems to have guided me through much difficulty, much and deep distress and perplexity of mind, I am still very calm, very inexpectant. What I taste of happiness is of the soberest order. I trust to love my husband — I am grateful for his tender love to me. I believe him to be an affectionate, a conscientious, a high-principled man; and if, with all this, I should yield to regrets, that fine / talents, congenial 113 tastes and thoughts are not added, it seems to me I should be most presumptuous and thankless.

Providence offers me this destiny. Doubtless then it is the best for me. Nor do I shrink from wishing those dear to me one not less happy.

. . . Yours affectionately,
C. Brontë

CHARLOTTE'S MARRIAGE AND DEATH, 1854 TO 1855

Charlotte's many misgivings were finally overcome and the wedding took place in June 1854 (see Mrs. Gaskell's account, V). Charlotte seems to have enjoyed the honeymoon drive through the romantic mountain scenery of North Wales, and she was unexpectedly pleased with her Irish in-laws. She probably anticipated that they would be poor like her father's people, but they were comfortably off and respectable. "I like my new relations," she wrote Miss Wooler, "My dear husband too appears in a new light here in his own country."

The nicest thing about Charlotte's married life is her astonished and growing pleasure in Mr. Nicholls' affection for her. His tenderness, his tact, his protectiveness, even his possessiveness evidently surprised and delighted her more than she had thought possible. The joy of being loved and looked after even by a perfectly ordinary person was evidently a revelation to her. So far the misgivings about the match — Mrs. Gaskell's, Ellen's, her father's, her own — seemed unnecessary. Whether if she had lived she might have felt she had paid dearly for "the purest gem life can give — genuine attachment" is only a matter for speculation.

Tragically, in November (see letter of Nov. 29) Charlotte caught cold. This was such a common occurrence with her that her family did not at first realize that she too was falling a victim to the disease which had carried off her sisters and her brother. She died March 31, 1855. The doctor's certificate reads "phthisis," *i.e.,* pulmonary tuberculosis. No doubt the exhaustion from the years of strain and sorrow and the complications attendant upon her pregnancy played their part in her decline.

Mr. Nicholls was faithful to his promise. As long as the Reverend Patrick Brontë lived, he shouldered the full responsibility for the parish of Haworth. Later he married again and retired to live in Ireland, where he died over fifty years after his famous wife.

IV,
114
115

153. TO E. N. [S. H.]

April 15th, '54

My own dear Nell, — ... / I suppose I shall have to go to Leeds. My purchases cannot be either expensive or extensive. You must just resolve in your head the bonnets and dresses; something that can be turned to decent use and worn after the wedding-day will be best I think.

I wrote immediately to Miss Wooler and received a truly kind letter from her this morning. If you think she would like to come to the marriage, I will not fail to ask her.

Papa's mind seems wholly changed about the matter, and he has said both to me and when I was not there, how much happier he feels since he allowed all to be settled. It is a wonderful relief for me to hear him treat the thing rationally, and quietly and amicably, to talk over with him themes on which once I dared not touch. He is rather anxious things should get forward now, and takes quite an interest in the arrangement of preliminaries. His health improves daily, though this east wind still keeps up a slight irritation in the throat and chest.

The feeling which had been disappointed in Papa was *ambition,* paternal pride — ever a restless feeling, as we all know. Now that this unquiet spirit is exorcised, justice, which was once quite forgotten, is once more listened to; and affection, I hope, resumes some power.

My hope is that in the end this arrange-ment will turn out more truly to Papa's advantage than any other it was in my power to achieve. Mr Nicholls only in his last letter refers touchingly to his earnest desire to prove his gratitude to Papa, by offering support and consolation to his declining age. This will not be mere *talk* with him; he is no talker, no dealer in professions. ...

— Yours affectionately, C. Brontë.

154. TO GEORGE SMITH [S. H.]

April 25th, 1854.

IV,
118

My dear Sir, — Thank you for your congratulations and good wishes; if these last are realised but in part — I shall be very thankful. ... / The step in contemplation is no hasty one; on the gentleman's side, at least, it has been meditated for many years, and I hope that, in at last acceding to it, I am acting right; it is what I earnestly wish to do. My future husband is a clergyman. He was for eight years my Father's curate. He left because the idea of this marriage was not entertained as he wished. His departure was regarded by the parish as a calamity, for he had devoted himself to his duties with no ordinary diligence. Various circumstances have led my Father to consent to his return, nor can I deny that my own feelings have been much impressed and changed by the nature and strength of the qualities brought out in the course of his long attachment. I fear I must accuse myself of having formerly done him less than justice. However, he is to come back now.

119

He has foregone many chances of preferment to return to the obscure village of
Haworth. I believe I do right in marrying
him. I mean to try to make him a good
wife. There has been heavy anxiety — but
I begin to hope all will end for the best.
My expectations however are very subdued
— very different, I dare say, to what *yours*
were before you were married. Care and
Fear stands so close to Hope, I sometimes
scarcely can see her for the shadows they
cast. And yet I am thankful too, and the
doubtful Future must be left with Providence.

On one feature in the marriage I can
dwell with unmingled satisfaction, with a
certainty of being right. It takes nothing
from the attention I owe to my Father. I
am not to leave him — my future husband
consents to come here — thus Papa secures
by the step a devoted and reliable assistant
in his old age.

There can, of course, be no reason for
withholding the intelligence from your
Mother and sisters; remember me kindly to
them whenever you write.

. . . In the course of the year that is gone,
Cornhill and London have receded a long
way from me; the links of communication
have waxed very frail and few. It must be
so in this world. All things considered, I
don't wish it otherwise. — Yours sincerely,
C. Brontë.

155.   TO E. N. [S. H.]

IV,
125
Haworth, May 14th, 1854.
My dear Ellen, — . . .

It was just 7 o'clock when I reached
home. I found Papa well. It seems he has
been particularly well during my absence
— but to-day he is a little sickly and only
preached once: however he is better again
this evening. . . .

Dear Ellen, I could not leave you with a
very quiet mind — or take away a satisfied
feeling about you — Not that I think that
bad cough lodged in a dangerous quarter —
but it shakes your system, wears you out
and makes you look ill. . . .

Take care of it — do dear Ellen avoid the
evening air for a time — and even in the
day-time — keep in the house when the
weather is cold. Observe these precautions
till the cough is quite gone — and you regain strength and feel better able to bear
chill and change. Believe me it does not
suit you at present to be much exposed to
variations of temperature. . . .

faithfully yours, C. Brontë 126

156.   TO E. N. [G.]

Haworth, May 22nd [1854] 393
[Dear Ellen, —] [. . .] Since I came home I
have been very busy stitching; the little
new room is got into order, and the green
and white curtains are up; they exactly suit
the papering, and look neat and clean
enough. I had a letter a day or two since,
announcing that Mr. Nicholls comes to-
morrow. I feel anxious about him; more
anxious on one point than I dare quite express to myself. It seems he has again been
suffering sharply from his rheumatic affection. I hear this not from himself, but from
another quarter. He was ill while I was in
Manchester and [Brookroyd]. He uttered
no complaint to me; dropped no hint on
the subject. Alas! he was hoping he had
got the better of it, and I know how this
contradiction of his hopes will sadden him.
For unselfish reasons he did so earnestly
wish this complaint might / not become 394
chronic. I fear — I fear; [. . .] but if he is
doomed to suffer, so much the more will he
need care and help. Well! come what may,
God help and strengthen both him and me!
I look forward to to-morrow with a mixture
of impatience and anxiety. [. . .]

[Yours affectionately, C. Brontë]

157.   TO E. N. [G.]

[June 16th, '54]
[My dear Ellen, —] . . . Mr. Nicholls is a 394
kind, considerate fellow. With all his masculine faults, he enters into my wishes about
having the thing done quietly, in a way that
makes me grateful; and if nobody interferes
and spoils his arrangements, he will manage it so that not a soul in Haworth shall
be aware of the day. He is so thoughtful,

too, about "the ladies," — that is, you and Miss Wooler. Anticipating, too, the very arrangements I was going to propose to him about providing for your departure, etc. . . .

[believe me faithfully yours, C. Brontë]

158. TO CATHERINE WINKWORTH [s. h.]

IV, 137

Cork, July 27th, 1854.

Dear Katie, — . . . Yes — I am married — a month ago this very day I changed my name — the same day we went to Conway — stayed a few days in Wales — then crossed from Holyhead to Dublin — after a short sojourn in the capital — went to the coast — such a wild, iron-bound coast — with such an ocean-view as I had not yet seen and such battling of waves with rocks as I had never imagined.

My husband is not a poet or a poetical man — and one of my grand doubts before marriage was about "congenial tastes" and so on. The first morning we went out on to the cliffs and saw the Atlantic coming in all white foam, I did not know whether /
138 I should get leave or time to take the matter in my own way. I did not want to talk — but I *did* want to look and be silent. Having hinted a petition, licence was not refused — covered with a rug to keep off the spray I was allowed to sit where I chose — and he only interrupted me when he thought I crept too near the edge of the cliff. So far he is always good in this way — and this protection which does not interfere or pretend is I believe a thousand times better than any half sort of pseudo sympathy. I will try with God's help to be as indulgent to him whenever indulgence is needed.

We have been to Killarney — I will not describe it a bit. We saw and went through the Gap of Dunloe. A sudden glimpse of a very grim phantom came on us in the Gap. The guide had warned me to alight from my horse as the path was now very broken and dangerous — I did not feel afraid and declined — we passed the dangerous part — the horse trembled in every limb and

slipped once but did not fall — soon after she (it was a mare) started and was unruly for a minute — however I kept my seat — my husband went to her head and led her — suddenly without any apparent cause — she seemed to go mad — reared, plunged — I was thrown on the stones right under her — my husband did not see that I had fallen — he still held her — I saw and felt her kick, plunge, trample round me. I had my thoughts about the moment — its consequences — my husband — my father — When my plight was seen, the struggling creature was let loose — she sprung over me. I was lifted off the stones neither bruised by the fall nor touched by the mare's hoofs. Of course the only feeling left was gratitude for more sakes than my own.

. . . I go home soon; goodbye, dear Katie.

. . . C. B. Nicholls.

159. TO E. N. [s. h.]

Haworth, Aug. 9th, 1854 IV, 145

Dear Ellen, — . . . Since I came home I have not had an unemployed moment; my life is changed indeed — to be wanted continually — to be constantly called for and occupied seems so strange: yet it is a marvellously good thing. As yet I don't quite understand how some wives grow so selfish — As far as my experience of matrimony goes — I think it tends to draw you out of, and away from yourself.

. . . Dear Nell — during the last 6 weeks — the colour of my thoughts is a good deal changed: I know more of the realities of life than I once did. I think many false ideas are propagated perhaps unintentionally. I think those married women who indiscriminately urge their acquaintance to marry — much to blame. For my part — I can only say with deeper sincerity and fuller sig-/nificance — what I always said 146 in theory — Wait God's will. Indeed — indeed Nell — it is a solemn and strange and perilous thing for a woman to become a wife. Man's lot is far — far different. Tell me when you think you can come. . . .

Yours faithfully, C. B. Nicholls

160. TO MARGARET WOOLER [G.]

[Haworth, August 22nd, 1954]

396 [My dear Miss Wooler, —] [. . .] I really seem to have had scarcely a spare moment since that dim quiet June morning, when you, [Ellen], and myself all walked down to Haworth Church. Not that I have been wearied or oppressed; but the fact is, my time is not my own now; somebody else wants a good portion of it, and says, "we must do so and so." We *do* so and so, accordingly; and it generally seems the right thing. * * * We have had many callers from a distance, and latterly some little occupation in the way of preparing for a small village entertainment. Both Mr. Nicholls and myself wished much to make some response for the hearty welcome and general goodwill shown by the parishioners on his return; accordingly, the Sunday and day scholars and teachers, the church-ringers, singers, etc., to the number of five hundred, were asked to tea and supper in the School-room. They seemed to enjoy it much, and it was very pleasant to see their happiness. One of the villagers, in proposing my husband's health, described him as a *"consistent Christian and a kind gentleman."* I own the words touched me deeply, and I thought (as I know *you* would have thought had you been present) that to merit and win such a character was better than to earn either wealth, or fame, or power. I am disposed to echo that high but simple eulogium. * * * My dear father was not well when we returned from Ireland. I am, however, most thankful to say that he is better now. May God preserve him to us yet for some years! The wish for his continued life, together with a certain solicitude for his happiness and health, seems, I scarcely know why, even stronger in me now than before I was married. Papa has taken no duty since we returned; and each time I see Mr. Nicholls put on gown or surplice, I feel comforted to think that this marriage has secured papa good aid in his old age. [. . .] [Yours always with true respect and warm affection,

C. B. Nicholls]

161. TO E. N. [S. H.]

Haworth, October 31st, 1854 IV,

Dear Ellen, — . . . Dear Ellen, Arthur com- 156 plains that you do not distinctly promise to burn my letters as you receive them. He says you must / give him a plain pledge to 157 that effect, or he will read every line I write and elect himself censor of our correspondence.

He says women are most rash in letter-writing, they think only of the trustworthiness of their immediate friend, and do not look to contingencies; a letter may fall into any hand. You must give the promise, I believe, at least he says so, with his best regards. . . . Write him out his promise on a separate slip of paper, in a legible hand, and send it in your next. . . .

yours faithfully, C. B. Nicholls

162. TO MARGARET WOOLER [S. H.]   IV,

Haworth, Novbr 15th, 1854 159

My dear Miss Wooler, — . . . / We are all — 160 indeed — pretty well — and for my own part — it is long since I have known such comparative immunity from head-ache, sickness and indigestion, as during the last three months.

My life is different to what it used to be. May God make me thankful for it! I have a good, kind attached husband and every day makes my own attachment to him stronger. . . .   Yours faithfully and affectionately, C. B. Nicholls

163. TO E. N. [G.]

[Haworth] Nov. 29 [1854]

[Dear Ellen, —] I intended to have written 398 a line yesterday, but just as I was sitting down for the purpose, Arthur called to me to take a walk. We set off, not intending to go far; but, though wild and cloudy, it was fair in the morning; when we had got about half a mile on the moors, Arthur suggested the idea of the waterfall; after the melted snow, he said, it would be fine. I had often wished to see it in its winter power, — so we walked on. It was fine indeed; a perfect torrent racing over the rocks, white and beautiful! It began to rain while

we were watching it, and we returned home under a streaming sky. However, I enjoyed the walk inexpressibly, and would not have missed the spectacle on any account. [. . .]
[yours faithfully, C. B. Nicholls]

164. TO E. N. [S. H.]

IV,   Haworth, December 7th, 1854
164 Dear Ellen, — I shall not get leave to go to Brookroyd before Christmas now, so do not expect me. For my own part I really should have no fear, and if it just depended on me, I should come; but these matters are not quite in my power now, another must be consulted, and where his wish and judgment have decided bias to a particular course, I make no stir, but just adopt it. Arthur is sorry to disappoint both you and me, but it is his fixed wish that a few weeks should be allowed yet to elapse before we meet. Probably he is confirmed in this desire by my having a cold at present. I did not achieve the walk to the waterfall with impunity, though I changed my wet things 165 immediately on re-/turning home, yet I felt a chill afterwards, and the same night had sore throat and cold; however, I am better now, but not quite well. . . . I am writing in haste. It is almost inexplicable to me that I seem so often hurried now, but the fact is, whenever Arthur is in, I must have occupations in which he can share, or which will not at least divert my attention from him; thus a multitude of little matters get put off till he goes out, and then I am quite busy. Good-bye, dear Ellen, I hope we shall meet soon. — Yours faithfully,   C. B. Nicholls.

165. TO LAETITIA WHEELWRIGHT [G.]

399   Feb. 15th [1855]
[Dear Laetitia, —] A few lines of acknowl-edgment your letter *shall* have, whether well or ill. At present I am confined to my bed with illness, and have been so for three weeks. Up to this period, since my marriage, I have had excellent health. My husband and I live at home with my father; of course, I could not leave *him*. He is pretty well, better than last summer. No kinder, better husband than mine, it seems to me, there can be in the world. I do not want now for kind companionship in health and the tenderest nursing in sickness. Deeply I sympathise in all you tell me about Dr. W. and your excellent mother's / anxiety. I trust he will not risk 400 another operation. I cannot write more now; for I am much reduced and very weak. God bless you all. — Yours affectionately,   C. B. Nicholls.

166. TO E. N. [G.]

[Haworth, February 21, 1855]
[My dear Ellen—] I must write one line out 399 of my dreary bed. The news of [Mercy's] probable recovery came like a ray of joy to me. I am not going to talk of my sufferings — it would be useless and painful. I want to give you an assurance, which I know will comfort you — and that is, that I find in my husband the tenderest nurse, the kindest support, the best earthly comfort that ever woman had. His patience never fails, and it is tried by sad days and broken nights. Write and tell me about Mrs. ——'s case; how long was she ill, and in what way? Papa — thank God! — is better. Our poor old Tabby is *dead* and *buried*. Give my kind love to Miss Wooler. May God comfort and help you.   C. B. Nicholls.[4]

[4] For other accounts of Charlotte's last months, see V.

BIOGRAPHICAL NOTICE OF ELLIS AND ACTON BELL

Prefaced to the second edition of *Wuthering Heights* and *Agnes Grey,* 3 vols., 1850; dated Sept. 19, 1850. This text is taken from the Modern Library College Edition of *Wuthering Heights,* ed. Royal A. Gettman, New York: Random House, 1950, pp. xix–xxvi.

This memoir, which cost Charlotte so much anguish to write, is of first importance since she must have known her shy sisters better than anyone. Even so, do not take all her judgments at face value. Some critics detect a tendency to undervalue Anne's talent and to misinterpret Emily's character. Perhaps Charlotte was too unlike "the sphinx of modern literature" to understand her. Her remarks on *Wuthering Heights* here and in her Editor's Preface to the novels are in some respects an apologia and should be compared to the reviews. Yet when all is said and done, the last paragraph reminds us that Charlotte was Emily's first admirer and remained to the end of her days the staunchest defender both of her book and her poems. She alone in her time saw that Emily was greater than herself.

xix IT has been thought that all the works published under the names of Currer, Ellis, and Acton Bell, were, in reality, the production of one person. This mistake I endeavoured to rectify by a few words of disclaimer prefixed to the third edition of "Jane Eyre." These, too, it appears, failed to gain general credence, and now, on the occasion of a reprint of "Wuthering Heights" I am advised distinctly to state how the case really stands.

Indeed, I feel myself that it is time the obscurity attending those two names — Ellis and Acton — was done away. The little mystery, which formerly yielded some harmless pleasure, has lost its interest; circumstances are changed. It becomes, then, my duty to explain briefly the origin and authorship of the books written by Currer, Ellis, and Acton Bell.

About five years ago, my two sisters and myself, after a somewhat prolonged period of separation, found ourselves reunited, and at home. Resident in a remote district, where education had made little progress, and where, consequently, there was no inducement to seek social intercourse beyond

xx our / own domestic circle, we were wholly dependent on ourselves and each other, on books and study, for the enjoyments and occupations of life. The highest stimulus, as well as the liveliest pleasure we had known from childhood upwards, lay in attempts at literary composition; formerly we used to show each other what we wrote, but of late years this habit of communication and consultation had been discontinued; hence it ensued, that we were mutually ignorant of the progress we might respectively have made.

One day, in the autumn of 1845, I accidentally lighted on a Ms. volume of verse in my sister Emily's handwriting. Of course, I was not surprised, knowing that she could and did write verse: I looked it over, and something more than surprise seized me, — a deep conviction that these were not common effusions, nor at all like the poetry women generally write. I thought them condensed and terse, vigorous and genuine. To my ear, they had also a peculiar music — wild, melancholy, and elevating.

My sister Emily was not a person of demonstrative character, nor one on the recesses of whose mind and feelings, even those nearest and dearest to her could, with impunity, intrude unlicensed; it took hours to reconcile her to the discovery I had made, and days to persuade her that such poems merited publication. I knew, however, that a mind like hers could not be without some latent spark of honourable ambition, and refused to be discouraged in my attempts to fan that spark to flame.

Meantime, my younger sister quietly produced some of her own compositions, intimating that, since Emily's had given me pleasure, I might like to look at hers. I could not but be a partial judge, yet I thought that these verses, too, had a sweet and sincere pathos of their own.

We had very early cherished the dream of one day becoming authors. This dream, never relinquished even when distance divided and absorbing tasks occupied us,

now suddenly acquired strength and con-
xxi sistency: it took the character of a / resolve.
We agreed to arrange a small selection of
our poems, and, if possible, get them
printed. Averse to personal publicity, we
veiled our own names under those of
Currer, Ellis, and Acton Bell; the ambigu-
ous choice being dictated by a sort of conscientious scruple at assuming Christian
names positively masculine, while we did
not like to declare ourselves women, because — without at that time suspecting that
our mode of writing and thinking was not
what is called "feminine" — we had a vague
impression that authoresses are liable to be
looked on with prejudice; we had noticed
how critics sometimes use for their chastisement the weapon of personality, and for
their reward, a flattery which is not true
praise.

The bringing out of our little book was
hard work. As was to be expected, neither
we nor our poems were at all wanted; but
for this we had been prepared at the outset;
though inexperienced ourselves, we had
read the experience of others. The great
puzzle lay in the difficulty of getting answers of any kind from the publishers to
whom we applied. Being greatly harassed
by this obstacle, I ventured to apply to the
Messrs. Chambers, of Edinburgh, for a
word of advice; *they* may have forgotten
the circumstance, but *I* have not, for from
them I received a brief and business-like,
but civil and sensible reply, on which we
acted, and at last made a way.

The book was printed: it is scarcely
known, and all of it that merits to be
known are the poems of Ellis Bell. The
fixed conviction I held, and hold, of the
worth of these poems has not indeed received the confirmation of much favourable
criticism; but I must retain it notwithstanding.

Ill-success failed to crush us: the mere
effort to succeed had given a wonderful zest
to existence; it must be pursued. We each
set to work on a prose tale: Ellis Bell produced "Wuthering Heights," Acton Bell
"Agnes Grey," and Currer Bell also wrote

a narrative in one volume. These Mss.
were perseveringly obtruded upon various
publishers for the space of a year and a
half; usually, their fate was an ignominious
and abrupt dismissal.

At last "Wuthering Heights" and "Agnes xxii
Grey" were accepted on terms somewhat
impoverishing to the two authors; Currer
Bell's book found acceptance nowhere, nor
any acknowledgment of merit, so that something like the chill of despair began to
invade his heart. As a forlorn hope, he
tried one publishing house more — Messrs.
Smith, Elder and Co. Ere long, in a much
shorter space than that on which experience had taught him to calculate — there
came a letter, which he opened in the
dreary expectation of finding two hard
hopeless lines, intimating that Messrs.
Smith, Elder and Co. "were not disposed
to publish the Ms.," and, instead, he took
out of the envelope a letter of two pages.
He read it trembling. It declined, indeed,
to publish that tale, for business reasons,
but it discussed its merits and demerits so
courteously, so considerately, in a spirit so
rational, with a discrimination so enlight-
ened, that this very refusal cheered the
author better than a vulgarly expressed
acceptance would have done. It was added,
that a work in three volumes would meet
with careful attention.

I was just then completing "Jane Eyre,"
at which I had been working while the
one-volume tale was plodding its weary
round in London: in three weeks I sent it
off; friendly and skilful hands took it in.
This was in the commencement of September 1847; it came out before the close of
October following, while "Wuthering
Heights" and "Agnes Grey," my sisters'
works, which had already been in the
press for months, still lingered under a
different management.

They appeared at last. Critics failed to
do them justice. The immature but very
real powers revealed in "Wuthering
Heights" were scarcely recognised; its import and nature were misunderstood; the
identity of its author was misrepresented;

it was said that this was an earlier and ruder attempt of the same pen which had produced "Jane Eyre." Unjust and grievous error! We laughed at it at first, but I deeply lament it now. Hence, I fear, arose a prejudice against the book. That writer who could attempt to palm off an inferior xxiii and imma-/ture production under cover of one successful effort, must indeed be unduly eager after the secondary and sordid result of authorship, and pitiably indifferent to its true and honourable meed. If reviewers and the public truly believed this, no wonder that they looked darkly on the cheat.

Yet I must not be understood to make these things subject for reproach or complaint; I dare not do so; respect for my sister's memory forbids me. By her any such querulous manifestation would have been regarded as an unworthy and offensive weakness.

It is my duty, as well as my pleasure, to acknowledge one exception to the general rule of criticism. One writer [See the *Palladium* for September, 1850.], endowed with the keen vision and fine sympathies of genius, has discerned the real nature of "Wuthering Heights," and has, with equal accuracy, noted its beauties and touched on its faults. . . .

Yet even the writer to whom I allude shares the mistake about the authorship, and does me the injustice to suppose that there was equivoque in my former rejection of this honour (as an honour I regard it). May I assure him that I would scorn in this and in every other case to deal in equivoque; I believe language to have been given us to make our meaning clear, and not to wrap it in dishonest doubt.

"The Tenant of Wildfell Hall," by Acton Bell, had likewise an unfavourable reception. At this I cannot wonder. The choice of subject was an entire mistake. xxiv Nothing less congru-/ous with the writer's nature could be conceived. The motives which dictated this choice were pure, but, I think, slightly morbid. She had, in the course of her life, been called on to contemplate, near at hand, and for a long time, the terrible effects of talents misused and faculties abused; hers was naturally a sensitive, reserved, and dejected nature; what she saw sank very deeply into her mind; it did her harm. She brooded over it till she believed it to be a duty to reproduce every detail (of course with fictitious characters, incidents, and situations), as a warning to others. She hated her work, but would pursue it. When reasoned with on the subject, she regarded such reasonings as a temptation to self-indulgence. She must be honest: she must not varnish, soften, or conceal. This well-meant resolution brought on her misconstruction, and some abuse, which she bore, as it was her custom to bear whatever was unpleasant, with mild, steady patience. She was a very sincere and practical Christian, but the tinge of religious melancholy communicated a sad shape to her brief, blameless life.

Neither Ellis nor Acton allowed herself for one moment to sink under want of encouragement; energy nerved the one, and endurance upheld the other. They were both prepared to try again; I would fain think that hope and the sense of power was yet strong within them. But a great change approached: affliction came in that shape which to anticipate is dread: to look back on, grief. In the very heat and burden of the day, the labourers failed over their work.

My sister Emily first declined. The details of her illness are deep-branded in my memory, but to dwell on them, either in thought or narrative, is not in my power. Never in all her life had she lingered over any task that lay before her, and she did not linger now. She sank rapidly. She made haste to leave us. Yet, while physically she perished, mentally she grew stronger than we had yet known her. Day by day, when I saw with what a front she met suffering, I looked on her with an anguish of wonder and love. I have seen nothing like it; but, indeed, I have never seen her parallel in anything. Stronger than a man, / simpler than a child, her xxv nature stood alone. The awful point was, that while full of ruth for others, on herself she had no pity; the spirit was inexorable to the flesh; from the trembling hand, the unnerved limbs, the faded eyes, the same service was exacted as they had rendered in health. To stand by and witness this, and not dare to remonstrate, was a pain no words can render.

Two cruel months of hope and fear passed painfully by, and the day came at last when the terrors and pains of death were to be undergone by this treasure, which had grown dearer and dearer to our hearts as it wasted before our eyes. Towards the decline of that day, we had nothing of Emily but her mortal remains as consumption left them. She died December 19, 1848.

We thought this enough: but we were utterly and presumptuously wrong. She was not buried ere Anne fell ill. She had not been committed to the grave a fortnight, before we received distinct intimation that it was necessary to prepare our minds to see the younger sister go after the elder. Accordingly, she followed in the same path with slower step, and with a patience that equalled the other's fortitude. I have said that she was religious, and it was by leaning on those Christian doctrines in which she firmly believed that she found support through her most painful journey. I witnessed their efficacy in her latest hour and greatest trial, and must bear my testimony to the calm triumph with which they brought her through. She died May 28, 1849.

What more shall I say about them? I cannot and need not say much more. In externals, they were two unobtrusive women; a perfectly secluded life gave them retiring manners and habits. In Emily's nature the extremes of vigour and simplicity seemed to meet. Under an unsophisticated culture, inartificial tastes, and an unpretending outside, lay a secret power and fire that might have informed the brain and kindled the veins of a hero; but she had no worldly wisdom; her powers were unadapted to the practical business of life: she would fail to defend her most manifest rights, to consult her most / legitimate advantage. xxvi An interpreter ought always to have stood between her and the world. Her will was not very flexible, and it generally opposed her interest. Her temper was magnanimous, but warm and sudden; her spirit altogether unbending.

Anne's character was milder and more subdued; she wanted the power, the fire, the originality of her sister, but was well endowed with quiet virtues of her own. Long-suffering, self-denying, reflective, and intelligent, a constitutional reserve and taciturnity placed and kept her in the shade, and covered her mind, and especially her feelings, with a sort of nun-like veil, which was rarely lifted. Neither Emily nor Anne was learned; they had no thought of filling their pitchers at the well-spring of other minds; they always wrote from the impulse of nature, the dictates of intuition, and from such stores of observation as their limited experience had enabled them to amass. I may sum up all by saying, that for strangers they were nothing, for superficial observers less than nothing; but for those who had known them all their lives in the intimacy of close relationship, they were genuinely good and truly great.

This notice has been written, because I felt it a sacred duty to wipe the dust off their gravestones, and leave their dear names free from soil.

September 19, 1850.   Currer Bell

III. Papers and Poems of Emily Jane Brontë and Anne Brontë

In his old age Charlotte's husband, Arthur Bell Nicholls, found in a tiny black box four papers carefully folded into squares smaller than a nickel. He sent them to the official Brontë biographer, Clement Shorter, commenting, "They are sad reading, poor girls." Presumably he meant that it was sad that their cheerfully expressed hopes for happiness and prosperity had not been fulfilled, for the early papers in particular are anything but sad reading, but delightul, frivolous, casual, and uninhibited. They speak well for the atmosphere of Haworth parsonage. Notice the variety of interests suggested and the mingling of the real and the imaginary.

Besides these papers and the published poems and novels, very few documents by Emily and Anne survive. There are three brief notes from Emily to Ellen Nussey, all having to do with Charlotte's absence from home; one hopes that Charlotte will "make the most of the next seven days and return stout and hearty." Few people knew Anne at all well (Ellen was one) and almost no one really knew Emily. Anne seems to have been closest to her. Together from childhood to at least 1845 they played the Gondal game and wrote the Gondal stories. Emily was strong-willed, independent, thoroughly self-sufficient. Anne, outwardly docile, conventional, and self-effacing, inwardly had great tenacity, courage, good sense, and independence of mind.

Emily Brontë left behind her almost two hundred poems. A substantial number of these — scholars disagree about how many — were written for the Gondal cycle, but students of the selection provided here should probably disregard for the most part this "bogus background," as Derek Stanford calls it and concentrate on the poems as poems and as revelations of Emily's personality and ideas. Many (though not all) of the Gondal poems are marred by melodramatic situations, false rhetoric, strained emotionalism, and other Gothic and Byronic excesses. The Gondal nobles were slaves of passion — vanity, pride, passion, and revenge — and their cycle was not life-like enough or universal enough to serve as an adequate vehicle for her poetry. Emily eventually transcended the Gondal atmosphere and freed herself from Byron's influence, though perhaps never completely. It is remarkable that one of her finest poems, the intense and powerful recollection (apparently) of a mystic experience (#15) is embedded in a pseudo-Gothic, pseudo-Byronic prison episode.

Other influences on Emily were more constructive. Muriel Spark has shown that, far from being an isolated figure in the history of English poetry, Emily was influenced by both eighteenth century and romantic traditions. All the young Brontës grew up with and loved Cowper, Burns, Scott, and the north country ballads. Emily's reading of Wordsworth, together with her drawing lessons and her absorption in the life of the moors, made her a careful observer of nature. Wordsworth could also provide her — temporarily anyway — with a theory of what nature could mean to "the heart that loved her." Emily's strongly individual mind soon made any adopted ideas her own. Another possible influence is Coleridge, whose delicate descriptions of nature and effective use of the supernatural sometimes seem to anticipate hers. Often, too, one is reminded of Blake, though there seems to be no proof that Emily read him. Perhaps, as in the case of the seventeenth century poets, the resemblance may be traced to some spiritual affinity.

Papers of Emily and Anne Brontë

1. DIARY PAPER [S. H.]

November the 24, 1834, Monday.

I,124 EMILY JANE BRONTË Anne Brontë I fed Rainbow, Diamond, Snowflake, Jasper pheasant [alias].

This morning Branwell went down to Mr Driver's and brought news that Sir Robert Peel was going to be invited to stand for Leeds. Anne and I have been peeling apples for Charlotte to make an apple pudding and for Aunt's . . . Charlotte said she made puddings perfectly and she . . . of a quick but lim[i]ted intellect. Taby said just now Come Anne pilloputate [*i.e.* peel a potato] Aunt has come into the kitchin just now and said Where are your feet Anne Anne answered On the floor Aunt. Papa opened the parlour door and gave Branwell a letter saying Here Branwell read this and show it to your Aunt and Charlotte. The Gondals are discovering the interior of Gaaldine. Sally Mosley is washing in the back kitchin.

It is past twelve o'clock Anne and I have not tid[i]ed ourselves, done our bed work, or done our lessons and we want to go out to play We are going to have for dinner Boiled Beef, Turnips, potatoes and apple pudding The kitchin is in a very untidy state Anne and I have not done our music exercise which consists of b *major* Taby said on my putting a pen in her face Ya pitter pottering there instead of pilling a potate. I answered O Dear, O Dear, O Dear I will derectly With that I get up, take a knife and begin pilling. Finished pilling the potatoes Papa going to walk Mr Sunderland expected.[1]

Anne and I say I wonder what we shall 125 be like and what we / shall be and where we shall be, if all goes well, in the year 1874 — in which year I shall be in my 57th year. Anne will be in her 55th year Branwell will be going in his 58th year and Charlotte in the 59th year Hoping we shall

all be well at that time We close our paper

Emily and Anne

November the 24, 1834

2. DIARY PAPER [B. S. T.]

XII, Pt.61, p.15

Monday evening June 26th 1837. A bit past 4 o'clock Charlotte working in Aunt's room Branwell reading Eugene Aram to her — Anne and I writing in the drawing-room [*sic*] — Anne a poem beginning "Fair was the evening and brightly the stars" — I Augustus-Almeda's life Ist, v, I-4th page from the last Fine rather coolish then grey cloudy but sunny day Aunt working in the little room Papa gone out Tabby in the kitchen The Emperors and Empresses of Gondal and Gaaldine preparing to depart from Gaaldine to Gondal to prepare for the coronation which will be on the 12th of July Queen Victoria ascended the throne this month.[2] Northangerland in Monkeys Isle — Zamorna at Eversham. All tight and right in which condition it is to be hoped we shall all be on this day 4 years at which time Charllotte will be 25 and 2 months — Branwell just 24 it being his birthday — myself 22 and 10 monthe and a peice [*sic*] Anne 21 and nearly a half I wonder where we shall be and how we shall be and what kind of a day it will be then let us hope for the best

Emily Jane Brontë — Anne Brontë

I guess that this day 4 years we shall all be in this drawing-room comfortable I hope it may be so.

Anne guesses we shall all be gone somewhere together comfortable. We hope it may be

. . . .

Aunt Come Emily, it's past 4 o'clock
Emily Yes Aunt

---

[1] The organist from Keighley, who taught all the children but Charlotte to play the piano.

[2] This time she means the real queen of England, who succeeded her uncle, William IV, June 20, 1837.

Anne Well, do you intend to write in the evening
Emily Well, what think you
(we agreed to go out Ist to make sure if we got into the humour. We may stay in

3. DIARY PAPER [S. H.]

I,238

A PAPER to be opened
when Anne is
25 years old,
or my next birthday after
if
all be well.

Emily Jane Brontë. July the 30th, 1841.

It is Friday evening, near 9 o'clock — wild rainy weather. I am seated in the dining-room alone, having just concluded tidying our desk boxes, writing this document. Papa is in the parlour — aunt upstairs in her room. She has been reading *Blackwood's Magazine* to papa. Victoria and Adelaide[3] are ensconced in the peat-house. Keeper is in the kitchen — Hero[4] in his cage. We are all stout and hearty, as I hope is the case with Charlotte, Branwell, and Anne, of whom the first is at John White, Esq., Upperwood House, Rawdon; the second is at Luddenden Foot; and the third is, I believe, at Scarborough, inditing perhaps a paper corresponding to this.

A scheme is at present in agitation for setting us up in a school of our own; as yet nothing is determined, but I hope and trust it may go on and prosper and answer our highest expectations. This day four years I wonder whether we shall still be dragging on in our present condition or established to our hearts' content. Time will show.

I guess that at the time appointed for the opening of this paper we *i.e.* Charlotte, Anne, and I, shall be all merrily seated in our own sitting-room in some pleasant and flourishing seminary, having just gathered in for the midsummer holyday. Our debts will be paid off, and we shall have cash in hand to a considerable amount. Papa, aunt,

and Branwell will either have been or be coming to visit us. It will be a fine warm summer evening, very different from this bleak look-out, and Anne and I will perchance slip out into the garden for a few minutes to peruse our papers. I hope either this or something better will be the case.

The *Gondalians* are at present in a threatening state, but there is no open rupture as yet. All the princes and princesses of the Royalty are at the Palace of Instruction. I have a good many books on hand, but I am sorry to say that as usual I make small progress with any. However, I have just made a new regularity paper! and I mean *verb sap* to do great things. And now I must close, sending from far an exhortation, "Courage, courage," to exiled and harassed Anne, wishing she was here.

4. DIARY PAPER [S. H.]

July the 30th, A.D. 1841.   I,239

This is Emily's birthday. She has now completed her 23rd year, and is, I believe, at home. Charlotte is a governess in the family of Mr White. Branwell is a clerk in the railroad station at Luddenden Foot, and I am a governess in the family of Mr Robinson. I dislike the situation and wish to change it for another. I am now at Scarborough. My pupils are gone to bed and I am hastening to finish this before I follow them.

We are thinking of setting up a school of our own, but nothing definite is settled about it yet, and we do not know whether we shall be able to or not. I hope we shall. And I wonder what will be our condition and how or where we shall all be on this day four years hence; at which time, if all be well, I shall be 25 years and 6 months old, Emily will be 27 years old, Branwell 28 years old and 1 month, and Charlotte 29 years and a quarter. We are now all separate and not likely to meet again for many a weary week, but we are none of us ill that I know of, and all are doing something for our own livelihood except Emily, who, however, is as busy as any of us, and

---

[3] The geese.
[4] A hawk.

in reality earns her food and raiment as much as we do.

How little know we what we are
How less what we may be!

Four years ago I was at school. Since then I have been a governess at Blake Hall, left it, come to Thorp Green, and seen the sea and York Minster. Emily has been a teacher at Miss Patchet's school, and left it. Charlotte has left Miss Wooler's, been a governess at Mrs Sidgwick's, left her, and gone to Mrs White's. Branwell has given up painting, been a tutor in Cumberland, left it, and become a clerk on the railroad. Tabby has left us, Martha Brown has come in her place. We have got Keeper, got a sweet little cat and lost it, and also got a hawk. Got a wild goose which has flown away, and three tame ones, one of which has been killed. All these diversities, with many others, are things we did not expect or foresee in the July of 1837. What will the next four years bring forth? Providence only knows. But we ourselves have sustained very little alteration since that time. I have the same faults that I had then, only I have more wisdom and experience, and a little more self-possession than I then enjoyed. How will it be when we open this paper and the one Emily has written? I wonder whether the *Gondalians* will still be flourishing, and what will be their condition. I am now engaged in writing the fourth volume of *Solala Vernon's Life*.

For some time I have looked upon 25 as a sort of era in my existence. It may prove a true presentiment, or it may be only a superstitious fancy; the latter seems most likely, but time will show.   Anne Brontë.

5. DIARY PAPER [S. H.]

II,49   Haworth, Thursday, July 30th, 1845.

My birthday — showery, breezy, cool. I am twenty-seven years old to-day. This morning Anne and I opened the papers we wrote four years since, on my twenty-third birthday. This paper we intend, if all be well, to open on my thirtieth — three years hence, in 1848. Since the 1841 paper the

following events have taken place. Our school scheme has been abandoned, and instead Charlotte and I went to Brussels on the 8th of February 1842.

Branwell left his place at Luddenden Foot. C. and I returned from Brussels, November 8th, 1842, in consequence of aunt's death.

Branwell went to Thorp Green as a tutor, where Anne still continued, January 1843.

Charlotte returned to Brussels the same month, and after staying a year, came back again on New Year's Day 1844.

Anne left her situation at Thorp Green of her own accord, June 1845.

Anne and I went our first long journey by ourselves together, leaving home on the 30th of June, Monday, sleeping at York, returning to Keighley Tuesday evening, sleeping there and walking home on Wednesday morning. Though the weather was broken we enjoyed ourselves very much, except during a few hours at Bradford. And during our excursion we were,[5] Ronald Macalgin, Henry Angora, Juliet Angusteena, Rosabella Esmaldan, Ella and Julian Egremont, Catharine Navarre, and Cordelia Fitzaphnold, escaping from the palaces of instruction to join / the Royalists 51 who are hard driven at present by the victorious Republicans. The Gondals still flourish bright as ever. I am at present writing a work on the First Wars. Anne has been writing some articles on this, and a book by Henry Sophona. We intend sticking firm by the rascals as long as they delight us, which I am glad to say they do at present. I should have mentioned that last summer the school scheme was revived in full vigour. We had prospectuses printed, despatched letters to all acquaintances imparting our plans, and did our little all; but it was found no go. Now I don't desire a school at all, and none of us have any great longing for it. We have cash enough for our present wants, with a prospect of accumulation. We are all in decent health, only that papa has a complaint in his eyes,

[5] Note the verb.

and with the exception of B., who, I hope, will be better and do better hereafter. I am quite contented for myself: not as idle as formerly, altogether as hearty, and having learnt to make the most of the present and long for the future with the fidgetiness that I cannot do all I wish; seldom or never troubled with nothing to do, and merely desiring that everybody could be as comfortable as myself and as undesponding, and then we should have a very tolerable world of it.

By mistake I find we have opened the paper on the 31st instead of the 30th. Yesterday was much such a day as this, but the morning was divine.

Tabby, who was gone in our last paper, is come back, and has lived with us two years and a half, and is in good health. Martha, who also departed, is here too. We have got Flossy; got and lost Tiger; lost the hawk Hero, which, with the geese, was given away, and is doubtless dead, for when I came back from Brussels, I inquired on all hands and could hear nothing of him. Tiger died early last year. Keeper and Flossy are well, also the canary acquired four years since. We are now all at home, and likely to be there some time. Branwell went to Liverpool on Tuesday to stay a week. Tabby has just been teasing me to turn as formerly to "Pilloputate." Anne and I should have picked the black currants if it had been fine and sunshiny. I must hurry off now to my turning and ironing. I have plenty of work on hands, and writing, and am altogether full of business. With best wishes for the whole house till 1848, July 30th, and as much longer as may be. — I conclude.   E. J. Brontë.

6. DIARY PAPER [S. H.]

II,52   Thursday, July the 31st, 1845. Yesterday was Emily's birthday, and the time when we should have opened our 1841 paper, but by mistake we opened it to-day instead. How many things have happened since it was written — some pleasant, some far otherwise. Yet I was then at Thorp Green, and now I am only just escaped from it. I was wishing to leave it then, and if I had known that I had four years longer to stay how wretched I should have been; but during my stay I have had some very unpleasant and undreamt-of experience of human nature. Others have seen more changes. Charlotte has left Mr White's, and been twice to Brussels, where she stayed each time nearly a year. Emily has been there too, and stayed nearly a year. Branwell has left Luddenden Foot, and been a tutor at Thorp Green, and had much tribulation and ill health. He was very ill on Thursday, but he went with John Brown to Liverpool, where he now is, I suppose; and we hope he will be better and do better in future. This is a dismal, cloudy, wet evening. We have had so far a very cold, wet summer. Charlotte has lately been to Hathersage, in Derbyshire, on a visit of three weeks to Ellen Nussey. She is now sitting sewing in the dining-room. Emily is ironing upstairs. I am sitting in the dining-room in the rocking-chair before the fire with my feet on the fender. Papa is in the parlour. Tabby and Martha are, I think, in the kitchen. Keeper and Flossy are, I do not know where. Little Dick is hopping in his cage. When the last paper was written we were thinking of setting up a school. The scheme has been dropt, and long after taken up again, and dropt again, because we could not get pupils. Charlotte is thinking about getting another situation. She wishes to go to Paris. Will she go? She has let Flossy in, by-the-by, and he is now lying on the sofa. Emily is engaged in writing the Emperor Julius's Life. She has read some of it, and I want very much to hear the rest. She is writing some poetry, too. I wonder what it is about? I have begun the third volume of *Passages in the Life of an Individual*.[6] I wish I had finished it. This afternoon I began to set about making my grey figured silk frock that was dyed at Keighley. What sort of a hand shall I make of it? E. and I have a

---

[6] Later *Agnes Grey*.

great deal of work to do. When shall we sensibly diminish it? I want to get a habit of early rising. Shall I succeed? We have not yet finished our *Gondal Chronicles* that we began three years and a half ago. When will they be done? The Gondals are at present in a sad state. The Republicans are uppermost, but the Royalists are not quite overcome. The young sovereigns, with their brothers and sisters, are still at the Palace of Instruction. The Unique /
53 Society, about half a year ago, were wrecked on a desert island as they were returning from Gaul. They are still there, but we have not played at them much yet. The Gondals in general are not in first-rate playing condition. Will they improve? I wonder how we shall all be, and where and how situated, on the thirtieth of July 1848, when, if we are all alive, Emily will be just 30. I shall be in my 29th year, Charlotte in her 33rd, and Branwell in his 32nd; and what changes shall we have seen and known; and shall we be much changed ourselves? I hope not, for the worse at least. I for my part cannot well be flatter or older

in mind than I am now. Hoping for the best, I conclude.   Anne Brontë.

7. TO ELLIS OR ACTON BELL [S. H.][7]
Dear Sir, — I am much obliged by your II,188 kind note and shall have great pleasure in making arrangements for your next novel. I would not hurry its completion for I think you are quite right not to let it go before the world until well satisfied with it, for much depends on your next work if it be an improvement on your first you will have established yourself as a first-rate novelist, but if it fall short the critics will be too apt to say that you have expended your talent in your first novel. I shall therefore have pleasure in accepting it upon the understanding that its completion be at your own time. — believe me, my dear Sir, yrs. sincerely,   T. C. Newby.
Feb. 15th, 1848

[7] This letter was found in Emily's desk, also an envelope exactly fitting it, addressed to "Ellis Bell, Esq." The letter suggests that Emily contemplated a second novel — unless, indeed, the letter was meant for "Acton Bell."

Emily Brontë

From *Poems,* selected with an Introduction by Philip Henderson. London: Lawson and Dunn, 1947.

8. ALL DAY I'VE TOILED
c. 1837[8]

4 All day I've toiled, but not with pain,
In learning's golden mine;
And now at eventide again
The moonbeams softly shine.

There is no snow upon the ground,
No frost on wind or wave:
The south wind blew with gentlest sound
And broke their icy grave.

[8] Another interesting poem of this period is "The Night Is Darkening Round Me," Hatfield, p. 56. The images of immobility and weight give it the quality of a familiar yet mysterious nightmare.

'Tis sweet to wander here at night
To watch the winter die,
With heart as summer sunshine light
And warm as summer sky.

O may I never lose the peace
That lulls me gently now,
Though time should change my youthful face,
And years should shade my brow!

True to myself, and true to all,
May I be healthful still,
And turn away from passion's call,
And curb my own wild will.

9. I'M HAPPIEST WHEN MOST AWAY
Early 1838

19 I'm happiest when most away
I can bear my soul from its home of clay
On a windy night when the moon is bright,
And the eye can wander through worlds of
  light, —

When I am not and none beside —
Nor earth nor sea nor cloudless sky —
But only spirit wandering wide
Through infinite immensity.

10. RICHES I HOLD IN LIGHT ESTEEM[1]
March 1, 1841

77 Riches I hold in light esteem
And Love I laugh to scorn
And Lust of Fame was but a dream
That vanished with the morn —

And if I pray — the only prayer
That moves my lips for me
Is — "Leave the heart that now I bear
And give me liberty."

Yes, as my swift days near their goal
'Tis all that I implore —
Through life and death, a chainless soul
With courage to endure!

11. SHALL EARTH NO MORE INSPIRE THEE?
May 16, 1841

79 Shall Earth no more inspire thee,
Thou lonely dreamer now?
Since passion may not fire thee
Shall Nature cease to bow?

Thy mind is ever moving
In regions dark to thee;
Recall its useless roving —
Come back and dwell with me.

I know my mountain-breezes
Enchant and soothe thee still —

1 Called "The Old Stoic" in the 1846 edition.

I know my sunshine pleases
Despite thy wayward will.

When day with evening blending
Sinks from the summer sky,
I've seen thy spirit bending
In fond idolatry.

I've watched thee every hour —
I know my mighty sway —
I know my magic power
To drive thy griefs away.

Few hearts to mortals given
On earth so wildly pine
Yet none would ask a Heaven
More like the Earth than thine.

Then let my winds caress thee —
Thy comrade let me be —
Since nought beside can bless thee
Return and dwell with me.

12. HOW CLEAR SHE SHINES!
April 13, 1843

How clear she shines! How quietly
I lie beneath her silver light
While Heaven and Earth are whispering me,
"To-morrow wake — but dream to-night."

Yes — Fancy come, my fairy love!
These throbbing temples, softly kiss,
And bend my lonely couch above
And bring me rest, and bring me bliss.

The world is going. Dark world adieu!
Grim world, go hide thee till the day:
The heart thou canst not all subdue
Must still resist if thou delay.

Thy love I will not — will not share
Thy hatred only wakes a smile
Thy griefs may wound — thy wrongs may tear
But O, thy lies shall not beguile.

While gazing on the stars that glow
Above me in that stormless sea
I long to hope that all the woe
Creation knows is held in thee!

And this shall be my dream to-night —
I'll think the heaven of glorious spheres
Is rolling on its course of light
In endless bliss, through endless years.

I'll think, there's not one world above,
Far as these straining eyes can see,
Where Wisdom ever laughed at Love —
Or Virtue crouched to Infamy.

Where writhing 'neath the strokes of Fate
The mangled wretch was forced to smile
To match his patience 'gainst her hate,
His heart rebellious all the while.

Where Pleasure still will lead to wrong
And helpless Reason warn in vain
And Truth is weak, and Treachery strong
And Joy the shortest path to pain:

And peace this lethargy of grief,
And Hope a phantom of the soul —
And Life a labour void and brief —
And Death the despot of the whole.

13. SONG
May 1, 1844

95 The linnet in the rocky dells,
The moor-lark in the air,
The bee among the heather-bells
That hide my lady fair —

The wild deer browse above her breast;
The wild birds raise their brood,
And they, her smiles of love caresst,
Have left her solitude!

I ween, that when the grave's dark wall
Did first her form retain,
They thought their hearts could ne'er recall
The light of joy again.

They thought the tide of grief would flow
Unchecked through future years
But where is all their anguish now,
And where are all their tears?

Well, let them fight for Honour's breath,
Or Pleasure's shade pursue —

The Dweller in the land of Death
Is changed and careless too.

And if their eyes should watch and weep
Till sorrow's source were dry
She would not in her tranquil sleep
Return a single sigh.

Blow, west-wind, by the lonely mound
And murmur, summer streams;
There is no need of other sound
To soothe my Lady's dreams.

14. R. ALCONA TO J. BRENZAIDA[2]
March 3, 1845

Cold in the earth and the deep snow piled 102
   above thee!
Far, far removed, cold in the dreary grave!
Have I forgot, my Only Love, to love thee,
Severed at last by Time's all-wearing wave?

Now, when alone, do my thoughts no longer
   hover
Over the mountains on Angora's shore;
Resting their wings where heath and fern-
   leaves cover
That noble heart for ever, ever more?

Cold in the earth, and fifteen wild Decembers
From those brown hills have melted into
   spring —
Faithful indeed is the spirit that remembers
After such years of change and suffering!

Sweet Love of youth, forgive if I forget thee
While the World's tide is bearing me along:
Sterner desires and darker hopes beset me,
Hopes which obscure but cannot do thee
   wrong.

[2] The title is Emily's own. The poem can be
read in manuscript in her "Gondal Poems" note-
book — in the British Museum. Rosina, princess
of Alcona, laments for Julius Brenzaida, conqueror
and emperor of all Gondal, long ago assassinated.
Generations of biographers have sought in vain
for some counterpart experience in Emily's life.
The more familiar title "Remembrance" was first
used in the 1846 edition of the poems. In that
edition the fourth line reads, "Severed at last
by time's all-severing wave," and there are other
minor changes.

No other Sun has lightened up my heaven;
No other Star has ever shone for me:
All my life's bliss from thy dear life was
    given —
All my life's bliss is in the grave with thee.

But when the days of golden dreams had
    perished
And even Despair was powerless to destroy,
Then did I learn how existence could be
    cherished,
Strengthened and fed without the aid of joy.

103 Then did I check the tears of useless passion,
Weaned my young soul from yearning after
    thine;
Sternly denied its burning wish to hasten
Down to that tomb already more than mine!

And even yet, I dare not let it languish,
Dare not indulge in Memory's rapturous pain:
Once drinking deep of that divinest anguish,
How could I seek the empty world again?

And behold, with tenfold increase blessing
Spring adorned the beauty-burdened spray;
Wind and rain and fervent heat caressing
Lavished glory on its second May.

High it rose; no wingéd grief could sweep it;
Sin was scared to distance with its shine:
Love and its own Life had power to keep it
From all wrong, from every blight but thine!

Heartless Death, the young leaves droop and
    languish!
Evening's gentle air may still restore —
No, the morning sunshine mocks my an-
    guish —
Time for me must never blossom more!

Strike it down — that other boughs may   105
    flourish
Where that perished sapling used to be;
Thus, at least, its mouldering corpse will
    nourish
That from which it sprung — Eternity.

15. DEATH
April 10, 1845

104 Death, that struck when I was most confiding
In my certain Faith of Joy to be,
Strike again, Time's withered branch dividing
From the fresh root of Eternity!

Leaves, upon Time's branch, were growing
    brightly
Full of sap and full of silver dew;
Birds, beneath its shelter, gathered nightly;
Daily, round its flowers, the wild birds flew.

Sorrow passed and plucked the golden blossom,
Guilt stripped off the foliage in its pride;
But within its parent's kindly bosom
Flowed forever Life's restoring tide.

Little mourned I for the parted Gladness,
For the vacant nest and silent song;
Hope was there and laughed me out of sad-
    ness,
Whispering, "Winter will not linger long."

16. JULIAN M. AND A. G. ROCHELLE[3]
October 9, 1845

. . .

"Yet, tell them, Julian, all, I am not doomed 115
    to wear
Year after year in gloom and desolate despair;
A messenger of Hope comes every night to me,
And offers, for short life, eternal liberty.

"He comes with western winds, with evening's
    wandering airs,
With that clear dusk of heaven that brings the
    thickest stars;
Winds take a pensive tone, and stars a tender 116
    fire,
And visions rise and change which kill me
    with desire —

"Desire for nothing known in my maturer
    years

---

[3] This religious lyric of matchless beauty, clarity, and power leaps to life from the middle of a piece of ersatz Byron, a prison scene in which Lord Julian finds the golden-haired companion of his youth lying in chains.

When joy grew mad with awe at counting
  future tears;
When, if my spirit's sky was full of flashes
  warm,
I knew not whence they came, from sun or
  thunderstorm;

"But first a hush of peace, a soundless calm
  descends;
The struggle of distress and fierce impatience
  ends;
Mute music soothes my breast — unuttered
  harmony
That I could never dream till earth was lost
  to me.

"Then dawns the Invisible, the Unseen its
  truth reveals;
My outward sense is gone, my inward essence
  feels —
Its wings are almost free, its home, its harbour
  found;
Measuring the gulf it stoops and dares the
  final bound!

"Oh dreadful is the check — intense the agony
When the ear begins to hear and the eye
  begins to see;
When the pulse begins to throb, the brain to
  think again;
The soul to feel the flesh and the flesh to feel
  the chain!

"Yet I would lose no sting, would wish no
  torture less;
The more that anguish racks the earlier it will
  bless;
And robed in fires of Hell, or bright with
  heavenly shine
If it but herald Death, the vision is divine!"

17. NO COWARD SOUL IS MINE[4]
January 2, 1846

No coward soul is mine   120
No trembler in the world's storm-troubled
      sphere
I see Heaven's glories shine
And Faith shines equal arming me from Fear.

O God within my breast
Almighty ever-present Deity
Life, that in me hast rest
As I, Undying Life, have power in Thee.

Vain are the thousand creeds
That move men's hearts, unutterably vain,
Worthless as withered weeds
Or idlest froth amid the boundless main

To waken doubt in one
Holding so fast by thy infinity
So surely anchored on
The steadfast rock of Immortality.

With wide-embracing love
Thy spirit animates eternal years
Pervades and broods above,
Changes, sustains, dissolves, creates and rears.

Though earth and moon were gone,
And suns and universes ceased to be
And thou wert left alone
Every Existence would exist in thee.

There is not room for Death   121
Nor atom that his might could render void
Since thou art Being and Breath
And what thou art may never be destroyed.

[4] Students of Emily's poetry should also look at
the poem beginning, "Often rebuked, yet always
back returning," Hatfield, pp. 255–256.

Anne Brontë

18. TO E. N. [S. H.]
April 5th, 1849.

1,320 My dear Miss Nussey, — I thank you greatly
for your kind letter, and your ready compliance with my proposal as far as the *will* can
go at least. I see, however, that your friends
are unwilling that you should undertake
the responsibility of accompanying me
under present circumstances. But I do not
think there would be any great responsibility in the matter. I know, and everybody
knows, that you would be as kind and help-

ful as any one could possibly be, and I hope I should not be very troublesome. It would be as a companion, not as a nurse, that I should wish for your company; otherwise I should not venture to ask it. As for your kind and often repeated invitation to Brookroyd, pray give my sincere thanks to your mother and sisters, but tell them I could not think of inflicting my presence upon them as I now am. It is very kind of them to
321 make so light of the trouble, / but still there must be more or less, and certainly no pleasure, from the society of a silent invalid stranger. I hope, however, that Charlotte will by some means make it possible to accompany me after all. She is certainly very delicate, and greatly needs a change of air and scene to renovate her constitution. And then your going with me before the end of May is apparently out of the question, unless you are disappointed in your visitors; but I should be reluctant to wait till then if the weather would at all permit an earlier departure. You say May is a trying month, and so say others. The early part is often cold enough, I acknowledge, but according to my experience, we are almost certain of some fine warm days in the latter half, when the laburnums and lilacs are in bloom; whereas June is often cold, and July generally wet. But I have a more serious reason than this for my impatience of delay. The doctors say that change of air or removal to a better climate would hardly ever fail of success in consumptive cases, if the remedy be taken *in time*; but the reason why there are so many disappointments is that it is generally deferred till it is too late. Now I would not commit this error; and, to say the truth, though I suffer much less from pain and fever than I did when you were with us, I am decidedly weaker, and very much thinner. My cough still troubles me a good deal, especially in the night, and, what seems worse than all, I am subject to great shortness of breath on going up stairs or any slight exertion. Under these circumstances, I think there is no time to be lost. I have no horror of death: if I thought it inevitable, I think I could quietly resign

myself to the prospect, in the hope that you, dear Miss Nussey, would give as much of your company as you possibly could to Charlotte, and be a sister to her in my stead. But I wish it would please God to spare me not only for papa's and Charlotte's sakes, but because I long to do some good in the world before I leave it. I have many schemes in my head for future practice, humble and limited indeed, but still I should not like them all to come to nothing, and myself to have lived to so little purpose. But God's will be done.[5] Remember me respectfully to your mother and sisters, and believe me, dear Miss Nussey, yours most affectionately,   Anne Brontë.

19. LAST VERSES
January 7 [1849], *B. S. T.*, VIII, Pt. 42   22

A dreadful darkness closes in
    On my bewildered mind;
O let me suffer and not sin,
    Be tortured yet resigned.

Through all this world of blinding [whelm-
        ing][6] mist
    Still let me look to thee,
And give me courage to resist
    The Tempter, till he flee.

Weary I am — O give me strength,
    And leave me not to faint:
Say thou wilt comfort me at length
    And pity my complaint.

I've begged to serve thee heart and soul,
To sacrifice to Thee
No niggard portion, but the whole
Of my identity.

I hoped amid the brave and strong[7]
    My portioned task might lie,

[5] For Ellen Nussey's account of Anne's death, see V; for Mrs. Gaskell's, see Ch. 17.
[6] This and other words enclosed in square brackets are alternatives left by Anne in her manuscript.
[7] The version Charlotte published after Anne's death began here.

To toil amid the labouring throng
  With purpose keen [pure] and high;

23 But thou has fixed another part,
  And thou hast fixed it well;
I said so with my bleeding [breaking] heart
  When first the anguish fell.

O [For] thou hast taken my delight
  And hope of life away,
And bid me watch the painful night
  And wait the weary day.

The hope and the delight were thine:
  I bless thee for their loan;
I gave thee while I deemed them mine
  Too little thanks, I own.

Shall I with joy thy blessings share
  And not endure their loss;
Or hope the martyr's crown to wear
  And cast away the cross?

[Anne left the poem at this point and returned
to it three weeks later.]

These weary hours will not be lost,
These days of passive misery,
These nights of darkness, anguish-tost,
If I can fix my heart on thee.

The wretch that weak and weary lies
  Crushed with sorrow, worn with pain,
Still to Heaven may lift his eyes
  And strive and labour not in vain;[8]

Weak and weary though I lie
  Crushed with sorrow, worn with pain,
I may lift to Heaven mine eye
  And strive and labour not in vain;[8]

That inward strife against the sins   . 24
  That ever wait on suffering
To strike wherever [watch and strike where]
    first begins
  Each ill [deed] that would corruption bring;

That secret labour to sustain
  With humble patience every blow;
To gather fortitude from pain
  And hope and holiness from wo.

Thus let me serve thee from my heart
  Whate'er [ever be may be] my written fate,
Whether thus early to depart
  Or yet a while to wait.   .

If thou shouldst bring me back to life,
  More humbled I should be,
More wise, more strengthened for the strife,
  More apt to lean on thee.

Should Death be standing at the gate,
  Thus should I keep my vow;
But hard whate'er my future fate,
  So let me serve thee now.
            Finished, Jan. 28, 1849.

[8] These were obviously different tries at the same
stanza.

IV. Contemporary Reviews of the Brontë Novels

Laura Hinkley calls *Jane Eyre* "the luck of the Brontës" because its "instant, overwhelming, universal appeal" aroused public interest in the other Brontë books (*Charlotte and Emily,* p. 250). It was also lucky in arriving on the literary scene when it did, when the novel as a respectable art was coming into its own. Earlier in the century its stock had not been high, attacked as it was by strict evangelicals as a lure contrived by the evil one, frowned upon by moralists who feared that anything read with ease and pleasure must be debilitating, and underrated by critics who disliked realism on principle. However, thanks to the reputations of Scott, Dickens, and Thackeray and to the urging of historians of the form, by the time the Brontës began to write, the novel was widely regarded as a reputable literary form and a substantial body of criticism was in existence. The anti-novel forces were on the defensive.

The part played by the reviewers of fiction in forming and altering public opinion was particularly important since they raised and debated some important issues. Should the novel provide a happy atmosphere into which the reader could escape (the word "sunshine" recurs), or should it stimulate the reader to reflection on this vale of tears? Should there be a moral? If so, should this moral be stated or implied? Should the story end in reward for the noble and punishment for the wicked, or should the unamiable (as in *Vanity Fair*) triumph? Should unity, probability, economy, and neatness of plot be the rules, after the precepts of Aristotle and the model of Jane Austen, or might the novel admit the variety and complexity of the epic, the panoramic, the picaresque? Should the author be remote, objective, standing aside while his creations enact their part, or should he involve himself in their story and comment on their predicament? Should the writer's work be based solely on his experience of the everyday world, or might it be informed by poetic intuition and transformed by allegory? The debate which opposed "realism" to "idealism" — the latter being equated with the use of allegory, symbol, fantasy, distortion, and the supernatural was a particularly warm one, and from it sprang, among other things, Dobell's defence of *Wuthering Heights*.

Curiously, at times the very people who demanded "real life" in the novel objected to the inclusion of the ugly, the painful, the passionate, and the hateful. Allied to this viewpoint was the characteristically Victorian attitude toward sex. Thackeray's lament that the novelist could no longer portray a "whole man" like Tom Jones is well known, yet he spoke of Balzac and George Sand as obscene and was himself very careful not to offend his readers by overt references to sex. Dickens (whom Thackeray praised for his "unsullied page"), though loud in his claims for the artist's freedom, was if possible more cautious in not violating conventions. Ironically both Thackeray and Dickens, as well as Bulwer, George Eliot, and even Kingsley, were at one time or another assailed for their part in lowering the standards of purity and wholesomeness which (it was thought) ought to prevail in the English novel — by using swear words, by describing slums and factory conditions, by displaying an interest in crime and illicit unions. Even Mrs. Gaskell, whose comments on the coarseness of *Jane Eyre* strike us today as an almost laughable example of Victorian prudery, was herself attacked because she discussed the problem of unmarried mothers and described the effects of the industrialism in Manchester.[1]

It is with the knowledge of these moral and aesthetic assumptions that the reviews

---

[1] For Mrs. Gaskell on C. B.'s "coarseness," see G. Ch. 26; later in the century George M. Smith tried to refute this charge, saying that the term as used by Mrs. Gaskell seemed to him quite inapplicable to Miss Brontë.

which follow should be read and against this background that the work of Charlotte and Emily judged, if their real originality is to be appreciated. Each in her own way frankly portrayed passion as she understood it, each showed heroines who were not afraid to declare that passion openly. This shocked some contemporaries, especially those who held that a woman's role ought to be passive and unaggressive. Only by realizing how great was the Brontës' break with this convention can we recognize fully how great was the originality, integrity, and independence of mind of the authors of *Jane Eyre* and *Wuthering Heights*.

Charlotte's own prefaces to *Jane Eyre, Wuthering Heights,* and *The Professor* might be read at this point, together with her letters to Lewes, Williams, and others (II). They show what she believed about the novel, the novelist, and the role of imagination.

Note: Most of these reviews have been cut, since in those leisurely Victorian times they were often enormously long. (A particular vice of reviewers was to give away the secrets of the plot in the same breath as they praised the author's handling of suspense!) They represented only a fraction of extant reviews — the second edition of *Jane Eyre,* for example, reprinted about two dozen rave notices — but give a fair sampling of opinions on *Jane Eyre* and *Wuthering Heights.* No attempt has been made to canvass opinions on *Shirley* and *Villette,* the articles by Lewes and Miss Martineau being included only because of their importance in Charlotte's relationship with these people. One favorable review of *Shirley* is inserted to balance Lewes' adverse criticism.

Students who read French and can get to a large library might be interested in the reviews of Brontë novels in the *Revue des Deux Mondes,* by Eugéne Forçade, whom Charlotte seems to have found particularly sympathetic. The review of *Jane Eyre* is in Volume XXXIV, 1045.

The Examiner

From Review of *Jane Eyre, The Examiner* (November 27 1847).

1

756 THERE can be no question but that *Jane Eyre* is a very clever book. Indeed it is a book of decided power. The thoughts are true, sound, and original; and the style, though rude and uncultivated here and there, is resolute, straightforward, and to the purpose. There are faults, which we may advert to presently; but there are also many beauties, and the object and moral of the work is excellent. Without being professedly didactic, the writer's intention (among other things) seems to be, to show how intellect and unswerving integrity may win their way, although oppressed by that predominating influence in society which is a mere consequence of the accidents of birth or fortune.

There are, it is true, in this autobiography (which though relating to a woman, we do not believe to have been written by a woman), struggles, and throes, and misgivings, such as must necessarily occur in a contest where the advantages are all on one side; but in the end, the honesty, kindness of heart, and perseverance of the heroine, are seen triumphant over every obstacle. We confess that we like an author who throws himself into the front of the battle, as the champion of the weaker party; and when this is followed up by bold and skillful soldiership, we are compelled to yield him our respect. . . .[1]

[1] This is only a sampling of scores of favorable reviews.

Westminster Review

From Review of *Jane Eyre, Westminster Review,* Vol. 48 (1847).

2

581   Decidedly the best novel of the season; and one, moreover, from the natural tone pervading the narrative, and the originality and freshness of its style, possessing the merit so rarely met with now-a-days in works of this class, of amply repaying a second perusal. Whoever may be the author, we hope to see more such books from *her* pen; for that these volumes are from the pen of a lady, and a clever one too, we have not the shadow of a doubt: nor can there be any question as to the *reality* of many of the scenes and personages so artistically depicted; the characters are too life-like to be the mere creations of fancy, and sketchy as some of them are, they are wondrous *telling:* several of them we almost feel persuaded we have met with in real life. The Rev. Mr. Brocklehurst, with his "straight, narrow, sable-clad shape, standing erect on the rug; the grim face at the top being like a carved mask, placed above the shaft by way of capital;" the lady-like Miss Temple; sweet Helen Burns, whose death-scene is so touchingly narrated; the neat and prim little Mrs. Fairfax, and the eccentric Mr. Rochester, whom with all his faults and eccentricities one can't help getting to like; are but a few of the characters in the drama, though essential ones, and cleverly struck off. . . .

[A substantial summary follows.]

There are many other passages we would 584 gladly quote, some perhaps of a more telling description . . . [but] the whole three volumes must be regularly read through, no skipping, no peeping, to see how Jane goes forward a few leaves later, or whether she gets married, or how her property comes to her. And thus perused, we venture to say no one will have regretted our advice to read *Jane Eyre.*

[G. H. Lewes]

From "Recent Novels French and English," *Fraser's Magazine* (December 1847).

3

690   After laughing over the *Bachelor of the Albany,* we wept over *Jane Eyre.* This, indeed, is a book after our own heart; and, if its merits have not forced it into notice by the time this paper comes before our readers, let us, in all earnestness, bid them lose not a day in sending for it. The writer is 691 evidently a woman, / and, unless we are deceived, new in the world of literature. But, man or woman, young or old, be that as it may, no such book has gladdened our eyes for a long while. Almost all that we require in a novelist she has: perception of character, and power of delineating it; picturesqueness; passion; and knowledge of life. The story is not only of singular interest, naturally evolved, unflagging to the last, but it fastens itself upon your attention, and will not leave you. The book closed, the enchantment continues. With the disentanglement of the plot, and the final release of the heroine from her difficulties, your interest does not cease. You go back again in memory to the various scenes in which she has figured; you linger on the way, and muse upon the several incidents in the life which has just been unrolled before you, affected by them as if they were the austere instructions drawn from a sorrowing existence, and not merely the cun-

ning devices of an author's craft. Reality — deep, significant reality — is the great characteristic of the book. It *is* an autobiography, — not, perhaps, in the naked facts and circumstances, but in the actual suffering and experience. The form may be changed, and here and there some incidents invented; but the spirit remains such as it was. The machinery of the story may have been borrowed, but by means of this machinery the authoress is unquestionably setting forth her own experience. This gives the book its charm: it is soul speaking to soul; it is an utterance from the depths of a struggling, suffering, much-enduring spirit: *suspiria de profundis!*

692   ... There are some defects in it — defects which the excellence of the rest only brings into stronger relief. There is, indeed, too much melodrama and improbability, which smack of the circulating-library, — we allude particularly to the mad wife and all that relates to her, and to the wanderings of Jane when she quits Thornfield; yet even those parts are powerfully executed. But the earlier parts — all those relating to Jane's childhood and her residence at Lowood, with much of the strange love story — are written with remarkable beauty and truth. The characters are few, and drawn with unusual mastery: even those that are but sketched — such as Mr. Brocklehurst, Miss Temple, Mrs. Fairfax, Rosamond, and Blanche — are sketched with a vividness which betrays the cunning hand: a few strokes, and the figure rises before you. Jane herself is a creation. The delicate handling of this figure alone implies a dramatic genius of no common order. We never lose sight of her plainness; no effort is made to throw romance about her — no extraordinary goodness or cleverness appeals to your admiration; but you admire, you love her, — love her for the strong will, honest mind, loving heart, and peculiar but fascinating person. A creature of flesh and blood, with very fleshly infirmities, and very mortal excellencies; a woman, not a pattern: that is the Jane Eyre here represented. Mr. Rochester is also well drawn, and from the life; but it is the portrait of a man drawn by a woman, and is not comparable to the portrait of Jane. The way in which the authoress contrives to keep our interest in this imperfect character is a lesson to novelists. St. John Rivers, the missionary, has a touch of the circulating-library, but not enough to spoil the truth of the delineation; there is both art and artifice in the handling, and, although true in the main, and very powerful in parts, one feels a certain misgiving about him: it is another example of the woman's pencil. Helen Burns is lovely and loveable; true, we believe, even in her exalted spirituality and her religious fervour: a character at once eminently ideal and accurately real.

. . . The style of *Jane Eyre* is peculiar; 693 but, except that she admits too many Scotch or North-country phrases, we have no objection to make to it, and for this reason: although by no means a fine style, it has the capital point of all great styles in being *personal,* — the written speech of an individual, not the artificial language made up from all sorts of books.

In philosophical remark she is sparing, and justly. It is what few women ever succeed in. . . .

Athenaeum

From Review of *Wuthering Heights* and *Agnes Grey, Athenaeum* (December 25 1847).

4

1324   "Jane Eyre," it will be recollected, was *edited* by Mr. Currer Bell. Here are two tales so nearly related to "Jane Eyre" in cast of thought, incident, and language as to excite some curiosity. All three might be the work of one hand, — but the first issued remains the best. In spite of much power and cleverness; in spite of its truth to life in the remote nooks and corners of England, "Wuthering Heights" is a disagreeable story. The Bells seem to affect painful and exceptional subjects: — the misdeeds and oppression of tyranny — the eccentricities of "woman's fantasy." They do not turn away from dwelling upon those physical acts of cruelty which we know to have their warrant in the real annals of crime and suffering, — but the contemplation of which true taste rejects. The brutal master of the lonely house on "Wuthering Heights" — a prison which might be pictured from life — has doubtless had his prototype in those ungenial and remote districts where human beings, like the trees, grow gnarled and dwarfed and distorted by the inclement climate; but he might have been indicated with far fewer touches, in place of so entirely filling the canvas that there is hardly a scene untainted by his presence. It was a like dreariness — a like unfortunate selection of / objects — which cut short the popularity of Charlotte Smith's novels, — rich though they be in true pathos and faithful descriptions of Nature. Enough of what is mean and bitterly painful and degrading gathers round every one of us during the course of his pilgrimage through this vale of tears to absolve the Artist from choosing his incidents and characters out of such a dismal catalogue; and if the Bells, singly or collectively, are contemplating future or frequent utterances in Fiction, let us hope that they will spare us further interiors so gloomy as the one here elaborated with such dismal minuteness. . . .

1325

The Examiner

From Review of *Wuthering Heights, The Examiner* (January 8 1848).

5

21   This is a strange book. It is not without evidences of considerable power: but, as a whole, it is wild, confused, disjointed, improbable; and the people who make up the drama, which tragic enough in its consequences, are savages ruder than those who lived before the days of Homer. With the exception of Heathcliff, the story is confined to the family of Earnshaw, who intermarry with the Lintons; and the scene of their exploits is a rude old-fashioned house, at the top of one of the high moors or fells in the north of England. . . .

This Heathcliff may be considered as the hero of the book, if a hero there be. He is an incarnation of evil qualities; implacable hate, ingratitude, cruelty, falsehood, selfishness, and revenge. He exhibits, moreover, a certain stoical endurance in early life, which enables him to "bide his time," and nurse up his wrath till it becomes mature and terrible; and there is one portion of his nature, one only, wherein he appears to approximate to humanity. Like the Corsair, and other such melodramatic heroes, he is

"Linked to one virtue and a thousand crimes;"

and it is with difficulty that we can prevail upon ourselves to believe in the appearance of such a phenomenon, so near our own dwellings as the summit of a Lancashire or Yorkshire moor. . . .

We are not disposed to ascribe any particular intention to the author in drawing the character of Heathcliff, nor can we perceive any very obvious moral in the story. There are certain good rough dashes at character; some of the incidents look like real events; and the book has the merit, which must not be undervalued, of avoiding common-place and affectation. The language, however, is not always appropriate; and we entertain great doubts as to the truth, or rather the *vraisemblance* of the main character. The hardness, selfishness, and cruelty of Heathcliff are in our opinion inconsistent with the romantic love that he is stated to have felt for Catherine Earnshaw. As Nelly Dean says, "he is hard as a whinstone." He has no gratitude, no affection, no liking for anything human except for one person, and that liking is thoroughly selfish and ferocious. He hates the son of Hindley, which is intelligible enough; but he also hates and tyrannizes over his own son and the daughter of his beloved Catherine, and this we cannot understand. . . .

22   If this book be, as we apprehend it is, the first work of the author, we hope that he will produce a second, giving himself more time in its composition than in the present case, developing his incidents more carefully, eschewing exaggeration and obscurity, and looking steadily at human life, under all its moods, for those pictures of the passions that he may desire to sketch for our public benefit. It may be well also to be sparing of certain oaths and phrases which do not materially contribute to any character and are by no means to be reckoned among the evidences of a writer's genius. We detest the affectation and effeminate frippery which is but too frequent in the modern novel, and willingly trust ourselves with an author who goes at once fearlessly into the moors and desolate places for his heroes; but we must at the same time stipulate with him that he shall not drag into light all that he discovers, of coarse and loathsome, in his wanderings, but simply so much good and ill as he may find necessary to elucidate his history — so much only as may be interwoven inextricably with the persons whom he professes to paint. It is the province of an artist to modify and in some cases refine what he beholds in the ordinary world. There never was a man whose daily life (that is to say, all his deeds and sayings, entire and without exception) constituted fit materials for a work of fiction.

Douglas Jerrold's Weekly Newspaper

From Review of *Wuthering Heights, Douglas Jerrold's Weekly Newspaper* (January 15 1848).

6

77   . . . "Wuthering Heights" is a strange sort of book, — baffling all regular criticism; yet it is impossible to begin and not finish it; and quite as impossible to lay it aside afterwards and say nothing about it. In the midst of the reader's perplexity the ideas predominant in his mind concerning this book are likely to be — brutal cruelty, and semi-savage love. What may be the moral which the author wishes the reader to deduce from his work, it is difficult to say; and we refrain from assigning any, because to speak honestly, we have discovered none but mere glimpses of hidden morals or secondary meanings. There seems to us great power in this book, but a purposeless power, which we feel a great desire to see turned to better account. We are quite confident that the writer of "Wuthering Heights" wants but the practised skill to make a great artist. . . . His qualities are, at present, excessive; a far more promising fault, let it be remembered, than if they were deficient. He may tone down, whereas the weak and inefficient writer, however carefully he may write by rule and line, will never work up his productions to the point of beauty in art. In "Wuthering Heights," the reader is shocked, disgusted, almost sickened by details of cruelty, inhumanity, and the most diabolical hate and vengeance, and anon come passages of pow-

erful testimony to the supreme power of love — even over demons in the human form. The women in the book are of a strange fiendish-angelic nature, tantalizing, and terrible, and the men are indescribable out of the book itself. Yet, towards the close of the story occurs the following pretty, soft picture, which comes like the rainbow after a storm.

[Here follows the scene where Cathy is teaching Hareton to read.]

We strongly recommend all our readers who love novelty to get this story, for we can promise them that they never have read anything like it before. It is very puzzling and very interesting, and if we had space we would willingly devote a little more time to the analysis of this remarkable story, but we must leave it to our readers to decide what sort of a book it is.

The Atlas

From Review of *Wuthering Heights, The Atlas* (January 22 1848).

7

59　About two years ago a small volume of poems by "Currer, Acton, and Ellis Bell" was given to the world. The poems were of varying excellence; those by Curser Bell, [*sic*] for the most part, exhibiting the highest order of merit; but, as a whole, the little work produced little or no sensation, and was speedily forgotten. Currer, Acton, and Ellis Bell have now all come before us as novelists, and all with so much success as to make their future career a matter of interesting speculation in the literary world.

Whether, as there is little reason to believe, the names which we have written are the genuine names of actual personages — whether they are, on the other hand, mere publishing names, as is our own private conviction — whether they represent three distinct individuals, or whether a single personage is the actual representative of the "three gentlemen at once" of the title-pages — whether the authorship of the poems and the novels is to be assigned to one gentleman or to one lady, to three gentlemen or three ladies, or to a mixed male and female triad of authors — are questions over which the curious may puzzle themselves, but are matters really of little account. One thing is certain; as in the poems, so in the novels, the signature of "Currer Bell" is attached to

pre-eminently the best performance. We were the first to welcome the author of *Jane Eyre* as a new writer of no ordinary power. A new edition of that singular work has been called for, and we do not doubt that its success has done much to ensure a favourable reception for the volumes which are now before us.

Wuthering Heights is a strange, inartistic story. There are evidences in every chapter of a sort of rugged power — an unconscious strength — which the possessor seems never to think of turning to the best advantage. The general effect is inexpressibly painful. We know nothing in the whole range of our fictitious literature which presents such shocking pictures of the worst forms of humanity. *Jane Eyre* is a book which affects the reader to tears; it touches the most hidden sources of emotion. *Wuthering Heights* casts a gloom over the mind not easily to be dispelled. It does not soften; it harasses, it extenterates. . . . [It] is a *sprawling* story, carrying us, with no mitigation of anguish, through two generations of sufferers — though one presiding evil genius sheds a grim shadow over the whole, and imparts a singleness of malignity to the somewhat disjointed tale. A more natural unnatural story we do not remember to have read. Inconceivable as are the combinations of human degradation which are here to be found moving within the circle of a few miles, the *vraisemblance* is so admirably preserved; there is so much truth in what we may call the *costumery* (not applying the word in its narrow acceptation) — the general mounting of the entire piece — that we readily identify the scenes and personages of the fiction; and when we lay aside the book it is some time before we can persuade ourselves that we have held nothing more than imaginary intercourse with the ideal creations of the brain. The reality of unreality has never been so aptly illustrated as in the scenes of almost savage life which Ellis Bell has brought so vividly before us.

The book sadly wants relief. A few glimpses of sunshine would have increased the reality of the picture and given strength rather than weakness to the whole. There is not in the entire *dramatis personæ* a single character which is not utterly hateful or thoroughly contemptible. If you do not detest the person, you despise him; and if you do not despise him, you detest him with your whole heart. Hindley, the brutal, degraded sot, strong in the desire to work all mischief, but impotent in his degradation; Linton Heathcliff, the miserable, drivelling coward, in whom we see selfishness in its most abject form; and Heathcliff himself, the presiding evil genius of the piece, the tyrant father of an imbecile son, a creature in whom every evil passion seems to have reached a gigantic excess — form a group of deformities such as we have rarely seen gathered together on the same canvas. The author seems to have designed to throw some redeeming touches into the character of the brutal Heathcliff, by portraying him as one faithful to the "idol of his boyhood" — loving to the very last — long, long after death had divided them, the unhappy girl who had cheered and brightened up the early days of his wretched life. Here is the touch of nature which makes the whole world kin — but it fails of the intended effect. There is a selfishness — a ferocity in the love of Heathcliff, which scarcely suffer it, in spite of its rugged constancy, to relieve the darker parts of his nature. Even the female characters excite something of loathing and much of contempt. Beautiful and loveable in their childhood, they all, to use a vulgar expression, "turn out badly." Catherine the elder — wayward, impatient, impulsive — sacrifices herself and her lover to the pitiful ambition of becoming the wife of a gentleman of station. Hence her own misery — her early death — and something of the brutal wickedness of Heathcliff's character and conduct; though we cannot persuade ourselves that even a happy love would have tamed down the natural ferocity of the tiger. Catherine the younger is more sinned against than sinning, and in spite of her grave moral defects, we have some hope of her at the last. . . .

The Christian Remembrancer

From Review of *Jane Eyre*, *The Christian Remembrancer*, XV (June 1848).

8

396   . . . The name and sex of the writer are still a mystery. Currer Bell (which by a curious Hibernicism[1] appears in the title-page as the name of a female autobiogra-pher) is a mere *nom de guerre* — perhaps an anagram. However, we, for our part, cannot doubt that the book is written by a female, and, as certain provincialisms indicate, by one from the North of England. . . . Yet we cannot wonder that the

---

[1] Irishism.

hypothesis of a male author should have been started, or that ladies especially should still be rather determined to uphold it. For a book more unfeminine, both in its excellences and defects, it would be hard to find in the annals of female authorship. Throughout there is masculine power, breadth and shrewdness, combined with masculine hardness, coarseness, and freedom of expression. Slang is not rare. The humour is frequently produced by a use of Scripture, at which one is rather sorry to have smiled. The love-scenes glow with a fire as fierce as that of Sappho, and somewhat more fuliginous. There is an intimate acquaintance with the worst parts of human nature, a practised sagacity in discovering the latent ulcer, and a ruthless rigour in exposing it, which /
397 must command our admiration, but are almost startling in one of the softer sex. Jane Eyre professes to be an autobiography, and we think it likely that in some essential respects it is so. If the authoress has not been, like her heroine, an oppressed orphan, a starved and bullied charity-school girl, and a despised and slighted governess (and the intensity of feeling which she shows in speaking of the wrongs of this last class seems to prove that they have been her own), at all events we fear she is one to whom the world has not been kind. And, assuredly, never was unkindness more cordially repaid. Never was there a better hater. Every page burns with moral Jacobinism. "Unjust, unjust," is the burden of every reflection upon the things and powers that be. All virtue is but well masked vice, all religious profession and conduct is but the whitening of the sepulchre, all self-denial is but deeper selfishness. In the preface to the second edition, this temper rises to the transcendental pitch. . . .

399   The plot is most extravagantly improbable, verging all along upon the supernatural, and at last running fairly into it. All the power is shown and all the interest lies in the characters. We have before intimated our belief, that in Jane Eyre, the heroine of the piece, we have, in some measure, a portrait of the writer. If not, it is a most skilful imitation of autobiography. The character embodied in it is precisely the same as that which pervades the whole book, and breaks out most signally in the Preface — a temper naturally harsh, made harsher by ill usage, and visiting both its defect and its wrongs upon the world — an understanding disturbed and perverted by cynicism, but still strong and penetrating — fierce love and fiercer hate — all this / viewed from within and coloured by self- 400 love. . . .

The character of Mr. Rochester, the hero, the lover, and eventually the husband, of Jane Eyre, we have already noticed as being, to our minds, the characteristic production of a female pen. Not an Adonis, but a Hercules in mind and body, with a frame of adamant, a brow of thunder and a lightning eye, a look and voice of command, all-knowing and all-discerning, fierce in love and hatred, rough in manner, rude in courtship, with a shade of Byronic gloom and appetizing mystery — add to this that when loved he is past middle age, and when wedded he is blind and fire-scarred, and you have such an Acis as no male writer would have given his Galatea, and yet what commends itself as a true embodiment of the visions of a female imagination. The subordinate characters almost all show proportionate power. Mr. Brocklehurst, the patron and bashaw of Lowood, a female orphan school, in which he practises self-denial, *alieno ventre,* and exercises a vicarious humility, is a sort of compound of Squeers and Pecksniff, but more probable than either, and drawn with as strong a hand. . . . His love of miracles of destruction is a true hit. *Those* miracles are still credible. . . . Mrs. Reed is a good type of the "strong-minded" and odious woman. Excellent too, in an artistic point of view, is the character of St. John Rivers, the Calvinist clergyman and missionary, with all its complex attributes and iridescent hues — self-denial strangely shot with selfishness — earthly pride and restless ambition blending and alternating with heaven-directed zeal, and resignation to the duties of a heavenly mission. The feeblest character in the book is that of Helen Burns, who is meant to be a perfect Christian, and is a simple seraph, conscious moreover of her own perfection. She dies early in the first volume, and our authoress might say of her saint, as Shakespeare said of his Mercutio,

401 "If I / had not killed her, she would have killed me." In her, however, the Christianity of Jane Eyre is concentrated, and with her it expires, leaving the moral world in a kind of Scandinavian gloom, which is hardly broken by the faint glimmerings of a "doctrine of the equality of souls," and some questionable streaks of that "world-redeeming creed of Christ," which being emancipated from "narrow human doctrines, that only tend to elate and magnify a few," is seldom invoked but for the purpose of showing that all Christian profession is bigotry and all Christian practice is hypocrisy. . . .

[Edwin Percy Whipple]

From Review of *Jane Eyre* and *Wuthering Heights, North American Review* (October 1848).

9

355 . . . Not many months ago, the New England States were visited by a distressing mental epidemic, passing under the name of the "Jane Eyre fever," which defied all the usual nostrums of the established doctors of criticism. Its effects varied with different constitutions, in some producing a soft ethical sentimentality, which relaxed all the fibres of conscience, and in others exciting a general fever of moral and religious indignation. It was to no purpose that the public were solemnly assured, through the intelligent press, that the malady was not likely to have any permanent effect either on the intellectual or moral constitution. The book which caused the distemper would probably have been inoffensive, had not some sly manufacturer of mischief hinted that it was a book which no respectable man should bring into his family circle. Of course, every family soon had a copy of it, and one edition after another found eager purchasers. . . .

356 The novel of Jane Eyre, which caused this great excitement, purports to have been edited by Currer Bell, and the said Currer divides the authorship, if we are not mis-informed, with a brother and sister. The work bears the marks of more than one mind and one sex, and has more variety than either of the novels which claim to have been written by Acton Bell. The family mind is strikingly peculiar, giving a strong impression of unity, but it is still male and female. From the masculine tone of Jane Eyre, it might pass altogether as the composition of a man, were it not for some unconscious feminine peculiarities, which the strongest-minded woman that ever aspired after manhood cannot suppress. These peculiarities refer not only to elaborate descriptions of dress, and the minutiæ of the sick-chamber, but to various superficial refinements of feeling in regard to the external relations of the sex. It is true that the noblest and best representations of female character have been produced by men; but there are niceties of thought and emotion in a woman's mind which no man can delineate, but which often escape unawares from a female writer. There are numerous examples of these in Jane Eyre. The leading characteristic of the novel, however, and the secret of its charm, is the / clear, 357 distinct, decisive style of its representation of character, manners, and scenery; and this

1 See Charlotte's letter to Williams, Nov. 22, 1848.

continually suggests a male mind. In the earlier chapters, there is little, perhaps, to break the impression that we are reading the autobiography of a powerful and peculiar female intellect; but when the admirable Mr. Rochester appears, and the profanity, brutality, and slang of the misanthropic profligate give their torpedo shocks to the nervous system, — and especially when we are favored with more than one scene given to the exhibition of mere animal appetite, and to courtship after the manner of kangaroos and the heroes of Dryden's plays, — we are gallant enough to detect the hand of a gentleman in the composition. There are also scenes of passion, so hot, emphatic, and condensed in expression, and so sternly masculine in feeling, that we are almost sure we observe the mind of the author of Wuthering Heights at work in the text.

The popularity of Jane Eyre was doubtless due in part to the freshness, raciness, and vigor of mind it evinced; but it was obtained not so much by these qualities as by frequent dealings in moral paradox, and by the hardihood of its assaults upon the prejudices of proper people. . . . The authors of Jane Eyre . . . confound vulgarity with truth, and awaken too often a feeling of unmitigated disgust. The writer who colors too warmly the degrading scenes through which his immaculate hero passes is rightly held as an equivocal teacher of purity; it is not by the bold expression of blasphemy and ribaldry that a great novelist conveys the most truthful idea of the misanthropic and the dissolute. The truth is, that the whole firm of Bell & Co. seem to have a sense of the depravity of human nature peculiarly their own. It is the yahoo, not the demon, that they select for representation; their Pandemonium is of mud rather than fire.

Britannia

From Review of *Wuthering Heights, Britannia,* 1848, as reprinted in *B. S. T.,* XI (Pt. LVII).

10

93   . . . It is humanity in [its] wild state that the author of "Wuthering Heights" essays to depict. His work is strangely original. It bears a resemblance to some of those irregular German tales in which the writers, giving the reins to their fancy, represent personages as swayed and impelled to evil by supernatural influences. But they gave spiritual identity to evil impulses, while Mr. Bell more naturally shows them as the natural offspring of the unregulated heart. He displays considerable power in his creations. They have all the angularity of misshapen growth, and form in this respect a striking contrast to those regular forms we are accustomed to meet with in English fiction. They exhibit nothing of the composite character. There is in them no trace of ideal models. They are so new, so grotesque, so entirely without art, that they strike us as / proceeding from a mind of 94 limited experience but of original energy and of a singular and distinctive cast.

In saying this we indicate both the merits and faults of the tale. It is in parts very unskilfully constructed; many passages in it display neither the grace of art nor the truth of nature, but only the vigour of one positive idea — that of passionate ferocity. It blazes forth in the most unsuitable circumstances and from persons the least likely to be animated by it. The author is a Salvator Rosa with his pen. He delineates forms of savage grandeur when he wishes to represent sylvan beauty. His Griseldas are furies and his swains Polyphemi. For this reason his narrative leaves an unpleasant effect on the mind. There are no green spots in it on which the mind can linger with satisfaction. The story rushes onwards with impetuous force, but it is the force of a dark and sullen torrent, flowing between high and rugged rocks. . . .

We must suppose that the characters are drawn from the very lowest of life; that they are the inhabitants of an isolated and uncivilized district, or that they are of some demoniac influence. It is difficult to pronounce any decisive judgment on a work in which there is so much rude ability displayed yet in which there is so much matter for blame. The scenes of brutality are unnecessarily long and unnecessarily frequent; and as an imaginative writer the author has to learn the first principles of his art. But there is singular power in his portraiture of strong passion. He exhibits it as convulsing the whole frame of nature,

distracting the intellect to madness, and snapping the heartstrings. The anguish of Heathcliff on the death of Catherine approaches to sublimity. . . .

We do not know whether the author writes with any purpose; but we can speak of one effect of his production. The story shows the brutalizing influence of unchecked passion. . . .

The tale . . . is but a fragment, yet of colossal proportion and bearing evidence of some great design. With all its power and originality, it is so rude, so unfinished and so careless, that we are perplexed to pronounce an opinion on it or to hazard a conjecture on the future of the author. As yet it belongs to the future to decide whether he will remain a rough hewer of marble or become a great and noble sculptor.

Anonymous

From Review of *Wuthering Heights,* source unknown (c. 1848).[1] Reprinted from Charles Simpson, *Emily Brontë,* London: Country Life, 1929.

11

177   This is a work of great ability, and contains many chapters, to the production of which talent of no common order has contributed. At the same time, the materials which the author has placed at his own disposal have been but few. In / the re-178 sources of his own mind, and in his own manifestly vivid perceptions of the peculiarities of character — in short, in his knowledge of human nature — has he found them all. An antiquated farm-house, a neighbouring residence of a somewhat more pretending description, together with their respective inmates, amounting to some half a dozen souls in each, constitute the material and the personal components of one of the

most interesting stories we have read for many a long day. The comfortable cheerfulness of the one abode, and the cheerless discomfort of the other — the latter being less the result of a cold and bleak situation, old and damp rooms, and (if we may use the term) of a sort of "haunted house" appearance, than of the strange and mysterious character of its inhabitants — the loves and marriages, separations and hatreds, hopes and disappointments, of two or three generations of the gentle occupants of the one establishment, and the ruder tenants of the other, are brought before us at a moment with a tenderness, at another with a fearfulness, which appeals to our sympathies with the truest tones of the voice of nature; and it is quite impossible to read the book — and this is no slight testimony to the merits of a work of the kind — without feeling that, if placed in the same posi-

[1] The source of this review, one of five left by Emily in her writing desk, is unknown. We must hope that this, apparently the one wholly favorable review she saw, gave Emily some of the pleasure she deserved. Mr. Simpson's book gives an interesting account of the contents of the desk.

tion as any one of the characters in any page of it, the chances would be twenty to one in favour of our conduct in that position being precisely such as the author has assigned to the personages he has introduced into his domestic drama. But we must at once impose upon ourselves a task — and we confess it is a hard one — we must abstain (from a regard to the space at our disposal) from yielding to the temptation by which we are beset to enter into that minute description of the plot of this very dramatic production to which such a work has an undoubted claim. It is not every day that so good a novel makes its appear-

ance; and to give its contents in detail would be depriving many a reader of half the delight he would experience from the perusal of the work itself. To its pages we must refer him, then; there will he have ample opportunity of sympathising — if he has one touch of nature / that "makes the whole 179 world kin" — with the feelings of childhood, youth, manhood, and age, and all the emotions and passions which agitate the restless bosom of humanity. May he derive from it the delight we have ourselves experienced, and be equally grateful to its author for the genuine pleasure he has afforded him.

[Elizabeth Rigby]

From *"Vanity Fair* — and *Jane Eyre," Quarterly Review*, Vol. 84 (December 1848).[1]

12

162   . . . "Jane Eyre," as a work, and one of equal popularity, is, in almost every respect, a total contrast to "Vanity Fair." The characters and events, though some of them masterly in conception, are coined expressly for the purpose of bringing out great effects. The hero and heroine are beings both so singularly unattractive that the reader feels they can have no vocation in the novel but to be brought together; and they do things which, though not impossible, lie utterly beyond the bounds of probability. . . . Jane Eyre is merely another Pamela, who, by the force of her character and the strength of her principles, is carried victoriously through

great trials and temptations from the man she loves. Nor is she even a Pamela adapted and refined to modern notions; for though the story is conducted without those derelictions of decorum which we are to believe had their excuse in the manners of Richardson's time, yet it is stamped / with a coarse- 163 ness of language and laxity of tone which have certainly no excuse in ours. It is a very remarkable book: we have no remembrance of another combining such genuine power with such horrid taste. Both together have equally assisted to gain the great popularity it has enjoyed; for in these days of extravagant adoration of all that bears the

---

[1] The author of this vituperative review — she had not, of course, any way of knowing the personal anguish "Currer Bell" was undergoing in December, 1848 — was a lady of otherwise blameless life, one Elizabeth Rigby, later Lady Eastlake. A native of Norwich, Norfolk, and a relative of the anthologist Palgrave, she had an excellent education in England and on the continent. Her background was Tory and orthodox, and her sympathy for governesses, though genuine, was paternalistic in the extreme. Even her recent biographer, Marion Lochhead, is at a loss to explain the "savagery" of the review which follows. It took all George Smith's tact to prevent Charlotte from replying to Lady Eastlake in a preface to *Shirley*.

She had to content herself with putting some of the words of the review into the mouth of the unpleasant Mrs. Hardman. Another puzzle is why Lockhart, the *Quarterly*'s editor, published this devastating article, since on December 29, 1847, he had written: "I have finished the adventures of Miss Jane Eyre and think her far the cleverest that has written since Austen and Edgeworth were in their prime. Worth fifty Trollopes and Martineaus rolled into one counterpane, with fifty Dickenses and Bulwers to keep them company; but rather a brazen Miss." — *The Life and Letters of John Gibson Lockhart,* ed. Andrew Long. London: J. C. Nimmo, 1897. See C. B.'s letters of Feb. 4, Mar. 2, 1849.

stamp of novelty and originality, sheer rudeness and vulgarity have come in for a most mistaken worship.

166 . . . Mr. Rochester is a man who deliberately and secretly seeks to violate the laws both of God and man, and yet we will be bound half our lady readers are enchanted with him for a model of generosity and honour. We would have thought that such a hero had had no chance, in the purer taste of the present day; but the popularity of Jane Eyre is a proof how deeply the love for illegitimate romance is implanted in our nature. Not that the author is strictly responsible for this. Mr. Rochester's character is tolerably consistent. He is made as coarse and as brutal as can in all conscience be required to keep our sympathies at a distance. In point of literary consistency the hero is at all events impugnable, though we cannot say as much for the heroine.

As to Jane's character — there is none of that harmonious unity about it which made little Becky so grateful a subject of anal-/
167 ysis — nor are the discrepancies of that kind which have their excuse and their response in our nature. The inconsistencies of Jane's character lie mainly not in her own imperfections, though of course she has her share, but in the author's. There is that confusion in the relations between cause and effect, which is not so much untrue to human nature as to human art. The error in Jane Eyre is, not that her character is this or that, but that she is made one thing in the eyes of her imaginary companions, and another in that of the actual reader. There is a perpetual disparity between the account she herself gives of the effect she produces, and the means shown us by which she brings that effect about. We hear nothing but self-eulogiums on the perfect tact and wondrous penetration with which she is gifted, and yet almost every word she utters offends us, not only with the absence of these qualities, but with the positive contrasts of them, in either her pedantry, stupidity, or gross vulgarity. She is one of those ladies who put us in the unpleasant predicament of undervaluing their very virtues for dislike of the person in whom they are represented. One feels provoked as Jane Eyre stands before us — for in the wonderful reality of her thoughts and descriptions, she seems accountable for all done in her name — with principles you must approve in the main, and yet with language and manners that offend you in every particular. Even in that *chef-d'œuvre* of brilliant retrospective sketching, the description of her early life, it is the childhood and not the child that interests you. The little Jane, with her sharp eyes and dogmatic speeches, is a being you neither could fondle nor love. There is a hardness in her infantine earnestness, and a spiteful precocity in her reasoning, which repulses all our sympathy. One sees that she is of a nature to dwell upon and treasure up every slight and unkindness, real or fancied, and such natures we know are surer than any others to meet with plenty of this sort of thing. As the child, so also the woman — an uninteresting, sententious, pedantic thing; with no experience of the world, and yet with no simplicity or freshness in its stead. . . .

[The author (Lady Eastlake) thinks that 169 in the dinner party scene Jane Eyre displays her own vulgarity as no ladies would really be so rude to servants. She also quotes part of the proposal scene, and on the embrace comments:]

Some ladies would have thought it high 170 time to leave the squire alone with chestnut tree; or at all events unnecessary to keep up that tone of high-souled feminine obtusity, which they are quite justified in adopting if a gentleman will not speak out — but Jane does neither. Not that we say she was wrong, but quite the reverse, considering the circumstances of the case — Mr. Rochester was her master, and "Duchess or nothing" was her first duty — only she was not quite so artless as the author would have us suppose. . . .

. . . Jane Eyre is throughout the personi- 173 fication of an unregenerate and undisciplined spirit, the more dangerous to exhibit from that prestige of principle and self-control which is liable to dazzle the eye too much for it to observe the inefficient and unsound foundation on which it rests. It is true Jane does right, and exerts great moral strength, but it is the strength of a mere heathen mind which is a law unto itself. No Christian grace is perceptible upon her. She has inherited in fullest measure the worst sin of our fallen nature — the sin of pride. Jane Eyre is proud, and therefore she is ungrateful too. It pleased God to make her an orphan, friendless, and penniless — yet she thanks nobody, and least of all Him, for the food and raiment, the friends, companions, and instructors of her helpless youth — for the care and education vouchsafed to her till she was capable in mind as fitted in years to provide for herself. On the contrary, she looks upon all that has been done for her not only as her undoubted right, but as falling far short of it. The doctrine of humility is not more foreign to her mind than it is repudiated by her heart. It is by her own talents, virtues, and courage that she is made to attain the summit of human happiness, and, as far as Jane Eyre's own statement is concerned, no one would think that she owed anything either to God above or to man below. . . .

Altogether the auto-biography of Jane Eyre is pre-eminently an anti-Christian composition. There is throughout it a murmuring against the comforts of the rich and against the privations of the poor, which, as far as each individual is concerned, is a murmuring against God's appointment — there is a proud and perpetual assertion of the rights of man, for which we find no / authority either in God's word or in God's providence — there is that pervading tone of ungodly discontent which is at once the most prominent and the most subtle evil which the law and the pulpit, which all civilized society in fact has at the present day to contend with. . . .

[She summarizes briefly the mystery of the Bells' identity.] . . . Whoever it be, it is a person who, with great mental powers, combines a total ignorance of the habits of society, a great coarseness of taste, and a heathenish doctrine of religion. . . . At all

174

175

events there can be no interest attached to the writer of "Wuthering Heights" — a novel succeeding "Jane Eyre," and purporting to be written by Ellis Bell — unless it were for the sake of more individual reprobation. For though there is a decided family likeness between the two, yet the aspect of the Jane and Rochester animals in their native state, as Catherine and Heathfield, is too odiously and abominably pagan to be palatable even to the most vitiated class of English readers. With all the unscrupulousness of the French school of novels it combines that repulsive vulgarity in the choice of its vice which supplies its own antidote. The question of authorship, therefore, can deserve a moment's curiosity only as far as "Jane Eyre" is concerned, and though we cannot pronounce that it appertains to a real Mr. Currer Bell and to no other, yet that it appertains to a man, and not, as many assert, to a woman, we are strongly inclined to affirm. Without entering into the question whether the power of the writing be above her, or the vulgarity below her, there are, we believe, minutiæ of circumstantial evidence which at once acquit the feminine hand. No woman — a lady friend, whom we are always happy to consult, assures us — makes mistakes in her own *métier* — no woman *trusses game* and garnishes dessert-dishes with the same hands, or talks of so doing in the same breath. Above all, no woman attires another in such fancy dresses as Jane's ladies assume — Miss Ingram coming down, irresistible, "in a *morning* robe of sky-blue crape, a gauze azure scarf twisted in her hair!!" No lady, we understand, when suddenly roused in the night, would think of hurrying on *"a frock."* They have garments more convenient for such occasions, and / more becoming too. This evidence seems incontrovertible. Even granting that these incongruities were purposely assumed, for the sake of disguising the female pen, there is nothing gained; for if we ascribe the book to a woman at all, we have no alternative but to ascribe it to one who has, for some sufficient reason, long forfeited the society of her own sex.

176

176- [Lady Eastlake comments on the isolation
177 of governesses, expected to behave like
ladies while they are treated like servants;
nevertheless she shows this isolation is inevitable, as the distance between employer
and employee *must* be preserved. She does,
however, recommend better pay for the
governesses and public support for institutions designed to educate and help them.][2]

[2] Useful background reading for Lady Eastlake's
article is Patricia Thompson's *The Victorian
Heroine: A Changing Ideal, 1837–1873*, London: Oxford University Press, 1956; particularly
Chapter XI, "That Noble Body of Governesses."

The Morning Chronicle

From Review of *Shirley, The Morning Chronicle* (December 25 1849).

13

7   Many were the sagacious critics who declared that "Jane Eyre" was the production
of a lady author, and that its delicate portraiture of character, its overflowing tenderness, and truth of sentiment, could only be
traceable to a female hand. It now appears,
however, that they were mistaken; and we
have to congratulate the writer of the present work upon having added to the laurels
which he gained by his first novel. "Shirley" is an admirable book — totally free
from cant, whining, affectation, or conventional tinsel of any kind; genuine English
in the independence and uprightness of the
tone of thought, in the purity of heart and
feeling which pervade it; genuine English
in the masculine vigor or rough originality
of its conception of character; and (a great
merit in these days of puff-paste composition) genuine English in style and diction.
Like the author's former work, it is a tale
of passion and character rather than of incident; and, thus considered, it is a veritable
triumph of psychology. Perhaps, indeed,
his searching investigation of the mysterious
workings of the human breast is pushed at
times almost to painfulness; but a clear
heart and a steady hand never desert him.
We would not be thought to imply that we
consider it deficient in incident, for there
is enough to furnish a sound basis for his
superstructure; but merely that mental
analysis and the portraiture of character are
its predominant features. . . .

[G. H. Lewes]

From "Currer Bell's *Shirley*," *Edinburgh Review* (January 1850), 158–161.

14

[Lewes begins with some rather heavy-
handed joking about the superiority of men
to women. Woman's "grand function," he
says, is maternal. Women writers such as
Mrs. Hemans, Miss Mitford, Miss Austen,
would do better not to try to write from the
men's point of view, not to attempt to rival
them. It takes him five pages to elucidate
this before he gets down to "Currer Bell."
For Charlotte's reaction, see her letters of
this period.]

. . . We take Currer Bell to be one of 158
the most remarkable of *female* writers; and
believe it is now scarcely a secret that
Currer Bell is the pseudonyme of a woman.
An eminent contemporary, indeed, has employed the sharp vivacity of a female pen
to prove "upon irresistible evidence" that

"Jane Eyre" *must be* the work of a man! But all that "irresistible evidence" is set aside by the simple fact that Currer Bell *is* a woman. We never, for our own parts, had a moment's doubt on the subject. That Jane herself was drawn by a woman's delicate hand, and that Rochester equally betrayed the sex of the artist, was to our minds so obvious, as absolutely to shut our ears to all the evidence which could be adduced by the erudition even of a *marchande des modes;* and that simply because we knew that there were women profoundly ignorant of the mysteries of the toilette, and the terminology of fashion (independent of the obvious solution, that such ignorance might be counterfeited, to mislead), and felt that there was no man who *could so* have delineated a woman — or *would so* have delineated a man. The fair and ingenious critic was misled by her own acuteness in the perception of details; and misled also in some other way, and more uncharitably, in concluding that the *author* of "Jane Eyre" was a heathen educated among heathens, — the *fact* being, that the *authoress* is the daughter of a clergyman!

This question of authorship, which was somewhat hotly debated a little while ago, helped to keep up the excitement about "Jane Eyre"; but, independently of that title to notoriety, it is certain that, for many years, there had been no work of such power, piquancy, and originality. Its very faults were faults on the side of vigour; and its beauties were all original. The grand secret of its success, however, — as of all genuine and lasting success, — was its *reality*. From out the depths of a sorrowing experience, here was a voice speaking to the experience of thousands. The aspects of external nature, too, were painted with equal fidelity, — the long cheerless winter days, chilled with rolling mists occasionally gathering into the strength of rains, — the bright spring mornings, — the clear solemn nights, — were all painted to your *soul* as well as to your eye, by a pencil dipped into a soul's experience for its colours. Faults enough the book has undoubtedly: faults

of conception, faults of taste, faults of ignorance, but in spite of all, it remains a book of singular fascination. A more masculine book, in the sense of vigour, was never written. Indeed that vigour often amounts to coarseness, — and is certainly the very antipode to "lady like."

This same over-masculine vigour is even more prominent in "Shirley," and does not increase the pleasantness of the book. / A 159 pleasant book, indeed, we are not sure that we can style it. Power it has unquestionably, and interest too, of a peculiar sort; but not the agreeableness of a work of art. Through its pages we are carried as over a wild and desolate heath, with a sharp east wind blowing the hair into our eyes, and making the blood tingle in our veins: There is health perhaps in the drive; but not much pleasantness. Nature speaks to us distinctly enough, but she does not speak sweetly. She is in her stern and sombre mood, and we see only her dreary aspects.

"Shirley" is inferior to "Jane Eyre" in several important points. It is not quite so true; and it is not so fascinating. It does not so rivet the reader's attention, nor hurry him through all obstacles of improbability, with so keen a sympathy in its reality. It is even coarser in texture, too, and not unfrequently flippant; while the characters are almost all disagreeable, and exhibit intolerable rudeness of manner. In "Jane Eyre" life was viewed from the standing point of individual experience; in "Shirley" that standing point is frequently abandoned, and the artist paints only a panorama of which she, as well as you, are but spectators. Hence the unity of "Jane Eyre" in spite of its clumsy and improbable contrivances, was great and effective: the fire of one passion fused the discordant materials into one mould. But in "Shirley" all unity, in consequence of defective art, is wanting. There is no passionate link; nor is there any artistic fusion, or intergrowth, by which one part evolves itself from another. Hence its falling-off in interest, coherent movement, and life. The book may be laid down at any chapter, and almost any chapter might be omitted. The various scenes are gathered up into three volumes, — they have not grown into a work. The characters often need a justification for their introduction; as in the case of the three Curates, who are offensive, uninstructive, and unamusing. That they are not *inventions,* however, we feel persuaded. For nothing but a strong sense of their reality could have seduced the authoress into such a mistake as admitting them at all. We are confident she has seen them, known them, despised them; and *therefore* she paints them! although they have no relation with the story, have no interest in themselves, and cannot be accepted as types of a class, — for they are not *Curates* but *boors:* and although not inventions, we must be permitted to say that they are *not true.* . . .

160 Again we say that "Shirley" cannot be received as a work of art. It is not a picture; but a portfolio of random sketches for one or more pictures. The authoress never seems distinctly to have made up her mind as to what she was to do; whether to describe the habits and manners of Yorkshire and its social aspects in the days of King Lud, or to paint character, or to tell a love story. All are by turns attempted and abandoned; and the book consequently moves slowly, and by starts — leaving behind it no distinct or satisfactory impression. Power is stamped on various parts of it; power unmistakeable, but often misapplied. Currer Bell has much yet to learn, — and, especially, the discipline of her own tumultuous energies. She must learn also to sacrifice a little of her Yorkshire roughness to the demands of good taste: neither saturating her writings with such rudeness and offensive harshness, nor suffering her style to wander into

such vulgarities as would be inexcusable — even in a man. No good critic will / object 161 to the homeliness of natural diction, or to the racy flavour of conversational idiom; but every one must object to such phrases as "Miss Mary, *getting up the steam* in her turn, now asked," &c., or as "making hard-handed worsted spinners *cash up to the tune of* four or five hundred per cent.," or as "Malone much chagrined at hearing him *pipe up in most superior style*"; all which phrases occur within the space of about a dozen pages, and that not in dialogue, but in the authoress's own narrative. And while touching on this minor, yet not trivial point, we may also venture a word of quiet remonstrance against a most inappropriate obtrusion of French phrases. . . .

To speak of a grandmother as *une grand'-mère,* and of treacle as *mélasse,* or of a young lady being angry as *courroucée,* gives an air of affectation to the style strangely at variance with the frankness of its general tone.

We scarcely know what to say to the impertinence which has been allowed to mingle so largely with the manners, even of the favourite actors in this drama. Their frequent harshness and rudeness is something which startles on a first reading, and, on a second, is quite inexplicable. Is this correct as regards Yorkshire, or is the fault with the artist? . . .

. . . But, to quit this tone of remonstrance, — which after all is a compliment, for it shows how seriously we treat the great talents of the writer, — let us cordially praise the real freshness, vividness, and fidelity, with which most of the characters and scenes are depicted.

Sydney Dobell

From "Currer Bell," *The Palladium*, I (September 1850).

15

162 . . . Who is Currer Bell? is a question which has been variously answered, and has lately, we believe, received, in well-informed quarters, a satisfactory reply. A year or two ago, we mentally solved the problem thus: Currer Bell is a woman. Every word she utters is female. Not feminine, but female. There is a sex about it which cannot be mistaken, even in its manliest attire. . . .

164   . . . For her most perfect work the world is still waiting, and will be content for some years to wait; and, placing in an assumed order of production (though not of publication) the novels called "Wuthering Heights," "Wildfell Hall," "Jane Eyre," and "Shirley," as the works of one author under sundry disguises, we should have deemed, a few days since, that an analysis of the first (and, by our theory, the earliest) of these was the amplest justice she could at present receive. Opening, however, the third edition of "Jane Eyre," published before the appearance of "Shirley," we find a preface in which all other works are disclaimed. A *nom de guerrist* has many privileges, and we are willing to put down to a *double entendre* all that is serious in this disclaimer. That any hand but that which shaped "Jane Eyre" and "Shirley" cut out the rougher earlier statues, we should require more than the evidence of our senses to believe. That the author of "Jane Eyre" need fear nothing in acknowledging these /

165 yet more immature creations of one of the most vigorous of modern idiosyncrasies, we think we shall shortly demonstrate.

Laying aside "Wildfell Hall," we open "Wuthering Heights," as at once the earlier in date and ruder in execution. We look upon it as the flight of an impatient fancy fluttering in the very exultation of young wings; sometimes beating against its solitary bars, but turning, rather to exhaust, in a circumscribed space, the energy and agility which it may not yet spend in the heavens — a youthful story, written for oneself in solitude, and thrown aside till other successes recall the eyes to it in hope. In this thought let the critic take up the book; lay it down in what thought he will, there are some things in it he can lay down no more.

That Catherine Earnshaw — at once so wonderfully fresh, so fearfully natural — new, "as if brought from other spheres," and familiar as the recollection of some woeful experience — what can surpass the strange compatibility of her simultaneous loves; the involuntary art with which her two natures are so made to co-exist, that in the very arms of her lover we dare not doubt her purity; the inevitable belief with which we watch the oscillations of the old and new elements in her mind, and the exquisite truth of the last victory of nature over education, when the past returns to her as a flood, sweeping every modern landmark from within her, and the soul of the child, expanding, fills the woman? Found at last, by her husband, insensible on the breast of her lover, and dying of the agony of their parting, one looks back upon her, like that husband, without one thought of accusation or absolution; her memory is chaste as the loyalty of love, pure as the air of the Heights on which she dwelt.

Heathcliff *might* have been as unique a creation. The conception in his case was as wonderfully strong and original, but he is spoilt in detail. The authoress has too often disgusted, where she should have terrified, and has allowed us a familiarity with her fiend which has ended in unequivocal contempt. If "Wuthering Heights" had been written as lately as "Jane Eyre," the figure of Heathcliff, symmetrised and elevated, might have been one of the most natural and most striking portraits in the gallery of fiction.

Not a subordinate place or person in this novel, but bears more or less the stamp of high genius. Ellen Dean is the ideal of the peasant playmate and servant of "the family." The substratum in which her mind moves is finely preserved. Joseph, as a specimen of the sixty years' servitor of "the house," is worthy a museum case. We feel that if Catherine Earnshaw bore her husband a child, it must be that Cathy Linton, and no other. . . .

166   But one looks back at the whole story as to a world of brilliant figures in an atmosphere of mist; shapes that come out upon the eye, and burn their colours into the brain, and depart into the enveloping fog. It is the unformed writing of a giant's hand; the "large utterance" of a baby god. In the sprawlings of the infant Hercules, however, there must have been attitudes from which the statuary might model. In the early efforts of unusual genius, there are not seldom unconscious felicities which maturer years may look back upon with envy. The child's hand wanders over the strings. It cannot combine them in the chords and melodies of manhood; but its separate notes are perfect in themselves, and perhaps sound all the sweeter for the Æolian discords from which they come.

We repeat, that there are passages in this book of "Wuthering Heights" of which any novelist, past or present, might be proud. [He asks the reader to look at the first six chapters.] There are few things in modern prose to surpass these pages for native power. We cannot praise too warmly the brave simplicity, the unaffected air of intense belief, the admirable combination of extreme likelihood with the rarest originality, the nice provision of the possible even in the highest effects of the supernatural, the easy strength and instinct of keeping with which the accessory circumstances are grouped, the exquisite but unconscious art with which the chiaro-scuro of the whole is managed, and the ungenial frigidity of place, time, weather, and persons, is made to heighten the unspeakable pathos of one ungovernable outburst.

The *thinking-out* of some of these pages . . . is the masterpiece of a poet, rather than the hybrid creation of the novelist. The mass of readers will probably yawn over the whole; but, in the memory of those whose remembrance makes *fame,* the images in these pages will live — when every word that conveyed them is forgotten — as a recollection of *things heard and seen.* This is the highest triumph of description; and perhaps every creation of the fancy is more or less faulty, so long as, in a mind fitted to reproduce them, the images co-exist only with the words that called them up. . . .

When Currer Bell writes her next novel, 168 let her remember, as far as possible, the frame of mind in which she sat down to her first. She cannot now commit the faults of that early effort; it will be well for her if she be still capable of the virtues. She will never sin so much against consistent keeping as to draw another Heathcliff; she is too much *au fait* of her profession to make again those sacrifices to machinery which deprive her early picture of any claim to be ranked as a work of art. Happy she, if her next book demonstrate the unimpaired possession of those powers of insight, that instinctive obedience to the nature within her, and those occurrences of infallible inspiration, which astound the critic in the young author of "Wuthering Heights." She will not let her next dark-haired hero babble away the respect of his reader and the awe of his antecedents; nor will she find another housekeeper who remembers two volumes *literatim.* Let her rejoice if she can again give us such an elaboration of a rare and fearful form of mental disease — so terribly strong, so exquisitely subtle — with such nicety in its transitions, such intimate symptomatic truth in its details, as to be at once a psychological and medical study. It has been said of Shakspere, that he drew cases which the physician might study; Currer Bell has done no less. She will not, again, employ her wonderful pencil on a picture so destitute of moral beauty and human worth. Let her exult, if she can still invest such a picture with such interest. We stand painfully before the portraits; but our eyes are drawn to them by the irresistible ties of blood relationship. Let her exult, if she can still make us weep with the simple pathos of that fading face, which looked from the golden crocuses on her pillow to the hills which concealed the old home and the churchyard of Gimmerton. . . .

[Harriet Martineau]

From Review of *Villette, Daily News* (February 3 1853).

16

2   Everything written by Currer Bell is remarkable. She can touch nothing without leaving on it the stamp of originality. Of her three novels, this is perhaps the strangest, the most astonishing, though not the best. The sustained ability is perhaps greater in "Villette" than in its two predecessors, there being no intervals of weakness, except in the form of a few passages, chiefly episodical, of over-wrought writing. . . . In regard to interest, we think this book will be pronounced inferior to "Jane Eyre," and superior to "Shirley." In point of construction it is superior to both; and this is a vast gain and a great encouragement to hope for future benefits from the same hand which shall surpass any yet given. The whole three volumes are crowded with beauties — with those good things for which we look to the clear sight, deep feeling, and singular, though not extensive, experience of life which we associate with the name of Currer Bell. But under all, through all, over all, is felt a drawback, of which we were anxious before, but which is terribly aggravated here — the book is almost intolerably painful. We are wont to say, when we read narratives which are made up of the external woes of life, such as may and do happen every day, but are never congregated in one experience — that the author has no right to make readers so miserable. We do not know whether the right will be admitted in the present case, on the ground of the woes not being external; but certainly we ourselves have felt inclined to rebel against the pain, and, perhaps, on account of its protraction, are disposed to deny its necessity and its truth. With all her objectivity, Currer Bell here afflicts us with an amount of subjective misery which we may fairly remonstrate against; and she allows us no respite, even while treating us with humour, with charming description, and the presence of those whom she herself regards as the good and gay. In truth, there is scarcely anybody that is good — serenely and cheerfully good, and the gaiety has pain in it. An atmosphere of pain hangs about the whole, forbidding that repose which we hold to be essential to the true presentment of any large portion of life and experience. In this pervading pain, the book reminds us of Balzac; and so it does in the prevalence of one tendency, or one idea, throughout the whole conception and action. All the female characters, in all their thoughts and lives, are full of one thing, or are regarded by the reader in the light of that one thought — love. It begins with the child of six years old, at the opening — a charming picture — and it closes with it at the last page: and, so dominant is this idea — so incessant is the writer's tendency to describe the need of being loved, that the heroine, who tells her own story, leaves the reader at last under the uncomfortable impression of her having either entertained a double love, or allowed one to supersede another without notification of the transition. It is not thus in real life. There are substantial, heartfelt inter-

ests for women of all ages, and under ordinary circumstances, quite apart from love: there is an absence of introspection, an unconsciousness, a repose in women's lives — unless under peculiarly unfortunate circumstances — of which we find no admission in this book: and to the absence of it may be attributed some of the criticism which the book will meet with from readers who are no prudes, but whose reason and taste will reject the assumption that events and characters are to be regarded through the medium of one passion only. . . .

The heroine, Lucy Snowe, tells her own story. Every reader of "Jane Eyre" will be glad to see the autobiographical form returned to. Lucy may be thought a younger, feebler sister of Jane. There is just enough resemblance for that: but she has not Jane's charm of mental and moral health, and consequent repose. She is in a state of chronic nervous fever, for the most part; is usually silent and suffering; when she speaks, speaks in enigmas or in raillery, and now and then breaks out under the torture of passion; but she acts admirably — with readiness, sense, conscience, and kindliness. Still we do not wonder that she loved more

than she was beloved; and the love at last would be surprising enough, if love could ever be so. Perhaps Paulina and her father are the best-drawn characters in the book, where all are more or less admirably delineated. We are not aware that there is one failure.

A striking peculiarity comes out in the third volume, striking, from one so large and liberal, so removed from ordinary social prejudices as we have been accustomed to think Currer Bell. She goes out of her way to express a passionate hatred of Romanism. It is not the calm disapproval of a ritual religion, such as we should have expected from her, ensuing upon a presentment of her own better faith. The religion she invokes is itself but a dark and doubtful refuge from the pain which compels the invocation; while the catholicism on which she enlarges is even virulently reprobated. We do not exactly see the moral necessity for this (there is no artistical necessity); and we are rather sorry for it, occurring as it does, at a time when catholics and protestants hate each other quite sufficiently; and in a mode which will not affect conversion. . . .

Two Nineteenth Century Estimates of Emily Brontë

When on the death of Thomas Hardy Sir James Barrie became president of the Incorporated Society of Authors, Playwrights, and Composers, he lamented that his predecessor always refused to read *Wuthering Heights* — he was afraid it would depress him! However, Barrie went on, it was not too late; surely Hardy would find a copy lying about somewhere in heaven. Then he lifted his glass and pronounced a simple toast: "Our greatest woman."[1]

This judgment would have staggered Emily's contemporaries, most of whom, as we have already seen, were variously confused, baffled, or shocked by a writer whose power they felt, but whose meaning they could not discern. Mrs. Gaskell probably spoke for the majority of educated readers in her day when she said the book "revolted many readers by the power with which wicked and exceptional characters are depicted" (p. 236). In fact, though her novel sold quite well, Emily's articulate admirers during her lifetime seem to have been limited to the anonymous reviewer and her sister Charlotte. (Newby, who published her book, did not really care for it.) Sydney Dobell's appreciation in the *Palladium* based on his vision of a great novel as ideal and poetic as

---

[1] Alexander Woollcott. " 'Our Greatest Woman' or Screen Credit for Emily," *The Portable Woollcott*. New York: Viking Press, 1946, p. 659.

opposed to "realistic" novel, gave Charlotte some comfort (see her letter to him, Dec. 8, 1850). After Charlotte's death and the publication of Mrs. Gaskell's *Life*, some critics reviewed the whole Brontë corpus once more. Emily's poems were beginning to be noticed, and here and there were notes of puzzled admiration, though the painful and amoral aspects of the novel were stressed rather than its careful structure, unsentimental observation of character, and lyric descriptive power.

Note: It has not been possible to include here criticisms on Emily's poetry; but their history forms much the same pattern as the history of her reputation as a novelist. Students of the early reviews and of this section should note the aesthetic and moral problems the novel posed for the critics and the various attempts to state the theme or central idea of the book. (They might also notice how young some of the early critics were!)

Algernon Charles Swinburne

From "Emily Brontë," *The Athenaeum* (June 16, 1883).[1]

17

762   From the first [in *Wuthering Heights*] we breathe the fresh dark air of tragic passion and presage; and to the last the changing wind and flying sunlight are in keeping with the stormy promise of the dawn.
763 There is no monotony, / there is no repetition, but there is no discord. This is the first and last necessity, the foundation of all labour and the crown of all success, for a poem worthy of the name; and this it is that distinguishes the hand of Emily from the hand of Charlotte Brontë. All the works of the elder sister are rich in poetic spirit, poetic feeling, and poetic detail; but the young sister's work is essentially and definitely a poem in the fullest and most positive sense of the term. It was therefore all the more proper that the honour of raising a biographical and critical monument to the author of "Wuthering Heights" should have been reserved for a poetess of the next generation to her own. And those who had already in their mind's eye the clearest and

most definite conception of Emily Brontë will be the readiest to acknowledge their obligation and express their gratitude to Miss Robinson for the additional light which she has been enabled to throw upon a great and singular character. . . .

. . . [T]he intelligent reader of "Wuthering Heights" cannot fail to recognize that what he is reading is a tragedy simply because it is the / work of a writer whose genius is essentially tragic. Those who believe that Heathcliff was called into existence by the accident that his creator had witnessed the agonies of a violent weakling in love and in disgrace might believe that Shakespeare wrote "King Lear" because he had witnessed the bad effects of parental indulgence, and that Æschylus wrote the "Eumenides" because he had witnessed the uncomfortable results of matricide. The book is what it is because the author was what she was; this is the main and central fact to be remembered. Circumstances have modified the details; they have not implanted the conception. If there were any need for explanation there would be no room for apology. As it is, the few faults of design or execution leap to sight at a first glance, and vanish in the final effect and unimpaired impression of the whole; while those who

[1] Like much of his poetry, the critical essays of Algernon Charles Swinburne (1837–1909) are often marred by flamboyancy and excess of emotion; nevertheless he must be credited with encouraging a fairer appraisal of some Elizabethan tragedians, of Blake, and of Emily Brontë. The article which follows was a review of A. F. M. Robinson's Life of Emily.

object to the violent illegalities of conduct with regard to real or personal property on which the progress of the story does undeniably depend — "a senseless piece of glaring folly," it was once called by some critic learned in the law — might as well complain, in Carlylesque phrase, that the manners are quite other than Belgravian.

It is a fine and accurate instinct that has inevitably led Miss Robinson to cite in chosen illustration of the book's quality at its highest those two incomparable pictures of dreamland and delirium which no poet that ever lived has ever surpassed or equalled for passionate and lifelike beauty of imaginative truth. . . . It is hardly ever safe to say dogmatically what can or cannot be done by the rarest and highest genius; yet it must surely be borne in upon us all that these two crowning passages could never have been written by any one to whom the motherhood of earth was less than the brotherhood of man — to whom the anguish, the intolerable and mortal yearning, of insatiate and insuppressible homesickness, was less than the bitterest of all other sufferings endurable or conceivable in youth. But in Emily Brontë this passion was twinborn with the passion for truth and rectitude. The stale and futile epithet of Titaness has in this instance a deeper meaning than appears; her goddess-mother was in both senses the same who gave birth to the divine martyr of Æschylean legend: Earth under one aspect and one name, but under the other Righteousness. And therefore was the first and last word uttered out of the depth of her nature a cry for that one thing needful without which all virtue is as worthless as all pleasure is vile, all hope as shameful as all faith is abject — a cry for liberty.

And therefore too, perhaps we may say, it is that any seeming confusion or incoherence in her work is merely external and accidental, not inward and spiritual. Belief in the personal or positive immortality of the individual and indivisible spirit was not apparently, in her case, swallowed up or nullified or made nebulous by any doc-

trine or dream of simple reabsorption into some indefinite infinity of eternal life. So at least it seems to me that her last ardent confession of dauntless and triumphant faith should properly be read, however capable certain phrases in it may seem of the vaguer and more impersonal interpretation. For surely no scornfuller or stronger comment on the "unutterable" vanity of creeds could pass more naturally into a chant expressive of more profound and potent faith; a song of spiritual trust more grave and deep and passionate in the solemn ardour of its appeal than the Hymn to God of Cleanthes. Her infrangible self-reliance and lonely sublimity of spirit she had in common with him and his fellows of the Porch; it was much more than "some shy ostrich prompting" which bade her assign to an old Stoic the most personal and characteristic utterance in all her previous poems; but the double current of imaginative passion and practical compassion which made her a tragic poet and proved her a perfect woman gives as it were a living warmth and sweetness to her memory, such as might well have seemed incompatible with that sterner and colder veneration so long reserved for her spiritual kinsmen of the past. As a woman we never knew her so well as now that we have to welcome this worthy record of her life, with deeper thanks and warmer congratulations to the writer than can often be due even to the best of biographers and critics. As an author she has not perhaps even yet received her full due or taken her final place. Again and again has the same obvious objection been taken to that awkwardness of construction or presentation which no reader of "Wuthering Heights" can undertake to deny. [Illustrations follow.]

. . . Yet all this we gladly and gratefully admit, without demur or cavil, to be thoroughly authentic and credible, because the whole matter of the report, however we get at it, is found when we do get at it to be vivid and lifelike as an actual experience of living fact. Here, if ever anywhere, the attainment of the end justifies the employment of the means. If we are to enjoy imaginative work at all, we must "assume the virtue" of imagination, even if we have it not; we must, as children say, "pretend" or make believe a little as a very condition of the game.

A graver and perhaps a somewhat more plausible charge is brought against the author of "Wuthering Heights" by those who find here and there in her book the savage note or the sickly symptom of a morbid ferocity. Twice or thrice especially the details of deliberate or passionate brutality in Heathcliff's treatment of his victims make the reader feel for a moment as though he were reading a police report or even a novel by some French "naturalist" of the latest and brutallest order. But the pervading atmosphere of the book is so high and healthy that the effect even of those "vivid and fearful scenes" which impaired the rest of Charlotte Brontë is almost at once neutralized — we may hardly say softened, but sweetened, dispersed, and transfigured — by the general impression of noble purity and passionate straightforwardness, which removes it at once and for ever from any such ugly possibility of association or comparison. The whole work is not more incomparable in the effect of its atmosphere or landscape than in the peculiar note of its wild and bitter pathos; but most of all is it unique in the special and distinctive character of its passion. The love which devours life itself, which devastates the present and desolates the future with unquenchable and raging fire, has nothing less pure in it than flame or sunlight. And this passionate and ardent chastity is utterly and unmistakably spontaneous and unconscious. Not till the story is ended, not till the effect of it has been thoroughly absorbed and digested, does the reader even perceive the simple and natural absence of any grosser element, any hint or suggestion of a baser alloy in the ingredients of its human emotion than in the splendour of lightning or the roll of a gathered wave. Then, as on issuing sometimes from the tumult of charging waters, he finds with something of wonder how absolutely pure and sweet was the element of living storm with which his own nature has been for a while made one; not a grain in it of soiling sand, not a waif of clogging weed. As was the author's life, so is her book in all things: troubled and taintless, with little of rest in it, and nothing of reproach. It may be true that not many will ever take it to their hearts; it is certain that those who do like it will like nothing very much better in the whole world of poetry or prose.

Angus M. Mackay

From "Emily Brontë," *Westminster Review*, Vol. 100 (August 1898).[1]

18

217   But . . . , Emily Brontë's rank as a poet is to be measured, not by her verse, but by her single romance. The quantity as well [as]

[1] Mackay, one of the soundest nineteenth century writers on the Brontës, begins this article with a careful study of her poetry, which he thinks has been underestimated. He remarks on her love of nature and of her home, her concern with her brother's failure, her imagination, and her "habit of pondering deeply the mysteries of human existence" (p. 213).

the quality of work must needs be taken into account in estimating the genius of a writer, and it may seem that a beginner's first volume forms a slender foundation for a claim to high rank. But if we look only to the *quality* of the imagination displayed in *Wuthering Heights* — its power, its intensity, its absolute originality — it is scarcely too much to say of Emily that she might have been Shakespeare's younger sister. To the many, of course, this will seem merely fantastic; but the few who have really learnt to appreciate *Wuthering Heights* will see no exaggeration in the title. Putting aside the clumsiness of the framework — the only mark of the prentice-hand in the whole book — what is there comparable to this romance except the greater tragedies of Shakespeare? The single peasant in the story, Joseph, is of the kin of Shakespeare's clowns, and yet is quite distinct from them. Heathcliffe is one of the most vivid creations in all literature; he fascinates the imagination, and in some scenes almost paralyses us with horror, and yet that subtle human touch is added which wrings from us pity and almost respect. He reminds us of Shylock and Iago — not, indeed, by any likeness to their characters, but by the sense of wonder he awakens in us at the power that could create such a being. Catherine Earnshaw, again, and Catherine Linton — are not these by their piquancy and winsomeness almost worthy of a place in Shakespeare's gallery of fair women? The whole story has something of the pathos of *King Lear* and much of the tragic force of *Macbeth,* and yet both characters and story are, perhaps, as absolutely original as any that can be named in English literature. It is not, of course, meant that Emily Brontë achieved anything comparable to Shakespeare's greatest work: Shakespeare lived to become a great artist, while Emily only once tried her prentice-hand; Shakespeare knew the world in all its phases, while Emily passed her life in the seclusion of a remote village: but the material out of which the two wrought their work, the protoplasm of their creations, so to speak, was the same. Suppose Shakespeare had died, as Emily did, after completing his first work — *Love's Labours Lost* — would he have lived in men's memories at all? Or suppose the great dramatist's career to have closed at the same age as Emily's — twenty-nine: he would then have written a group of five complete plays, many of them comparatively immature, and none of them of the first rank as showing the real supremacy of his genius. Thus considered, the claim that Emily Brontë's creative power had something of the nature of Shakespeare's will not appear extravagant to those who can justly estimate what she has accomplished in *Wuthering Heights*.

It would be profitless, perhaps, to speculate on the work which this powerful imagination might have achieved had time been granted; let us rather be grateful for the imperishable work with which she has enriched our literature, and cherish the careless preludes which show how great a poet was lost to the world when Emily Brontë died.

V. Letters and Reminiscences

The Brontës apparently destroyed most letters written to them, so the first part of this section consists mainly of letters *about* Charlotte or her work. Immediately after her death began the flood of writings on the family which to this day shows no signs of diminishing. The items included here (from #15 on) are limited to accounts by people who had first-hand acquaintance with the Brontës or the Hegers or Ellen Nussey. The degree of intimacy and any possible bias are important factors to keep in mind in estimating the value of the source. You will find at the front of this book an alphabetical list of some of the people mentioned here and in Charlotte's letters whose acquaintance with the Brontës was of some substance. Other writers are identified in footnotes. It has not been thought necessary to describe major Victorian figures such as Thackeray, Arnold, or Miss Martineau, who can be looked up in encyclopedias.

Information on Mrs. Gaskell, too, is easy to find, but perhaps something should be said of her life of Charlotte, a few excerpts from which are given here. Curious students will want to read the whole work and should be aware of its limitations as well as its importance.

Mrs. Gaskell certainly had the very highest intentions in writing the *Life,* as her own words show: "I did so try to tell the truth. . . . I weighed every line with my whole power and heart, so that every line should go to its great purpose of making her known and valued, as one who had gone through such a terrible life with such a brave and faithful heart."[1] To Mr. Brontë, too, she must have seemed an ideal choice. She had made a good impression on him personally. She had known and liked Charlotte. She was in touch with the literary world of which they had both been a part. She was already well known as a writer. Her novels, many of them exposés of the ill effects of industrialism on the working class, were remarkable for their insight into human nature, graceful style, quaint touches of humor, and fidelity to life. Her ability and integrity were unquestioned. Yet shrewd Mary Taylor, far away in New Zealand, wrote in surprise, "Mrs. Gaskell seems far too able a person to put her head into such a wasps' nest, as she would raise about her by speaking the truth of living people."[2]

However, even before Mr. Brontë's letter came, Mrs. Gaskell had written to Charlotte's publishers suggesting a short collection of her memories about Charlotte. She was delighted with the project and set about it with enthusiasm and thoroughness. She obtained letters from Charlotte's correspondents and copied them (not always accurately). She got Mr. Brontë, Ellen, Mary, and others to write down their recollections. She visited almost every place connected with Charlotte and talked with people who had known her. She even went to Brussels: Mme. Heger would not see her, but M. Heger was kind and suggested that she read his letters to Charlotte which contained, he said, advice on her conduct and studies. These had, unfortunately, disappeared. Mrs. Gaskell saw Charlotte's letters to her "master" — at least parts of them — but naturally did not print them. In a letter to a friend she expressed the pious hope that M. Heger was too good a man to reveal their contents to the public.

The *Life* came out early in 1857 and had gone into a second edition before Mrs. Gaskell, who had traveled to Italy for a rest, returned to England. The book had had good reviews and was selling well, but the wasps were gathering. Mr. Brontë (presumably Mr. Nicholls read him a judiciously cut version) was pleased, and even later, when he had been told of some criticisms she had made, remained substantially loyal

---

1 Quoted in S. H. IV, 218–219.
2 Letter to E. N., April 19, 1856; quoted in S. H. IV, 198.

to her. But Mr. Nicholls, though silent, had never liked the idea of a biography and probably did not relish hints that he was not appreciative of Charlotte as a literary figure. The servants were furious at being called wasteful, other local people were up in arms that a Lancashire woman should write of Yorkshire as a rough, barbarous place, and a reference to a Haworth girl said to have been seduced gave offence. Miss Martineau was put out that Mrs. Gaskell had not seen fit to apply to her for more information, and John Stuart Mill was hurt at some comments in one of Charlotte's letters on his wife's "Emancipation of Women." But all this was as nothing compared to the furor aroused by two passages in particular: the account of Cowan Bridge School and the open implication that Branwell owed his downfall to the evil character of Mrs. Robinson. The first brought forth a flood of charges and counter-charges, while the attack on Mrs. Robinson, by then Lady Scott, nearly brought about a libel action. Mrs. Gaskell was obliged to publish a retraction in the *Times*. The third edition of the *Life* attempted to satisfy some of these complaints, but met with some criticism, for example from Mary Taylor, who wrote Ellen: "Libellous or not, the first edition was all true and . . . useful to be published." She had already told Mrs. Gaskell that the *Life* was "not so gloomy as the truth," but probably "as much as people will accept without calling it exaggerated." She was indignant that the third edition had been "mutilated."

Robert Southey

1

TO C. B. [G.][1]

[Keswick, March 1837]

102 MADAM, —] [. . .] It is not my advice that you have asked as to the direction of your talents, but my opinion of them, and yet the opinion may be worth little, and the advice much. You evidently possess, and in no inconsiderable degree, what Wordsworth calls the "faculty of verse." I am not depreciating it when I say that in these times it is not rare. . . . Whoever, therefore, is ambitious of distinction in this way ought to be prepared for disappointment.

But it is not with a view to distinction that you should cultivate this talent, if you consult your own happiness. I, who have made literature my profession, and devoted my life to it, and have never for a moment repented of the deliberate choice, think myself, nevertheless, bound in duty to caution every young man who applies as an aspirant to me for encouragement and advice,

[1] Robert Southey (1774–1843) had been Poet Laureate since 1813. For Charlotte's reply, see March 16, 1837.

against taking so perilous a course. You will say that a woman has no need of such a caution; there can be no peril in it for her. In a certain sense this is true; but there is a danger of which I would, with all kindness and all earnestness, warn you. The day dreams in which you habitually indulge are likely to induce a distempered state of mind; and in proportion as all the ordinary uses of the world seem to you flat and unprofitable, you will be unfitted for them without becoming fitted for anything else. Literature cannot be the business of a woman's life, and it ought not to be. The more she is engaged in her proper duties, the less leisure will she have for it, even as an accomplishment and a recreation. To those duties you have / not yet been called, 103 and when you are you will be less eager for celebrity. You will not seek in imagination for excitement, of which the vicissitudes of this life, and the anxieties from which you must not hope to be exempted, be your state what it may, will bring with them but too much.

But do not suppose that I disparage the

gift which you possess; nor that I would discourage you from exercising it. I only exhort you so to think of it, and so to use it, as to render it conducive to your own permanent good. Write poetry for its own sake; not in a spirit of emulation, and not with a view to celebrity; the less you aim at that the more likely you will be to deserve and finally to obtain it. So written, it is wholesome both for the heart and soul; it may be made the surest means, next to religion, of soothing the mind and elevating it. You may embody in it your best thoughts and your wisest feelings, and in so doing discipline and strengthen them.

Farewell, madam. It is not because I have forgotten that I was once young myself, that I write to you in this strain; but because I remember it. You will neither doubt my sincerity nor my good will; and however ill what has here been said may accord with your present views and temper, the longer you live the more reasonable it will appear to you. Though I may be but an ungracious adviser, you will allow me, therefore, to subscribe myself, with the best wishes for your happiness here and hereafter, your true friend,   Robert Southey.

2

Keswick, March 22, 1837.
105 Dear Madam, — Your letter has given me great pleasure, and I should not forgive myself if I did not tell you so. You have received admonition as considerately and as kindly as it was given. Let me now request that, if you ever should come to these lakes while I am living here, you will let me see you. You would then think of me afterwards with the more goodwill, because you would perceive that there is neither severity nor moroseness in the state of mind to which years and observation have brought me. . . .

And now, Madam, God bless you!

Farewell, and believe me to be your sincere friend,   Robert Southey.

C. Heger

3

TO PATRICK BRONTË[1]
Saturday, November 5th [1842]
My dear Sir, — A very sad event has made your daughters decide to return suddenly to England. Their departure, which grieved us very much, has, however, my complete approval; it is quite natural that by being with you they should seek to console you for what Heaven has taken from you, by reminding you of what it leaves you still. I hope you will pardon me, Sir, for taking advantage of this circumstance to convey to you this expression of my respect; I do not have the honor of knowing you personally, and nevertheless I entertain for you a feeling of sincere admiration, for in judging a father by his children, one is not likely to be deceived, and in this respect the education and the sensibilities that we have found in your daughters have given us a very high opinion of your worth and of your character. Without doubt you will learn with pleasure that your children have made very remarkable progress in all branches of instruction, and that this progress is due entirely to their love for study and to their perseverance.

Mlle. Emily was studying the piano; taking lessons from the best professor we have in Belgium, and already she herself had some little pupils; she was losing thereby what was left of ignorance, and what was still more troublesome, a last vestige of shy-

[1] Translated from the original French (S. H. I, pp. 278–280) by Giselle Guerre and Beatrice Shuttleworth.

ness; Mlle. Charlotte was beginning to give English lessons, and to acquire that assurance and poise so necessary in teaching; one year more at the most and the work would have been accomplished and well accomplished. Then we would have been able, if it had been agreeable to you, to offer your daughters, or at least to one of the two, a position which would have given her that agreeable independence so difficult for a young person to secure. This is not, believe me sincerely, Sir, a question of selfish interest, it is a question of affection; you will pardon me if we speak to you about your children, if we concern ourselves with their future as though they were part of our family; their personal qualities, their willingness, their extraordinary zeal are the only reasons that impel us to venture thus.

We know, Sir, that you will weigh with greater maturity and greater wisdom, the consequences for the future that a total interruption in your two daughters' studies would have. You will decide what must be done, and you will forgive our frankness if you take into consideration that the motive which prompts our action is a truly disinterested affection, already saddened at the thought of being no longer of assistance to your children.

May I beg you, Sir, to accept the respectful expression of my highest regard.

C. Heger

William Makepeace Thackeray

4

TO W. S. WILLIAMS [S. H.]
II,149
Oct. 23rd, 1847
I wish you had not sent me *Jane Eyre*. It interested me so much that I have lost (or won if you like) a whole day in reading it at the busiest period with the printers I know wailing for copy. Who the author can be I can't guess, if a woman she knows her language better than most ladies do, or has had a "classical" education. It is a fine book though, the man and woman capital, the style very generous and upright so to speak. I thought it was Kinglake for some time. The plot of the story is one with wh. I am familiar. Some of the love passages made me cry, to the astonishment of John, who came in with the coals. St John the Missionary is a failure I think but a good failure, there are parts excellent. I don't know why I tell you this but that I have been exceedingly moved and pleased by *Jane Eyre*. It is a woman's writing, but whose? Give my respects and thanks to the author, whose novel is the first English one (and the French are only romances now) that I've been able to read for many a day.

George Eliot

As reprinted in *The Life of George Eliot*, ed. J. W. Cross, 3 vols. Edinburgh: Blackwood, 1885.

5

TO CHARLES BRAY
I,154
June, 1848
I have read *Jane Eyre*, and shall be glad to know what you admire in it. All self-sacrifice is good, but one would like it to be in a somewhat nobler cause than that of a diabolical law which chains a man soul and body to a putrefying carcase. / However, 155 the book *is* interesting; only I wish the characters would talk a little less like the heroes and heroines of police reports.

Elizabeth Gaskell

6

TO ANN SHAEN [S. H.]

II,57   December 21st, 1849.

. . . Have you heard that Harriet Martineau has sworn an eternal friendship with the authoress of "Shirley," if not I'll tell you. She sent "Shirley" to Harriet Martineau. H. M. acknowledged it in a note directed to Currer Bell Esq. — but inside written to a *lady*. Then came an answer requesting a personal interview. This was towards or about last Saturday week, and the time appointed was 6 o'clock on Sunday Eveng and the place appointed was at Mr Richard Martineau's . . . in Hyde Park Square, so Mr and Mrs R. Martineau and Harriet M. sat with early tea before them, awaiting six o'clock, and their mysterious visitor, when lo! and behold, as the clock struck in walked a little, very little, bright haired sprite, looking not above 15, very unsophisticated, neat and tidy. She sat down and had tea with them, her name being still unknown; she said to H. M. "What did you really think of 'Jane Eyre'?" H. M. "I thought it a first rate book." Whereupon the little sprite went red all over with pleasure. After tea Mr and Mrs R. M. withdrew, and left sprite to a 2 hours tête à tête with H. M. to whom she revealed her name and the history of her life. . . .

7

TO CATHERINE WINKWORTH [G.][1]

[August 25, 1850]

309 [My dearest Katie, . . .] Dark when I got to Windermere station; a drive along the level road to Low-wood; then a stoppage at a pretty house, and then a pretty drawing-room, in which were Sir James and Lady Kay Shuttleworth, and a little lady in a black-silk gown, whom I could not see at first for the dazzle in the room; she came up and shook hands with me at once. I went up to unbonnet, etc.; came down to tea; the little lady worked away and hardly spoke, but I had time for a good look at her. She 310 is (as she calls herself) / undeveloped, thin, and more than half a head shorter than I am; soft brown hair, not very dark; eyes (very good and expressive, looking straight and open at you) of the same colour as her hair; a large mouth; the forehead square, broad, and rather overhanging. She has a very sweet voice; rather hesitates in choosing her expressions, but when chosen they seem without an effort admirable, and just befitting the occasion; there is nothing overstrained, but perfectly simple. * * * After breakfast, we four went out on the lake, and Miss Brontë agreed with me in liking Mr. Newman's *Soul*, and in liking *Modern Painters*, and the idea of the *Seven Lamps*; and she told me about Father Newman's lectures at the Oratory in a very quiet, concise, graphic way. * * * She is more like Miss [Fox] than any one in her ways — if you can fancy Miss [Fox] to have gone through suffering enough to have taken out every spark of merriment, and to be shy and silent from the habit of extreme, intense solitude. Such a life as Miss Brontë's I never heard of before. . . .

We were only three days together; the greater part of which was spent in driving about, in order to show Miss Brontë the Westmoreland scenery, as she had never been there before. We were both included in an invitation to drink tea quietly at Fox How; and I then saw how severely her nerves were taxed by the effort of going amongst strangers. We knew beforehand that the number of the party would not exceed twelve; but she suffered the whole day

[1] Mrs. Gaskell had been visiting the Kay-Shuttleworths at their home near Windermere. Fox How was Arnold's home.

from an acute headache brought on by apprehension of the evening.

. . . I was struck by Miss Brontë's careful examination of the shape of the clouds and the signs of the heavens, in which she read, as from a book, what the coming weather would be. I told her that I saw she must have a view equal in extent at her own home. She said that I was right, but that the character of the prospect from Haworth was very different; that I had no idea what a companion the sky became to any one living in solitude, — more than any inanimate object on earth, — more than the moors themselves.

[Yours very affectionately, E. C. Gaskell]

Bessie Parkes

8

III,
167

TO E. G. [S. H.][1]

October 3rd, 1850.

Though the weather was drizzly we resolved to make our long-planned excursion to Haworth; so we packed ourselves into the buffalo skin, and that into the gig, and set off about eleven. The rain ceased, and the day was just suited to the scenery — wild and chill — with great masses of cloud glooming over the moors, and here and there a ray of sunshine covertly stealing through, and resting with a dim magical light upon some high bleak village; or darting down into some deep glen, lighting up the tall chimney, or glistening on the windows and wet roof of the mill which lies couching in the bottom. The country got wilder and wilder as we approached Haworth; for the last four miles we were ascending a huge moor, at the very top of which lies the dreary, black-looking village of Haworth. The village street itself is one of the steepest hills I have ever seen, and the stones are so horribly jolting that I should have got out and walked with W——, if possible, but, having once begun the ascent, to stop was out of the question. At the top was the inn where we put up, close by the church; and the clergyman's house, we were told, was at the top of the churchyard. So through that we went — a dreary, dreary place, literally *paved* with / rain-blackened tombstones, and all on the 168 slope; for at Haworth there is on the highest height a higher still, and Mr. Brontë's house stands considerably above the church. There was the house before us, a small oblong stone house, with not a tree to screen it from the cutting wind; but how we were to get at it from the churchyard we could not see! There was an old man in the churchyard, brooding like a ghoul over the graves, with a sort of grim hilarity on his face. I thought he looked hardly human; however, he was human enough to tell us the way, and presently we found ourselves in the little bare parlour. Presently the door opened, and in came a superannuated mastiff, followed by an old gentleman very like Miss Brontë, who shook hands with us, and then went to call his daughter. A long interval, during which we coaxed the old dog, and looked at a picture of Miss Brontë, by Richmond, the solitary ornament of the room, looking strangely out of place on the bare walls, and at the books on the little shelves, most of them evidently the gift of the authors since Miss Brontë's celebrity. Presently she came in, and welcomed us very kindly, and took me upstairs to take off my bonnet, and herself brought me water and towels. The uncarpeted pine stairs and floors, the old drawers propped on wood, were all scrupulously clean and neat. When we went into

[1] Elizabeth (Bessie) Parkes, later Belloc (1829–1925), a member of a radical and Unitarian family who later became a Roman Catholic, was a minor writer of the day. Hilaire Belloc was her son. Compare this description with Mrs. Gaskell's when she visited Charlotte in 1853. (*Life of Charlotte Brontë*, Ch. 27.)

the parlour again we began talking very comfortably. . . .

169   Miss Brontë put me so in mind of her own "Jane Eyre." She looked smaller than ever, and moved about so quietly, and noiselessly, just like a little bird, as Rochester called her, barring that all birds are joyous, and that joy can never have entered that house since it was first built; and yet, perhaps, when that old man married, and took home his bride, and children's voices and feet were heard about the house, even that desolate crowded graveyard and biting blast could not quench cheerfulness and hope. Now there is something touching in the sight of that little creature entombed in such a place, and moving about herself like a spirit, especially when you think that the slight still frame encloses a force of strong fiery life, which nothing has been able to freeze or extinguish.

Matthew Arnold

As reprinted in *Letters of Matthew Arnold,* 2 vols. London: Macmillan and Co., 1895.

9

TO MISS WIGHTMAN
[Fox How, Dec. 21, 1850]
I,13   . . . At seven came Miss Martineau and Miss Brontë (*Jane Eyre*); talked to Miss Martineau (who blasphemes frightfully) about the prospects of the Church of England, and, wretched man that I am, promised to go and see her cow-keeping miracles to-morrow — I, who hardly know a cow from a sheep. I talked to Miss Brontë (past thirty and plain, with expressive grey eyes, though) of her curates, of French novels, and her education in a school at Brussels, and sent the lions roaring to their dens at half-past nine. . . .

Elizabeth Gaskell

As reprinted in Elizabeth Haldane, *Mrs. Gaskell and Her Friends.* London: Hodder and Stoughton, 1930. Reprinted by permission of the publisher and Mrs. Haldane.

10

TO JOHN FORSTER[1]
150   April 23rd, 1854
. . . Yes! she is going to be married! to Mr Nicholls, who has returned to Haworth. He made some kind of renewed application to her father to be allowed to see them from time to time as an acquaintance, in January; in February he again spoke to her; and

1 John Forster (1812–76), critic and friend and biographer of Dickens. Mrs. Gaskell's brand of nonconformity (Unitarianism) would be particularly objectionable to Mr. Nicholls, a strict Anglican.

she says she cannot tell all the details in a letter, but "events have so flowed out of each other that now she finds herself what people called engaged." . . . The "old, the poor, the very young" among the Haworth people are delighted, which speaks well for Mr. Nicholls / I'm sure. I am terribly 151 afraid he won't let her go on being intimate with us heretics. I see she is, too, a little. However, she is coming to us in May, and I must make the most of her then, and hope for the future. I fancy him very good, but *very* stern and bigoted; but I daresay that is partly fancy. Still, it arises from what she told me. He sounds vehemently in love with her. And I like his having known her dead sisters and dead brother and all she has gone through of home trials, and being no person who has just fancied himself in love with her because he was dazzled by her genius. Mr. N. never knew till long after "Shirley" was published that she wrote books; and came in, cold & disapproving one day, to ask her if the report he had heard at Keighley was true &c. Fancy him an Irish curate, loving her even then, reading that beginning of "Shirley"! However, with all his bigotry and sternness it must be charming to be loved with all the strength of his heart as she sounds to be. Mr. Shaen accuses me always of being "too much of a woman" in always wanting to obey somebody — but I am sure that Miss Brontë could never have borne not to be well-ruled and ordered — Well! I think I have got into a fiasco and I have hardly any right to go on discussing what she could or she could not do — but I mean that she would never have been happy but with an exacting, rigid, law-giving passionate man — only you see, I'm afraid one of his laws will be to shut us out, and so I am making a sort of selfish moan over it & have got out of temper I suppose with the very thing I have been wanting for her this six months past. . . .

11

TO JOHN FORSTER [HALDANE]

153

May, 1854.

I troubled you with my groans, my dear Mr. Forster, so now you see I am going to send you my reliefs — selfish the first is. I don't believe Miss Brontë will *soon* become bigoted, or *ever* lose her true love for me — but I do fear a *little* for her happiness just because he is narrow and she is not. Good, true, pure & / affectionate he is, but 154 he is also narrow, and she can never be so. . . .[1]

[1] Ellen, too, had misgivings about Charlotte's happiness; see the reminiscences of Reid, below.

Catherine Winkworth

12

TO EMMA SHAEN [S. H.]

IV,
121

Alderley Edge, May 8th, 1854
. . . I suppose you will have heard that [Miss Brontë] is to be married in a few weeks to a clergyman, a Mr. Nicholls, who was for eight years curate to her father, was then sent off in a hurry for his audacity in falling in love with the rector's daughter, but is now coming back to be curate and / 122 son-in-law. Alas! alas! I am very glad for Miss Brontë's sake, but sorry for ours, for we can never reckon on seeing her much again when she is "a married woman." Emily and I both went over on Tuesday to see her. . . . [A]t parting Miss Brontë said to me: "I hope I shall see you again." So I went in on Wednesday. Lily [Mrs G.] drew me in directly to the room, whispering: "Say something about her marriage." . . . When she was summoned away I began: "I was very glad to hear something Mrs Gaskell told me about you." "What was it?" "That you are not going to be alone any more." She leant her head on her hand and said very quickly: "Yes, I am going to be married in June." "It will be a great happiness for you to have someone to care for, and make happy." "Yes; and it is a great thing to be the first object with any one." "And you must be very sure of that with Mr Nicholls; he has known you and wished for this so long, I hear." "Yes, he has more

than once refused preferment since he left my father, because he knew he never could marry me unless he could return to Haworth; he knew I could not leave my father." She stopped, and then went on: "But, Katie, it has cost me a good deal to come to this." "You will have to care for his things, instead of his caring for yours, is that it?" "Yes, I can see that beforehand." "But you have been together so long already that you know what his things are, very well. He is very devoted to his duties, is he not? — and you can and would like to help him in those?" "I have always been used to those, and it is one great pleasure to me that he is so much beloved by all the people in the parish; there is quite a rejoicing over his return. But those are not everything, and I cannot conceal from myself that he is *not* intellectual; there are many places into which he could not follow me intellectually." "Well; of course every one has their own tastes. For myself, if a man had a firm, constant, affectionate, reliable nature, with tolerable practical sense, I should be much better satisfied with him than if

123 he had an intellect far / beyond mine, and brilliant gifts without that trustworthiness. I care most for a calm, equable atmosphere at home." "I do believe Mr Nicholls is as reliable as you say, or I wouldn't marry him." "And you have had time to prove it; you are not acting in a hurry." "That is true; and, indeed, I am quite satisfied with my decision; still" — here Lily came in, and Miss Brontë repeated what I had been saying, ending with — "still such a character would be far less amusing and interesting than a more impulsive and fickle one; it might be dull!" "Yes, indeed," said Lily. "For a day's companion, yes," I said, "but not for a life's: one's home ought to be the one fixed point, the one untroubled region in one's lot; at home one wants peace and settled love and trust, not storm and change and excitement; besides such a character would have the advantage that one might do the fickleness required one's self, which would be a relief sometimes." "Oh, Katie, if *I* had ever said such a wicked thing,"

cried Lily; and then Miss Brontë: "Oh, Katie, I never thought to hear such a speech from *you!*" "You don't agree with it?" "Oh, there is truth in it; so much that I don't think *I* could ever have been so candid," Miss Brontë said; "And there is danger, too, one might be led on to go too far." "I think not," I said; "the steadiness and generosity on the other side would always keep one in check." But they made a great deal of fun and laughing about this, and then Lily was called away again, and Miss Brontë went on: "He is a Puseyite[1] and very stiff; I fear it will stand in the way of my intercourse with some of my friends. But I shall always be the same in my heart towards them. I shall never let him make me a bigot. I don't think differences of opinion ought to interfere with friendship, do you?" "No." And we talked about this a little, and then I said: "Perhaps, too, you may do something to introduce him to goodness in sects where he has thought it could not be." "That is what I hope; he has a most sincere love of goodness wherever he sees it. I think if he could come to know Mr Gaskell it would change his feeling." Then, quite suddenly, she said: "Tell me about your sister. Is she happy in her married life?" "Yes, very happy indeed." "Sincerely?" "Yes, she not only says so, but it shines out in everything that she is happier than ever before in her life." "And what is your brother-in-law like?" So I had to describe Will, thinking privately that it did not sound as though Mr Nicholls would make half such a good husband, but did not say so, and to tell her a good deal about their en-/gagement. What she cared most 124 about hearing about Will was, whether he was selfish about small things, whether he took his share of small economies, or whether he appreciated Emily's endeavours and small self-denials, &c. Concerning which he had been praising Emily to me the last time he was here, so I edified her

[1] A follower of Pusey, one of the leaders of the Oxford Movement which advocated the revival of Catholic doctrine and practice in the Church of England.

with reporting that, and gave him generally "an excellent character," as people say of servants. About Emily she wanted to know what variations of mood, what doubts and fears, she had felt about her marriage beforehand. Had she felt any, or was she always light-hearted during the time? So I said that no one could be exactly always light-hearted, I thought, who was not very young and thoughtless, whereat it came out that she thought Emily not twenty-five now. And then we talked over all the natural doubts that any thoughtful woman would feel at such a time, and my own mother's early married life, and when Lily returned she said she felt greatly comforted; and thereupon Lily set off praising *her* husband for being a good sick nurse and so good to the children, and how very winning that was to the mother. Afterwards, Miss Brontë asked me a good deal about you, with a great deal of kindly interest. . . .

Patrick Brontë

13

IV, 177

Haworth, nr Keighley, March 30th, 1855.

My dear Madam, — We are all in great trouble, and Mr Nicholls so much so that he is not so sufficiently strong and composed as to be able to write. I therefore devote a few moments to tell you that my dear Daughter is very ill, and apparently on the verge of the grave. If she could speak she would no doubt dictate to us while answering your kind letter, but we are left to ourselves to give what answer we can. The Doctors have no hope of her case, and fondly as we a long time cherished hope that hope is now gone, and we have only to look forward to the solemn event with prayer to God that He will give us grace and strength sufficient unto our day.

Will you be so kind as to write to Miss Wooler, and Mrs Joe Taylor, and inform them that we requested you to do so, telling them of our present condition? — Ever truly and respectfully yours, P. Brontë

[1] See Mrs. Gaskell's account of Charlotte's last months.

Arthur Bell Nicholls

14

TO E. N. [S. H.]

IV, 177

Haworth, March 31st, 1855.

Dear Miss Nussey, — Mr Brontë's letter would prepare you for the sad intelligence I have to communicate. Our dear Charlotte is no more. She died last night of exhaustion. For the last two or three weeks we had become very uneasy about her, but it / was not until Sunday evening that it became apparent that her sojourn with us was likely to be short. We intend to bury her on Wednesday morning. — Believe me, sincerely yours,

A. B. Nicholls

Harriet Martineau

15

"Death of Currer Bell," *Daily News* (April 6 1855).

5   "Currer Bell" is dead! The early death of the large family of whom she was the sole survivor prepared all who knew the circumstances to expect the loss of this gifted creature at any time: but not the less deep will be the grief of society that her genius will yield us nothing more. We have three works from her pen which will hold their place in the literature of our country; and, but for her frail health, there might have been three times three, — for she was under forty — and her genius was not of an exhaustible kind. If it had been exhaustible, it would have been exhausted some time since. She had every inducement that could have availed with one less high-minded to publish two or three novels a year. Fame waited upon all she did; and she might have enriched herself by very slight exertion: but her steady conviction was that the publication of a book is a solemn act of conscience — in the case of a novel as much as any other kind of book. She was not fond of speaking of herself and her conscience; but she now and then uttered to her very few friends things which may, alas! be told now, without fear of hurting her sensitive nature; things which ought to be told in her honour. Among these sayings was one which explains the long interval between her works. She said that she thought every serious delineation of life ought to be the product of personal experience and observation of a normal, and not of a forced or special kind. "I have not accumulated, since I published 'Shirley'," she said, "what makes it needful for me to speak again, and, till I do, may God give me grace to be dumb!" She had a conscientiousness which could not be relaxed by praise or even sympathy — dear as sympathy was to her sensitive nature. She had no vanity which praise could aggravate or censure mortify. She calmly read all adverse reviews of her books, for the sake of instruction; and when she could not recognise the aptness of criticism, she was more puzzled than hurt or angry. The common flatteries which wait upon literary success she quizzed with a charming grace; and any occasional severity, such as literary women are favoured with at the beginning of their course, she accepted with a humility which was full of dignity and charm. From her feeble constitution of body, her sufferings by the death of her whole family, and the secluded and monotonous life she led, she became morbidly sensitive in some respects; but in her high vocation, she had, in addition to the deep intuitions of a gifted woman, the strength of a man, the patience of a hero, and the conscientiousness of a saint. In the points in which women are usually most weak — in regard to opinion, to appreciation, to applause, — her moral strength fell not a whit behind the intellectual force manifested in her works. Though passion occupies too prominent a place in her pictures of life, though women have to complain that she represents love as the whole and sole concern of their lives, and though governesses especially have reason to remonstrate, and do remonstrate, that their share of human conflict is laid open somewhat rudely and inconsiderately and sweepingly to social observation, it is a true social blessing that we have had a female writer who has discountenanced sentimentalism and feeble egotism with such practical force as is apparent in the works of Currer Bell. Her heroines love too readily, too vehemently, and sometimes after a fashion which their female readers may resent; but they do their duty through everything, and are healthy in action, however morbid in passion.

[Miss Martineau speaks of experiences which lead to the writing of *Wuthering Heights* and *Wildfell Hall*, and continues:] Such an experience as this indicates is really perplexing to English people in general; and all that we have to do with it is to bear it in mind when disposed to pass criticism on the coarseness which, to a certain degree, pervades the works of all the sisters, and the repulsiveness which makes the tales by Emily and Ann really horrible to people who have not iron nerves.

"Jane Eyre" was naturally and universally supposed to be Charlotte herself; but she always denied it, calmly, cheerfully, and with the obvious sincerity which characterised all she said. She declared that there was no more ground for the assertion than this. She once told her sisters that they were wrong — even morally wrong — in making their heroines beautiful, as a matter of course. They replied that it was impossible to make a heroine interesting on other terms. Her answer was, "I will prove to you that you are wrong. I will show you a heroine as small and as plain as myself who shall be as interesting as any of yours." "Hence, 'Jane Eyre'," said she in telling the anecdote; "but she is not myself, any further than that." As the work went on the interest deepened to the writer. When she came to "Thornfield" she could not stop. Being short-sighted to excess, she wrote in little square paper books, held close to her eyes, and (the first copy) in pencil. On she went, writing incessantly for three weeks; by which time she had carried her heroine away from Thornfield, and was herself in a fever, which compelled her to pause. The rest [i.e. of her work] was written with less vehemence, and more anxious care. . . .

"Shirley" was conceived and wrought out in the midst of fearful domestic griefs. Her only brother, a young man of once splendid promise which was early blighted, and both her remaining sisters, died in one year. There was something inexpressibly affecting in the aspect of the frail little creature who had done such wonderful things, and who was able to bear up, with so bright an eye and so composed a countenance, under such a weight of sorrow, and such a prospect of solitude. In her deep mourning dress (neat as a quaker's), with her beautiful hair, smooth and brown, her fine eyes blazing with meaning, and her sensible face indicating a habit of self-control, if not of silence, she seemed a perfect household image — irresistibly recalling Wordsworth's description of that domestic treasurer. . . . In so utter a seclusion as she lived in — in those dreary wilds, where she was not strong enough to roam over the hills,[1] in that retreat where her studious father rarely broke the silence — and there was no one else to do it; in that forlorn house, planted on the very clay of the churchyard, where the graves of her sisters were before her window; in such a living sepulchre her mind could not prey upon itself; and how it did suffer, we see in the more painful portions of her last novel — "Villette." . . .

[1] On this sentence Mrs. Gaskell (p. 319) comments as follows:

A friend of [Charlotte's], who wrote to me on the appearance of the eloquent article in the *Daily News* upon the "Death of Currer Bell," gives an anecdote which may well come in here.

"They are mistaken in saying she was too weak to roam the hills for the benefit of the air. I do not think any one, certainly not any woman, in this locality, went so much on the moors as she did, when the weather permitted. Indeed, she was so much in the habit of doing so, that people, who live quite away on the edge of the common, knew her perfectly well. I remember on one occasion an old woman saw her at a little distance, and she called out, 'How! Miss Brontë! Hey yah (have you) seen ought o' my cofe (calf)?' Miss Brontë told her she could not say, for she did not know it. 'Well!' she said, 'Yah know, it's getting up like nah (now), between a cah (cow) and a cofe — what we call a stirk, yah know, Miss Brontë; will yah turn it this way if yah happen to see't, as yah're going back, Miss Brontë; nah *do*, Miss Brontë.' "

Matthew Arnold

From *Poetical Works*. London: Macmillan and Co., 1907.

16

HAWORTH CHURCHYARD
Written April, 1855

299 Where, under Loughrigg,[1] the stream
Of Rotha sparkles through fields
Vested for ever with green,
Four years since, in the house
Of a gentle spirit, now dead —
Wordsworth's son-in-law,[2] friend —
I saw the meeting of two
Gifted women. The one,
Brilliant with recent renown, /

300 Young, unpractised, had told
With a master's accent her feign'd
Story of passionate life;
The other, maturer in fame,
Earning, she too, her praise
First in fiction, had since
Widen'd her sweep, and survey'd
History, politics, mind.

The two held converse; they wrote
In a book which of world-famous souls
Kept the memorial; — bard,
Warrior, statesman, had sign'd
Their names; chief glory of all,
Scott had bestow'd there his last
Breathings of song, with a pen
Tottering, a death-stricken hand.

Hope at that meeting smiled fair.
Years in number, it seem'd,
Lay before both, and a fame
Heighten'd, and multiplied power. —

Behold! The elder, to-day,
Lies expecting from death,
In mortal weakness, a last
Summons![3] the younger is dead!

First to the living we pay
Mournful homage; — the Muse
Gains not an earth-deafen'd ear.

Hail to the steadfast soul,
Which, unflinching and keen,
Wrought to erase from its depth
Mist and illusion and fear! /
Hail to the spirit which dared   301
Trust its own thoughts, before yet
Echoed her back by the crowd!
Hail to the courage which gave
Voice to its creed, ere the creed
Won consecration from time!

Turn we next to the dead.
— How shall we honour the young,
The ardent, the gifted? how mourn?
Console we cannot, her ear
Is deaf. Far northward from here,
In a churchyard high 'mid the moors
Of Yorkshire, a little earth
Stops it for ever to praise.

Where, behind Keighley, the road
Up to the heart of the moors
Between heath-clad showery hills
Runs, and colliers' carts
Poach the deep ways coming down,
And a rough, grimed race have their homes —
There on its slope is built

[1] Loughrigg is a high hill or "fell" which overlooks Grasmere Lake and Rydall Lake. The stream Rotha runs from Grasmere to Rydal and then to Lake Windermere. Fox How, Arnold's own home, was on the west side of the Rotha, about a mile down stream from Rydal Mount.

[2] This was Edward Quillinan (1791–1851), who married Wordsworth's daughter Dorothy in 1841.

[3] Harriet Martineau had at that time been told by a specialist that her heart was in bad condition; neither she nor her family and friends expected her to live. Even the newspapers speculated as to when she might die. Well-wishers sent her evangelical pamphlets and a New Testament so that she might repent her heresies before death overtook her. In actual fact, she lived until 1876, reading widely and writing energetically to the end!

The moorland town. But the church
Stands on the crest of the hill,
Lonely and bleak; — at its side
The parsonage-house and the graves.

Strew with laurel the grave
Of the early-dying! Alas,
Early she goes on the path
To the silent country, and leaves
Half her laurels unwon,
Dying too soon! — yet green /
302 Laurels she had, and a course
Short, but redoubled by fame.

And not friendless, and not
Only with strangers to meet,
Faces ungreeting and cold,
Thou, O mourn'd one, to-day
Enterest the house of the grave!
Those of thy blood, whom thou lov'dst,
Have preceded thee — young,
Loving, a sisterly band;
Some in art, some in gift
Inferior — all in fame.
They, like friends, shall receive
This comer, greet her with joy;
Welcome the sister, the friend;
Hear with delight of thy fame!

Round thee they lie — the grass
Blows from their graves to thy own!
She, whose genius, though not
Puissant like thine, was yet
Sweet and graceful; — and she
(How shall I sing her?) whose soul
Knew no fellow for might,
Passion, vehemence, grief,
Daring, since Byron died,
That world-famed son of fire — she, who sank
Baffled, unknown, self-consumed;

[4] Derek Stanford (*Emily Brontë: Her Life and Work*, p. 183) observes that in this stanza Arnold "anticipated the full course of Emily's thought on the issues of nature, immortality, and death," although he could hardly have seen the unpublished "I See Around Me Tombstones Grey," which offers "the silent dead" the same alternatives Arnold suggests here. Perhaps he was influenced by the closing paragraphs of *Wuthering Heights*.

Whose too bold dying song
Stirr'd like a clarion-blast my soul.[4]

Of one, too, I have heard,
A brother — sleeps he here? /
Of all that gifted race   303
Not the least gifted; young,
Unhappy, eloquent — the child
Of many hopes, of many tears.
O boy, if here thou sleep'st, sleep well!
On thee too did the Muse
Bright in thy cradle smile;
But some dark shadow came
(I know not what) and interposed.

Sleep, O cluster of friends,
Sleep! — or only when May,
Brought by the west-wind, returns
Back to your native heaths,
And the plover is heard on the moors,
Yearly awake to behold
The opening summer, the sky,
The shining moorland — to hear
The drowsy bee, as of old,
Hum o'er the thyme, the grouse
Call from the heather in bloom!
Sleep, or only for this
Break your united repose!

EPILOGUE

So I sang; but the Muse,
Shaking her head, took the harp —
Stern interrupted my strain,
Angrily smote on the chords.

April showers
Rush o'er the Yorkshire moors. /
Stormy, through driving mist,   304
Loom the blurr'd hills; the rain
Lashes the newly-made grave.

Unquiet souls!
— In the dark fermentation of earth,
In the never idle workshop of nature,
In the eternal movement,
Ye shall find yourselves again!

Patrick Brontë

17

IV,
194

TO E. G. [S. H.]

Haworth, August 27th, 1855

... My children generally, and my dear daughter Charlotte in particular, were both kind, liberal and affable with the inhabitants. A thorough sense of this proceeding was not wanting on the death of each of them — and when the last death took place, when my dear Charlotte was no more, both rich and poor throughout the village and the neighbourhood, both publicly and privately, gave sure proofs of genuine sorrow. ... a poor blind girl who received an annual donation from my daughter, after her death required to be led four miles to be at my daughter's funeral, over which she wept many tears of gratitude and sorrow. In her acts of kindness my dear daughter was, as I thought, often rather impulsive. Two or three winters ago a poor man fell on the ice and broke his thigh, and had to be carried home to his comfortless cottage, where he had a wife with twins and six other small children. My daughter having heard of their situation sent the servant to see how they were. On her return she made a very eloquent and pathetic report. My daughter being touched, got up directly and sent them a sovereign, to their great astonishment — and pleasure — for which they have been ever afterwards grateful. Though I could not help being pleased with this act — though hardly in accordance with my daughter's means — I observed to her that women were often impulsive in deeds of charity. She jocularly replied "In deeds of charity men reason much and do little; women reason little and do much, and I will act the woman still."　　P. Brontë

Ellen Nussey

Account of A. B.'s Death (from notes made at the time), written for Mrs. Gaskell, probably August, 1855. [G.]

18

271　She left her home May 24th, 1849 — died May 28th. Her life was calm, quiet, spiritual: *such* was her end. Through the trials and fatigues of the journey, she evinced the pious courage and fortitude of a martyr. Dependence and helplessness were ever with her a far sorer trial than hard, racking pain.

The first stage of our journey was to York; and here the dear invalid was so revived, so cheerful, and so happy, we drew consolation, and trusted that at least temporary improvement was to be derived from the change which *she* had so longed for, and her friends had so dreaded for her.

By her request we went to the Minster, and to her it was an overpowering pleasure; not for its own imposing and impressive grandeur only, but because it brought to her susceptible nature a vital and overwhelming sense of omnipotence. She said, while gazing at the structure, "If finite power can do this, what is the . . . ?" and here emotion stayed her speech, and she was hastened to a less exciting scene. . . .

On the 25th we arrived at Scarborough; our dear invalid having, during the journey, directed our attention to every prospect worthy of notice.

On the 26th she drove on the sands for an hour; and lest the poor donkey should be urged by its driver to a greater speed than her tender heart thought right, she took the reins, and drove herself. When joined by her friend, she was charging the boy-master of the donkey to treat the poor animal well. She was ever fond of dumb things, and would give up her own comfort for them.

On Sunday, the 27th, she wished to go 272 to church, and her / eye brightened with the thought of once more worshipping her God amongst her fellow-creatures. We thought it prudent to dissuade her from the attempt, though it was evident her heart was longing to join in the public act of devotion and praise.

She walked a little in the afternoon, and meeting with a sheltered and comfortable seat near the beach, she begged we would leave her, and enjoy the various scenes near at hand, which were new to us but familiar to her. She loved the place, and wished us to share her preference.

The evening closed in with the most glorious sunset ever witnessed. The castle on the cliff stood in proud glory gilded by the rays of the declining sun. The distant ships glittered like burnished gold; the little boats near the beach heaved on the ebbing tide, inviting occupants. The view was grand beyond description. Anne was drawn in her easy chair to the window, to enjoy the scene with us. Her face became illumined almost as much as the glorious scene she gazed upon. Little was said, for it was plain that her thoughts were driven by the imposing view before her to penetrate forwards to the regions of unfading glory. . . .

The night was passed without any apparent accession of illness. She rose at seven o'clock, and performed most of her toilet herself, by her expressed wish. Her sister always yielded such points, believing it was the truest kindness not to press inability when it was not acknowledged. Nothing occurred to excite alarm till about 11 A.M. She then spoke of feeling a change. "She believed she had not long to live. Could she reach home alive, if we prepared immediately for departure?" A physician was sent for. Her address to him was made with perfect composure. She begged him to say "How long he thought she might live; — not to fear speaking the truth, for she was not afraid to die." The doctor reluctantly admitted that the angel of death was already arrived, and that life was ebbing fast. She thanked him for his truthfulness, and he departed to come again very soon. She still occupied her easy chair, looking so serene, so reliant: there was no opening for grief as yet, though all knew the separation was at hand. She clasped her hands, and reverently invoked a blessing from on high; first upon her sister, then upon her friend, to whom she said, "Be a sister in my stead. Give Charlotte as much of your company as you can." She then thanked each for her kindness and attention.

Ere long the restlessness of approaching death appeared, and she was borne to the sofa; on being asked if she were easier, she looked gratefully at her questioner, and said, "It is not *you* who can give me ease, but soon all will be well, through the merits of our Redeemer." Shortly after this, seeing that her sister could hardly restrain her grief, she said, "Take courage, Charlotte; take courage." Her faith never failed, and her eye never dimmed till about two o'clock, when she calmly and without a sigh passed from the temporal to the eternal. So still, and so hallowed were her last hours and moments. . . .

Mary Taylor

19

65   [Jan. 18, 1856]

I first saw her coming out of a covered cart, in very old-fashioned clothes, and looking very cold and miserable. She was coming to school at Miss Wooler's. When she appeared in the schoolroom, her dress was changed, but just as old. She looked a little old woman, so short-sighted that she always appeared to be seeking something, and moving her head from side to side to catch a sight of it. She was very shy and nervous, and spoke with a strong Irish accent. When a book was given her, she dropped her head over it till her nose nearly touched it, and when she was told to hold her head up, up went the book after it, still close to her nose, so that it was not possible to help laughing.

We thought her very ignorant, for she had never learnt grammar at all, and very little geography.

66   She would confound us by knowing things that were out of our range altogether. She was acquainted with most of the short pieces of poetry that we had to learn by heart; would tell us the authors, the poems they were taken from, and sometimes repeat a page or two, and tell us the plot. She had a habit of writing in italics (printing characters) and said she had learnt it by writing in their magazine. They brought out a "magazine" once a month, and wished it to look as like print as possible. She told us a tale out of it. No one wrote in it, and no one read it, but herself, her brother, and two sisters. She promised to show me some of these magazines, but retracted it afterwards, and would never be persuaded to do so. In our play hours she sate, or stood still, with a book, if possible. Some of us once urged her to be on our side in a game at ball. She said she had never

¹ Mrs. Gaskell's text is faulty and there are some omissions, which she does not indicate.

played, and could not play. We made her try, but soon found that she could not see the ball, so we put her out. She took all our proceedings with pliable indifference, and always seemed to need a previous resolution to say "No" to anything. She used to go and stand under the trees in the playground, and say it was pleasanter. She endeavoured to explain this, pointing out the shadows, the peeps of sky, etc. We understood but little of it. She said that at Cowan Bridge she used to stand in the burn, on a stone, to watch the water flow by. I told her she should have gone fishing; she said she never wanted. She always showed physical feebleness in everything. She ate no animal food at school. It was about this time I told her she was very ugly. Some years afterwards, I told her I thought I had been very impertinent. She replied, "You did me a great deal of good, Polly, so don't repent of it." She used to draw much better, and more quickly, than anything we had seen before, and knew much about celebrated pictures and painters. Whenever an opportunity offered of examining a picture or cut of any kind, she went over it piecemeal, with her eyes close to the paper, looking so long that we used to ask her "what she saw in it." She could always see plenty, and explained it very well. She made poetry and drawing, at least exceedingly interesting to me; and then I got the habit, which I have yet, of referring / mentally to her opinion on all matters of that   67 kind, along with many more, resolving to describe such and such things to her, until I start at the recollection that I never shall.

We used to be furious politicians, as one could hardly help being in 1832. She knew the names of the two ministries; the one that resigned, and the one that succeeded and passed the Reform Bill. She worshipped the Duke of Wellington, but said that Sir Robert Peel was not to be trusted; he did not act from principle like the rest, but from expediency. I, being of the furious radical party, told her "how could any of them trust one another; they were all of them rascals!" Then she would launch out into praises of the Duke of Wellington, referring to his actions; which I could not contradict, as I knew nothing about him. She said she had taken interest in politics ever since she was five years old. She did not get her opinions from her father — that is, not directly — but from the papers, etc., he preferred.

68   She used to speak of her two elder sisters, Maria and Elizabeth, who died at Cowan Bridge. I used to believe them to have been wonders of talent and kindness. She told me, early one morning, that she had just been dreaming; she had been told that she was wanted in the drawing-room, and it was Maria and Elizabeth. I was eager for her to go on, and when she said there was no more, I said, "but go on! *Make it out! I know you can.*" She said she would not; she wished she had not dreamed, for it did not go on nicely; they were changed; they had forgotten what they used to care for. They were very fashionably dressed, and began criticising the room, etc.

This habit of "making out" interests for themselves, that most children get who have none in actual life, was very strong in her. The whole family used to "make out" histories, and invent characters and events. I told her sometimes they were like growing potatoes in a cellar. She said, sadly, "Yes! I know we are!"

100   . . . She visited us twice or thrice when she was at Miss Wooler's. We used to dispute about politics and religion. She, a
101 Tory and clergyman's / daughter, was always in a minority of one in our house of violent Dissent and Radicalism. She used to hear over again, delivered *with authority,* all the lectures I had been used to give her at school on despotic aristocracy, mercenary priesthood, etc. She had not energy to defend herself; sometimes she owned to a *little* truth in it, but generally said nothing. Her feeble health gave her her yielding manner, for she could never oppose any one without gathering up all her strength for the struggle. Thus she would let me advise and patronise most imperiously, sometimes picking out any grain of sense there might be in what I said, but never allowing any one materially to interfere with her independence of thought and action. Though her silence sometimes left one under the impression that she agreed when she did not, she never gave a flattering opinion, and thus her words were golden, whether for praise or blame. . . .

Three years after [the Roe Head period] 92 I heard that she had gone as teacher to Miss Wooler's. I went to see her, and asked how she could give so much for so little money, when she could live without it. She owned that, after clothing herself and Anne, there was nothing left, though she had hoped to be able to save something. She confessed it was not brilliant, but what could she do? I had nothing to answer. She seemed to have no interest or pleasure beyond the feeling of duty, and, when she could get [the opportunity], used to sit alone, and "make out." She told me afterwards, that one evening she had sat in the dressing-room until it was quite dark, and then observing it all at once, had taken sudden fright.

From that time her imaginations became gloomy or frightful; she could not help it, nor help thinking. She could not forget the gloom, could not sleep at night, nor attend in the day. . . .

When I last saw Charlotte (Jan. 1845), 190 she told me she had quite decided to stay at home. She owned she did not like it. Her health was weak. She said she should like any change at first, as she had liked Brussels at first, and she thought that there must be some possibility for some people of having a life of more variety and more communion with human kind, but she saw none for her. I told her very warmly, that she ought not to stay at home; that to spend the next five years at home, in solitude, and weak health, would ruin her; that she would never recover it. Such a dark shadow came over her face when I said, "Think of what you'll be five years hence!" that I stopped, and said "Don't cry, Charlotte!" She did not cry, but went on walking up and down the room, and said in a little while, "But I intend to stay, Polly." . . .

401 She thought much of her duty, and had loftier and clearer notions of it than most people, and held fast to them with more

success. It was done, it seems to me, with much more difficulty than people have of stronger nerves, and better fortunes. All her life was but labour and pain; and she never threw down the burden for the sake of present pleasure. I don't know what use you can make of all I have said. I have written it with the strong desire to obtain appreciation for her. . . .

20

TO E. N. [S. H.]

IV,   Wellington, April 19th, '56.
198 Dear Ellen, — . . . Your letter is most interesting concerning poor Charlotte's "Life." If, for the sake of those who behaved ill to her, the truth cannot be spoken, still people should not tell lies. The fact reached me even here that Mr. Brontë did not choose his daughter should marry — she wrote to me that she once dismissed Mr. Nicholls because he (her papa) was so angry that she was frightened — frightened for *him*. It was long after, years I think, that she told him she had determined to see Mr. Nicholls again, and without positively saying yes, to retract her refusal. I can never think without gloomy anger of Charlotte's sacrifices to the selfish old man. How well we know that, had she left him entirely and succeeded in gaining wealth, and name, and influence, she should have had all the world

lauding her to the skies for any trivial act of generosity that would have cost her nothing! . . . / I wish I could set the world 199 right on many points, but above all respecting Charlotte. It would do said world good to know her and be forced to revere her in spite of their contempt for poverty and helplessness. No one ever gave up more than she did and with full consciousness of what she sacrificed. I / don't think my- 200 self that women are justified in sacrificing themselves for others, but since the world generally expects it of them, they should at least acknowledge it. But where much is given we are all wonderfully given to grasp at more. If Charlotte had left home and made a favour of returning, she would have got thanks instead of tyranny. . . .

Yours affectionately,
Mary Taylor.

Elizabeth Gaskell

From *Life of Charlotte Brontë*, published March, 1857; these extracts are from the Everyman Library edition cited above. [G.]

21

[HAWORTH AND THE PARSONAGE]

3   . . . Right before the traveller on this road [from Keighley] rises Haworth village; he can see it for two miles before he arrives, for it is situated on the side of a pretty steep hill, with a background of dun and purple moors, rising and sweeping away yet higher

than the church, which is built at the very summit of the long narrow street. All round the horizon there is this same line of sinuous wave-like hills; the scoops into which they fall only revealing other hills beyond, of similar colour and shape, crowned with wild, bleak moors — grand, from the ideas of solitude and loneliness which they suggest, or oppressive from the feeling which they give of being pent-up by some monotonous and illimitable barrier, according to the mood of mind in which the spectator may be.

For a short distance the road appears to turn away from Haworth, as it winds round the base of the shoulder of a hill; but then it crosses a bridge over the "beck," and the ascent through the village begins. The flagstones with which it is paved are placed end-ways, in order to give a better hold to the horses' feet; and, even with this help, they seem to be in constant danger of slipping backwards. The old stone houses are high compared to the width of the street, which makes an abrupt turn before reaching the more level ground at the head of the village, so that the steep aspect of the place, in one part, is almost like that of a wall. But this surmounted, the church lies a little off the main road on the left; a hundred yards, or so, and the driver relaxes his care, and the horse breathes more easily, as they pass into the quiet little by-street that leads to Haworth Parsonage. . . .

28   Haworth Parsonage is . . . an oblong stone house, facing down the hill on which the village stands, and with the front door right opposite to the western door of the church, distant about a hundred yards. Of this space twenty yards or so in depth are occupied by the grassy garden, which is scarcely wider than the house. The graveyard goes round house and garden, on all sides but one. The house consists of four rooms on each floor, and is two stories high. When the Brontës took possession, they made the larger parlour, to the left of the entrance, the family sitting-room, while that on the right was appropriated to Mr. Brontë as a study. Behind this was the kitchen; behind the former, a sort of flagged store-room. Up-stairs were four bed-chambers of similar size, with the addition of a small apartment over the passage, or "lobby" as we call it in the north. This was to the front, the staircase going up right opposite to the entrance. There is the pleasant old

fashion of window seats all through the house; and one can see that the parsonage was built in the days when wood was plentiful, as the massive stair-bannisters, and the wainscots, and the heavy window frames testify.

This little extra up-stairs room was appropriated to the children. Small as it was, it was not called a nursery; indeed, it had not the comfort of a fireplace in it; the servants — two ROUGH,[1] affectionate, warm-hearted, WASTEFUL sisters, who cannot now speak of the family without tears — called the room the "children's study." The age of the eldest student was perhaps by this time seven.

[THE HOUSEHOLD AT HAWORTH]

MR. BRONTË WISHED TO MAKE HIS CHIL- 31 DREN HARDY, AND INDIFFERENT TO THE PLEASURES OF EATING AND DRESS. . . .

His strong, passionate, Irish nature was, in general, compressed down with resolute stoicism; but it was there notwithstanding all his philosophic calm and dignity of demeanour. HE DID NOT SPEAK WHEN HE WAS ANNOYED OR DISPLEASED, but worked off his volcanic wrath by firing pistols out of the back-door in rapid succession. Mrs. Brontë, lying in bed up-stairs, would hear the quick explosions, and know that something had gone / wrong; BUT HER SWEET NATURE 32 THOUGHT INVARIABLY OF THE BRIGHT SIDE, AND SHE WOULD SAY, "OUGHT I NOT TO BE THANKFUL THAT HE NEVER GAVE ME AN ANGRY WORD?" NOW AND THEN HIS ANGER TOOK A DIFFERENT FORM, BUT STILL WAS SPEECHLESS. ONCE HE GOT THE HEARTH-RUG, AND STUFFING IT UP THE GRATE, DELIBERATELY SET IT ON FIRE, AND REMAINED IN THE ROOM IN SPITE OF THE STENCH, UNTIL IT HAD SMOULDERED AND SHRIVELLED AWAY INTO USELESSNESS. ANOTHER TIME HE TOOK SOME CHAIRS, AND SAWED AWAY AT THE BACKS TILL THEY WERE REDUCED TO THE CONDITION OF STOOLS.

[1] The expressions and passages appearing throughout this account in small capitals were cancelled in later editions at Mr. Brontë's request and the sentences were rewritten where necessary.

He was an active walker, stretching away over the moors for many miles, noting in his mind all natural signs of wind and weather, and keenly observing all the wild creatures that came and went in the loneliest sweeps of the hills. He has seen eagles stooping low in search of food for their young; no eagle is ever seen on those mountain slopes now. He fearlessly took whatever side in local or national politics appeared to him right. In the days of the Luddites, he had been for the preemptory interference of the law, at a time when no magistrate could be found to act, and all the property in the West Riding was in terrible danger. He became unpopular there among the mill-workers, and he esteemed his life unsafe if he took his long and lonely walks unarmed; so he began the habit, which has continued to this day, of invariably carrying a loaded pistol about with him. It lay on his dressing-table with his watch; with his watch it was put on in the morning; with his watch it was taken off at night. Many years later, during his residence at Haworth, there was a strike; the hands in the neighbourhood felt themselves aggrieved by the masters, and refused to work; Mr. Brontë thought that they had been unjustly and unfairly treated, and he assisted them by all the means in his power to "keep the wolf from their doors," and avoid the incubus of debt. Several of the more influential inhabitants of Haworth and the neighbourhood were mill-owners; they remonstrated pretty sharply with him, but he believed that his conduct was right, and persevered in it. . . .

50   . . . Miss Branwell instructed the children at regular hours in all she could teach, making her bed-chamber into their school-room. Their father was in the habit of relating to them any public news in which he felt an interest; and from the opinions of his strong and independent mind they would gather much food for thought; but I do not know whether he gave them any direct instruction. Charlotte's deep thoughtful spirit appears to have felt almost painfully the tender responsibility which rested

upon her with reference to her remaining sisters. She was only eighteen months older than Emily; but Emily and Anne were simply companions and playmates, while Charlotte was motherly friend and guardian to both; and this loving assumption of duties beyond her years, made her feel considerably older than she really was.

Patrick Branwell, their only brother, was a boy of remarkable promise, and, in some ways, of extraordinary precocity of talent. Mr. Brontë's friends advised him to send his son to school; but, remembering both the strength of will of his own youth and his mode of employing it, he believed that Patrick was better at home, and that he himself could teach him well, as he had taught others before. So Patrick, or as his family called him — Branwell, remained at Haworth, working hard for some hours a day with his father; but, when the time of the latter was taken up with his parochial duties, the boy was thrown into chance companionship with the lads of the village — for youth will to youth, and boys will be boys. . . .

. . . [N]otwithstanding that Miss Bran- 124 well might be occasionally unreasonable, she and her nieces went on smoothly enough; and though they might now and then be annoyed by petty tyranny, she still inspired them with sincere respect, and not a little affection. They were, moreover, grateful to her for many habits she had enforced upon them, and which in time had become second nature: order, method, neatness in everything; a perfect knowledge of all kinds of household work; an exact punctuality, and obedience to the laws of time and place, of which no one but themselves, I have heard Charlotte say, could tell the value in after-life; with their impulsive natures, it was positive repose to have learnt implicit obedience / to external laws. 125 People in Haworth have assured me that, according to the hour of day — nay, the very minute — they could have told what the inhabitants of the parsonage were about. At certain times the girls would be sewing in their aunt's bedroom — the chamber which, in former days, before they had outstripped her in their learning, had served them as a schoolroom; at certain (early) hours they had their meals; from six to eight, Miss Branwell read aloud to Mr. Brontë; at punctual eight, the household assembled to evening prayers in his study; and by nine he, Miss Branwell, and Tabby, were all in bed, — the girls free to pace up and down (like restless wild animals) in the parlour, talking over plans and projects, and thoughts of what was to be their future life. . . .

49   . . . About this time [1825] an elderly woman of the village came to live as servant at the parsonage. She remained there, as a member of the household, for thirty years; and from the length of her faithful service, and the attachment and respect which she inspired, is deserving of mention. Tabby was a thorough specimen of a Yorkshire woman of her class, in dialect, in appearance, and in character. She abounded in strong practical sense and shrewdness. Her words were far from flattery; but she would spare no deeds in the cause of those whom she kindly regarded. She ruled the children pretty sharply; and yet never grudged a little extra trouble to provide them with such small treats as came within her power. In return, she claimed to be looked upon as a humble friend; . . .

35 . . . The children did not want [i.e. lack] society. To small infantine gaieties they were unaccustomed. They were all in all to each other. I do not suppose that there ever was a family more tenderly bound to each other. Maria read the newspapers, and reported intelligence to her younger sisters which it is wonderful they could take an interest in. But I suspect that they had no "children's books," and that their eager minds "browsed undisturbed among the wholesome pasturage of English literature," as Charles Lamb expresses it. The servants of the household appear to have been much impressed with the little Brontës' extraordinary cleverness. In a letter which I had from him on this subject, their father writes: — "The servants often said that they

had never seen such a clever little child" (as Charlotte), "and that they were obliged to be on their guard as to what they said and did before her. Yet she and the servants always lived on good terms with each other."

[COWAN BRIDGE]

. . . I now come to a part of my subject which 39 I find great difficulty in treating, because the evidence relating to it on each side is so conflicting that it seems almost impossible to arrive at the truth. Miss Brontë more than once said to me, that she should not have written what she did of Lowood in *Jane Eyre,* if she had thought the place would have been so immediately identified with Cowan's Bridge, although there was not a word in her account of the institution but what was true at the time when she knew it; she also said that she had not considered it necessary, in a work of fiction, to state every particular with the impartiality that might be required in a court of justice, nor to seek out motives, and make allowances for human feelings, as she might have done, if dispassionately analysing the conduct of those who had the superintendence of the institution. I believe she herself would have been glad of an opportunity to correct the over-strong impression which was made upon the public mind by her vivid picture, though even she, suffering her whole life long, both in heart and body, from the consequences of what happened there, might have been apt, to the last, to take her deep belief in facts for the facts themselves — her conception of truth for the absolute truth.

A wealthy CLERGYMAN, LIVING NEAR KIRBY LONSDALE, THE REVEREND WILLIAM CARUS WILSON, WAS THE PRIME MOVER IN THE ESTABLISHMENT OF THIS SCHOOL. HE WAS AN ENERGETIC MAN, SPARING NO LABOUR FOR THE ACCOMPLISHMENT OF HIS ENDS, and willing to sacrifice everything but power. He saw that it was an extremely difficult task for clergymen with limited incomes to provide for the education of their children; and he devised a scheme, /

40 by which a certain sum was raised annually in subscription, to complete the amount required to furnish a solid and sufficient English education, for which the parent's payment of £14 a year would not have been sufficient. Indeed that made by the parents was considered to be exclusively appropriated to the expenses of lodging and boarding, and the education provided for by the subscriptions. Twelve trustees were appointed; Mr. Wilson being not only a trustee, but the treasurer and secretary; in fact, taking most of the business arrangements upon himself; a responsibility which appropriately fell to him, as he lived nearer the school than any one else who was interested in it. So his character for prudence and judgment was to a certain degree implicated in the success or failure of Cowan's Bridge School; and the working of it was for many years the great object and interest of his life. But he was apparently unacquainted with the prime element in good administration — seeking out thoroughly competent persons to fill each department, and then making them responsible for, and judging them by, the result, without perpetual and injudicious interference with the details. So great was the amount of good which Mr. Wilson did, by his constant, unwearied superintendence, that I cannot help feeling sorry that, in his old age and declining health, the errors, which he certainly committed, should have been brought up against him in a form which received such wonderful force from the touch of Miss Brontë's great genius. . . .

42 Mr. Wilson felt, most probably, that the responsibility of the whole plan rested upon him. The payment made by the parents was barely enough for food and lodging; the subscriptions did not flow very freely into an untried scheme; and great economy was necessary in all the domestic arrangements. He determined to enforce this by frequent personal inspection; and his love of authority seems to have led to a great deal of unnecessary and irritating meddling with little matters. Yet, although there was economy in providing for the household, there does not appear to have been any parsimony. The meat, flour, milk, etc., were contracted for, but were of very fair quality; and the dietary, which has been shown to me in manuscript, was neither bad not unwholesome; nor, on the whole, was it wanting in variety. Oatmeal porridge for breakfast; a piece of oat-cake for those who required luncheon; baked and boiled beef, and mutton, potato-pie, and plain homely puddings of different kinds for dinner. At five o'clock, bread and milk for the younger ones; and one piece of bread (this was the only time at which the food was limited) for the elder pupils, who sat up till a later meal of the same description. Mr. Wilson himself ordered in the food, and was anxious that it should be of good quality. But the cook, who had much of his confidence, and against whom for a long time no one durst utter a complaint, was careless, dirty, and wasteful. To some children oatmeal porridge is distasteful, and consequently unwholesome, even when properly made; at Cowan's Bridge School it was too often sent up, not merely burnt, but with offensive fragments of other substances discoverable in it. The beef, that should have been carefully salted before it was dressed, had often become tainted from neglect; and girls, who were schoolfellows with the Brontës, during the reign of / the 43 cook of whom I am speaking, tell me that the house seemed to be pervaded, morning, noon, and night, by the odour of rancid fat that steamed out of the oven in which much of their food was prepared. There was the same carelessness in making the puddings; one of those ordered was rice boiled in water, and eaten with a sauce of treacle and sugar; but it was often uneatable, because the water had been taken out of the raintub, and was strongly impregnated with the dust lodging on the roof, whence it had trickled down into the old wooden cask, which also added its own flavour to that of the original rain water. The milk, too, was often "bingy," to use a country expression for a kind of taint that is far worse than sourness, and suggests the

idea that it is caused by want of cleanliness about the milk pans, rather than by the heat of the weather. On Saturdays, a kind of pie, or mixture of potatoes and meat, was served up, which was made of all the fragments accumulated during the week. Scraps of meat from a dirty and disorderly larder, could never be very appetising; and, I believe, that this dinner was more loathed than any in the early days of Cowan's Bridge School. One may fancy how repulsive such fare would be to children whose appetites were small, and who had been accustomed to food, far simpler perhaps, but prepared with a delicate cleanliness that made it both tempting and wholesome. Many a meal the little Brontës went without food, although craving with hunger. They were not strong when they came, having only just recovered from a complication of measles and hooping-cough; indeed, I suspect they had scarcely recovered; for there was some consultation on the part of the school authorities whether Maria and Elizabeth should be received or not, in July, 1824. Mr. Brontë came again, in the September of that year, bringing with him Charlotte and Emily to be admitted as pupils.[2]

It appears strange that Mr. Wilson should not have been informed by the teachers of the way in which the food was served up; but we must remember that the cook had been known for some time to the Wilson family, while the teachers were brought together for an entirely different work — that of education. They were expressly given to understand that such was their department; the BUYING IN AND MANAGEMENT OF THE PROVISIONS RESTED WITH MR. WILSON AND THE COOK. THE TEACHERS WOULD, OF COURSE, BE UNWILLING TO LAY ANY COMPLAINTS ON THE SUBJECT BEFORE him; and when he heard of them, his reply was to the effect that the children were to be trained up to regard /
44 higher things than dainty pampering of the appetite, and (apparently unconscious of

the fact, that daily loathing and rejection of food is sure to undermine the health) he lectured them on the sin of caring overmuch for carnal things.

There was another trial of health common to all the girls. The path from Cowan's Bridge to Tunstall Church, where Mr. Wilson preached, and where they all attended on the Sunday, is more than two miles in length, and goes sweeping along the rise and fall of the unsheltered country, in a way to make it a fresh and exhilarating walk in summer, but a bitter cold one in winter, especially to children whose thin blood flowed languidly in consequence of their half-starved condition. The church was not warmed, there being no means for this purpose. It stands in the midst of fields, and the damp mists must have gathered round the walls, and crept in at the windows. The girls took their cold dinner with them, and ate it between the services, in a chamber over the entrance, opening out of the former galleries. The arrangements for this day were peculiarly trying to delicate children, particularly to those who were spiritless, and longing for home, as poor Maria Brontë must have been. For her ill health was increasing; the old cough, the remains of the hooping-cough, lingered about her; she was far superior in mind to any of her play-fellows and companions, and was lonely amongst them from that very cause; and yet she had faults so annoying that she was in constant disgrace with her teachers, and an object of merciless dislike to one of them, who is depicted as "Miss Scatcherd" in *Jane Eyre,* and whose real name I will be merciful enough not to disclose. I need hardly say, that Helen Burns is as exact a transcript of Maria Brontë as Charlotte's wonderful power of reproducing character could give. Her heart, to the latest day on which we met, still beat with unavailing indignation at the worrying and the cruelty to which her gentle, patient, dying sister had been subjected by this woman. Not a word of that part of *Jane Eyre* but is a literal repetition of scenes between the pupil and the teacher.

[2] Inexact; see chronology.

Those who had been pupils at the same time knew who must have written the book, from the force with which Helen Burns' sufferings are described. They had, before that, recognised the description of the sweet dignity and benevolence of Miss Temple as only a just tribute to the merits of one whom all that knew her appear to hold in honour; but when Miss Scatcherd was held up to opprobrium they also recognised in the writer of *Jane Eyre* an unconsciously avenging sister of the sufferer.[3]

45 One of these fellow-pupils of Charlotte and Maria Brontë's, among other statements even worse, gives me the following: — The dormitory in which Maria slept was a long room, holding a row of narrow little beds on each side, occupied by the pupils; and at the end of this dormitory there was a small bed-chamber opening out of it, appropriated to the use of Miss Scatcherd. Maria's bed stood nearest to the door of this room. One morning, after she had become so seriously unwell as to have had a blister applied to her side (the sore from which was not perfectly healed), when the getting-up bell was heard, poor Maria moaned out that she was so ill, so very ill, she wished she might stop in bed; and some of the girls urged her to do so, and said they would explain it all to Miss Temple, the superintendent. But Miss Scatcherd was close at hand, and her anger would have to be faced before Miss Temple's kind thoughtfulness could interfere; so the sick child began to dress, shivering with cold, as, without leaving her bed, she slowly put on her black worsted stockings over her thin white legs (my informant spoke as if she saw it yet, and her whole face flashed out undying indignation). Just then Miss Scatcherd issued from her room, and, without asking for a word of explanation from the sick and frightened girl, she took her by the arm, on the side to which the blister had been applied, and by one vigorous movement whirled her out into the middle of the floor, abusing her all the time for dirty and untidy habits. There she left her. My informant says, Maria hardly spoke, except to beg some of the more indignant girls to be calm; but, in slow, trembling movements, with many a pause, she went down stairs at last — and was punished for being late. . . .

BEFORE MARIA BRONTË'S DEATH, THAT LOW FEVER BROKE OUT, / IN THE SPRING 46 OF 1825, WHICH IS SPOKEN OF IN *Jane Eyre*. MR WILSON WAS EXTREMELY ALARMED AT THE FIRST SYMPTOMS OF THIS; his self-confidence was shaken; he did not understand what kind of illness it could be, that made the girls too dull and heavy to understand remonstrances, or be roused by texts and spiritual exhortation; but caused them to sink away into dull stupor, and half-unconscious listlessness. He went to a kind motherly woman, who had had some connection with the school — as laundress, I believe — and asked her to come and tell him what was the matter with them. She made herself ready, and drove with him in his gig. When she entered the school-room, she saw from twelve to fifteen girls lying about; some resting their aching heads on the table, others on the ground; all heavy-eyed, flushed, indifferent, and weary, with pains in every limb. Some peculiar odour, she says, made her recognise that they were sickening for "the fever"; and she told Mr. Wilson so, and that she could not stay there for fear of conveying the infection to her own children; but he half commanded, and half intreated her to remain and nurse them; and finally mounted his gig and drove away, while she was still urging that she must return to her own house, and to her domestic duties, for which she had provided no substitute. However, when she was left in this unceremonious manner, she determined to make the best of it; and a most efficient nurse she proved, although, as she says, it was a dreary time. Mr. Wilson supplied everything ordered by the doctors of the best quality, and in the most liberal manner; he even sent for additional

---

[3] Readers of Dickens' *Nicholas Nickleby* will see why comparisons were made between it and *Jane Eyre*. An early critic of *Jane Eyre* called Lowood "a sort of do-the-girls-Hall."

advice, in the person of his own brother-in-law, a very clever medical man in Kirby, with whom he had not been on good terms for some time previously; and it was this doctor who tasted and condemned the daily food of the girls by the expressive action of spitting out a portion which he had taken in order to taste it. About forty of the girls suffered from this fever, but none of them died at Cowan's Bridge, though one died in her own home, sinking under the state of health which followed it. None of the Brontës had the fever. But the same causes, which affected the health of the other pupils through typhus, told more slowly, but not less surely, upon their constitutions. The principal of these causes was the food.

The bad management of the cook was chiefly to be blamed for this; she was dismissed, and the woman who had been forced against her will to serve as head nurse, took the place of housekeeper; and henceforward the food was so well prepared 47 / that no one could ever reasonably complain of it. Of course it cannot be expected that a new institution, comprising domestic and educational arrangements for nearly a hundred persons, should work quite smoothly at the beginning, and all this occurred during the first two years of the establishment. But Mr. Wilson seems to have had the unlucky gift of irritating even those to whom he meant kindly, and for whom he was making perpetual sacrifices of time and money, by never showing any respect for their independence of opinion and action. He had, too, so little knowledge of human nature as to imagine that, by constantly reminding the girls of their dependent position, and the fact that they were receiving their education from the charity of others, he could make them lowly and humble. Some of the more sensitive felt this treatment bitterly, and instead of being as grateful as they should have been for the real benefits they were obtaining, their mortified pride rose up from its fall a hundred-fold more strong. Painful impressions sink deep into the hearts of delicate

and sickly children. What the healthy suffer from but momentarily, and then forget, those who are ailing brood over involuntarily, and remember long — perhaps with no resentment, but simply as a piece of suffering that has been stamped into their very life. The pictures, ideas, and conceptions of character received into the mind of the child of eight years old, were destined to be reproduced in fiery words a quarter of a century afterwards. She saw only one side, and that the unfavourable side of Mr. Wilson; but many of those who knew him, assure me of the wonderful fidelity with which his disagreeable qualities, his spiritual pride, his love of power, his ignorance of human nature and consequent want of tenderness are represented; while, at the same time, they regret that the delineation of these should have obliterated, as it were, nearly all that was noble and conscientious.

[M. HEGER]

After consulting with his wife, Mr. 151 Héger told them that he meant to dispense with the old method of grounding in grammar, vocabulary, etc., and to proceed on a new plan — something similar to what he had occasionally adopted with the elder among his French and Belgian pupils. He proposed to read to them some of the master-pieces of the most celebrated French authors / . . . and after having thus impressed the complete effect of the whole, to 152 analyse the parts with them, pointing out in what such or such an author excelled, and where were the blemishes. He believed that he had to do with pupils capable, from their ready sympathy with the intellectual, the refined, the polished, or the noble, of catching the echo of a style, and so reproducing their own thoughts in a somewhat similar manner.

After explaining his plan to them, he awaited their reply. Emily spoke first; and said that she saw no good to be derived from it; and that, by adopting it, they should lose all originality of thought and expression. She would have entered into an argument on the subject, but for this, M. Héger had no time. Charlotte then spoke; she also doubted the success of the plan; but she would follow out M. Héger's advice, because she was bound to obey him while she was his pupil. . . .

158 When they had made further progress, M. Héger took up a more advanced plan, that of synthetical teaching. He would read to them various accounts of the same person or event, and make them notice the points of agreement and disagreement. Where they were different, he would make them seek the origin of that difference by causing them to examine well into the character and position of each separate writer, and how they would be likely to affect his conception of truth. For instance, take Cromwell. He would read Bossuet's description of him in the "Oraison Funèbre de la Reine d'Angleterre," and show how in this he was considered entirely from the religious point of view, as an instrument in the hands of God, pre-ordained to His work. Then he would make them read Guizot, and see how, in his view, Cromwell was endowed with the utmost power of free will, but governed by no higher motive than that of expediency; while Carlyle regarded him as a character regulated by a strong and conscientious desire to do the will of the Lord. Then he would desire them to remember that the Royalist and Commonwealth man had each their different opinions of the great Protector. And from these conflicting characters he would require them to sift and collect the elements of truth, and try to unite them into a perfect whole.

This kind of exercise delighted Charlotte. It called into play her powers of analysis, which were extraordinary, and she very soon excelled in it.

[THE RECEPTION OF "JANE EYRE"]

229 The sisters had kept the knowledge of their literary ventures from their father, fearing to increase their own anxieties and disappointment by witnessing his; for he took an acute interest in all that befell his children, and his own tendency had been towards literature in the days when he was young and hopeful. It was true he did not much manifest his feelings in words; he would have thought that he was prepared for disappointment as the lot of man, and that he could have met it with stoicism; but words are poor and tardy interpreters of feelings to those who love one another, and his daughters knew how he would have borne ill-success worse for them than for himself. So they did not tell him what they were undertaking. He says now that he suspected it all along, but his suspicions could take no exact form, as all he was certain of was, that his children were perpetually writing — and not writing letters. We have seen how the communications from their publishers were / received "under 230 cover to Miss Brontë." Once, Charlotte told me, they overheard the postman meeting Mr. Brontë, as the latter was leaving the house, and inquiring from the parson where one Currer Bell could be living, to which Mr. Brontë replied that there was no such person in the parish. . . .

Now, however, when the demand for the work had assured success to *Jane Eyre*, her sisters urged Charlotte to tell their father of its publication. She accordingly went into his study one afternoon after his early dinner, carrying with her a copy of the book, and one or two reviews, taking care to include a notice adverse to it.

She informed me that something like the following conversation took place between her and him. (I wrote down her words the day after I heard them; and I am pretty sure they are quite accurate.)

"Papa, I've been writing a book."

"Have you, my dear?"

"Yes, and I want you to read it."

"I am afraid it will try my eyes too much."

"But it is not in manuscript: it is printed."

"My dear! you've never thought of the expense it will be! It will be almost sure to be a loss, for how can you get a book sold? No one knows you or your name."

"But, papa, I don't think it will be a loss; no more will you, if you will just let me read you a review or two, and tell you / 231 more about it."

So she sate down and read some of the reviews to her father; and then, giving him the copy of *Jane Eyre* that she intended for him, she left him to read it. When he came in to tea, he said, "Girls, do you know Charlotte has been writing a book, and it is much better than likely?"

[MRS. GASKELL'S VISIT TO HAWORTH]

387 We went, not purposely, but accidentally, to see various poor people in our distant walks. From one we had borrowed an umbrella; in the house of another we had taken shelter from a rough September storm. In all these cottages, her quiet presence was known. At three miles from her home, the chair was dusted for her, with a kindly "Sit ye down, Miss Brontë;" and she knew what absent or ailing members of the family to inquire after. Her quiet, gentle words, few though they might be, were evidently grateful to those Yorkshire ears. Their welcome to her, though rough and curt, was sincere and hearty.

We talked about the different courses through which life ran. She said, in her own composed manner, as if she had accepted the theory as a fact, that she believed some were appointed beforehand to sorrow and much disappointment; that it did not fall to the lot of all — as Scripture told us — to have their lines fall in pleasant places; that it was well for those who had rougher paths, to perceive that such was God's will concerning them, and try to moderate their expectations, leaving hope to those of a different doom, and seeking patience and resignation as the virtues they were to cultivate. I took a different view: I thought that human lots were more equal than she imagined; that to some happiness and sorrow came in strong patches of light and shadow, (so to speak), while in the lives of others they were pretty equally blended throughout. She smiled, and shook her head, and said she was trying to school herself against ever anticipating any pleasure; that it was better to be brave and submit faithfully. . . .

[CHARLOTTE'S MARRIAGE]

It was fixed that the marriage was to take 394 place on the 29th of June. Her two friends arrived at Haworth Parsonage the / day 395 before; and the long summer afternoon and evening were spent by Charlotte in thoughtful arrangements for the morrow, and for her father's comfort during her absence from home. When all was finished — the trunk packed, the morning's breakfast arranged, the wedding-dress laid out, — just at bedtime, Mr. Brontë announced his intention of stopping at home while the others went to church. What was to be done? Who was to give the bride away? There were only to be the officiating clergyman, the bride and bridegroom, the bridesmaid, and Miss Wooler present. The Prayer-book was referred to; and there it was seen that the Rubric enjoins that the Minister shall receive "the woman from her father's or *friend's* hands," and that nothing is specified as to the sex of the "friend." So Miss Wooler, ever kind in emergency, volunteered to give her old pupil away.

The news of the wedding had slipt abroad before the little party came out of church, and many old and humble friends were there, seeing her look "like a snowdrop," as they say. Her dress was white embroidered muslin, with a lace mantle, and white bonnet trimmed with green leaves, which perhaps might suggest the resemblance to the pale wintry flower. . . .

[CHARLOTTE'S LAST ILLNESS AND DEATH]

On Christmas-day she and her husband 398 walked to [a] poor old woman * * * carrying with them a great spice-cake to make glad her heart. On Christmas-day many a humble meal in Haworth was made more plentiful by her gifts.

Early in the new year (1855), Mr. and Mrs. Nicholls went to visit Sir James Kay Shuttleworth at Gawthorpe. They only remained two or three days, but it so fell out that she increased her lingering cold, by a long walk over damp ground in thin shoes.

Soon after her return, she was attacked by new sensations of perpetual nausea, and ever-recurring faintness. After this state of things had lasted for some time, she yielded 399 to Mr. / Nicholls' wish that a doctor should be sent for. He came, and assigned a natural cause for her miserable indisposition; a little patience, and all would go right. She, who was ever patient in illness, tried hard to bear up and bear on. But the dreadful sickness increased and increased, till the very sight of food occasioned nausea. "A wren would have starved on what she ate during those last six weeks," says one. Tabby's health had suddenly and utterly given way, and she died in this time of distress and anxiety respecting the last daughter of the house she had served so long. Martha tenderly waited on her mistress, and from time to time tried to cheer her with the thought of the baby that was coming. "I dare say I shall be glad some time," she would say; "but I am so ill — so weary —" Then she took to her bed, too weak to sit up. . . .

. . . Long days and longer nights went 400 by; still the same relentless nausea and faintness, and still borne on in patient trust. About the third week in March there was a change; a low wandering delirium came on; and in it she begged constantly for food and even for stimulants. She swallowed eagerly now; but it was too late. Wakening for an instant from this stupor of intelligence, she saw her husband's woe-worn face, and caught the sound of some murmured words of prayer that God would spare her. "Oh!" she whispered forth, "I am not going to die, am I? He will not separate us, we have been so happy."

Early on Saturday morning, March 31st, the solemn tolling of Haworth church-bell spoke forth the fact of her death to the villagers who had known her from a child, and whose hearts shivered within them as they thought of the two sitting desolate and alone in the old grey house.

Patrick Brontë

22

TO E. G. [S. H.]

IV, 220
Haworth, near Keighley,
April 2nd, 1857.

My dear Madam, — I thank you for the books you have sent me containing the Memoir of my daughter. I have perused them with a degree of pleasure and pain which can be known only to myself. . . . 221 You have not only given a picture of my dear daughter Charlotte, but of my dear wife, and all my dear children, and such a picture, too, as is full of truth and life. The picture of my brilliant and unhappy son is a masterpiece. Indeed, all the pictures in the work have vigorous, truthful, and delicate touches in them, which could have been executed only by a skilful female hand. There are a few trifling mistakes, which, should it be deemed necessary, may be corrected in the second edition. Mr Nicholls joins me in kind and respectful regards to you, Mr Gaskell, and your family, wishing you greatest good in both the words. — I remain, my dear Madam, Yours respectfully and truly,

P. Brontë.

W[illiam] M[akepeace] T[hackeray]

From "The Last Sketch," *Cornhill Magazine,* 1860, I.

23

486 ... I can only say of this lady, *vidi tantum.* I saw her first just as I rose out of an illness from which I had never thought to recover. I remember the trembling little frame, the little hand, the great honest eyes. An impetuous honesty seemed to me to characterize the woman. . . . She spoke
487 her mind out. . . . / New to the London world, she entered it with an independent, indomitable spirit of her own; and judged of contemporaries, and especially spied out arrogance or affectation, with extraordinary keenness of vision. She was angry with her favourites if their conduct or conversation fell below her ideal. Often she seemed to me to be judging the London folk prematurely: but perhaps the city is rather angry at being judged. I fancied an austere little Joan of Arc marching in upon us, and rebuking our easy lives, our easy morals. She gave me the impression of being a very pure, and lofty, and high-minded person. A great and holy reverence of right and truth seemed to be with her always. Such, in our brief interview, she appeared to me. . . .

Meta Gaskell

24

TO EMILY (WINKWORTH) SHAEN [S. H.]
[November 6th, 1860.]
IV, My dearest Emily, — . . . What I want
239 really to tell you about, is a visit which Mama and I paid to old Mr Brontë to-day. . . . We were taken into his bedroom; where everything was delicately clean and white, and there he was sitting propped up in bed in a clean nightgown, with a clean towel laid just for his hands to play upon — looking Oh! very different from the stiff scarred face above the white walls of cravat in the photograph — he had a short soft white growth of beard on his chin; and such a gentle, quiet, sweet, half-pitiful expression on his mouth, a good deal of soft white hair, and spectacles on. He shook hands with us, and we sat down, and then said how glad he was to see Mama — and she said how she had hesitated about coming, — feeling as if he might now have unpleasant associations with her — which never seemed to have entered into his head — then he asked her how, since he last saw her, she had passed through this weary and varied world — in a sort of half grandiloquent style —/ . . . . He said to Mama — "As 240 I told you in my first letter, the Memoir is a book which will hand your name down to posterity," and that there was only one fault he had to find with it; might he speak out openly before me? Mama told him he might, and we both sat expecting some allusion to the Lady S[cott][1] but — but what he said was that the statement that he had not allowed his children to have meat till they were (a certain age) had been quoted by either Mr Carus Wilson, or his defenders, as more likely to have been the cause of their delicacy than the fare they subsequently had at Cowan's Bridge. Now — this statement was a mistake. His children had always been allowed meat; but

[1] Previously Mrs. Robinson, the lady Branwell claimed was in love with him; attacked by Mrs. Gaskell in Chs. 13 and 16.

he said he had chosen not to defend himself at the expense of proving Mama inaccurate: and so giving a handle to those who accused her of mis-statements — I wish I could remember more of what he said. He very soon turned the conversation to politics: asked Mama whether she thought the English ought to interfere in Italian affairs at present, or wait till the Italians asked for help; and seemed very much pleased when she said she thought we ought to hold back for the present. "You see we agree in politics as in everything else." . . . He alluded to his own "eccentricity" with a certain pride; and his "independence," too, of other people's opinion; not but what he valued the opinion of good people — Mama said: "Yes — I was just telling my daughter as we came up the hill, that I thought you had always done what you thought right." — "And so I have," he said, "and I appeal to God." There was something very solemn in the way he said it; and in him altogether — None of the sternness I had fancied — Mama said something about our not staying too long to tire him and that we were going, for me to make a sketch; And he said, "There are certain circumstances, you see," looking very knowing, "which make it desirable that when you leave in 5 minutes or so, we should shake hands — and I give your daughter free leave to make a sketch, or do anything *outside* the house. Do you understand Latin? Mrs Gaskell does at any rate, well, *verbum sap.*, a word to the wise," and then he chuckled very much; the gist of it was, as Mama saw, and I guessed, that he feared Mr Nicholls' return from the school — and we were to be safely out of the house before that. Mama is telling Mr Shaen all about the sexton. Just before leaving Haworth we went to call on John Greenwood; and whilst Mama was talking

to him, his wife volunteered to me how she disliked Mr N., as they all seemed to do . . . . — Mrs Greenwood had a puny, precocious little lad clinging to her dress, about 1½ years old — so of course I asked its name, and she said "Brontë, Miss. Eh, Mr Nicholls was angry a' that." He heard they were going to give it the name; and said in Mr B's hearing that he wouldn't christen the child, whereupon Mr B. sent word by Martha of his determination to the Greenwoods, to spare them the annoyance of a direct refusal, so they kept the child unchristened till it was 6 months old when it became so ailing that they thought it wouldn't live; and Mr B. hearing of this, sent for it (as far as I understand) to his own bedroom (it is a year since his health began to fail) and christened it there; having the Register-book for baptisms, and writing down its name with his own hand. It was years since he had christened a child. Of course the next baby Mr N. condescended to christen, he went to write its name down, and there saw Mr B's registration of the christening of little Brontë Greenwood. Mrs G. said that there and then he strode straight back to the Parsonage, and up into Mr B's bedroom; and "So I see you have christened your / namesake." 241 And Mr. B. got out of it by saying that he had done it to save Mr. N. from the terrible scrape in which he would have found himself, had the child died unchristened, etc.[2] But this is a specimen of Mr. N.'s sullen, obstinate rooted objection to any reverence being paid to Miss B. one might almost say at any rate to people caring to remember her as an authoress. . . .

M. E. Gaskell 242

[2] This boy, Brontë Greenwood, later went to America, served in the U. S. Navy, settled in Philadelphia and died there.

Ellen Nussey

From "Reminiscences of Charlotte Brontë," *Scribner's Monthly* II, May, 1871. See also *B.S.T.* II, Part X, pp. 58–83.

25

18 Arriving at school about a week after the general assembling of the pupils, I was not expected to accompany them when the time came for their daily exercise, but while they were out, I was led into the school-room, and quietly left to make my observations. I had come to the conclusion it was very nice and comfortable for a school-room, though I had little knowledge of school-rooms in general, when, turning to the window to observe the look-out I became aware for the first time that I was not alone; there 19 / was a silent, weeping, dark little figure in the large bay-window: she must, I thought, have risen from the floor. As soon as I had recovered from my surprise, I went from the far end of the room, where the book-shelves were, the contents of which I must have contemplated with a little awe in anticipation of coming studies. A crimson cloth covered the long table down the center of the room, which helped, no doubt to hide the shrinking little figure from my view. I was touched and troubled at once to see her so sad and so tearful.

I said *shrinking*, because her attitude, when I saw her, was that of one who wished to hide both herself and her grief. She did not shrink, however, when spoken to, but in very few words confessed she was "home-sick." After a little of such comfort as could be offered, it was suggested to her that there was a possibility of her too having to comfort the speaker by and by for the same cause. A faint quivering smile then lighted her face; the tear-drops fell; we silently took each other's hands, and at once we felt that genuine sympathy which always consoles, even though it be unexpressed. . . . Miss Wooler's system of education required that a good deal of her pupils' work should be done in classes, and to effect this, new pupils had generally a season of solitary study; but Charlotte's fervent application made this period a very short one to her, — she was quickly up to the needful standard, and ready for the daily routine and arrangement of studies, and as quickly did she outstrip her companions, rising from the bottom of the classes to the top, a position which, when she had once gained, she never had to regain. She was first in everything but play, yet never was a word heard of envy or jealousy from her companions; every one felt she had won her laurels by an amount of diligence and hard labor of which they were incapable. She never exulted in her successes or seemed conscious of them; her mind was so wholly set on attaining knowledge that she apparently forgot all else.

Charlotte's appearance did not strike me at first as it did others. I saw her grief, not herself particularly, till afterwards. She never seemed to me the unattractive little person others designated her, but certainly she was at this time anything but *pretty*; even her good points were lost. Her naturally beautiful hair of soft silky brown being then dry and frizzy-looking, screwed up in tight little curls, showing features that were all the plainer from her exceeding thinness and want of complexion, she looked "dried in." A dark, rusty green stuff dress of old-fashioned make detracted still more from her appearance; but let her wear what she might, or do what she would, she / had ever the demeanour of a born gentle- 20 woman; vulgarity was an element that never won the slightest affinity with her nature. Some of the elder girls, who had been years at school, thought her ignorant. This was true in one sense; ignorant she was indeed in the elementary education which is given in schools, but she far surpassed her most advanced school-fellows in knowledge of what was passing in the world at large and in the literature of her country. She knew a thousand things in these matters unknown to them.

She had taught herself a little French before she came to school; this little knowledge of the language was very useful to her when afterwards she was engaged in translation or dictation. She soon began to make a good figure in French lessons. Music she wished to acquire, for which she had both ear and taste, but her nearsightedness caused her to stoop so dreadfully in order to see her notes, she was dissuaded from persevering in the acquirement, especially as she had at this time an invincible objection to wearing glasses. . . .

21   . . . She always seemed to feel that a deep responsibility rested upon her; that she was an object of expense to those at home, and that she must use every moment to attain the purpose for which she was sent to school, *i.e.*, to fit herself for governess life. She had almost too much opportunity for her conscientious diligence; we were so little restricted in our doings, the industrious might accomplish the appointed tasks of the day and enjoy a little leisure, but she chose in many things to do *double* lessons when not prevented by class arrangement or a companion. . . . She liked the stated task to be over, that she might be free to pursue her self-appointed ones. Such, however, was her conscientiousness that she never did what some girls think it generous to do; generous and unselfish though she was, she never whispered help to a companion in class (as she might have done), to rid herself of the trouble of having to appear again. All her school-fellows regarded her, I believe, as a model of high rectitude, close application, and great abilities. She did not play or amuse herself when others did. When her companions were merry round the fire, or otherwise enjoying themselves during the twilight, which was always a precious time of relaxation, she would be kneeling close to the

window busy with her studies, and this would last so long that she was accused of seeing in the dark; yet though she did not play, as girls style play, she was ever ready to help with suggestions in those plays which required taste or arrangement.

Charlotte [once] caused . . . a panic of terror by her thrilling relations of the wanderings of a somnambulist. She brought together all the horrors her imagination could create, from surging seas, raging breakers, towering castle walls, high precipices, invisible chasms and dangers. Having wrought these materials to the highest pitch of effect, she brought out, in almost cloud-height, her somnambulist, walking on shaking turrets, — all told in a voice that conveyed more than words alone can express. A shivering terror seized the recovered invalid; a pause ensued; then a subdued cry of pain came from Charlotte herself, with a terrified command to others to call for help. She was in bitter distress. Something like remorse seemed to linger in her mind after this incident; for weeks there was no prevailing upon her to resume her tales, and she never again created terrors for her listeners. . . .

At the close of the first half-year, Charlotte bore off three prizes. For once she had to draw lots with her friend — a moment of painful suspense to both; for neither wished to deprive the other of her reward. Happily, Charlotte won it, and so had the gratifying pleasure of carrying home three tangible proofs of her goodness and industry. . . .

In these early days, whenever she was 22 certain of being quite alone with her friend, she would talk much of her two dead sisters, Maria and Elizabeth. Her love for them was most intense; a kind of adoration dwelt in her feelings which, as she conversed, almost imparted itself to her listener.

She described Maria as a little mother among the rest, superhuman in goodness and cleverness. But the most touching of all were the revelations of her sufferings, — how she suffered with the sensibility of a grown-up person, and endured with a patience and fortitude that were Christ-like. Charlotte would still weep and suffer when thinking of her. She talked of Elizabeth also, but never with the anguish of expression which accompanied her recollections of Maria. When surprise was expressed that she should know so much about her sisters when they were so young, and she herself still younger, she said she began to analyze character when she was five years old, and instanced two guests who were at her home for a day or two, and of whom she had taken stock, and of whom after-knowledge confirmed first impressions. . . .

In the seldom recurring holidays Charlotte made sometimes short visits with those of her companions whose homes were within reach of the school. Here she made acquaintance with the scenes and prominent characters of the Luddite period; her father materially helped to fix her impressions, for he had held more than one curacy in the very neighbourhood which she describes in *Shirley*. He was present in some of the scenes, an active participator as far as his position permitted. Sometimes on the defensive, sometimes aiding the sufferers, uniting his strength and influence with the Mr. Helstone of *Shirley*.[1] . . .

23   I must not forget to state that no girl in the school was equal to Charlotte in Sunday lessons. Her acquaintance with Holy Writ surpassed others in this as in everything else. She was very familiar with all the sublimest passages, especially those in Isaiah, in which she took great delight. Her confirmation took place while she was at school, and in her preparation for that, as in all other studies, she distinguished herself by application and proficiency.

At school she acquired that habit which she and her sisters kept up to the very last, that of pacing to and fro in the room. In days when out-of-door exercise was impracticable, Miss Wooler would join us in our evening hour of relaxation and converse (for which she had rare talent); her pupils used to hang about her as she walked up

[1] The Reverend Hammond Roberson; see Mrs. Gaskell's *Life*, Ch. 6.

and down the room, delighted to listen to her, or have a chance of being nearest in the walk. The last day Charlotte was at school she seemed to realize what a sedate, hard-working season it had been to her. She said, "I should for once like to feel *out and out* a school-girl; I wish something would happen! Let us run round the fruit garden [running was what she never did]; perhaps we shall meet some one, or we may have a fine for trespass." She evidently was longing for some never-to-be-forgotten incident. Nothing, however, arose from her little enterprise. She had to leave school as calmly and quietly as she had there lived.

Charlotte's first visit from Haworth was made about three months after she left school. She travelled in a two-wheeled gig, the only conveyance to be had in Haworth except the covered cart which brought her to school. Mr. Brontë sent Branwell as an escort; he was *then* a very dear brother, as dear to Charlotte as her own soul; they were in perfect accord of taste and feeling, and it was mutual delight to be together.

Branwell probably had never been far from home before! he was in wild ecstasy with everything. He walked about in unrestrained boyish enjoyment, taking views in every direction of the old turret-roofed house, the fine chestnut trees on the lawn (one tree especially interested him because it was "iron-garthed," having been split by storms, but still flourishing in great majesty), and a large rookery, which gave to the house a good background — all these he noted and commented upon with perfect enthusiasm. He told his sister he "was leaving her in Paradise, and if she were not intensely happy she never would be!" Happy, indeed, she then was, *in himself*, for she, with her own enthusiasms, looked forward to what her brother's great promise and talent might effect. He would at this time be between fifteen and sixteen years of age.

The visit passed without much to mark it (at this distance of time) except that we crept away together from household life as much as we could. Charlotte liked to pace the plantations or seek seclusion in the fruit garden! she was safe from visitors in these retreats. She was so painfully shy she could not bear any special notice. One day, on being led in to dinner by a stranger, she trembled and nearly burst into tears; but 24 notwithstanding her / excessive shyness, which was often painful to others as well as herself, she won the respect and affection of all who had opportunity enough to become acquainted with her. . . .

My first visit to Haworth was full of novelty and freshness. The scenery for some miles before we reached Haworth was wild and uncultivated, with hardly any population; at last we came to what seemed a terrific hill, such a steep declivity no one thought of riding down it; the horse had to be carefully led. We no sooner reached the foot of this hill than we had to begin to mount again, over a narrow, rough, stone-paved road; the horses' feet seemed to catch at boulders, as if climbing. When we reached the top of the village there was apparently no outlet, but we were directed to drive into an entry which just admitted the gig; we wound round in this entry and then saw the church close at hand, and we entered on the short lane which led to the parsonage gateway. Here Charlotte was waiting, having caught the sound of the approaching gig. When greetings and introductions were over, Miss Branwell (the aunt of the Brontës) took possession 25 of their guest and / treated her with the care and solicitude due to a weary traveller. Mr. Brontë, also, was stirred out of his usual retirement by his own kind consideration, for not only the guest but the man-servant and the horse were to be made comfortable. He made enquiries about the man, of his length of service, &c., with the kind purpose of making a few moments of conversation agreeable to him.

Even at this time, Mr. Brontë struck me as looking very venerable, with his snow-white hair and powdered coat-collar. His manner and mode of speech always had the tone of high-bred courtesy. He was con-sidered somewhat of an invalid, and always lived in the most abstemious and simple manner. His white cravat was not then so remarkable as it grew to be afterwards. He was in the habit of covering this cravat himself. We never saw the operation, but we always had to wind for him the white sewing-silk which he used. Charlotte said it was her father's one extravagance — he cut up yards and yards of white lutestring (silk) in covering his cravat. . . .

Miss Branwell, their aunt, was a small, antiquated little lady. She wore caps large enough for half a dozen of the present fashion, and a front of light auburn curls over her forehead. She always dressed in silk. She had a horror of the climate so far north, and of the stone floors of the parsonage. She amused us by clicking about in pattens whenever she had to go into the kitchen or look after household operations.

Emily Brontë had by this time acquired a lithesome, graceful figure. She was the tallest person in the house, except her father. Her hair, which was naturally as beautiful as / Charlotte's was in the same 26 unbecoming tight curl and frizz, and there was the same want of complexion. She had very beautiful eyes — kind, kindling, liquid eyes; but she did not often look at you; she was too reserved. Their color might be said to be dark gray, at other times dark blue, they varied so. She talked very little. She and Anne were like twins — inseparable companions, and in the very closest sympathy, which never had any interruption.

Anne — dear, gentle Anne — was quite different in appearance from the others. She was her aunt's favorite. Her hair was a very pretty, light brown, and fell on her neck in graceful curls. She had lovely violet-blue eyes, fine penciled eyebrows, and clear, almost transparent complexion. She still pursued her studies, and especially her sewing, under the surveillance of her aunt. Emily had now begun to have the disposal of her own time.

Branwell studied regularly with his father, and used to paint in oils, which was regarded as study for what might be eventually his profession. All the household entertained the idea of his becoming an artist, and hoped he would be a distinguished one.

In fine and suitable weather delightful rambles were made over the moors, and down into the glens and ravines that here and there broke the monotony of the moorland. The rugged bank and rippling brook were treasures of delight. Emily, Anne, and Branwell used to ford the streams, and sometimes placed stepping-stones for the other two; there was always a lingering delight in these spots, — every moss, every flower, every tint and form, were noted and enjoyed. Emily especially had a gleesome delight in these nooks of beauty, — her reserve for the time vanished. One long ramble made in these early days was far away over the moors to a spot familiar to Emily and Anne, which they called "The Meeting of the Waters." It was a small oasis of emerald green turf, broken here and there by small clear springs; a few large stones served as resting-places; seated here, we were hidden from all the world, nothing appearing in view but miles and miles of heather, a glorious blue sky, and brightening sun. A fresh breeze wafted on us its exhilarating influence; we laughed and made mirth of each other, and settled we would call ourselves the quartette. Emily, half reclining on a slab of stone, played like a young child with the tadpoles in the water, making them swim about, and then fell to moralizing on the strong and the weak, the brave and the cowardly, as she chased them with her hand. No serious care or sorrow had so far cast its gloom on nature's youth and buoyancy, and nature's simplest offerings were fountains of pleasure and enjoyment.

27   The interior of the now far-famed parsonage lacked drapery of all kinds. Mr. Brontë's horror of fire forbade curtains to the windows; they never had these accessories to comfort and appearance till long after Charlotte was the only inmate of the family sitting-room, — she then ventured on the innovation when her friend was with her; it did not please her father, but it was not forbidden.

There was not much carpet anywhere except in the sitting-room, and on the study floor. The hall floor and stairs were done with sand-stone, always beautifully clean, as everything was about the house; the walls were not papered, but stained in a pretty dove-coloured tint; hair-seated chairs and mahogany tables, book-shelves in the study, but not many of these elsewhere. Scant and bare indeed, many will say, yet it was not a scantness that made itself felt. Mind and thought, I had almost said elegance but certainly refinement, diffused themselves over all, and made nothing really wanting.

A little later on, there was the addition of a piano. Emily, after some application, played with precision and brilliancy. Anne played also, but she preferred soft harmonies and vocal music. She sang a little; her voice was weak, but very sweet in tone.

Mr. Brontë at times would relate strange 28 stories, which had been told to him by some of the oldest inhabitants of the parish, of the extraordinary lives and doings of people who had resided in far-off, out-of-the-way places, but in contiguity with Haworth, — stories which made one shiver and shrink from hearing; but they were full of grim humor and interest to Mr. Brontë and his children, as revealing the characteristics of a class in the human race, and as such Emily Brontë has stereotyped them in her *Wuthering Heights*.

During Miss Branwell's reign at the parsonage, the love of animals had to be kept in due subjection. There was then but one dog, which was admitted to the parlor at stated times. Emily and Anne always gave him a portion of their breakfast, which was, by their own choice, the old north country diet of oatmeal porridge. Later on, there were three household pets — the tawny, strong-limbed "Keeper," Emily's favorite: he was so completely under her control, she could quite easily make him spring and roar like a lion. She taught him this kind of occasional play without any coercion. "Flossy," — long, silky-haired, black and white "Flossy," — was Anne's favorite; and black "Tom," the tabby, was everybody's favorite. It received such gentle treatment it seemed to have lost cat's nature, and subsided into luxurious amiability and contentment. The Brontës' love of dumb creatures made them very sensitive of the treatment bestowed upon them. For any one to offend in this respect was with them an infallible bad sign, and a blot on the disposition.

[After describing with some regret the "improvements" in the house and garden after Mr. Brontë's time, Ellen goes on:]

But after-thought shows the folly of such regret; for what the Brontës cared for and *lived* in most were the surroundings of nature, the free expanse of hill and mountain, the purple heather, the dells, and glens, and brooks, the broad sky view, the whistling winds, the snowy expanse, the starry heavens, and the charm of that solitude and seclusion which sees things from a distance without the disturbing atmosphere which lesser minds are apt to create. For it was not the seclusion of a *solitary* person, such as Charlotte endured in after days, and which in time becomes awfully oppressive and injurious. It was solitude and seclusion shared and enjoyed with intelligent companionship, and intense family affection. 29

Harriet Martineau

From *Autobiography,* 3 vols., London: Smith and Elder, 1877.

26

II,323   On the last evening of my stay . . . a parcel arrived for me, enclosing a book, and a note which was examined as few notes ever are. The book was "Shirley;" and the note was from "Currer Bell." . . .

We examined this note to make out whether it was written by a man or a woman. The hand was a cramped and nervous one, which might belong to anybody who had written too much, or was in bad health, or who had been badly taught. . . .

324   I had made up my mind, as I had / repeatedly said, that a certain passage in "Jane Eyre," about sewing on brass rings, could have been written only by a woman or an upholsterer. I now addressed my reply externally to "Currer Bell, Esq.," and began it "Madam." — I had more reason for interest than even the deeply-interested public in knowing who wrote "Jane Eyre;" for, when it appeared, I was taxed with the authorship by more than one personal friend, and charged by others, and even by

relatives, with knowing the author, and having supplied some of the facts of the first volume from my own childhood. . . .

A month after my receipt of "Shirley," I removed, on a certain Saturday, from the house of a friend in Hyde Park Street to that of a cousin in Westbourne Street, in time for a dinner party. [There Miss Martineau received another note from Currer Bell, who was forthwith invited to dine.]

. . . The servant was sent with this invi- 325 tation on Sunday morning, and brought back the following reply.

My dear Madam,

I hope to have the pleasure of seeing you at six o'clock today: — and I shall try now to be patient till six o'clock comes.

I am, &c., &c.

"That is a woman's note," we agreed. We were in a certain state of excitement all day, and especially towards evening. The footman would certainly announce this mysterious personage by his or her right name; and, as I could not hear the announcement, I charged my cousins to take care that I was duly informed of it. A little before six, there was a thundering rap: — the drawing-room door was thrown open, and in stalked a gentleman six feet high. It was not "Currer," but a philanthropist, who had an errand about a model lodging-house. Minute by minute I, for 326 one, wished him away; and he did go / before any body else came. Precisely as the time-piece struck six, a carriage stopped at the door; and after a minute of suspense, the footman announced "Miss Brogden;" whereupon, my cousin informed me that it was Miss Bronti;" for we had heard the name before, among others, in the way of conjecture. — I thought her the smallest creature I had ever seen (except at a fair) and her eyes blazed, as it seemed to me. She glanced quickly round; and my trumpet pointing me out, she held out her hand frankly and pleasantly. I introduced her, of course, to the family; and then came a moment which I had not anticipated. When she was seated by me on the sofa, she cast up at me such a look, — so loving, so appealing, — that, in connexion with her deep mourning dress, and the knowledge that she was the sole survivor of her family, I could with the utmost difficulty return her smile, or keep my composure. I should

have been heartily glad to cry. We soon got on very well; and she appeared more at her ease that evening than I ever saw her afterwards, except when we were alone. My hostess was so considerate as to leave us together after tea, in case of C. B. desiring to have private conversation with me. She was glad of the opportunity to consult me about certain strictures of the reviewers which she did not understand, and had every desire to profit by. I did not approve the spirit of those strictures; but I thought them not entirely groundless. She besought me then, and repeatedly afterwards, to tell her, at whatever cost of pain to herself, if I saw her afford any justification of them. I believed her, (and I now believe her to have been) perfectly sincere: but when the time came (on the publication of "Villette," in regard / to which she had expressly 327 claimed my promise a week before the book arrived) she could not bear it. There was never any quarrel, or even misunderstanding between us. She thanked me for my sincere fulfilment of my engagement; but she could not, she said, come "at present" to see me, as she had promised: and the present was alas! all that she had to dispose of. She is dead, before another book of hers could (as I hoped it would) enable her to see what I meant, and me to reestablish a fuller sympathy between us. — . . .

Anne Thackeray Ritchie

From *Chapters from Some Memoirs,* London: Macmillan and Co., 1894.

27

60 One of the most notable persons who ever came into our bow-windowed drawing-room in Young Street is a guest never to be forgotten by me — a tiny, delicate, little person, whose small hand nevertheless grasped a mighty lever which set all the

[1] Anne Isabella Thackeray, later Lady Ritchie (1837–1919), eldest daughter of the novelist, edited his works and wrote novels and biographies.

literary world of that day vibrating. I can still see the scene quite plainly — the hot summer evening, the open windows, the carriage driving to the door as we all sat silent and expectant; my father, who rarely waited, waiting with us; our governess and my sister and I all in a row, and prepared for the great event. We saw the carriage stop, and out of it sprang the active, well-knit figure of Mr George Smith, who was bringing Miss Brontë to see our father. My father, who had been walking up and down the room, goes out into the hall to meet his guests, and then, after a moment's delay, the door opens wide, and the two gentlemen come in, leading a tiny, delicate, serious, little lady, pale, with fair straight hair, and steady eyes. She may be a little over thirty; she is dressed in a little *barège* dress, with a pattern of faint green moss. She 61 enters in / mittens, in silence, in seriousness; our hearts are beating with wild excitement. This, then, is the authoress, the unknown power whose books have set all London talking, reading, speculating; some people even say our father wrote the books — the wonderful books. To say that we little girls had been given *Jane Eyre* to read scarcely represents the facts of the case; to say that we had taken it without leave, read bits here and read bits there, been carried away by an undreamed-of and hitherto unimagined whirlwind into things, times, places, all utterly absorbing, and at the same time absolutely unintelligible to us, would more accurately describe our state of mind on that summer's evening as we look at Jane Eyre — the great Jane Eyre — the tiny little lady. The moment is so breathless that dinner comes as a relief to the solemnity of the occasion, and we all smile as my father stoops to offer his arm; for, though genius she may be, Miss Brontë can barely reach his elbow. My own personal impressions are that she is somewhat grave and stern, especially to forward little girls who wish to chatter. Mr George Smith 62 has since told / me how she afterwards remarked upon my father's wonderful forbearance and gentleness with our uncalled-for incursions into the conversation. She sat gazing at him with kindling eyes of interest, lighting up with a sort of illumination every now and then as she answered him. I can see her bending forward over the table, not eating, but listening to what he said as he carved the dish before him.

I think it must have been on this very occasion that my father invited some of his friends in the evening to meet Miss Brontë — for everybody was interested and anxious to see her. Mrs Crowe, the reciter of ghost-stories, was there. Mrs Brookfield, Mrs Carlyle, Mr Carlyle himself was present [and a number of other persons]. / It 63 was a gloomy and a silent evening. Every one waited for the brilliant conversation which never began at all. Miss Brontë retired to the sofa in the study and murmured a low word now and then to our kind governess, Miss Truelock. The room looked very dark, the lamp began to smoke a little, the conversation grew dimmer and more dim, the ladies sat round still expectant, my father was too much pertubed by the gloom and the silence to be able to cope with it at all. Mrs Brookfield, who was in the doorway by the study, near the corner in which Miss Brontë was sitting, leant forward with a little commonplace, since brilliance was not to be the order of the evening. "Do you like London, Miss Brontë?" she said; another silence, a pause, then Miss Brontë answers, "Yes and No," very gravely. Mrs Brookfield has herself reported the conversation. My sister and I were much too young to be bored in those days; alarmed, impressed we might be, but not / yet bored. 64 A party was a party, a lioness was a lioness; and — shall I confess it? — at that time an extra dish of biscuits was enough to mark the evening. We felt all the importance of the occasion: tea spread in the dining-room, ladies in the drawing-room. We roamed about inconveniently, no doubt, and excitedly, and in one of my incursions crossing the hall, after Miss Brontë had left, I was surprised to see my father opening the front door with his hat on. He put his fingers to his lips, walked out into the darkness, and shut the door quietly behind him. When I went back to the drawing-room again, the ladies asked me where he was. I vaguely answered that I thought he was coming back. I was puzzled at the time, nor was it all made clear to me till long years afterwards, when one day Mrs Procter asked me if I knew what had happened once when my father had invited a party to meet Jane Eyre at his house. It was one of the dullest evenings she had ever spent in her life, she said. And then with a good deal of humour she described the situation — the ladies who had all come expecting so much delightful conversation, and the gloom and the / constraint, and how, 65 finally, overwhelmed by the situation, my father had quietly left the room, left the house, and gone off to his club. . . .

George M. Smith

From "Charlotte Brontë," *Cornhill Magazine*, N. S., Vol. IX (December 1900).

28

780 . . . In July 1847 a parcel containing a MS. reached our office addressed to the firm, but bearing also the scored-out addresses of three or four other publishing houses; showing that the parcel had been previously submitted to other publishers. This was not calculated to prepossess us in favour of the MS. It was clear that we were offered what had been already rejected elsewhere.

The parcel contained the MS. of "The Professor," by "Currer Bell," a book which was published after Charlotte Brontë's death. Mr. Williams, the "reader" to the firm, read the MS., and said that it evinced great literary power, but he had doubts as to its being successful as a publication. We decided that he should write to "Currer Bell" a letter of appreciative criticism declining the work, but expressing an opinion that he could produce a book which would command success. . . .

782 . . . The MS. of "Jane Eyre" was read by Mr. Williams in due course. He brought it to me on a Saturday, and said that he would like to read it. There were no Saturday half-holidays in those days, and, as was usual, I did not reach home until late. I had made an appointment with a friend for Sunday morning; I was to meet him about twelve o'clock, at a place some two or three miles from our house, and ride with him into the country.

After breakfast on Sunday morning I took the MS. of "Jane Eyre" to my little study, and began to read it. The story quickly took me captive. Before twelve o'clock my horse came to the door, but I could not put the book down. I scribbled two or three lines to my friend, saying I was very sorry that circumstances had arisen to prevent my meeting him, sent the note off by my groom, and went on reading the MS. Presently the servant came to tell me that luncheon was ready; I asked him to bring me a sandwich and a glass of wine, and still went on with "Jane Eyre." Dinner came; for me the meal was a very hasty one, and before I went to bed that night I had finished reading the manuscript.

The next day we wrote to "Currer Bell" accepting the book for publication. I need say nothing about the success which the book achieved, and the speculations as to whether it was written by a man or a woman. For my own part I never had much doubt on the subject of the writer's sex; but then I had the advantage over the general public of having the handwriting of the author before me. There were qualities of style, too, and turns of expression, which satisfied me that "Currer Bell" was a woman, an opinion in which Mr. Williams concurred. We were bound, however, to respect the writer's anonymity, and our letters / con- 783 tinued to be addressed to "Currer Bell, Esq." Her sisters were always referred to in the correspondence as "Messrs. Ellis and Acton Bell." The works of Ellis and Acton Bell had been published by a Mr. Newby, on terms which rather depleted the scanty purses of the authors. When we were about to publish "Shirley" — the work which, in the summer of 1848, succeeded "Jane Eyre" — we endeavoured to make an arrangement with an American publisher to sell him advance sheets of the book, in order to give him an advantage in regard to time over other American publishers. There was, of course, no copyright with America in those days. We were met during the negotiations with our American correspondents by the statement that Mr. Newby had informed them that he was about to publish the next book by the author of "Jane Eyre," under her other *nom de plume* of Acton Bell — Currer, Ellis, and Acton Bell being in fact, according to him, one person. We wrote to "Currer Bell" to say that we should be glad to be in a position to contradict the statement, adding at the same time we were quite sure Mr. Newby's assertion was untrue. Charlotte Brontë has related how the letter affected her. She was persuaded that her honour was impugned [and she and Anne set out for London.] . . .

That particular Saturday morning I was at work in my room, when a clerk reported that two ladies wished to see me. I was very busy and sent out to ask their names. The clerk returned to say that the ladies declined to give their names, but wished to see me on a private matter. After a moment's hesitation I told him to show them in. I was in the midst of my correspondence, and my thoughts were far away from "Currer Bell" and "Jane Eyre." Two rather quaintly dressed little ladies, pale-faced and anxious-looking, walked into my room; one of them came forward and presented me with a letter addressed, in my own handwriting, to "Currer Bell, Esq." I noticed 784 that the letter / had been opened, and said, with some sharpness, "Where did you get this from?" "From the post-office," was the reply; "it was addressed to me. We have both come that you might have ocular proof that there are at least two of us." This then was "Currer Bell" in person. I need hardly say that I was at once keenly interested, not to say excited. Mr. Williams was called down and introduced, and I began to plan

all sorts of attentions to our visitors. . . .

This is the only occasion on which I saw Anne Brontë. She was a gentle, quiet, rather subdued person, by no means pretty, yet of pleasing appearance. Her manner was curiously expressive of a wish for protection and encouragement, a kind of constant appeal which invited sympathy.

I must confess that my first impression of Charlotte Brontë's personal appearance was that it was interesting rather than attractive. She was very small, and had a quaint old-fashioned look. Her head seemed too large for her body. She had fine eyes, but her face was marred by the shape of the mouth and by the complexion. There was but little femine charm about her; and of this fact she herself was uneasily and perpetually conscious. It may / seem strange 785 that the possession of genius did not lift her above the weakness of an excessive anxiety about her personal appearance. But I believe that she would have given all her genius and her fame to have been beautiful. Perhaps few women ever existed more anxious to be pretty than she, or more angrily conscious of the circumstance that she was *not* pretty.

Charlotte Brontë stayed with us several times. The utmost was, of course, done to entertain and please her. We arranged for dinner-parties, at which artistic and literary notabilities, whom she wished to meet, were present. . . .

Her letters show that she enjoyed the 787 recollection of these visits, and the society at our house; but my mother and sisters / found her a somewhat difficult guest, and I 788 am afraid she was never perfectly at her ease with them. Strangers used to say that they were afraid of her. She was very quiet and self-absorbed, and gave the impression that she was always engaged in observing and analysing the people she met. She was sometimes tempted to confide her analysis to the victim. . . .

When I first asked Thackeray to dine to 790 meet Charlotte Brontë, he offended her by failing to respect the anonymity behind which, at that time, she was very anxious to screen herself. On another occasion Thackeray roused the hidden fire in Charlotte Brontë's soul, and was badly scorched himself as the result. My mother and I had taken her to one of Thackeray's lectures on "The English Humourists." After the lecture Thackeray came down from the platform and shook hands with many of the audience, receiving their congratulations and compliments. He was in high spirits, and rather thoughtlessly said to his mother — Mrs. Carmichael Smyth — "Mother, you must allow me to introduce you to Jane Eyre." This was uttered in a loud voice, audible over half the room. Everybody near turned round and stared at the disconcerted little lady, who grew confused and angry when she realised that every eye was fixed upon her. My mother got her away as quickly as possible.

On the next afternoon Thackeray called. I arrived at home shortly afterwards, and when I entered the drawing-room found a scene in full progress. Only these two were in the room. Thackeray was standing on the hearthrug, looking anything but happy. Charlotte Brontë stood close to him, with head thrown back and face white with anger. The first words I heard were, "No, Sir! If *you* had come to our part of the country in Yorkshire, what would you have thought of me if I had introduced you to my father, before a mixed company of 791 strangers, as 'Mr. / Warrington'?" Thackeray replied, "No, you mean 'Arthur Pendennis.'" "No, I *don't* mean Arthur Pendennis!" retorted Miss Brontë; "I mean Mr. Warrington, and Mr. Warrington would not have behaved as you behaved to me yesterday." . . .

Thackeray shocked Charlotte Brontë sadly by the fashion of his talk on literary subjects. The truth is, Charlotte Brontë's heroics roused Thackeray's antagonism. He declined to pose on a pedestal for her admiration, and with characteristic contrariety of nature he seemed to be tempted to say the very things that set Charlotte Brontë's teeth, so to speak, on edge, and affronted all her ideals. He insisted on discussing his books very much as a clerk in a bank would discuss the ledgers he had to keep for a salary. But all this was, on Thackeray's part, an affectation; an affectation into which he was provoked by what he considered Charlotte Brontë's high falutin'. Miss Brontë wanted to persuade him that he was a great man with a "mission"; and Thackeray, with many wicked jests, declined to recognize the "mission.". . .

After Charlotte Brontë's first visit to our house her anonymity was dropped, and people naturally tried to draw her out. She shrank from this, or resented it, and seemed to place herself under my mother's care for protection. My mother accepted the position, and was generally equal to it, but sometimes, when accident left Charlotte Brontë exposed to a direct attack, the fire concealed beneath her mildness broke out. The first time this / happened I was not a 792 little surprised. G. H. Lewes, who was lunching with us, had the indiscretion to say across the table, "There ought to be a bond of sympathy between us, Miss Brontë, for we have both written naughty books!" This fired the train with a vengeance, and an explosion followed: I listened with mingled admiration and alarm to the indignant eloquence with which that impertinent remark was answered.

By way of parenthesis, I may say that *Jane Eyre* was really considered in those days by many people to be an immoral book. My mother told me one evening that Lady Herschel, having found the book in her drawing-room, said: "Do you leave such a book as *this* about, at the risk of your daughter reading it?" Charlotte Brontë herself was quite unconscious that the book possessed in any degree a reputation of this sort. . . .

Sir Wemyss Reid

From *Memoirs*. London: Cassell & Co., 1905.[1]

29

239   As I have said already, when I first wrote about the Brontës there were many still living who had known the sisters well. Of these Miss Nussey was the chief and it may be of interest to repeat a few of the statements which from time to time she made to me with regard to Charlotte. One of the most striking of these was her account of the single visit which she paid to Haworth after Charlotte became the wife of Mr. Nicholls. Miss Nussey told me that she 240 accompanied Charlotte and her / husband one day on a walk over the moors. In the course of their conversation she asked Charlotte if she was writing another book "No," replied Charlotte; "Arthur says I have no time for writing now, as I must attend to my duties as a clergyman's wife." She said it in such a tone as to convince her friend that she was not satisfied with her husband's decision, and Miss Nussey, plucking up her courage, remonstrated with him upon his refusal to allow Charlotte to exercise her great gift. Mr. Nicholls's response was short and to the point. "I did not marry Currer Bell, the novelist, but Charlotte Brontë, the clergyman's daughter. Currer Bell may fly to heaven tomorrow for anything I care." I do not vouch for the absolute truth of this story, but I give it as I heard it from Miss Nussey, and I am quite sure that when she told it to me she believed it to be true.

1 Sir Thomas Wemyss Reid (1842–1905), journalist and biographer, editor of the *Leeds Mercury* (1870–87). In estimating the value of this anecdote, the reader should be aware that Ellen's attitude to Mr. Nicholls was not very friendly; see her correspondence with George Smith, SH IV, 251–60.

Frederika Macdonald

From *The Secret of Charlotte Brontë*. London: T. C. and E. C. Jack, 1914.[1] Reprinted by permission of the publisher.

30

145   The basis of the "Problem [of Charlotte Brontë]" was the alleged "dissonance" between Charlotte's personality and her genius — between her dreary, desolate, dull, well-tamed existence, uncoloured, untroubled by romance (as Mrs. Gaskell painted it), and the passionate atmosphere of her novels, where all events / and personages 146 are seen through the medium of one sentiment — tragical romantic love.

We know now that the dissonance did not exist; that from her twenty-sixth year

1 Frederika Macdonald, née Richardson, attended the Pensionnat Heger from 1859–61, unaware then that the school and the Hegers were allegedly pictured in *Villette*. Though much younger than Charlotte (she was fourteen when she entered), she was, like her, a foreigner and a Protestant. However, blessed perhaps with a happier disposition, she found the Belgian girls kind, friendly, even generous. Her impression of the Hegers, too, was very different from Charlotte's. Mme. Heger she remembered with deep affection and "a sentiment of reverence" for her "Tranquillité, Douceur, Bonté," her "serene sweetness, a kindness without preferences, covering her little world of pupils and teachers with watchful care" (p. 165). Though both Mrs. Macdonald and her

downwards, Charlotte's life was, not only coloured, but governed by a tragical romantic love: that, in its first stage, threw her into a hopeless conflict against the force of things and broke her heart: but that, because the battle was fought in the force, and in the cause, of noble emotions, saved her soul alive; and called her genius forth to life: so that it rose as an immortal spirit from the grave of personal hopes.

158 ... I myself owe to M. Heger, not only admirable rules for criticism and practice, that have always claimed and still claim my absolute belief, but also I owe to him, as she did, a full enjoyment of beautiful

159 thoughts, beautifully expressed, / and of treasures of the mind and of the imaginations, that, lying outside of the recognised paths of English study, I might never have found, nor even have recognised as treasures, had I not been cured of insularity of taste by M. Heger. ... But if my judgment of M. Heger, as a Professor, coincides with Charlotte's, my judgment of him, outside of this capacity, does not show him to me at all as the model of the man from whom

she painted Paul Emanuel. In other words, I never found nor saw in the real Monsieur Heger the lovableness under the outward harshness, — the depths of tenderness under the very apparent severity and irritability, — the concealed consideration for the feelings of others, under the outer indifference to the feelings of any one who ruffled his temper; nor yet did I ever discover meekness and / modesty in him, under the dog- 160 matic and imperious manner that swept aside all opposition. In fact, I never found out that M. Heger wore a mask. But, irritable, imperious, harsh, not *unkind,* but certainly the reverse of tender, and without any consideration for any one's feelings, or any respect for any one's opinions, thus, *just as he seemed to be, so in reality, in my opinion, M. Heger actually was.* And what one must remember is that Charlotte's point of view, from which she formed the opinion that M. Heger *was* tender-hearted, and modest and meek, was the point of view of a woman in love; and this standpoint is not one that ensures impartiality.

Sir George M. Smith

From *The House of Smith and Elder,* Privately printed, 1923; as reprinted in *The Brontës, Their Lives Recorded by Their Contemporaries,* compiled by E. M. Delafield, London: Hogarth Press, 1935. Reprinted by permission of the publisher.

31

176 Charlotte Brontë was devoured with curiosity to meet Thackeray, to whom she had dedicated the second edition of her book. I told Thackeray there would be no one with us except Sir John Forbes, and explained that Miss Brontë was incognito in London, and begged him not to say or indicate his knowledge of her identity as the

authoress of *Jane Eyre.* He replied in his large way: "I see! It will be all right; you are speaking to a man of the world."

But unhappily it was not all right. When the ladies had left the dining room I offered Thackeray a cigar. The custom of smoking after dinner was not common then, but I had been told he liked a cigar, and so pro-

brother, the Abbé Richardson, later had nothing but praise for M. Heger as a teacher, the schoolgirl of fourteen, stumbling along in her imperfect French, found him, though amusing and stimulating, an exacting master, unsympathetic, unjust, "not a loveable but a formidable man: a Terror ... some one who is sure to appear upon the

scene when one is / least prepared to face him, and who is constantly finding fault with one" (pp. 160–61). Mrs. Macdonald's recollections both illuminate and temper Charlotte's portraits of the Hegers, and her account should be compared with Charlotte's earlier impressions as well as her later emotional attitudes.

vided for his tastes. To my dismay, when we rejoined the ladies in the drawing-room, he approached Miss Brontë and quoted a familiar and much criticised passage from *Jane Eyre*. It was that in which she describes "the warning fragrance" which told of the approach of Mr. Rochester:

"Sweetbriar and southern wood, jasmine, pink and rose, had long been yielding their evening sacrifice of incense. This new scent was neither shrub nor flower. It was — I knew it well — it was Mr. Rochester's cigar!"

The quotation, in one sense, was happy enough, and it did credit to Thackeray's memory of *Jane Eyre;* but not to his memory of his agreement with me. Miss Brontë's face showed her discomposure, and in a chilly fashion she turned off the allusion. But I was almost as much discomposed as Miss Brontë by this sudden assault on what she was so anxious / to guard — her identity 177 as the authoress of *Jane Eyre*. She cast an accusing look at me.

Thackeray, however, had no sense of either awkwardness or guilt. From my house he went to the smoking-room of the Garrick Club and said: "Boys! I have been dining with 'Jane Eyre!'!"

VI. The Cowan Bridge Controversy

One repercussion from publication of Mrs. Gaskell's life of Charlotte was the renewed controversy over Charlotte's depiction of the charity school in *Jane Eyre*. The Carus Wilson family, still involved in Casterton School, the successor to Cowan Bridge, had been much distressed by the identification of Lowood with the earlier school. Mrs. Gaskell, who had taken the trouble to visit Casterton while doing the research for the *Life,* undoubtedly tried to be fair, but her sympathy with Charlotte's sufferings led her into criticisms of the school regime which Mr. Carus Wilson and his supporters deeply resented and which provoked much correspondence, including the exhibits printed below. It is interesting that in spite of his hatred of publicity Mr. Nicholls felt he must defend his wife's honor. It was partly as a result of the controversy that Mrs. Gaskell made the changes in her chapter on the school. The reader who studies this section, Section I, and *Jane Eyre,* will have sufficient evidence to judge whether or not Lowood is a fair picture of Cowan Bridge. More is extant, but the old arguments are only repeated. The debate continued fitfully even after Mrs. Gaskell's death. The last item in this section, from a magazine controversy of the sixties, is included for its somewhat fresh restatement. It is interesting that Emma Jane Warboise, the author of *Thorneycroft Hall,* another novel about the school, speaks well of Mr. Carus Wilson: "His works of love and mercy were manifold. He was thoroughly sincere and unostentatiously generous. A kinder man I never knew."

W. W. Carus Wilson

1

TO THE LEEDS MERCURY

May 16, 1857[1]

GENTLEMEN, — May I ask for a corner for the following taken out of a Review, which is a complete answer to the statements in *The Life of Charlotte Brontë* regarding my father's charitable institutions. —

Yours, W. W. Carus Wilson

[The reviewer quotes from a letter by A. H. ("a former superintendent") written in 1855.] The columns of the leading papers have for some time past been occupied with obituary notices of the late Miss Brontë, and many conveying the impression that her treatment at the Clergy Daughters' School when at Cowan Bridge, was of a character not only to affect her health but to darken her prospects in after life. Now, as I have it in my power to refute these charges, I should consider myself guilty in a measure concerning them, did I not make known to the world the truth of the case, and thereby exonerate an excellent and eminently useful clergyman from the imputations cast on him in *Jane Eyre,* as well as vindicate an institution which has been to the poverty-stricken clergy a blessing of inestimable value. In July 1824, Mr. Brontë arrived at Cowan Bridge with two of his daughters, Maria and Elizabeth; the children were so delicate that there were doubts whether they could be admitted into the school. They were received, and went on so well that their father brought in September two more, Charlotte and Emily.[2] During both these visits Mr. Brontë stayed

[1] Dates given throughout this section are dates of publication. Page numbers are not available.

[2] Not exact; see chronology.

at the school, sat at the table with the pupils, and saw the whole routine of the establishment.

They all inherited consumption from their mother, and were taken home; none of them, as has been stated, had any attack of fever or died at the school. I can truly say that none of the pupils were denied a sufficient quantity of good food; they were never limited: meat, vegetables, and puddings daily in abundance; any statement to the contrary is most false. Charlotte was a bright, clever, happy little girl, never in disgrace. . . . Let us hope that in caricaturing an institution which has been such a blessing to the daughters of her own church, she had no injurious motives, but, misled by a vivid imagination, and a dim recollection of thirty years, when she was but a child, she published in an unguarded moment, unmindful of the consequences, misstatements, the tendency of which has been to calumniate a most excellent institution, and to bring disgrace on religion.

[After quoting A. H.'s letter, Mr. Wilson goes on.] . . . We would take the testimony of hundreds of pupils, who with their parents have gratefully acknowledged the advantages they received at these institutions, rather than the account of one, however talented, who when but a child of nine left the establishment, and has so ungenerously cast an odium upon him who first planned such a help to our poorer clergy, and who has yearly undertaken the risk of the support of near 300 pupils and teachers, for, including a preparatory school, there are about 150 daughters of clergymen boarded, clothed, and educated, at only £14 a year each, including everything, and in the "Servants' School," above 100 girls trained for service, each paying only £10 a year.

The schools are situated in Westmoreland, built on Mr. Carus Wilson's property, half a mile from Casterton Hall, his residence. They stand amid beautiful scenery, on high and healthy situations. They require above £1,000 a year, in addition to the payments of the pupils, to cover all expenses.

Arthur Bell Nicholls

2

TO THE LEEDS MERCURY
May 23, 1857

Gentlemen, — On Saturday last you published, by request of Mr W. W. Carus Wilson, an extract from a review, containing, he says, "a complete answer to the statements regarding his father's charitable institutions."

. . . Now let us examine the "complete answer," and see how these charges are disposed of. And first, the reviewer assumes that these statements rest solely on the testimony "of one who, when but a child of nine, left the establishment"; a reference, however, to the *Life of Charlotte Brontë* will show that this is a *false* assumption. He praises the situation of the school, "on Mr Carus Wilson's property, half a mile from Casterton Hall, high and healthy"; but he has not the candour to state that this description applies to the *present* site, and *not to that referred to in "Jane Eyre."*

He eulogises Mr Wilson's liberality, but omits to state that funds are raised from the public for the support of the establishment which Mr W. W. Carus Wilson modestly calls his "father's charitable institutions."

. . . [A. H.] eulogises Mr Wilson; asseverates her own impartiality . . . makes a somewhat erroneous statement respecting Mr Brontë's family; hazards some conjectures about the intentions of the author of *Jane Eyre*; and lays before us a bill of fare at Cowan Bridge — "Meat, vegetables, and puddings, daily in abundance." Very good, madam! But what about the *cooking* that spoiled these provisions, boiled the puddings in unclean water, compounded the Saturday's nauseous mess from the fragments accumulated in a dirty larder during the week, and too often sent up the porridge, not merely burnt, but with offensive fragments of other substances discoverable in it? . . .

Jane Eyre was published in 1847; Lowood was almost immediately identified with Cowan Bridge, yet "the lady, who was superintendent in 1824," was discreetly silent for more than *seven* years, in fact until the author was laid in her grave. So were Mr W. W. Carus Wilson and the Reviewer, for aught I know. . . .

To the day of her death "Currer Bell" maintained that the picture drawn in *Jane Eyre* was on the whole a true picture of Cowan Bridge School, as she knew it by experience: that the institution was subsequently greatly improved she knew and stated in the same work in which she exposed its former mismanagement.

Trusting to your sense of justice to give this letter a place in your Saturday's impression, I am, gentlemen, your obedient servant,   A. B. Nicholls.

W. W. Carus Wilson

3

May 28, 1857

Gentlemen, — If the Rev. A. Nicholls will refer to the refutation which in your paper of last Thursday he endeavours to answer, he will see that the reviewer particularly stated that he wished there had been space to have inserted *all* the letter of the lady who was over the Cowan Bridge School when C. Brontë was there. . . . [He quotes from the letter.] During the Spring of 1825 a low fever, though not an alarming one, (Mr N. says it "scourged the school") prevailed, and the managers, naturally anxious to know if any local cause occasioned it, asked the doctor's opinion of the food that had happened to be on the table. I recollect he spoke rather scornfully of a baked rice pudding, but as the ingredients were rice, sugar and milk, its effects could hardly have been so serious as have been affirmed. . . .

In addition to the above, my father has denied the accounts in *Jane Eyre,* and declared he was most particular about the food at Cowan Bridge.

I leave your readers to form their own judgment between the testimony of this lady and my father, and a child who left the institution when but nine years old.

If there are any besides, perhaps a dismissed pupil or teacher, who can bear out C. Brontë's assertions, there are many more Cowan Bridge pupils who have written to me during the last month saying "how happy they were there, how all loved my father, how entirely false the character Mrs Gaskell has sketched of him, and how good the food was, better (some have said) than they got at their own home."

Mr Nicholls complains of the expression "My father's charitable institutions." It was my father who first established them, had them built on his own property, collected single-handed for thirty years all subscriptions for them, running the risk himself of their yearly support, and thereby doing for his brother clergy what no other man has done. No "Committee of management was formed" till about six years ago, when ill-health obliged my father to live abroad. . . .

Mr N. is surprised that no defence was made on the publication of *Jane Eyre.* But that was a novel, and persons and places were not publicly and certainly identified till the obituary notices of the press in 1855 and the memoir of C. Brontë appeared. It was in 1855 that the letter of refutation was sent to a Review by the lady who was over Cowan Bridge School, when C. Brontë was there. . . .

It is only natural that Mr N. should seek to defend his wife's assertions, but considering that to add force to her fiction she casts odium on an invaluable institution, and a public benefactor to mankind, which as Mrs Gaskell says she often afterwards regretted, I think Mr N. should be the first to share in that regret and to repair the great injury that has been done. — Yours, etc.,

W. W. Carus Wilson.

Arthur Bell Nicholls

4

TO THE HALIFAX GUARDIAN
June 6, 1857

Sir, — . . . Let me . . . thank Mr Wilson for his last letter. In his former statement all was perfection at Cowan Bridge, now we have the following points *admitted*: That "during the spring of 1825 there prevailed a low fever, though not an alarming one" (what would *alarm* Mr W. if the illness of about forty girls failed to do so?); that "the doctor rather scornfully" condemned the girls' food. . . .

But mark how easily Mr Wilson disposes of adverse testimony; "if there *are* any besides (C. Brontë), perhaps a dismissed pupil or teacher."

Now even at the risk of incurring such a summary dismissal I cannot forbear giving him the following extract from a letter which I have received from a former pupil at Cowan Bridge:

"On first reading *Jane Eyre* several years ago I recognised immediately the picture there drawn, and was far from considering it any way exaggerated; in fact, I thought at the time, and still think the matter rather understated than otherwise. I suffered so severely from the treatment that I was never in the schoolroom during the last three months I was there, until about a week before I left, and was considered to be far gone in consumption. My mother (whose only child I was) was never informed of my illness, and I might certainly have died there without her being informed of it, had not a severe illness of her own caused her hastily to summon me home. She was so much shocked at my appearance that she refused to allow me to return, though pressed to do so. . . . I attribute my illness to the unhealthy situation of the school, the long walks to church in bad weather (for in winter our feet were often wet during the whole of the service), and the scanty and ill-prepared food. . . . The housekeeper was very dirty with the cooking. I have frequently seen grease swimming on the milk and water we had for breakfast, in consequence of its having been boiled in a greasy copper, and I perfectly remember once being sent for a cup of tea for a teacher, who was ill in bed, and no spoon being at hand, the housekeeper stirred it with her finger, she being engaged in cutting up raw meat at the time. I could give you scores of such instances as these which fell under my own observation. Our food was almost always badly cooked, and besides that we certainly had not enough of it, whatever may be said to the contrary. . . . In a word, the system at Cowan Bridge was a very harsh one, and I was very glad to hear that an improvement took place after the school was removed to Casterton, for it was much needed. I had no knowledge whatever of Mrs Nicholls personally, therefore my statement may fairly be considered an impartial one. You are quite welcome to make what use you think proper of this letter." . . . A. B. Nicholls.

Sarah Baldwin

5

June 13, 1857

Sir, — . . . It gives me inexpressible pain to see the repeated attempts made, by the distortion and exaggeration of facts, and what looks very like wilful misrepresentations of character, to disparage a valuable institution, and to cast odium upon a venerated minister of our church, who has spent his best days in energetic labours in his Master's cause, and for the benefit of the families of his poorer brethren in the ministry.

As an old pupil, both of the school at Cowan Bridge, and at Casterton, I claim to be heard.

Charlotte Brontë was, if I have been correctly informed, a pupil at Cowan Bridge about nine months. I was a pupil there for two years; and subsequently at Casterton for more than seven years; thus my residence extended over a period of more than nine years. . . .

I was one of the victims of that visitation of fever at Cowan Bridge, about which so much has been said, and to this hour I have a vivid recollection of the motherly care and attention I received, and the tender solicitude shown towards me on that trying occasion. Nor have I the slightest reason to think that I was treated better than my fellow-pupils. Nor do I for a moment believe that the fever took its rise from the quantity or quality of the food provided, but was introduced to the school from the village, or by a pupil returning to the school.

. . . I solemnly affirm that our food was uniformly abundant, good, and generally well cooked; but no reasonable person could expect that in a large establishment like that, any more than in a private family, a failure in cooking should not sometimes happen.

And as to the pupils walking to the church in wet weather, and sitting the whole time of service with wet and cold feet, I do not say this never occurred; but this I do say, that it was the usual practice for the pupils not to go to church in wet weather, but to have prayers and a sermon at the school; so that this occurrence must have been rare indeed. . . .

The character of the founder of that institution has been cruelly and falsely assailed, as all who know him will readily admit; but he will think it no dishonour "to suffer for righteousness' sake."

It would be almost too much to expect that no injury should be sustained by the institution from the repeated attacks made upon it with such perverse energy; most thankful therefore should I be could I enlist the sympathies of the wealthy in this locality in its behalf, and add to the numbers of its subscribers. I know of no institution that has a stronger claim to the sympathies and support of the Christian Church.

Trusting to your sense of justice and impartiality to insert this in your next publication, — I remain, sir, your obedient servant,   Sarah Baldwin

Arthur Bell Nicholls

6

TO THE HALIFAX GUARDIAN
July 4, 1857

Sir, — . . . Mrs. Baldwin says that she has "had more ample opportunities of forming a judgment on the management of Cowan Bridge School than Charlotte Brontë." Now, Charlotte Brontë described the institution as she found it. Mrs Baldwin was not there at the time, consequently she cannot personally know whether the statements in *Jane Eyre* are true or false. Hear the testimony of a lady who *was* at the school with Miss Brontë: — "I would rather see a child of mine in its grave than subjected to the treatment I endured, and which I shall never forget."

. . . Mrs. Baldwin, after informing us that she is "preparing to send two of her own dear little girls" (a first instalment, I presume) to "the charitable institution" already so liberally patronised by her family, proceeds to do a little congenial business, and with exquisite taste presents a begging box to the Halifax gentry. Surely such a graceful and disinterested appeal cannot be made in vain.

. . . I am, sir, your obliged and obedient servant,　　　　　　　　A. B. Nicholls

Sarah Baldwin

7

TO THE HALIFAX GUARDIAN
July 11, 1857

Sir, — . . . Mr. Nicholls's letter is written in a style so coarse and unusual among educated people, that it is quite undeserving of notice, and would have been allowed to pass at once into oblivion, but for one or two misstatements it contains. . . .

. . . He intimates that because I was not at the school at the identical time with Charlotte Brontë, therefore I cannot know whether the statements in *Jane Eyre* be true or false. . . . I do not pretend to know by personal observation whether all these statements are true or not; but I have very satisfactory evidence, of a personal nature and of other kinds, that they are not; and especially so to Mr Wilson, the accusations against whom, and the misrepresentations of whose character are, to my mind, the gravest part of the whole question. I think I may be allowed to speak with some confidence, because for nearly ten years I knew him intimately, and had full opportunity of observing his religious character, his temper, disposition, and general treatment of the pupils; and it was such as to produce in me, and in the good majority of them, feelings of unaffected love and veneration. This testimony is founded upon nearly ten years' experience. Charlotte Brontë speaks only from personal observation and experience, extending over a period of nine months and when she was a mere child, a little more than nine years old. I went to the school at Cowan Bridge about a year after she left, when, I believe, the state of things was much as during her stay there. . . .

With your permission, I will now give the testimony of one of the first pupils at Cowan Bridge. "As a pupil at Cowan Bridge in its first days, I feel it a privilege to be able to bear testimony in direct opposition to Miss Brontë. I could mention many interesting little incidents corroborative of my opposite testimony, calculated to account for the affectionate feeling with which I myself, and my fellow-pupils, regarded the kind Carus Wilson family. I have not read *Jane Eyre*, for I felt it a waste of time to read tales founded on falsehoods; but when I have heard remarks made upon it, and now on the *Memoir*, it has afforded me satisfaction to refute the ungrateful slander cast on Mr Wilson, and to bear my testimony to the practical consistency of his character, which, with me, gave weight to all his religious instructions. My annual subscription for many years to the school betokens my interest in it; and I now send a little donation as a further proof of my regard for him and it."

This is one of more than three hundred letters that have been received by Mr W. W. C. Wilson within the last few weeks, almost all grieving over the assertions made in *Jane Eyre* and in the *Life of Charlotte Brontë*, which crush entirely any testimony that can be produced to the contrary. . . .

The "Miss Temple" of *Jane Eyre* is exhibited in a most favourable light by Charlotte Brontë herself, and is spoken of in highly eulogistic terms by the authoress of the *Life of Charlotte Brontë*. The following is from a clergyman, the husband of the lady who is represented under the name of Miss Temple, and who died only last year. "Often," he says, "have I heard my late dear wife speak of her sojourn at Cowan Bridge. I never heard her speak otherwise than in terms of admiration at Mr Carus Wilson's personal sacrifices, and of the parental affection he manifested towards the pupils. Of the food and treatment of the children she always spoke in terms of general approval. I have heard her allude to some unfortunate cook, who used at times to spoil the food, but she said she was soon dismissed." This testimony from such a quarter is strong indeed. . . .

I have as little inclination as Mr Nicholls to continue the correspondence, especially as it is conducted by himself in defiance of all the rules of courtesy and propriety. Having borne my humble, but most conscientious, testimony in this matter on the side of truth and justice, I am so far satisfied. With many thanks for your kind indulgence, — I am, sir, your obedient servant,

Sarah Baldwin.

W. W. Carus Wilson

8

TO THE HALIFAX GUARDIAN
July 18, 1857

Sir, — I don't wish to make any defence for Mrs Baldwin. Your readers will, I am sure, agree with me, that she is *quite* able to take care of herself: neither do I wish to notice the strain of Mr Nicholls's letter, at which many have expressed to me (to use the lightest term) their astonishment; but I hope I may now be able to close this controversy by saying, that in a correspondence I have had with Mrs Gaskell, I have found her most willing to rectify the injury she has done to my father and his institutions, and I believe her third edition will be a work which none can cavil at, but all extol.

I gladly do her justice in saying that I am sure she only desires to elicit truth. I do think she is more to blame than C. Brontë, for having too much endorsed as facts the exaggerated fictions of *Jane Eyre*.

C. Brontë's wonderful writings being but novels, we must allow her gifted pen more licence. . . .

It has been said that the statements of pupils who were not at school with C. Brontë are of no avail. But I have seen the testimony of teachers and pupils who were *with* her, and those who followed her, as did Mrs Baldwin (who finds from her father now that she was at Cowan Bridge for a much longer period than she stated in her first letter), would surely have heard of the horrors depicted in *Jane Eyre,* if they had had any reality. And as regards my father's conduct towards the pupils, those at Casterton, as well as Cowan Bridge, can give evidence about that. . . .

I am ready to give your readers the addresses of any of my correspondents, and I only wish they could read a tithe of the letters I have had from old pupils.

The testimony Mrs Baldwin gives in her last letter is from Miss Frizell, residing with the Hon. J. Tollemache, M.P., Ham House, Surrey, and the "Miss Temple's" husband, the Rev. J. Connor, Melton Mowbray.

Shortly after C. Brontë left Cowan Bridge, which has been designated as a second Dotheboys' Hall (though now the whole tone of the reviews and magazines for this month has been turned towards the truth, and I have seen more than a dozen), the late Bishop of London visited the school with Mrs Blanfield, and after an examination of the classes, and a careful inspection of the whole establishment, observed to my father, that "if it should please God to deprive his daughters of their parents, he knew no institution where he could more desire them to be placed."

I do trust that this letter may close this controversy. — Yours,

W. W. Carus Wilson.

Arthur Bell Nicholls

9

July 18, 1857

Sir, — I regret to find that Mrs Baldwin takes such strong exception to my last letter, but if she indulges in charges of "distortion and exaggeration of facts and wilful misrepresentation," she must not feel surprised if she be answered in a manner less gentle than one would wish to use in replying to a lady.

She cannot, it seems, perceive the fallacy in her argument, and yet it is very plain. She assumes that because the management was good in *her* time, it must have been so *always*. With equal correctness might she argue that because she is *now* in a position to "send two of her dear little girls" to "my father's charitable institution," she has been *always* in a similar interesting situation. For the statements I have made I have produced proof. Mr. Wilson's friends have not, that I am aware of, produced the testimony of a single pupil who was at the institution with Charlotte Brontë. . . .

Mrs Baldwin says she went to Cowan Bridge about a year after Miss Brontë left it. This can hardly be so, for in that case she must have been *sixteen* years at school instead of nine, as she says herself. This, however, is of little consequence. I merely wish to point out the inconsistency. But contrast the testimony of a lady who *did* go to the school at that time.

The following extract is from a letter addressed to me by her husband, a clergyman: — "Feeling interested, in common with thousands, in the fame of C. Brontë, and indignant at the aspersions cast on her veracity, I think it may not be disagreeable to you to receive from an independent source a statement confirmatory in some respects of the account of the Clergy Daughters' School given by your late lamented wife.

My own wife and one of her sisters (E.) were educated at Cowan Bridge, entering shortly after Miss Brontë left, and remaining there five years. At the time of their entrance, the school was considered to be in a course of progressive improvement, and my wife makes no complaint of dirt, but her account of the food supplied during the early part of her residence is very *unfavourable* in respect to the *quantity* and *quality*.

The breakfast consisted of ill-made porridge, without bread. Many girls from the southern counties, unused to such food at home, could not eat it, and for six months my wife and her sister E. had no breakfast whatever. On one occasion it was observed that E. was not taking her porridge. She was required to eat it. Attempting to do so, her stomach rejected it, upon which she was treated, not to a meal of bread or other wholesome food, but to a *strong dose of senna tea*.

The dinner was sufficient, but not good. . . . The evening meal consisted of a cup of milk and water, and *one small piece of bread, not weighing two ounces*.

Many of the girls being thus always hungry, there were continual attempts to procure bread clandestinely. This was brought to light by the following incident. It was usual for each pupil to repeat on Sunday morning a text of her own choice; and one, who had, I believe, been punished for stealing bread, repeated in her turn the verse which declares that men do not despise a thief who steals bread to satisfy his hunger. This girl died shortly after of consumption.

My own wife, on her return home for the first vacation, was considered by her family to be half starved, and her brother, a medical man, has told me, that in his opinion, her health suffered for years from the consequences of insufficient nourishment. . . ."

My sole desire in this controversy has been to defend the dead from the aspersions cast on her by interested individuals. Against the Clergy Daughters' School, as at present conducted, the author of *Jane Eyre* has not written a line, nor have I. The management is, I am told, unexceptionable. . . . I am, sir, your much obliged and obedient servant,   A. B. Nicholls.

Sarah Baldwin

10

TO THE HALIFAX GUARDIAN
August 1, 1857

Sir, — . . . Mr Nicholls's misapprehension as to the duration of my residence at the school is easily rectified. The only uncertainty in my mind was the date of the removal of the school from Cowan Bridge to Casterton; it was at a later period than I thought; so that I was at Cowan Bridge a longer, and at Casterton a shorter, period than I at first stated. This, it will be perceived, adds some strength to my former testimony. . . .

In dismissing, as I hope finally, this subject, I must observe that in what I have said I have been influenced only by a regard for justice and truth, and of gratitude to Mr Wilson. The school and Mr Wilson were misrepresented and misunderstood, and no voice lifted up here in defence. Many of my former fellow-pupils in other parts of the country had stood forward with their favourable testimony. I felt constrained to use my feeble powers and influence in the same cause. I feel thankful that I have done so, and thus been enabled to discharge in some small degree the debt of gratitude I, in common with the hundreds, owe to the excellent and benevolent founder of the school.   Sarah Baldwin.

Arthur Bell Nicholls

11

TO THE HALIFAX GUARDIAN
August 8, 1857

Sir, — . . . The question, stripped of extraneous matter, is simply this: What was the state of the school *during the time that Miss Brontë was there?*

She and others described the treatment as harsh; the food as indifferent and insufficient. Up started Mrs Baldwin, and, asserting her own superior means of information, said in effect: Don't believe a word of it; hear me. I went to Cowan Bridge *seven years* (according to Mr Wilson's date) *after C. Brontë left,* and "I solemnly affirm that the food was uniformly abundant and good." I pointed out to her that she could not personally know whether the statements were true or not, because she was not at "my father's charitable institution" at the time referred to. She *then* said: "*I do not pretend to know by personal observation whether the statements are true or not. I* went to the school about *a year after she left,* when, *I believe,* the state of things was *much* as during her stay." How conclusive! But Mr Wilson has "300 testimonials" in his favour — he may have 500 — and all just as worthless as Mrs Baldwin's, unless proved to have been written by pupils who were at school *with* Miss Brontë, which has not been done in a single instance. You will observe that "E." *admits* that she was treated as described by my correspondent; and Mrs. Baldwin does not deny that the girls were driven by hunger to steal bread. . . .

Of Rev. C. Wilson I know nothing personally. I would only say that I have heard him spoken of by clergymen, who agree with him in sentiment, in terms very different from those employed by Mrs Baldwin.

And now, sir, I have done with this subject. I have discharged a painful but necessary duty. Henceforth Charlotte Brontë's assailants may growl and snarl over her grave undisturbed by me. — I am, sir, your obedient servant,

A. B. Nicholls.

The Reverend H. Shepheard

12

From *A Vindication of the Clergy Daughters' School* . . . London: Seeley, Jackson, and Halliday, 1857.[1]

8   Mrs. Gaskell is so incorrect in some of her statements as to matters of fact, that one stands in doubt how she can have been so misinformed on a subject which she professes to have investigated.

She states, for example, that "Mr. Wilson was 'a wealthy clergyman.'" No one could have written this otherwise than by guess. Those who knew Mr. Carus Wilson as a young man, or even, as I did myself, twenty years ago, would bear witness to the remarkable simplicity and economy of all his habits and household; and those who were acquainted with his circumstances would know that Mrs. Gaskell's description did not apply to him.

Again, she says, "Mr. Wilson opened the school with from 70 to 80 pupils, as far as I can make out." The real number was *sixteen!* as appears from the school books. The whole number admitted during the

[1] Mr. Shepheard, Mr. Wilson's son-in-law, wrote a point-by-point refutation of Mrs. Gaskell's remarks on the school.

first eighteen months, up to the time when Charlotte Brontë left the school, was 53. 9 It would be well if / Mrs. Gaskell had been more careful in making out facts, both here and in matters of greater moment. . . .

Once more — either through want of information, or through negligence (a serious fault, when character is attacked), Mrs. Gaskell has failed to correct a misrepresentation in "Jane Eyre," which conveys an unfounded and injurious insinuation. Mr. Carus Wilson's wife and daughters are described, under the names of "Mrs. and the Misses Brocklehurst," as presenting a striking contrast in dress and fashionable appearance to the rigid plainness enforced by the lectures in the school-room. Now, at the time when Charlotte Brontë was at Cowen Bridge, Mr. Carus Wilson's oldest children were hardly out of the nursery, and could not, therefore, have furnished the originals of the "Misses Brocklehurst," — "fine girls of 16 or 17," — with their "hats" and "feathers" and "profusion of curls." The *animus* of this misrepresentation need not be pointed out.

Anonymous

13

TO THE EDITOR OF BELGRAVIA
V, 1868

243 I think that we may refer to the old precedent of the gold and silver shield, and say that each writer is right from her own point of view. My experience of the "C. D. S." at Cowan Bridge is two years later than that of "Jane Eyre," and began in 1827. I have a feeling of the strongest respect and gratitude towards my old school, both for the principles instilled, and for the thorough conscientious teaching which we received in all branches of our education. The food was abundant, good, and well-prepared. But there were traditions of things having been very differently managed under former superintendence and service; and to that time "Jane Eyre's" experiences, coloured by her vivid imagination, may refer. Numerous as we were, a somewhat Spartan discipline was perhaps necessary, and a Spartan tone was cultivated by the girls themselves. Any tendency to "softness," in the north-country depreciatory phrase, was avoided by us. Girls would protest that they were well, and faint as the words were uttered. To young delicate children, peculiarly reared and peculiarly constituted, as "Jane" and her sisters were — and I may say to *any* invalids — the "C. D. S." was scarcely fitted. The general feeling towards Mr. Carus Wilson was one of the deepest reverence — I may say, of a more unquestioning and implicit reverence than might have been expected in so *very* Protestant a school. His colossal stature doubtless *told* in the impression he effected amongst us. . . . All justice, by showing the other side of the shield, is due to a school which has benefited so many hundreds directly, and through them so many more.